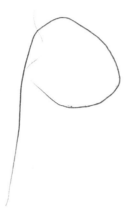

Educational Administration
3rd Edition

Jeffrey S. Kaiser, Ph.D.

Stylex Publishing Co., Inc.
529 East Maple Lane
Mequon, WI 53092
Phone: (262) 241-8347
Fax: (262) 241-8348
Email: info@stylexonline.com
Web: http://www.stylexonline.com

Contents

Chapter 3
Legal and Financial Aspects of Public School Administration
Sandra Lowery and George Garrett

Chapter 4
Community Relations
Sondra Estep

Chapter 5
The Role of the Administrator in Curriculum
David I Blood

Chapter 6
Strategic Planning and Program Evaluation
Marcus Ahmed and John Borsa

Chapter 7
Administrative Assessment
Jack Klotz

Chapter 8
Personnel Administration and Empowerment
Peter Strodl

Chapter 9
Staff Development
Linda J. Schmidt*

Chapter 10
Microcomputers in Educational Administration
J. Fred Schouten and Jeffrey S. Kaiser

Chapter 11
Conflict
Jeffrey S. Kaiser

Chapter 12
Violence and Safe Schools
Sandra L. Harris, Garth Petrie, and Jamey E. Harris

Chapter 13
Educational Choice
Bernard Brogan

Chapter 14
Stress and Time Management
Jeffrey S. Kaiser

Preface

The first edition of this book appeared more than 10 years ago. Two editions later, the chaos in American education continues.

The calm of earlier decades gave way back in the 1960s to a lack of harmony among parents, students, teachers, administrators, school boards, state legislatures, federal and state courts, and ethnic cultures. It all looked hopeless to the administrative novice then and likely appears that way to many now. Administrators still operate in what appears to be an ever-shrinking power base, an ever-increasing milieu of litigation, and an even more unruly, less respectful student body.

Although feelings of powerlessness plague administrators, alternatives to such feelings come from knowledge of options. Court cases continue, but a greater knowledge of what can and can't be done exists because our predecessors blazed a trail for us. That is the perspective of this book. There are sufficient numbers of repetitive patterns, even within chaos, to allow study, postulation, research, and solution. Many problems have already been solved. For those that appear to allude solution, patterns are starting to become clearer. Those patterns form the basis for knowledge. And, when examined closely, the patterns are not all that unfamiliar. They make sense. We have seen it all before. The combinations and intensities may have changed administrators' roles, but our new technology is helping us manage the vastness of it all. The one constant is that people, however, never change.

The approach of this textbook is that of learned balance . . . a balance between old wisdom and new understandings, between theory and practice, and between conception and implementation. If the approach leans in any one direction, it is toward the practical. If a source is sought, it is the solid grounding in administrative theory and administrative experience.

The approaches herein are the products of discussions among experienced administrators and seasoned professors throughout the country. Everyone writing in the original edition of this book agreed that the various educational administration books used in U.S. universities and available to practicing administrators needed to be better. The books were too long, too short, theoretical, too boring, not practical enough, or so over-simplified as to be insulting. None of them were written in a style aimed at the way adults learn best.

So, for the last two years year, sixteen of us, with expertise in specific chapter areas, put our heads together and wrote, re-wrote, and wrote again. We think we have something good here—the most readable and informative book in the field. Each chapter provides just the right amount of background information to bring the reader in step with current understandings. Charts, diagrams, checklists, instruments, and graphic illustrations provide the reader with learning devices that speed comprehension. And, chapter summaries are often followed by a case problem, which can be solved with the knowledge from the chapter.

The content of *Educational Administration 3rd Edition* was designed by persons with expertise at all levels of education including teaching, building level administration, central office administration, superintendency, university professorship, and university administration. All chapter contributors are experienced administrators, authors, and most are now full-time professors.

Dr. Jeffrey S. Kaiser holds a Ph. D. from the State University of New York at Buffalo and is University Professor of Educational Administration at Governors State University in University Park, Illinois where he is recipient of Academic Excellence and Performance Appraisal Awards for teaching, research, and service. He has experience as a teacher, a school administrator, a central office administrator, a college administrator, and has lectured in Australia, New Zealand, Canada, and the United States. With offices in Milwaukee and Chicago, he has conducted administrative training programs for numerous school systems and multi-national corporations such as Miller Brewing Company, Delco/GM, Rexnord, Kerney & Trecker, Jacobsen/Textron, and many others. The author of numerous articles in national and international journals, he is co-author of *Complete Guide to Administering School Services* (Parker/Prentice-Hall, 1980), *The Principalship* (Burgess/Macmillan/Kaiser & Associates, 1985, 1988, and 1991), *The Principalship: A Software Tutorial* (Kaiser & Associates, 1991), earlier editions of the textbook *Educational Administration* (Stylex Publishing Co., Inc.*, 1993, 1994) Stress Management* (management training software for Telelearning's Electronic University, *The 21st Century Principal* (Stylex Publishing Co., Inc., 1995) and *The Adventures of Reality Jones* (Stylex Publishing Co., Inc., 1996) and *The Adventures of Integrity Gonzales* (CD-ROM software for administrative training from Stylex Publishing Co., Inc., 2000). He is in numerous listings such as *Who's Who in the World* and has served on the editorial review boards of the *Journal of Teacher Education, The Personnel Administrator, Record in Educational Administration*, and the *Journal of Research in Education.*

Dr. Marcus Ahmed was a teacher and administrator with the Chicago Board of Education for many years before joining the faculties of Southern Illinois University in Edwardsville and then Governors State University (GSU) in University Park, Illinois. His scholarly interests include strategic management, the school improvement process, teacher evaluation, site-based management, middle schools, and principal/administrator professional development. Dr. Ahmed is University Professor of Educational Administration and has been coordinator of the Graduate Program in Educational Administration at GSU.

Dr. David G. Blood is University Professor of Computer Education at Governors State University. He has been a teacher and school administrator and is a recipient of the National Rural and Small Schools Exemplary Award for Research and Evaluation. Dr. Blood is listed in Who's Who in American Education and published in the areas of Educational Reform, Curriculum Development, and Applications of Psychological Type in Education. He is a frequent consultant to school districts in curriculum alignment and reform.

Dr. John Borsa was a teacher, superintendent, and professor of educational administration at Southern Illinois University in Edwardsville, Illinois. His contributions to the field of administration were prolific. Dr. Borsa passed away after a brief illness in 2001.

Dr. Bernard R. Brogan is a professor of educational administration at Widener University with experience in a public school teaching and higher education administration. His research and writing interests are in the areas of school choice and school leadership.

Dr. Sondra Estep is a professor of educational administration at Governors State University and a former school principal and district level administrator. Her current interests are in teaching administrators their important role as leaders of technology integration and their role in building school community relationships. She is currently administering a national grant she was awarded to develop a wireless computer laboratory for administration students further emphasizing her commitment to technology and leadership.

Dr. George Garrett holds an Ed. D. from Texas A&M University-Commerce and has over 30 years experience in school administration and higher education. His teaching emphasis is in school law, finance, and research in educational administration. He has published several monographs and numerous articles. He has served as coordinator of the Educational Administration program at the University of Texas - San Antonio and as Chairperson of the Division of Education at Governors State University.

Jamey E. Harris Pinkerton, JD is a graduate of the University of Texas at Austin and the Texas Tech School of Law. She has a special interest in child advocacy and school law and has served as a legislative aide for a state representative. She has worked in the Lubbock and Dallas District Attorney offices. Her experiences include working at a program for at-risk children. She has co-authored an article on school violence and is currently an assistant district attorney in the Felony Division for Harris County in Houston, Texas.

Dr. Sandra Harris is a professor of educational leadership at Stephen F. Austin State University with 30 years experience in public and private schools. She has published articles in national journals on many topics including school violence. She edited a book on school choice, *A School for Every Child: School Choice in America Today*, and co-authored a soon-to-be released book *Standards-Based Leadership: A Case Study Book for the Superintendency*. Dr. Harris has also completed a book on peer harassment: *Bullies, Bullied, and Bystanders: Victims All*.

Dr. Jack Klotz has served as a teacher, principal, superintendent, and professor of educational administration at the University of Southern Mississippi and now serves as head of the graduate program in educational administration at the University of Central Arkansas. Dr. Klotz is a frequent speaker at national educational conferences and an author of numerous articles in educational administration in areas of school governance.

Dr. Georgia J. Kosmoski is an experienced classroom teacher, assistant principal, principal, assistant superintendent, and is currently University Professor of educational administration at Governors State University in University Park, Illinois. She is author of *Supervision*, 2nd Ed. (Stylex Publishing Co., Inc., 2000) and has published books in administrative job acquisition and conflict. She is a frequent speaker at national conventions, schools, and universities and is a recipient of GSU's Performance Appraisal award.

Dr. Sandra Lowery's areas of expertise are the principalship, the superintendency and superintendent/school board relations, school choice, regional education service centers, school standards. She is an editorial board member of Advancing Women in Leadership and a member of the Texas Association of School Administrators. Dr. Lowery is a professor and chairperson of the Department of Secondary Education and Educational Leadership at Stephen F. Austin State University in Nacogdoches, Texas.

Dr. Garth Petrie is a professor in educational leadership at Stephen F. Austin University. He has 12 years experience as a teacher, principal, and assistant superintendent and nearly 30 years at the university. Dr. Petrie has published numerous journal articles and several book chapters and has current interest in gangs, school violence, and principals' use of power.

Dr. Linda J. Schmidt has served as a Professor of Curriculum and Instruction and a member of the Graduate Faculty of Chicago State University in Chicago, Illinois. She is an internationally known author in Special Education and Education in professional journals. She has conducted presentations in the United States, China and Yugoslavia in the area of Special Education Administration, and has conducted inservice training programs throughout the State of Illinois on Special Education Management.

Dr. Fred Schouten has been a teacher and administrator of computer services with school districts. Dr. Schouten teaches *The Administrative Use of Computers* course at Governors State University and is a frequent consultant to school districts on administrative problem solving.

Dr. Peter Strodl has eight years experience as a school administrator, and has served on the faculties of Long Island University, the University of Hartford, and at the University of Alabama with an additional administrative role in bilingual educational administration at Long Island. He also served as professor de la formation de maitre for the Commission Scolaire Crie where he taught courses in teacher education on Indian reservations in the James Bay region of northern Quebec under the sponsorship of the Universitie de Quebec a' Chicoutimi. Dr. Strodl is founder and has been chair of the Eastern Educational Research Association's, Division of Urban Education Research.

-Jeffrey S. Kaiser-

Chapter 1
Leadership:
Ascendancy, Maintenance, and Excellence
Jeffrey S. Kaiser

The process of attaining a leadership position is quite different from the requirements for maintaining that same position. Neither the ascendance to nor maintenance of a leadership position necessarily relates to leadership excellence. This chapter will distinguish among ascendancy, maintenance, and excellence in leading others to higher levels of performance.

Introduction

Thirty years ago, I stood as a tourist on a river bank in the interior of Bali in Indonesia. My wife, my guide, and I had arrived at the location using motorcycles because of the inaccessibility of the area by car. This was truly rural Bali. When looking upstream, I noticed that people were using the river to dispose of personal waste. My glance downstream found a small group of women washing their clothes and their cooking pots. I was moved to ask my guide if Balinese people were schooled in understanding the danger of using the same water as a bathroom and a washing facility. He laughed. *"Oh! You are talking about those things you Westerners call germs. I heard about that. We don't believe what we can't see."*

Theories are often difficult to grasp and often more difficult to apply to real-world problem solving. Like my Balinese guide, we just don't see them and aren't readily willing to accept them. It is understandable why Missouri is called the "Show me" state. It seems altogether natural that we take caution when undergoing change.

Owens (2001) describes the history of germ theory from the initial work of Joseph Lister, who, in 1865 discovered an antiseptic for killing microorganisms. The theory of germs caught on, until in 1874, Robert Johnson developed ready-to-use sterile dressings and eventually, the Johnson and Johnson Company of Band-Aid fame. Of course, research in germ theory has since saved millions of lives through the practical application of antibiotics.

The interaction of theory and practice has been simultaneously analyzed, glorified, and castigated. This chapter ties together administrative and management theory epistemologically through the use of logical application of logical thinking and the direct application of research. To suggest that excellence in leadership can exist without theoretical ties to reality would be a disservice to readers. Excellence in practice interacts with the excellence of reasoned thought.

Ascendancy

Successful leadership is measured by the improvement of the performance of others. Success in attaining a position of leadership is a different matter.

The movement from a position of follower to a position of leader requires the aspirant to pay strict attention to the needs of two distinct groups of people. Teachers aspiring to administrative positions must convince peers that the needs of teachers will be fulfilled and they must simultaneously convince superordinate administrators that the needs of administrators will be fulfilled. Successful aspirants neglect neither of these two constituencies. Such negligence results in the loss of opportunity to lead and the subsequent loss of opportunity to provide an even wider range of power to affect education.

Influencing peers or superordinate administrators to support one's ascendancy is the most important aspect of the ascendancy process. The large number of inept people in leadership positions is evidence that the ability to lead is not the most important ingredient in ascendancy. While it may be a factor, perceived ability may be quite different from actual ability. At the stage of ascendancy, it is only perceptions that count.

Perceptions, which are more often individualistic than collective, are based on the history of interactions between the individual constituent and the aspirant. Although constituents may consult with others before deciding for or against an aspirant, in the end, constituents judge the aspirant as capable or incapable of providing the means to fulfill the constituent's needs (Kaiser, (1977). Constituent needs may or may not be what is best for the organization, and may or may not be what are actually best for constituents, but they are what are best for the aspirant.

Identifying Constituent Need. Successful aspirants understand that they are always dealing with individuals. Political candidates are good at distinguishing between those voters who need to have their babies kissed and those who need to have their Social Security checks protected. They kiss the babies and protect the Social Security checks, but they never confuse the two. Both ends of the spectrum are promised and both ends are cared for. The extent to which both ends believe in the undivided attention of the candidate will determine the candidate's success.

Organizational constituents are not unlike political constituents. They have individual needs for support and informal affiliations with informal special interest groups. Their individual needs change with time, as do their affiliations. In fact, constituencies may be considered a moving target.

Although aspirants may be perceived to have control of the means to satisfy constituent needs, constituents have tremendous power over aspirants. Constituent power comes not merely from the ability to support or withhold support from an aspirant, but also from the ability to control needs.

Aspirants who offer the means to satisfy nonexistent needs have little chance of ascendancy. Although this may seem self-explanatory, it is probably the least understood aspect of the concept of followership power. Aspirants who promise constituents "excellence in administrative efficiency" are offering little to those constituents who hold "salary increases" as their immediate priority. Superordinate constituents may have the need for "keep the lid on" or "align the curriculum to meet state guidelines." It is the needs that determine the successful aspirant.

Only to the extent that aspirants can determine constituent needs can aspirants offer the means to fulfill them. Aspirants must suppress their own needs. Constituent needs must always take precedence during aspirant ascendancy.

Being in the right place at the right time is very helpful. However, whether the aspirant is in a pluralistic-collegial organization or a monocratic-bureaucratic one, as described below, convincing all diverse constituencies of the need for aspirant means is the key.

Understanding Your Type of Organization

Pluralistic-collegial and monocratic-bureaucratic. Pluralistic-collegial organizations are those where decisions are made with much input from everyone who has anything to offer and anyone who may be involved with decision outcomes. Monocratic-bureaucratic organizations are taller and characterized by downward decision flows, less upward communication, and highly territorial decision making. Stereotypical bureaucracies are those in which the bosses make all the decisions without regard to subordinate input. Stereotypical plurocracies are those that involve the maximum number of individuals in decisions.

Figure 1-1 depicts both types of formal organizational structures and their inherent power distributions. Note the double arrow pointing down in both structures. No matter what the shape and no matter what lip service is given to pluralistic decision structures, there is always more power at the top flowing downward than in any other direction. Witness what happens to power in collective bargaining associations such as unions. While much is said for pluralism and collegiality in unions, eventually, the key decisions are made at the top and most of the legwork is at the bottom. This is true in all organizations and appears to increase with organizational maturation (Weber, 1957).

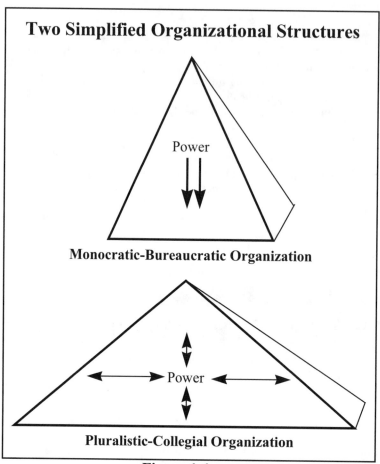

Figure 1-1

Mintzberg (1979) defined five types of organizations: (a) Simple Structure, characterized by top-down administration; (b) Machine Bureaucracy, characterized by highly bureaucratic structure; (c) Professional Bureaucracy, characterized by a strong bureaucracy and standardization, but with less centralized decision-making; (d) Divisionalized Organization, characterized by strong control by division heads (middle management); and (e) Adhocracy, characterized by support staff as the primary coordinators. Of the five types, Simple Structure, Machine Bureaucracy, and Professional Bureaucracy are the most prevalent in schools. Logic would tell us that Professional Bureaucracy would produce the most productivity of the three.

Hoy and Miskel (1996) identified four types of schools: (a) Weberian schools are characterized as High Bureaucracy-High Professionalism; (b) Authoritarian schools are characterized as High Bureaucracy-Low Professionalism; those within the organization that choose not to do what is expected from the top receive immediate retributions; (c) Shared Decision-making schools are characterized by high professionalism and reasonably low bureaucratic structure; and (d) Chaotic schools are characterized by low bureaucratic structure and low professionalism, resulting in more discipline problems and higher staff turnover.

Successful ascendancy requires a clear understanding of the power relationships in the organization. Since monocratic-bureaucratic systems are controlled from the top, it is highly likely that superordinate administrators needs take priority over the needs of teachers and other constituents. Power is not always found on the organization chart. The informal networks, friendships, and leverage in organizations often account for what the more naive describe as surprise appointments and dismissals. These, however, are only surprises to those out of touch with the informal network.

Organizational Purpose. Understanding the purpose of your organization is helpful in orienting your thinking toward organizational missions and goals. Here are a couple of ways to think about the purpose of your organization:

Parsons (1960) classified organizations depending on their *social functions.* Chance and Chance (2002) described their classifications as follows:

- Economic organizations that serve to solve the problem of adaptation, or acquiring sufficient resources and adapting to environmental demands.

- Political organizations that operate to achieve basic societal goals.

- Integrative organizations, such as courts and social agencies, that serve to maintain solidarity and unity within society.

- Pattern-maintenance organizations, such as schools and churches, that operate to preserve and transmit a society's culture.

Blau and Scott (1962) classified organizations by those *who benefit from them*:

- Mutual benefit organizations where the prime beneficiaries are the members of the organization. Examples include labor unions, political parties, professional associations, and churches.

- Business organizations where the main beneficiaries are the owners, such as corporations and businesses for profit.

- Commonweal organizations where the primary beneficiary is the public, such as the military, police, and fire departments.

- Service organizations where the main beneficiary is the public being served by the organization. Examples would include schools, prisons, hospitals, and mental health clinics.

Climate, Culture, and Fit. Understanding the climate and culture of an organization can help you determine whether your thinking has a good *fit* with that of the organization. Without a rich and willing interplay among the three, your own productivity and that of the organization will suffer as stress levels proliferate. Organizational ascendancy is affected by this *goodness of fit*.

Climate consists of the totality the interplay among structure, leadership style, and culture. The most well known instrument to measure organizational climate is Halpin and Croft's (1962) Organizational Climate Description Questionnaire (OCDQ). Administration of the OCDQ results in a climate being described (by teachers) along a continuum from open to closed. Open climates have free-flowing communication among managers and workers, administrators, and teachers. The result is a highly committed group of employees who are not restricted or directed by their administrations. Closed climates are characterized as, restrictive, bureaucratic, and directive resulting in frustrated, divided, and uncommitted teachers. Two clusters of factors described teachers' perceptions.

Cluster 1 consists of four factors describing teachers' perceptions of teachers as a human group:
- Intimacy (the degree of social cohesiveness among teachers in the school)
- Disengagement: (the degree to which teachers are involved and committed to achieving school goals)
- Espirit (the apparent morale of the group)
- Hindrance: The extent to which teachers see rules, paperwork, and "administrivia" as impeding their work.

Cluster 2 consists of four factors describing teachers' perceptions of their principal:
- Thrust (the principal's dynamism in modeling hard-working behavior)
- Consideration (the principal's treatment of teachers with dignity and concern)
- Aloofness (the principal's behavior maintaining social distance or being warm and friendly)
- Production emphasis (the principal's behavior in getting teachers to work harder through close supervision and directive principal behavior).

Halpin and Croft's (1962) research found that teachers' descriptions in Cluster 1 were related to their descriptions in Cluster 2. Negative descriptions tended to coexist in what became known as *Closed Climates*. Positive descriptions tended to coexist in what became known as *Open Climates*. While controversy exists as to the best way to measure organizational climate, the extent to which climate affects performance is clear. Climates such as those described by Halpin and Croft as "closed" do little to motivate teachers.

Moos (1979) reported the results of large-scale research supporting the contention that organizational culture affects student learning and development. Cultures with factors such as emphasizing rules and fostering competition were related to student dissatisfaction with learning, student rate of absence, and grades earned.

The Getzels and Guba model (1957) has described the relationship between the individuals in an organization and the organization itself. They use they word "Nomothetic" to describe the formal organization's roles, bureaucracy, and expectations. They use the word "Idiographic" to describe the needs, wants, and personalities of the people in the organization. The interaction between the nomothetic and the idiographic components define the organization's culture.

Owens (2001) refers to organizational culture as the norms about what is acceptable behavior and what is not, the values that the organization cherishes, the basic assumptions and beliefs shared by the organization's members, the rules of the game for individual member survival, and the philosophy of the organization that guides it in dealing with its employees and clients.

Organizational culture changes to adapt to pressures from within the organization and from its environment outside the organization. As the culture changes, so do expectations about teacher dispositions and behavior. To the extent that there exists a dissonance between culture and fit, teacher willingness to cooperate and teacher motivation is affected. High-performing organizations owe their longevity to this goodness of fit.

Peters & Waterman (1982) argue that organizations may have different cultures, but that successful organizations are filled with highly motivated employees working in an atmosphere that fosters self actualization.

Remaining Flexible

All organizations, including school districts, can be seen as either youthful, middle-aged, or mature (see Figure 1-2). Youthful organizations rely heavily on participative decisions. Middle-aged organizations become heavily bureaucratic. The organizations that survive over long periods of time usually have made peace with power and often choose decision-making strategies based on situational needs instead of territorial imperatives. Mature organizations are lead by people who are well aware of the need to adapt to changes in the environment. Adaptation is necessary for all organizations, whether biological, mechanical, or social. Successful aspirants to leadership positions examine the organization they have applied to, identify the needs of the organization's most powerful constituencies, and sell those constituencies on the means to fulfill those needs. Choosing a healthy organization is important for self-health. Owens (2001) defines organizational health in terms of its (a) ability to achieve goals, (b) ability to maintain itself internally, and (c) adaptation to its environment. Joining an unhealthy environment can be unhealthy for the employee.

Public, bureaucratic organizations, such as school systems, are so vulnerable to outside influences that it is difficult to determine constituent needs very far in advance. Superordinate constituents' needs change with political winds. Teacher needs, while more predictable, also change in reaction to the external political changes. Still, there are some long-range trends. Teachers traditionally push for greater autonomy. Administrators, under great pressure to react to change, look for greater and quicker flexibility in subordinates.

Longevity is directly related to the ability to adapt to the changes in one's environment. Organizations remaining inflexible and stoic often remain stable for a short time, but they eventually die. The same is true of the longevity of people in organizations. Figure 1-2 depicts the longevity of organizations and individuals over time.

Flexibility also requires of the ascendant the ability to fill the appropriate position when the time is correct. One often hears of candidates obtaining teaching positions because of their ability to coach sports. All other things being even, it may be the ability to coach that accounts for the start of a career in teaching social studies. A social studies teaching position applicant with higher grades, better recommendations, a second master's degree, and a Rhodes scholarship in Asian Studies may lose to someone who can coach football. The reason may seem illogical to the scholar in social studies. It is, however, completely reasonable to the superordinate administrator, who has a different set of needs from the scholar.

The answer to the scholar's problem is a very simple one. Learn to coach football. Unfortunately, there is no other means to get that position in that particular district. The same logic holds for administrative aspirants. All the politics in the world will not help an unlicensed aspirant in a state that enforces administrative licensure. Some districts circumvent the law by appointing people to acting positions or by appointing unlicensed people to positions named with nonadministrative sounding titles. But, the ascendant is usually in a much more advantageous position when fully credentialed with the degrees and licenses appropriate for the position. The aspirants with the most applicable credentials usually get the job, because those credentials fulfill the needs of the hiring administrator.

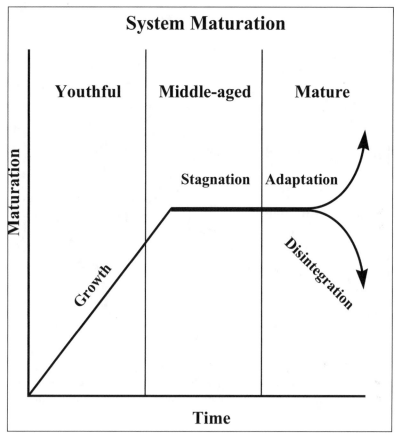

Figure 1-2

Of course, times change. As they change, so do the needs of individuals and organizations. The survivors are those that are most flexible, whether individuals or organizations. The ability to react quickly to changes in the needs of significant others in one's environment is crucial. The story is an old one: the better the formal education, experience, knowledge of position aspired to, knowledge of all the actors in the situation, and knowledge of which way the wind is blowing, the better the chances of the aspirant (see Figure 1-3).

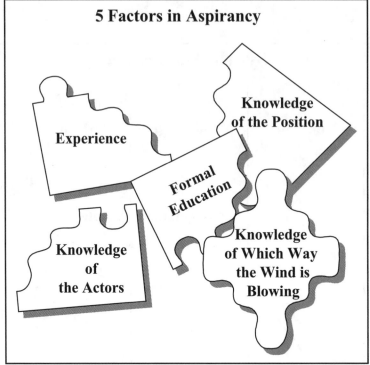

5 Factors in Aspirancy

Knowledge of the Position

Experience

Formal Education

Knowledge of the Actors

Knowledge of Which Way the Wind is Blowing

Figure 1-3

The idea of fairness is too abstract. It is usually in the mind of the beholder, is less objective, and much more difficult to define. Morality plays a role in the selection of the successful aspirant only to the extent that the players are, they themselves, moral.

Maintenance

Our knowledge of successful management is rich but incomplete. Blueprints for successful self-management date back to before the Old Testament. However, few historical references are available on the management of organizations other than the interpretations of classic works such as those of Plato and Machiavelli. Organized research into appropriate philosophies and functions of management are generally a phenomenon of the past one hundred years.

Philosophies are different from functions. Philosophies of management are guidelines for thinking and theories offered as truths. Functions offer us the categories within which we are to structure our behaviors despite our chosen philosophy. The two concepts are not mutually exclusive, but the distinction is clear enough to allow easy discussion and important enough for that discussion to be an early mandate in developing understanding.

Philosophies

Acceptable philosophies concerning the management of people and the management of organizations have varied over time. Eras of management thought have emerged, often related to economic trends and the supply of and demand for labor (Etzioni, 1964).

Scientific Management.

Scientific management. The Industrial Revolution and large-scale immigration to the United States resulted in an oversupply of labor at the end of the 1800s. The early 1900s prevailing philosophy of management resulted from these economic factors and from the work of Frederick W. Taylor and others (Taylor, 1911). Taylor, an industrialist, was concerned with increasing efficiency within industry. He is most well known for his human motion studies and for his attempts to design more efficient tooling, including a more efficiently shaped shovel. Frank and Lillian Gilbreth pioneered time and motion studies at the turn of 20th century.

Henry Fayol (born 1841) also associated with the era of scientific management, studied managers. Fayol's Principles:

- *Division of Work*: Reducing the number of tasks for an employee will increase productivity.
- *Authority and Responsibility*: Authority is the right to give orders, responsibility is the obligation to complete jobs. Authority and responsibility go hand in hand.
- *Discipline*: Discipline implies obedience and respect for agreements.
- *Unity of Command*: Employees should receive orders from one supervisor only.
- *Unity of Direction*: Activities and objectives should relate to one plan with one supervisor.
- *Subordination*: Individual interests should give way to group interests. The interests of the larger organization prevail.
- *Remuneration of Employees*: A fair wage maintains loyalty and support.
- *Centralization*: Centralization is natural; its extent is situational.
- *Scalar Chain*: The scalar chain is the chain of command among managers. It should be followed except when it is a detriment to the organization.
- *Order*: A place for everything and everything in its place.
- *Equity*: Equity is kindliness and justice.
- *Tenure*: High turnover decreases efficiency. A reliable but mediocre manager is preferable to those excellent managers who come and go.

- ***Initiative***: Organizational energy comes from thinking out a plan and ensuring its success.
- ***Esprit de corps***: Strength comes from unity. Unity comes from harmony of personnel.

Taylor studied employees. To Taylor, employees were expendable and replaceable. Taylor's efforts were seen by his contemporaries as more scientific than ever before. Hence, the term *scientific management* was coined. Some stereotypical views from the Era of Scientific management are in Figure 1-4.

Principles of Scientific Management

Industry

- Both hands should begin and end a task at the same time.

- Smooth hand motion is preferable to zig zag motion.

- The better the lighting, the higher the productivity.

- All tools should be left in their proper place

- Pay should be based on merit and nothing else. However, if time units must be paid, they should be paid in small increments.

Education

- When reading, the index finger should always touch the book and move with the eyes.

- All studens shall form a single line when passing through the halls.

- The better the lighting the better the learning.

- Desk compartments shall be kept neat.

- Merit pay for all teachers based on student achievement.

Figure 1-4

The management of education at the start of the 1900s paralleled that of industry and was similar to that of post-Civil War America. Curriculum was controlled by local power figures often allied with the needs of local farmers or industrialists. It was expected that teachers espouse the local philosophy, use teaching methods approved by school masters and school boards, dress according to strict Victorian standards, and behave according to rules that often specified marital status, where to live, and how often to attend church (see Figure 1-5).

Teacher Contract: 1919

This constitutes agreement between Miss Sally Mae Butons and the Homesweet Board of Education whereby Miss Buttons agrees to teach from September 1, 1919 to May 15, 1920. The Board of Education agrees to pay Miss Buttons $75 per month. Miss Buttons agrees to the following in consideration:

1. Not to marry. This contract is null and void if the teacher gets married.

2. Not to keep company with men.

3. To be home between 8 PM and 6 AM.

4. Not to loiter.

5. Not to smoke cigarettes.

6. Not to leave town without permission of the board.

7. Not to drink beer, wine, whisky, or other spirits.

8. Not to ride in a carriage with any man except her brother or father.

9. Not to dress in bright colors; not to wear makeup.

10. Not to wear dresses more than 2 inches above the ankles.

Figure 1-5

Classical Organization Theory

Classical Organization Theory is associated with the first half of the 20th century and most closely associated with the period of time up to World War II. The leaders in organization theory were Gulik and Urwick (1937) and Max Weber (Weber, 1957). Classical Organization Theory is concerned with the organization of the organization. Specifically, it is concerned with bureaucracy and division of labor. Weber's concern was with the structure of the organization, which was seen as a contributor to the cohesiveness of those within it and the productivity of the organization as a whole. Gulik and Urwick concerned themselves with role theory, power theory, and, along with Daniel Griffiths' (Griffiths, 1959), decision-making theory.

Division of labor. Division of labor had fervent believers for many years. The idea is that the more a task can be broken into its parts (by a centralized authority), the more specialized and skilled the workers. Figure 1-6 lists four ways of dividing tasks.

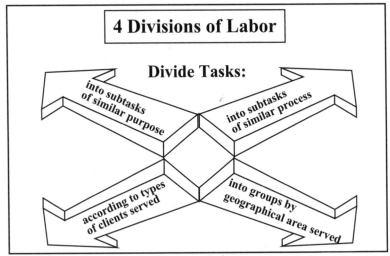

4 Divisions of Labor

Divide Tasks:

into subtasks of similar purpose

into subtasks of similar process

according to types of clients served

into groups by geographical area served

Figure 1-6

The rationale for the usual division of school district services by grade level is being questioned (Cushman, 1990). Division of educational services by geographic region based on municipal boundaries has been under scrutiny for 30 years because of defacto segregation. The growth of regional service agencies such as New York State's BOCES, Illinois' ESCs, and Wisconsin's CESAs suggests that a more efficient mechanism for providing services to children may depend on the density of children per square mile rather than on municipal boundaries.

Redistricting school boundaries is highly political because it challenges a basic foundation of education in the United States, local control of schools.

There are advantages and disadvantages to the strict implementation of division of labor. They are listed in Figure 1-7.

Pros and Cons of Division of Labor	
Advantages	Disadvantages
Efficient utilization of labor	Routine, repetitive jobs
Reduced training costs	Reduced job satisfaction
Increased uniformity of output	Decreased employee commitment
Increased expertise	Increased alienation

Figure 1-7

Bureaucracy. Max Weber defined organizations in terms of hierarchical structures where all power flows from superordinates to subordinates. Figure 1-8 lists assumptions of monocratic-bureaucratic systems.

Assumptions of Monocratic-Bureaucratic Organizations
1. Leadership is only allowed for those holding the position proper for the occasion. Therefore, it is the position that is important, not the person.
2. Subordinates must accept the decisions of superordinates.
3. Authority and power can be delegated, responsibility cannot.
4. Superordinates must defend their subordinates—right or wrong.
5. Unity of purpose is secured through loyalty to superordinates.
6. Since money is the most important thing in determining the prestige and status of a person in an organization, the most superordinate person should be the most highly paid.
7. Maximum productivity and performance are attained in a climate of competition and pressure.
8. Authority is the right and privilege of persons holding a hierarchical position.
9. The individual is expendable.
10. Labor should have distinct divisions, each filled by an expert.
11. The hierarchy of positions establishes the chain of command.
12. Rules should be abstract but consistent. This ensures uniform performance.
13. Business should be impersonal, with social distance between management and labor.
14. Employment and advancement should be based on expertise.
15. Evaluation is the prerogative of the superordinate.

Figure 1-8

Assumptions of Monocratic-Bureaucratic Organizations

There are weaknesses inherent in large bureaucracies. Goal displacement occurs when the original goals of the organization are somehow lost over time. A most obvious example could be made from a large-city school district with very noble goals to serve the educational needs of all children with the district.

After years of frustration dealing with legal challenges to the rights of administrators, continuous strife from special interest groups, and lack of sufficient funding, the goal of principals might easily become that of survival. Other examples of goal displacement would include continuous district-wide efforts to cut staff and other budgetary expenditures. When the goals become that of maintaining one's job or political game playing, the original goals of serving the educational needs of students have been lost.

Bureaucracies are known for rules and regulations. Often rules and regulations are decreed before there is a thorough understanding of their ramifications. Further, the unanticipated consequences of rules often create obstacles to getting things done. For example, a strictly enforced central office rule prohibiting faculty from using district vehicles in a mid-South school district kept a faculty member from getting to an important meeting at city hall. The faculty member had been appointed acting superintendent during the superintendent's illness. No one had notified the motor pool that the rules could be bent in such situations, or that the term "acting" gave the faculty member all the authority of the superintendency. The rules were then changed to prevent further embarrassment.

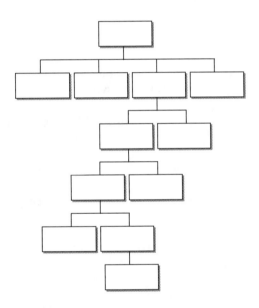

Large bureaucracies replete with sharply defined divisions of labor often result in organizational incumbents trained only for very specific jobs. When the wind changes, calling for new skills, such specific expertise becomes trained incapacity.

Bureaucracies often result in stifled creativity and initiative. If sufficient numbers of hurdles are placed between a person and his or her goals, the person will either (a) quit and move to a job allowing achievement, or (b) stay on the job, learning to do the minimum necessary to keep

> Those at the top are caught in the middle as the rest of us.
> -Peter Block

that job and paycheck. During times of decreased educator mobility, bureaucratic organizations foster increased bureaucratic behavior. This is especially true when the risk of failure outweighs the value of the reward. If there is little chance of receiving rewards from risky creativity, and if the punishments for failure are great, the best bet is simply not to play.

Human Relations Theory

Employment was very high during World War II, and women entered the workforce to replace men in positions vacated while they were away at war. There were jobs for everyone. Although there were some theoreticians who believed management would have a difficult time leading employees who could quit and work elsewhere, the opposite occurred. A high level of patriotism resulted in excellent productivity and high-spirited workers.

After World War II, the United States economy boomed. The excess capital investment in plant and equipment no longer needed for supporting the war effort was turned into the production of consumer goods. And the consumers consumed. Electronic appliances, televisions, automobiles, and housing became available for a larger percentage of the population. The effort of the 1950s toward understanding organizational behavior was turned toward increasing the productivity of current employees. No longer were there throngs of immigrants waiting for jobs at plant gates. Instead, there were employers always seeking more employees.

Management's desire to learn how to increase the productivity of workers currently employed necessitated a second look at some old research and designs for new research. Since acting tough only caused employees to leave, it is understandable that managers would believe that acting nice would cause employees to stay and to improve. The pendulum began to swing toward the direction opposite of scientific management. The era of Human Relations Theory was born. Its birth was a reaction to the old ways, and the idea had its inception in the original Hawthorne Electric studies of decades before.

Human relations theory was a reaction to scientific management and classical organization theory. The results of many studies within the realm of human relations are summarized in Figure 1-9.

Generalized Findings of Human Relations Research
• Human productivity is not only determined by physical capacity; interpersonal relations at the work place are a very important factor as well.
• Human productivity is not only determined by economic rewards, but also by noneconomic rewards.
• High specialization of labor is not the best form of the division of labor.
• Employees do not only react to supervisors as individuals, but as members of groups.

Figure 1-9

The Hawthorne, Illinois, plant of Western Electric had been the site of a famous study in 1927 directed by Elton Mayo (Mayo, 1933). Among the findings were that: (a) increasing the level of lighting does not always result in increased productivity, (b) increasing the number of employee rest breaks does not always result in increased productivity, (c) productivity can be increased by changing the social situation of the worker, and (d) monetary incentives do not always work when peer group pressures to conform to low levels of productivity are strong. New terminology had come out of the Hawthorne studies. A rate-buster and a speed-king were names given by workers to coworkers who produced too much. Many workers believed that rate-busters and speed-kings were hurting their fellow workers by letting management know how much productivity was actually possible. Workers feared that management would increase their expectations of workers without increasing worker pay. What was formerly acceptable to management might no longer suffice. If 70 pieces per day were the expected standard from each worker, managers might soon expect 75 or 80. The concern was that the standard might continue to increase.

Although the Hawthorne studies were completed decades before the popularity of human relations research, they are indeed the cornerstones in the understanding of the effect of interpersonal relations in organizations. Mayo's work also resulted in the coining of the phrase the Hawthorne effect. The phrase is used to define the effect that research experiments often have on the subjects of those experiments.

The work of Mary Parker Follett (born in 1868) is also associated with the era of *Human Relations*. Follett's work (in Metcalf and Urwick, 1940) and Mayo's work might have received more attention had they not been completed during the era of scientific management and classical organization theory. Their work was the foundation of many studies completed during the 1950s and early 1960s during the era of human relations.

> Our most productive plant is our least automated. So, it's not just technology.
>
> -Lee Iacocca

Lewin completed a well-known study of the effect of involvement in decision-making on behavior (Lewin, Lippit, & White, 1939). The purpose of the study was to get mothers to feed their new babies cod-liver oil (a vitamin) and orange juice. Two methods were tried: (a) lecture and (b) discussion. The results were that more mothers in the discussion groups fed their babies cod-liver oil and orange juice than did mothers in lecture groups. The conclusion was that people react as members of groups as well as just individuals.

Lewin, Lippitt and White (1939) were interested in determining which of the following three leadership styles is best: (a) authoritarian, (b) democratic, or (c) laissez-faire. They used three different types of leaders to direct three separate groups in an arts and crafts project. The results were as follows:

1. The group lead by the authoritarian (autocratic) leader produced the most output, but it was of poor quality. The children needed constant leadership and seemed lost when on their own. Some were rebellious and some were apathetic.

2. The group lead by the democratic (shared decision-making) leader was friendly, could work without the leader present, and produced the highest quality product.

3. The group lead by the laissez-faire (let the group lead itself) leader produced the least and worst products. The children seemed uncooperative among themselves and seemed very frustrated.

> Running a business is about 95% people and 5% economics.
>
> -The Economic Press

The Coch and French Harwood Manufacturing Company study on techniques for innovation used three innovation methods on three different groups (Coch &French, 1948). Method #1 was to give the group of workers only a short announcement about the coming change. Method #2 gave the workers an announcement of the necessity of the change and asked them to appoint representatives to devise the necessary retraining program. Method #3 involved all the workers. The results were that Method #3 yielded the highest productivity, followed by Method #2 and finally Method #1. The overwhelming conclusion was that the more pluralistic the decision-making process, the better the outcome.

Another result of the inquiry into organizational behavior was a clearer understanding of the differences between monocratic-bureaucratic organizations and pluralistic-collegial organizations. Pluralistic-collegial organizations (see Figure 1-10) tend to have higher productivity. While no organization is purely monocratic-bureaucratic or pluralistic-collegial, there is a sense of a continuum between the two extremes. Compare Figure 1-10 with Figure 1-8.

Assumptions of Pluralistic-Collegial Organizations
• Emergent leaders should be encouraged.
• Good human relations cause increased productivity.
• Responsibility, power, and authority can be shared.
• Those affected by a decision should share in its planning.
• People are more secure when they determine their own fate.
• Unity of purpose is secured through consensus and group loyalty.
• Maximum productivity is secured in a threat-free climate.
• The use of line and staff is limited to dividing labor, not status.
• The situation, not the position, determines the right and privilege.
• The individual is not expendable.
• Evaluation is a group responsibility.

Figure 1-10

Despite the growing trend toward decentralization of educational decision-making power in American schools in the early 1990s, President Bush and U.S. Secretary of Education Lamar Alexander promulgated the idea of national testing to provide norms for use by schools to assess themselves and by universities and colleges to consider student applications for admission. This centralized testing, coupled with a more decentralized school choice (such as voucher plans) and an experimental schools (such as Comer's School Development Program, administered at Yale University [see Chapter 10]) agenda, may provide the controversy necessary for school improvement. The testing is touted as providing a centralized accountability. The school choice provides the decentralized, pluralistic, and collegial decision making. (DeLoughry, 1991).

Systems Analysis Theory

During the 1960s, much attention turned toward the possibility of solving the myriad of school problems by computer analysis and computerization. This hope was fueled by the increasing affordability of mainframe computers. The trend of thought at the time was linear, involving step-by-step thinking and the reduction of as much as possible to that of quantitative formulas. Computer analysis of such formulas, it was hoped, would help generate larger formulas to aid decision-making and management.

Although few administrators believed that computers could solve all the problems, there was indeed an optimism, a belief in the possibility of a jet-propelled administrative process. Even if computers could not make all the decisions, they might at least help with the tedium of data synthesis, form reporting, check writing, encumbrance accounting, census data analysis, and report card generation. By the early 1970s, most medium- sized school districts had central office computers or purchased computer services from cooperative agencies or outside contractors.

Models of schools (see Figure 1-11) often depicted students, faculty, money, materials, and utilities as inputs. The school building, the curriculum, and the efforts of faculty, administration, and staff were viewed as throughput. The educated graduates were seen as the output.

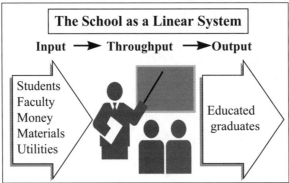

Figure 1-11

Although such an approach may appear trite, it serves an excellent purpose: it forces educators to think seriously about the management of schools. Its thesis is that curriculum is only a means, not an end. Educational philosophies and theories are useful only to the extent that they can serve a purpose, but this focus on purpose became a logical epistemology during this era. Districts concentrated on a step-by-step process for planning and implementing educational programs, a process that involves combining the tried-and-true management-by-objectives (MBO) approach (see Figure 1-12) with systems analysis.

The first step in this process is to come to agreement on the mission of the district. Lengthy discussions regarding the purpose of education ensued, usually because districts define missions differently. Controversy about the meaning of words such as citizenship, rounded education, liberal education, college oriented, life skills, and core curriculum usually emerges.

The second step is to define major goals with the understanding that they will likely take at least one year to achieve. The wording of the goal statements is important. They must guarantee, upon completion, that the mission is accomplished.

The third step in planning is to define more specific and short-term goals called objectives. Objectives are written in behavioral terms so that their achievement can be easily monitored. Objectives appear to be less obtuse than long-term goals and philosophical mission statements. Some districts delineate the plans even further by specifying elements of each portion of the curriculum that lead to the accomplishment of objectives. One can easily imagine program elements being reduced to specific teacher behaviors on specific weeks of the year.

Figure 1-12

The fourth step is to build in feedback mechanisms (see Figure 1-13) to measure progress toward each objective. Feedback mechanisms vary with the type of objective being measured. Feedback on excellence in human relations might be obtained through questionnaires on organizational climate administered to faculty and community. Feedback on objectives regarding the reading program might be obtained via nationally normed test scores.

The importance of feedback is that it helps administrators measure whether the plans are actualized. Feedback that actual performance matches planned performance suggests excellence in performance. Conversely, discrepancies between actual performance and planned performance provide the administrator with the information necessary for revising the throughput. The 1970s and early 1980s focused on the design of acceptable feedback systems, although the move toward nationalization of acceptable tests for measuring verbal and quantitative skills resulted in much controversy. The fourth step has been accepted as a most significant step forward, one that moves away from the input-throughput-output linearity of early systems theory. Feedback forms a loop from output back to input, and each cycle of the system more finely tunes the system.

System with Feedback

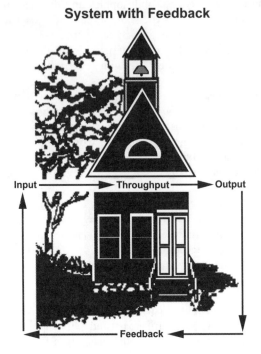

Figure 1-13

New terminology and acronyms emerged in the 1960s and 1970s. Planning-Programming-Budgeting Systems (PPBS) became popular for those districts that were concerned with tracking the dollars spent on each specific educational program. The older, line-item budgeting system grouped expenditures by categories having nothing to do with goals or objectives. For example, all teachers' salaries under a line-item budgeting system usually appear in one category, categorized by school or by educational level within the district (elementary, junior high school, high school). That type of budgeting system provides little information on how much money is being spent on moving the district toward achievement of literacy goals or citizenship goals.

In contrast, program budgets categorize expenditures by educational programs or goals. Dade County, Florida, and Montgomery County, Maryland, pioneered much of the effort toward fiscal accountability in schools. Other efforts toward Program Evaluation and Review Techniques (PERT) provided educators with a structure for evaluation previously nonexistent in schools. Management Information Systems (MIS) were adapted for educational administration from the business world. These structured systems for gathering information from within one's own district often required computer systems to process the data.

All of these new ways of thinking were, of course, not new at all. They were mechanisms taken from industrial models for increasing productivity. A search for the source of those industrial models eventually leads back to the logical thinking of the scientific method taught in schools for decades. It seems that educators are slow at practicing what they preach.

General Systems Theory

As the 1980s progressed into the 1990s, schools became increasingly aware of their role and priority in American society. Pressures on schools became immense, but the increased pressures did not come with increased dollars. Further, the growing inability of parents and guardians to instill values similar to those of teachers augmented the difficulty of classroom management and front-office management. The rise in single-parent families, two-working-parent families, latch key children, sexual promiscuity, and chemically dependent children began to take its toll on schools. Still, society looked to schools for solutions. Unwilling or unable to accept their own responsibility, many parents, the news media, and government officials decided that the major responsibility for unacceptable student achievement lay with largely ineffective teachers. After decades of respect for teachers, a general dissatisfaction with educators swept the United States. During a time of decreased tax support for schools, eroded teacher salaries, and inflated teacher workloads, teachers and administrators were used as scapegoats for societal ills and political gain.

It soon became obvious to educators that a school was no longer an oasis in a desert of chaos, no longer a bastion of common sense isolated from temporary societal swings. Administrators and teachers became painfully aware that schools are merely components of society. The technology of the news media had grown and contributed to everyone's understanding of the interrelatedness of the entire planet. For better or worse, schools were forced to join society.

General Systems Theory (GST) asserts that there are sufficient similarities among biological, mechanical, and social systems as to warrant the study of systems in general. Ludwig von Bertalanffy, an Austrian cytologist, pioneered the theory in the 1960s. Notables such as Margaret Mead became active in the International Society for General Systems Research, a special interest group of the American Association for the Advancement of Science (AAAS). GST became a crossdisciplinary approach to problem-solving. It utilized principles from seemingly disparate systems to understand whole systems and systems within systems. While all of this appeared esoteric, it made its way into university curricula in the training of business administration majors and graduate students in educational administration. Then, with the softening of the iron curtain in the early 1990s, the understanding of interconnectedness made its way into most parts of the curriculum. The study of school/community relations changed from that of a transplant from the business world to that of viewing the school as part of its environment. Von Bertalanffy's terminology, such as subsystems, component boundaries, and feedback, had slowly crept into vocabulary in common use.

> Andrew Carnegie was once asked what he considered most important in industry: labor, capital, or brains. With a laugh he replied,
> *Which is the most important leg of a three-legged stool?*
> -The Economic Press

Although traditional American values had remained intact, the rapidly changing society called for schools to be able to adapt quickly to its environment. The structures of schools seemed to change regularly to match environmental demands. Changes in technology, including the rapid rise in the availability of microcomputers, caused schools to change. Instead of organizational needs driving the use of technology, technology began to drive the organization. Leaders learned to modify their behaviors to meet the demands of all stakeholders. The increased lack of respect for educational authorities made it increasingly more difficult for dogmatic leaders to hold their ground. The move toward increased flexibility, while necessary for organizational maintenance, became a move away from the very anchors so necessary in times of rapid change. Inventor and philosopher Marshall McLuhan's "global village" seemed closer to reality. Author and lecturer R. Buckminster Fuller's definition of humans, written decades before, seemed at once more accurate and more appalling (Fuller, R.B., 1963). The following is his definition:

A self balancing, 28-jointed adapter-base biped; an electro-chemical reduction-plant, integral with segregated stowages of special energy extracts in storage batteries, for subsequent actuation of thousands of hydraulic and pneumatic pumps, with motors attached; 62,000 miles of capillaries; millions of warning signal, railroad and conveyor systems; crushers and cranes (of which the arms are magnificent 23-jointed affairs with self-surfacing and lubricating systems, and a universally distributed telephone system needing no service for 70 years if well managed); the whole extraordinarily complex mechanism guided with exquisite precision from a turret in which are located telescopic and microscopic self-registering and recording range finders, a spectroscope, et cetera, the turret control being closely allied with an air conditioning intake-and-exhaust, and a main fuel intake.

Within the few cubic inches housing the turret mechanisms, there is room, also, for two sound-wave and sound-direction-finder recording diaphragms, a filing and instant reference system, and an expertly devised analytical laboratory large enough not only to contain minute records of every last and continual event of up to 70 years' experience, or more, but to extend, by computation and abstract fabrication, this experience with relative accuracy into all corners of the observed universe. There is, also, a forecasting and tactical plotting department for the reduction of future possibilities and probabilities to generally successful specific choice.

Finally, the whole structure is not only directly and simply mobile on land and in water, but indirectly and by exquisite precision of complexity, mobile in air, and even in the intangible mathematically sensed electrical "world", by means of the extension of the primary integral mechanism to secondary mechanical compositions of its own devising, operable either by a direct mechanical hook-up with the device, or by indirect control through wired or wire-less electrical impulses.

Organized Anarchy

Over a quarter century ago, Cohen and March (1974) described schools as having unclear goals, uncertain technology, and fluid participation. In the decades since then, schools have changed. The 1980s, 1990s, and 2000s brought fiscal austerity, declining enrollment, larger class sizes, fewer administrators to do more work, and greater accountability with less control. Responsibility without control was soon recognized as the major culprit in the cause of stress. All of this accompanied lower real income for all educators as states arranged for property tax freezes, effectively prohibiting any real salary increases for teachers.

The extent of organized anarchy in schools grew. The 1990s was considered the age of organized anarchy (see Figure 1-14). The 2000s may well be seen as the battle for public or private control of schools.

Controversy over goals. There has always been controversy over the goals of education. There are those who argue for different goals, objectives, and curricula for urban schools. Rural schools often have a curricula matching their local lifestyle, folkways, and mores. Suburban schools often boast of their college-bound curriculum, with less attention paid to technological occupations.

> If we give the principal real input into decision making, we take the first step toward building trust and confidence between teachers and principals and between principals and superintendents.
> -Tingley

Large cities, such as Chicago and New York, have decentralized decision-making with a move toward school-based management and local citizen council empowerment (see Chapter 10). However, Dade County, Florida (Miami area), schools have moved toward empowering teachers with control of many school functions. The rightness or wrongness of missions, goals, objectives, or the means by which to accomplish them, became situational and temporary.

Schools as Organized Anarchies
• Controversy Over Goals
• Uncertain Control
• Moving Objectives
• Uncertain Funding
• Uncertain Success

Figure 1-14

Uncertain control. The inadequacies of relying on short-range problem-solving resulted in the need for greater attention to long-range planning. Strategic planning models were developed (see Chapter 6) to call attention to the need for a decision-making process dedicated to more than putting out day-to-day fires. A major benefit of long-rang planning is the decrease in the ability of new actors to subvert the process. Once goals are in place and resources are committed, changes in political realities have a diminished chance at changing direction. However, with frequent changes in memberships on boards of education and rapid turnover in school superintendencies come administrators who learn to play the short-run. Their argument is that there is no long run.

Educational administrators are not the only managers blamed for playing the short run. Chief executive officers in industry also receive blame. The pressure on CEOs to increase short-run profits is great, and the easiest way to do this is to decrease staff size and cut expenses. The result is a short-run increase in profits at the expense of the long run. But to CEOs who are concerned with contract renewal in the short run, long-run plans that may result in short-run losses also result in termination. A logical game plan, then, is to play the short run and be prepared to keep your bags packed. After a few years of cutting the organization to the bare bones, there is nothing left to cut.

> If you're going to take out a long-term car loan, don't buy a short-term car.
> -K. Blanchard and S. Johnson

When no more profits can be squeezed out of cost-cutting and people-cutting, companies begin to realize the financial loss that long-term planning may have prevented.

If CEOs and superintendents lack control of their companies and school systems, the control must lie in the hands of boards of directors and board of education. Boards of education are often made up of expert plumbers, interested homemakers, local medical doctors and dentists, and aspiring politicians. Expertise in managing education is usually lacking. Skills in long-range planning are usually lacking, and understanding of organizational behavior is often lacking. Any control that does exist is often based on temporary power bases.

Moving objectives. With the change in power bases and board membership often comes the change in objectives. With each new federal commission studying education comes new moves toward accountability, new goals, new objectives for meeting those goals, and new methods for accomplishing the objectives. Consider the many programs promulgated by the federal, state, or local level over just a few years: The Hunter Approach, Left Brain Thinking, Cooperative Learning, Critical Thinking, Gifted and Talented Programs, PPBS, LD, BD, CD, ED, EMR, TMR, Student Assistance Programs, Curriculum Realignment, Global Education, Back to the Basics, Computerized Learning, Core Curriculum, Assertive Discipline, Bilingual Education, Early Childhood Education, Crises Management, RIF Management, and Writing Across the Curriculum, to name just a few.

Uncertain funding. As younger families move to newer neighborhoods, the empty nesters left behind tend not to vote for increased funding for education. As the federal government increases its concern for what it has termed as crises in education and a nation at risk, it has decreased its funding of educational programs. As the income level in inner-city households decreases, the local base of financial support for education decreases. And as state budgets decrease, state financing of local education decreases as well. Next year's funding of education no longer has a basis in high local, state, or federal priorities for education. Attitudes toward future funding are usually less than optimistic.

Uncertain success. With lack of funding for programs, decreased budgets for personnel, a continuous barrage of federal criticism from national and local media, loss of autonomy over curricula, eroding autonomy over methods of

> Chancellor Joseph A. Fernandez, New York City Schools, had to warranty that graduates can read and calculate.
>
> **-NY Times**

instruction, continuously changing directions of goals, and perceived legal constraints came great uncertainty of success. The expectation of failure always carries the danger of a negative self-fulfilling prophecy. To many educators, healthy skepticism turned into unhealthy cynicism based on loss of control over schools and individual classrooms. The goals became survival, and survival depended on keeping the lid on things and risking as little as possible. That attitude causes leaders to develop skills in leadership maintenance but not leadership excellence.

Functions

Operative Functions. Operative functions are the day-to-day tasks associated with specific jobs, and they differ depending on the job. The manager in the payroll department usually spends time arranging for checks to be printed. A postal worker usually spends time sorting the mail. An assistant principal usually spends time monitoring the lunch room or halls. Operative functions are different from management functions.

Management Functions. Management functions are the same no matter what is being managed. Whether a superintendent of schools, a chief executive office of a corporation, a principal of a school, or an owner and manager of a frozen yogurt stand, every manager is more or less involved with the management functions listed in Figure 1-15. Urwick also included reporting and budgeting (Gulik and Urwick, (1937).

Management Functions
• Planning
• Organizing
• Staffing
• Directing
• Controlling

Figure 1-15

Planning encompasses the setting of goals and determination of how to get there. Short-range planning usually refers to one year or less, medium-range planning to one to five years, and long-range planning to five years or more. The length of the planning range increases with the level in the organizational hierarchy. The design of missions, goals, and objectives, no matter what the extent of collaboration, is part of the planning process. The methods used for attaining goals and objectives include: setting priorities, establishing deadlines, preparing for contingencies, and constructing a feedback design.

Most planning done by low-level administrators is short range; the long range is usually planned by top level administrators. Techniques of planning vary. Strategic planning is a process that sets critical direction and guides the allocation of resources for an organization. It is usually done at the top level, with involvement from various levels of the organization. See Chapter 6 for more information on strategic planning.

Organizing clarifies channels of communication, job design, procedures, activities, scheduling of evaluative tasks, remediation, responsibility (who is obligated to perform), accountability (the requirement of a subordinate to answer for results), and the chain of command.

Staffing involves assessing the needs for personnel, writing and reviewing job descriptions, interviewing, selecting, hiring, orienting, providing initial training, developing, and outprocessing. The ability to recruit may be affected by a school district's salary schedule for teachers. In 1990, for example, 50% of the U.S. population polled thought that teachers' salaries were too low (Elam, 1990).

Directing involves educating, communicating, facilitating, guiding, supporting, recycling evaluation results, negotiating, manipulating, coopting, and coercing subordinates. Directing appropriate to organizational goals may necessitate all of these. Seasoned administrators know that all of these are not just unavoidable, but necessary at various times. They also know that there are prices paid for the less palatable choices.

Controlling involves the designing of evaluative feedback mechanisms to assure that subordinates and projects stay on track. It also involves time management to assure planned unavailability and interruption control. For more information on time management, see Chapter 14.

The extent to which administrators are successful in management functions appropriate to their administrative levels is directly related to the length of time that they are allowed to remain in their leadership positions.

Maintaining a position of leadership requires skills in managing people, managing operative functions, and managing management functions. Managing teachers, staff, and the entire school district requires great attention to the continuing development and redevelopment of those skills as the philosophies, missions, goals, and objectives change through the years.

Although the process of keeping one's job as leader may appear to be self-serving and often manipulative, it is quite different. Maintaining a position of leadership over time requires a sincere and intense desire to do what is right for students. The perception is that once that desire is lost, a less sincere, Machiavellian attitude will result in short-run management. Such crisis management serves only to extinguish the fires without rebuilding the forests. The philosophy of caring for students is a major part of the culture of education. It is engrained in the hearts and minds of the school boards and communities that do the hiring. It is threatened during times of fiscal constraint and chaos, but also provides the strength necessary to rise above maintenance and strive for the excellence still available to the skillful.

Excellence

Problems often give birth to new opportunities. The multitude of problems coexisting with short-run thinking initiate a strong need for leadership excellence. Such excellence cannot be developed in a climate of organized anarchy, but its birth is often dependent on the existence of such a climate. The answer lies in understanding the nature of leadership excellence and its difference from leadership maintenance.

> Philosophies and functions drive managers, but leaders drive philosophies and functions.
> -JK

Leadership is excellent when it results in the long-term increased performance of the entire organization. That is much more than keeping the lid on. Although leadership excellence can exist at any level of the organization, it is most commonly associated with the top administrative position in the organization of focus. Such focus may be at the department level, school level, or system level, but the difficulty of achieving excellence at the lower hierarchical level has to do with the pressure of the multitude of operative functions inherent in lower-level administrative positions.

Philosophies and functions drive managers involved with position maintenance; in contrast, leaders seeking excellence drive philosophies and functions. The manner in which teachers, staff, management functions, and operative functions are driven is referred to as leadership style. Leadership style is an outgrowth of the leader's attitudes.

Leadership Attitudes

Douglas McGregor (1960) wrote extensively on the effect of leadership attitudes on subordinate performance. He is most well known for his definition of two different attitudes sets that leaders may have about subordinates. These attitudes sets can be seen as a continuum between the Theory X set of attitudes and the Theory Y set of attitudes.

Administrators with a Theory X set of assumptions have a low opinion about subordinates in general. These Theory X-thinking bosses do not do well. Their subordinates can feel the distain of the boss and often react by doing the least possible to keep their jobs. Such subordinates believe that it is a waste of time and energy to try to convince their boss otherwise.

Administrators with a Theory Y set of assumptions have a high opinion about subordinates in general. These Theory Y-thinking bosses tend to get more productivity and higher performance from their subordinates. Subordinates of Theory Y bosses understand that their boss has high expectations of them and faith in them. Such subordinates appear to have a natural tendency to work harder. In actuality, it is their Theory Y-thinking boss that has made the difference.

Siepert & Likert (1973) had a similar way of looking at management attitudes. In Likert's four-system model, a System 1 organization is described as one in which management has no trust in subordinates. A System 2 organization is one in which management has condescending confidence and trust in subordinates. In a System 3 organization, management has substantial, but not complete trust in subordinates, and in System 4, management has complete trust and confidence in subordinates.

McGregor's work and Likert's work were not concerned with being leaders nice to people. They were concerned with finding the leader attitudes that result in the best performance. Theory Y and System 4 work the best.

Robert Rosenthal and Robert K. Merton made significant advances in understanding how a leader's expectations affect subordinate performance. In a classic study in the 1960s, an

> Attitudes are caught, not taught.
> -Elwood N. Chapman

elementary school teacher was given the names of four children she would be getting in next year's class. She was told that testing had found these children to be extremely bright and ready to "bloom". In reality, the children's names were chosen from her next year's class at random (Rosenthal and Merton, 1990) .

As the year progressed, the children did indeed bloom. They had received better grades from the teacher, they were chosen as the best by their classmates, and they actually improved on standardized tests more than any of their peers. Although the teacher believed that she had treated them the same as she had treated all of the other students, she had obviously treated them differently. Whatever she had done had emanated from her belief that they would bloom. It became a self-fulfilling prophecy (Rosenthal, 1991).

The self-fulfilling prophecy is also referred to as the Pygmalion Effect. Pygmalion was a character out of Greek and Roman mythology who set out to carve a statue of the ideal woman. He worked long and hard on the project until, in his own mind, he succeeded. His

> The Master doesn't talk, he acts. When his work is done, the people say,
> "Amazing: we did it, all by ourselves"
> -Lao-tzu- (551-479 B.C.E.)

strong belief in and love for the statue would have presented many problems had not the deities of Mt. Olympus interceded and caused the statue to come to life. Pygmalion and the statue lived happily ever after.

Since the original studies of the Pygmalion Effect in the classroom, the self-fulfilling prophecy has been tested in many authority-subordinate relationships. The consensus is that most often what a boss thinks about subordinates comes true. It is not magic. It has to do with the overt or slight nuances and nonverbal behavior of a boss that is received loud and clear by subordinates. What one expects from subordinates are very often what one will get from subordinates. Management attitudes have a tremendous effect on excellence in performance.

I'm just a plowhand from Arkansas, but I have learned how to hold a team together. How to lift some men up, how to calm down others, until finally they've got one heartbeat together, a team. There are just three things I'd ever say:
If anything goes bad, I did it.
If anything goes semi-good, then we did it.
If anything goes real good, then you did it.
That's all it takes to get people to win football games for you.

-Bear Bryant

Pygmalion's statue had the name Galatea, a name now associated with the belief that self-concept is also responsible for motivation and resultant productivity. To the extent that self-concept is affected by the history of one's personal treatment by others, the interaction of the Pygmalion Effect and the Galatea Effect becomes extremely useful (The Galatea Effect, 1989) .

The effect of a boss's low expectations on a subordinate's own low self-concept can have disastrous effects on productivity. Leaders can work toward eliminating the effects of various Pygmalion-Galatea interactions by tailoring their own behavior to the specific interacting effects (see Figure 1-16).

Pygmalion & Galatea Interaction

Pygmalion

		High	Low
Galatea	**High**	Danger of coasting	Encourage subordinates to take risks
	Low	•Clarify assignments •Encourage with step-by-step successes	•Wrong assignment? •Reassign

Figure 1-16

In a low Pygmalion-low Galatea situation, a boss has low expectations for the subordinate and the subordinate has low self-expectations. Appropriate leader behavior in such a situation is to consider the possibility that the subordinate has been given an inappropriate assignment. Reassigning the subordinate to a more appropriate task would be the method of choice.

In a low Pygmalion-high Galatea situation, a boss has low expectations for the subordinate, but the subordinate has high self-expectations. Appropriate leader behavior in such a situation is to give the subordinate the benefit of the doubt and encourage the subordinate to take risks. As the subordinate's success becomes more apparent to the boss, the boss' expectations of the subordinate should become positive. This behavior is often difficult for a low Pygmalion to adopt. It takes discipline and a clear understanding of the effects of the self-fulfilling prophecy.

In a high Pygmalion-low Galatea situation, a boss has high expectations for the subordinate, but the subordinate has low self-expectations. Appropriate leader behavior in such a situation is to be sure that the subordinate understands assignments, to partition the structure of each assignment in such a way as to provide the subordinate the opportunity to see every step of success toward longer-term goals, and to encourage the subordinate as much as possible.

In a high Pygmalion-high Galatea situation, a boss has high expectations for the subordinate and the subordinate has high self-expectations. This situation provides the opportunity for the highest and -productivity. Bosses can err in such a situation by abdicating their own leadership responsibilities and providing no leadership for the subordinate. Because there is always danger in coasting, leaders still must provide appropriate levels of structure, direction, and human interaction for productivity to remain high.

A more linear approach, yet intriguing to those administrators believing in teacher rewards through concepts such as merit pay is the concept of *expectancy theory* (Kaiser, 1991). See Figure 1-17.

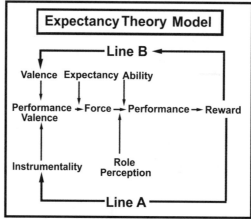

Figure 1-17

From the original work of Lawler (1973) and Vroom (1960), administrators are to look at the diagram above and ask themselves a question regarding each part. For example, if the *reward* offered for high performance is a salary bonus such as merit pay, the first question is with regard to *valence*, the reward's ability to attract the subordinate. If the merit pay is insufficiently important to the teacher, the entire system becomes a waste of time.

The same is true for all parts of the system. If the teacher has no *performance valence* (the desire to perform at the required level), the system will not work either. Expectancy is the teacher's belief that performing at the high level will actually lead to the reward. Of course, if the teacher has been denied the reward despite previous high performance, the system will not work. *Expectancy* is the teacher's belief (or disbelief) that achievement is actually possible. *Role perception* is the teacher's belief that the expected level of performance is appropriate for such a reward. Then, of course, the teacher has to actually put forth the effort (*force*), *perform*, and receive the *reward*. Lines A and B are paths taken by the teacher after the required level of performance is achieved. Line A is where the teacher reexamines the future desirability of the reward (was it worth it?), and Line B is where the teacher decides whether the performance actually resulted in the reward.

What becomes immediately apparent in such an expectancy theory model is the tremendous number of hurdles necessary to make it work as a motivator. There are also the high probabilities that not every teacher would be motivated to receive the same type of reward. Merit systems, which often bog down in paperwork monitoring teacher performance, are often discarded in a few years by the school districts implementing them.

Leadership Behavior

Leadership behavior is directly related to leadership excellence. Although the understanding of organizational behavior is in its infancy, there are already significant findings from research that help to predict which behaviors work best.

The belief that physical traits predict leadership excellence has lost its followers. So has the study of phrenology. Cunningham and Gephart (1973) and Stogdill (1969) reviewed many studies lending some credence to the trait approach. Most are seen as an attempt to oversimplify a complex issue. Although there may be the mistaken notion that tall, handsome males have a better chance to ascend to leadership positions, the belief does little to explain the ascendance of short, stocky Napoleon. Although there is no denying that American political parties often spend vast sums on assuring that their presidential candidates look their physical best, there is no significant relationship between physical traits and leadership excellence once the ascendant is in a leadership position.

However, there are indeed broad personality traits that contribute to leadership effectiveness. Yukl (1994) identified these as *energy and stress tolerance, self-confidence, internal locus of control, emotional maturity, integrity, power motivation, achievement orientation, and need for affiliation*. Yukl also identified actual skills necessary for leadership as *technical, interpersonal*, and *conceptual*.

Although the physical traits of leaders appear to have little relationship to leadership excellence, leadership behaviors are very important. In 1930, Lippitt and White identified three different leadership styles that result in different levels of subordinate productivity (Hillriegel & Slocum, 1978).

Four Traits of Successful Schools
• Clear goals
• Ambitious academic programs
• Strong leadership with a degree of autonomy for the principal
• A dedicated workforce of teachers
-Jeanne Allen

Figure 1-18

Autocratic leaders are task oriented; closely supervise subordinates; foster competition; are critical and authoritarian; and punish poor performance. Subordinate productivity under autocratic leadership may be temporarily high, but quality is low.

Democratic leadership, on the other hand, involves subordinates in the decision-making process and gives subordinates more responsibility for their own tasks. Responsibility is clarified through discussion and consensus. Democratic leadership results in the highest level of teamwork, the lowest antiorganizational behavior, the lowest turnover, the most commitment, and the highest-quality product.

Laissez-faire leadership leaves employees with the least guidance, least supervision, and least direction. Employees working for a laissez-faire boss are frustrated and produce the poorest quality and quantity (Kaiser, 1991).

In 1959, Andrew Halpin furthered the understanding of the effects of differing leadership styles on subordinate performance by identifying two separate aspects of leadership behavior having a significant effect on subordinate performance. Halpin found that leaders elicit higher levels of subordinate performance when they initiate structure in their subordinates' tasks and when they are highly considerate of subordinate needs. Initiation of structure refers to a leader's behavior in delineating the leaders' relationship with subordinates, and in establishing patterns of organization, channels of communication, and methods of procedure. Consideration refers to leaders' behaviors indicative of friendship, trust, and mutual respect in warm relations with subordinates. Halpin's instrument, the Leadership Behavior Description Questionnaire (LBDQ), contains questions measuring leaders' placements on both continua. When the instrument is completed by subordinates, the leader, and superordinates of that leader, the results are a very useful means of identifying a leader's ability as perceived from differing levels of the hierarchy.

Use and Abuse of Power

French and Raven (1968) studied the sources of power and the effects of the use of such power. Figure 1-19 contains their categories of sources and what administrators might expect from their usages. More information on the effects of power abuse can be found in the chapter on Conflict, Stress, and Time Management.

Sources and Results of Power Usage	
Type of Power	**Expected Result**
Reward Power: The leader has the ability to give out rewards to subordinates.	Compliance
Coercive power: The leader has the ability to threaten punishment or threaten the withholding of expected perquisites.	Compliance
Legitimate Power: The leader's power comes from the formal organizational position held by the leader.	Compliance
Expert Power: The followers believe that the leader has the best skills and knowledge to achieve goals.	Commitment
Referent Power: The followers admire the leader because of leader charisma and because of their need to gain the leader's approval.	Commitment

Figure 1-19

Situational and Contingency Leadership

More recent interest in leadership behavior has focused on the possibility that leaders ought to act differently depending on the situations within which they find themselves. The suggestion is that there are times and situations that call for leadership behaviors quite uncalled for in other situations and at other times. The difficulty in such a logical approach is to define the appropriate situation-leadership behavior pairs.

Hersey and Blanchard (1972) theorized that the maturity level of subordinates should determine the appropriate leadership behavior. When the subordinate maturity level is low, the style of the leader should be more task oriented and authoritarian. Moderately low maturity levels would be met by a leadership style characterized by the leader who comes up with almost all the ideas and tries to sell subordinates on or coach subordinates into adopting such ideas. Such subordinates would not be expected to come up with many ideas on their own. Moderately mature subordinates would be allowed to collaborate in decision-making, but they would need much attention paid to their human relations needs. For highly mature subordinates, the appropriate leadership style would be closer to a laissez-faire model. They theorized that highly mature subordinates need very little structure and very little attention paid to their human relations needs.

The major concern about this situational leadership model is the lack of conclusive evidence that maturity levels can be judged in such isolation from other factors. There is also a great concern with any theory that suggests that immature subordinates have less need for human relations than more highly mature subordinates do. Reason would suggest that the feelings of insecurity accompanying such immaturity necessitate excellence in leader human relation skills.

Fiedler (1976) not only theorized situational factors, but also engaged in statistical studies to test the theories. His work resulted in significant understanding of the relationship between situational factors and appropriate leadership styles. Fiedler's work is known as *contingency theory* or *contingency leadership*. Fiedler's studies and many follow-up replication studies have identified the three organizational factors, shown in Figure 1-20 upon which leadership style is contingent. The solid line is the result of a number of validation studies. The dotted line is the result of the original studies.

The first factor, leader-member relations, refers to a leader's personal relations with subordinates. Although principals are not in complete control of their relations with their teaching and nonteaching staff, the relationships have a direct effect on the best style or behavior of leadership appropriate for such situations.

The second factor, task structure, is the degree of structure in the task that the subordinates are assigned. The task structure of a teacher is usually considered unstructured compared to an extreme, such as assembly line work. However, there are some school districts that mandate much more structure in the paperwork, accountability, curriculum, and even the teaching methods of teachers.

The third factor, position power, refers to the power of the hierarchical position held by the leader, not to the leader's personality. The position is the principalship, not the principal. In some districts, administrative positions carry tremendous power no matter who holds the positions. A position of the same title, but in a neighboring district, may carry little or no power. Fiedler found that the power of the position itself is a significant factor in the determination of the appropriate leadership style for the situation.

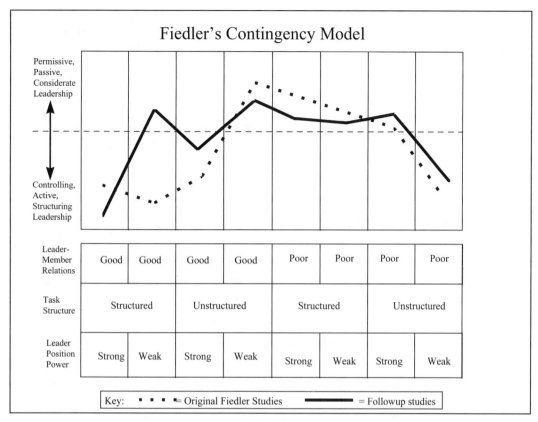

Figure 1-20

All three of these factors interact to determine appropriate leadership style. None should be taken in isolation from the other two. Fiedler used an instrument called the LPC, which requires leaders to describe their *least preferred coworker*, past or present. The idea of the instrument is for leaders to identify the traits liked least about their least preferred coworker.

In visualizing such traits, leaders are likely to describe the opposite of what they, themselves, value the most. Such values are categorized as typical of leadership along a continuum from two extremes of controlled, active, structuring leadership to permissive, passive, considerate leadership. No one is expected to be at the extremes, but there are significant differences in the leadership styles of leaders who are more successful in some situations than others. Figure 1-20 delineates leadership behavior eliciting the highest subordinate productivity in various situations. The educational adaptation of the LPC for educational administrators is called the LPEC, the least preferred educational coworker scale (Kaiser, 1991)

The Path-Goal theory of House (1971) describes the effects of four kinds of leader behavior on subordinates' attitudes and expectations. *Directive leadership* is preferred during ambiguous tasks or when organizational policies are not clear. A directive leadership style is preferred by closed-minded (dogmatic) subordinates. A *supportive* leadership style, characterized by friendship, concern, and trust, is preferred when tasks are stressful or dissatisfying. An *achievement-oriented leadership* style, emphasizing challenging goals, excellence, and confidence in subordinates, is preferred when tasks are ambiguous and nonrepetitive. *Participative leadership* is preferred when the task is ambiguous and the subordinates are highly ego-involved in the task. Personality characteristics do not play a role here.

Decision making

Regardless of who makes a decision—management, employees, or combinations of both—each decision ought to follow a logical process. Many rules for the proper process of decision making likely stem from the age-old scientific method.

Drucker (1974) defines a five-step process for decision making: (a) define the problem, (b) analyze the problem, (c), develop alternative solutions, (d) decide on the best solution, and (e) convert decisions into effective actions.

Hoy and Miskel (1996) view the decision-making process as one in which steps may occur simultaneously: (a) recognize and define the problem or issue, (b) analyze the difficulties in the existing situation, (c) establish criteria for problem resolution, (d) develop a plan or strategy for action, and (e) initiate the plan of action.

Decision-making processes are not as smooth as the above lists suggest. Lindblom (1959) described a process of muddling through little by little with the occurrence of simultaneous events. March (1988) described decision making as bounded rationality wherein the bounds are often political limits, organizational limits, and skill limits affecting the process.

Vroom and Yetton (1973) argue that the extent to which the entire organization ought to participate in the decision-making process is dependent on the situation.

Complex problems requiring both speed and accuracy require the maximum number of stakeholders to be involved. For simple problems, a minimum number of people will speed the process and produce a high-quality decision.

Cohen, March, and Olsen (1972) remind us all that decisions are the result of the complex interaction among the problem, the solution, the people involved, and the choices. Since all of these are acting independently of each other, problem-solving is often coincidental

Change and Innovation

Many models have been put forth for the correct way to innovate. Figure 1-21 emphasizes the situational variables inherent in the use of various methods for dealing with resistance to change. It is synthesized from an approach originally promulgated by Kotter & Schlesinger (1979).

Situational Change Strategies			
Approach	**Used Where**	**Advantages**	**Disadvantages**
Education & Communication	There is a lack of information	Persuaded people understand	Time, if many people are involved
Participation and Involvement	Lack of Information and where there is high power to resist	Increases commitment	Time, if employees design a poor change
Facilitation and Support	Resistance is an adjustment problem	Removes the barriers	Time, effort, resources
Negotiation	Need to create Win-Win	Ease	Encourages negotiations for future compliance
Manipulation & Co-optation	There is little left to try	Quick	Future morale problems
Coercion	Speed is a must & boss has high power	Quick	Anti-organizational behavior

Figure 1-21

Kotter (2002) approaches innovation as another administrative uphill battle. He defines 8 stages or steps for successful large-scale change. 1) Create a sense of urgency among the staff. 2) Put together a guiding team with the credibility, skills, connections, reputations, and formal authority necessary to get the job done. 3) Have the guiding team create clear and simple uplifting visions and set strategies. 4) Communicate the vision and strategies directly to the staff. Symbols speak louder than lots of words. 5) Empower all to do their jobs. The empowerment should cut through any bureaucracy. 6) Provide situations that allow short-term wins. Nothing succeeds in the future like success right now. 7) Don't let up even for a moment. Continuous effort is necessary. 8) Once the change is in place, make it stick. Develop a new culture based on the shared values learned over the process. If necessary, change the structure of the organization to assure that old traditions give way to new ones.

> School reform effects have had little or no effect on Illinois school districts
> -Thomas E. Glass-

Ethics and Dispositions

Much has been argued over the centuries on the role of morality and ethics in management and administration. Although management may indeed be manipulation, certainly Machiavellian behavior and management power, for that matter, can be misused to cause pain in others. University educator-licensing programs in their partnerships with states often attend to student dispositions. These universities may require their graduates to meet standards related to dispositions toward diversity, scholarly collaboration with colleagues, commitment to ethical behavior, commitment to life-long learning, and enhanced habits of mind related to the conceptual framework of the licensing institution. The American Association of School Administrators (AASA) has developed a statement on ethical standards that guide us through both easy and difficult political times. It is not presented here as a complete guide to morality. That ought to be left for elsewhere. Still, AASA's list can be used as a basis for checking our professional legitimacy

An educational administrator's professional behavior must conform to an ethical code. Although a code must be idealistic, it must also be operational so that it can apply reasonably to educational administrators.

Schools belong to the public they serve for the purpose of providing educational opportunities to all. However, administrators assume responsibility for providing professional leadership in schools and therefore in their communities. Such responsibility requires administrators to maintain standards of exemplary professional conduct. Administrators' actions are viewed and appraised by their communities, professional associates, and students.

To these ends, administrators subscribe to the following statements of standards.

The educational administrator:

1. Makes the well-being of students the fundamental value of all decision-making and actions.
2. Fulfills professional responsibilities with honesty and integrity.
3. Supports the principle of due process and protects the civil and human rights of all individuals.
4. Obeys local, state, and national laws and does not knowingly join or support organizations that advocate, directly or indirectly, the overthrow of the government.
5. Implements the governing board of education's policies and administrative rules and regulations.
6. Pursues appropriate measures to correct those laws, policies and regulations that are not consistent with sound educational goals.
7. Avoids using positions for personal gain through political, social, religious, economic or other influences.
8. Accepts academic degrees or professional certification only from duly accredited institutions.

9. Maintains the standards and seeks to improve the effectiveness of the profession through research and continuing professional development.
10. Honors all contracts until fulfillment, release or dissolution mutually agreed upon by all parties to contract.

Summary

Ascending to a position of leadership requires skills quite different from those necessary to maintain the position.

> The Master allows things to happen. She shapes events as they come [and then] she steps out of the way . . .
> -Lao-Tsu

Ascendancy requires combinations of experience, formal education, knowledge of the position, and political savvy.

Maintaining a position of leadership requires knowledge of bureaucratic structures, divisions of labor, decision-making strategies, and great flexibility during short-run policy changes. Neither the ascendance to, nor maintenance of, a leadership position necessarily relates to leadership excellence. Excellence comes from the immediate and prolonged increase in the performance of subordinates. Burns (1978) discussed *transformational* leadership as that which results in both leaders and followers raising each others' performance to higher levels or motivation and morality. He contrasted transformational leadership with that of *transactional* leadership, which usually involves the need to exchange something valued by both follower and leader in order to increase performance. Successful leaders have more positive attitudes toward their subordinates than that which is characterized by having to buy their compliance. Those positive attitudes result in leadership behavior characterized by strength in human relations and strength in the ability to provide direction and structure.

Of tantamount importance is the understanding that Rome was not built in a day. Bad leadership interspersed with short spurts of good leadership just does not work. In mastering the quest for high-quality output, a continuous behavior of excellent leadership is much better than a ridiculous attempt at a quick fix through the use of motivational speakers or bandwagon snake oil. From the work of Deming (1982), the Japanese term *kaizen* comes into play. It is the emphasis on *continuous improvement* that increases the quality of performance.

The human relations abilities, directing abilities, and structuring abilities are gained through the experiential and formal educational acquisition of knowledge about people and the organizations within which they work. Success is predicated on the notion that these abilities incorporate the dispositions and ethical standards of the local community, the profession, and the country.

Case Problem: Cortland's New Environment

Cortland High School (CHS) was within a suburban district in the innermost ring around a large city district. Its faculty mean age was fifty. Its community, once a wealthy suburb, was aging. The large brick, four- or five-bedroom homes that distinguished the community for fifty years were still magnificent, but populated by older people whose children had chosen to settle in suburbs further from the city.

CHS's student population was declining and integrating. People now referred to CHS as "United Nations High School" because it was attended by students from diverse ethnic populations. Declining budgets over many years had forced the school board to increase class size, decrease the number of administrative support staff, and decrease the percentage of the budget available to individual schools and departments for discretionary spending. Teachers' salaries remained competitive, but as with surrounding districts, teacher real income had actually dropped over the past 10 years. Discipline problems were increasing, as were the frequency of complaints from teachers about the lack of administrative support for teachers who tried to hold the line against what they perceived as chaos in the halls and classrooms. With each teacher complaint came what appeared to be a distancing of administrators from the faculty.

With the simultaneous retirement of the CHS principal and the district's superintendent came the opportunity for the school board to make a real difference. They decided to hire a superintendent from a nearby district. He was known for his tough, hard-nosed stance with faculty, for cracking the whip, for trimming budgets to the bone, and for skillful politics with his former school board. He hired a new principal for CHS, a former colleague who saw things in a similar way. When she arrived at CHS, she called a faculty meeting to let everyone know how things were going to be in the future.

What would you predict would be the effect on CHS faculty performance resulting from the behaviors of the new superintendent and new principal?

References

Allen, J A. (1991, January 20). What business can teach teachers: Report on the Chubb-Moe study. *The New York Times*.

American Association of School Administrators (2002) *Ethical Standards*. Retrieved September 20, 2002 from http://www.aasa.org.

Bits & pieces (1981). Fairfield, NJ: The Economic Press, Inc., D, (4A) p. 4.

Blanchard, K., & Johnson, S. (1982). *The one-minute manager*. New York: Berkley Books.

Blau, P., & Scott, W. (1962). *Formal organizations: A comparative approach*. San Francisco: Chandler.

Block, P. (1987). *The empowered manager: Positive political skills at work*. San Francisco: Jossey-Bass Publishers, p. 59.

Bryant, B. (1987). *Bits & pieces*. Fairfield, NJ: The Economic Press, 1(1) p. 5.

Burns, J. (1978). *Leadership*. NY: Harper and Row.

Carnegie, A. (1981). *Bits & pieces*. D (4A), p.4.

Chance, P., & Chance, E. ((2002). *Educational leadership and organizational behavior*. Larchmont, NY. Eye on Education, Inc..

Chapman, E. N. (1988). The 50-minute supervisor. (2nd ed.). Los Altos, CA: Crisp Publications, p.10.

Coch, L., & French, J. R. P. (1948). Overcoming resistance to change. *Human Relations (. 1)*, pp. 512-532.

Cohen, M. & March, J., and Olsen, J.(1972). A garbage can model of organizational choice. *Administrative Science Quarterly*, 17, 1-25

Cohen, M., & March, J. (1974). *Leadership and ambiguity*. New York: McGraw-Hill.

Cunningham, L. L. and Gephart, W. J. (1973). *Leadership: The science and art today*. PDK: F.E.Peacock.

Cushman, K. (1990, Summer). The whys and hows of the multi-age primary classroom. *American Educator*, 28-32.

DeLoughry, T. J. (1991, April 24). Bush proposes populist crusade to reform education: Colleges would help to develop schools, train adults. *The Chronicle of Higher Education, XXXVII (32)*, A21, A23.

Deming, W. (1982). *Out of the crisis: Quality, productivity and competitive position.* Cambridge: Cambridge University Press.

Drucker, P. (1974). *Management: tasks, responsibilities, and practices.* NY: Harper and Row.

Elam, S. M. (1990, September).The 22nd annual gallup poll of public's attitudes toward the public schools. *Phi Delta Kappan, 72* (1) 41-55.

Etzioni, A. (1964). *Modern organizations.* Englewood Cliffs, NJ: Prentice-Hall.

Fiedler, F. E. (1976, Winter). The leadership game: matching the man to the situation. *Organizational Dynamics, 4*, (c).

French, J., & Raven, B. (1968). Bases of social power. In D. Cartwright & A. Zander (Eds.), *Group dynamics: research and theory* (pp. 259-270). New York, NY: Harper and Row.

Fuller, R. B. (1963). *Nine chains to the moon.* Carbondale, IL: Southern Illinois University Press, pp . 18-19.

Galatea Effect, The. (1989). Del Mar, CA: CRM/McGraw-Hill Films.

Getzels, J., and Guba, E. (1957). Social behavior and the administrative process. *School Review, 65*, 423-441.

Glass, T. E. (1988, September) *The Illinois school superintendency: A summary report of the 1988 Survey of Illinois Superintendents.* Springfield, IL: Illinois Association of School Administrators.

Griffiths, D. E. (1959). *Administrative theory.* New York: Appleton-Century-Crofts.

Gulik, L. and Urwick, L., eds. (1973). *Papers on the science of administration.* New York: Columbia University Institute of Public Administration.

Halpin, A. (1959). The leadership behavior of school superintendents. Chicago: University of Chicago Midwest Administration Center. .

Halpin, A., & Croft, D. (1963). *The organizational climate of schools.* Chicago: University of Chicago Midwest Administration Center..

Hersey, P., and Blanchard, K. (1972). *Management of organizational behavior.* (2nd ed.) Englewood Cliffs, NJ: Prentice-Hall.

Hillriegel, D., and Slocum, J. (1978). Management: contingency approaches. New York: Addison-Wesley.

House, R (1971). A path-goal theory of leader effectiveness. *Administrative Science Quarterly, 16*(3), 321-338.

Hoy, W., & Miskel, C. (1996). *Educational administration: Theory, research, and practice.* (5th ed.) New York: McGraw-Hill.

Iacocca, L. (1990, November 12). Commonwealth Press Club. [Radio broadcast]. Washington, DC: National Public Radio.

Kaiser, J. (1977, Fall). *The rise to leadership: born leaders, good role players, and just basic luck.* Forward.

Kaiser, J. (1991). *The principalship.* Mequon, WI: Kaiser and Associates (reprinted from Macmillan edition,1988).

Lawler, E.E., III. (1973). Motivation in work organizations. Monterey, CA: Brooks/Cole Publishing Co.

Kotter, J.(2002) *The Heart of Change.* Boston: Harvard Business School Press

Kotter, J., & Schlesinger, L. (1979) Choosing strategies for change. *Harvard Business Review,* March-April, p. 111

Lao-tsu. (1988). *Tao te ching.* (S. Mitchell, Trans.) New York: Harper & Row, Publishers, Inc. (Original published c. 479 B.C.E.)

Lewin, K., Lippitt, R., and White, R. K. (1939) Patterns of aggressive behavior in experimentally created social climates. *Journal of Social Psychology, 10,* 271-299.

Lindblom, C. E. (1959). The science of muddling through. Public Administration Review. 19, 79-99

March, J. (1988). *Decisions and organizations.* Oxford: Blackwell.

Mayo, E. (1993). *The human problems of an industrial civilization.* New York: Macmillan.

McGregor, Douglas. (1960). The human side of enterprise. New York: McGraw-Hill.

Metcalf, H. C., and Urwick, L. (Eds.) (1940). *Dynamic administration: The collected papers of Mary Parker Follett.* New York: Harper and Row.

Mintzberg, H. (1979). *The structuring of organizations.* Englewood Cliffs, NJ: Prentice-Hall.

Moos, R. (1979) *Evaluating educational environments.* Palo Alto, CA: Consulting Psychologists Press.

NEA Today. (1990, April/May).

The New York Times (1991, February). For schools chancellor, no hat and no rabbit. Sec E. p. 19.

Office of Educational Research and Improvement, U.S. Department of Education (1991, May). *Developing leaders for restructuring schools: new habits of mind and heart.* Bitnet Electronic Mail Distribution.

Owens, R. (2001). *Organizational behavior in education.* Needham Heights, MA:. Allyn and Bacon

Parsons, T. (1960). *Structure and process in modern societies.* Glencoe, IL: Free Press

Peters, T. J., & Waterman, R. H. (1982). *In search of excellence: Lessons from America's best run companies.* New York: Harper and Row

Rosenthal, R., & Merton, R. K. (1990). *Productivity and the self-fulfilling prophecy: The Pygmalion effect.* [Motion picture]. New York: McGraw-Hill Films

Rosenthal, R. (1991, Spring). Teacher expectancy effects: a brief update 25 years after the Pygmalion experiment. *Journal of Research in Education, 1* (1), 3-12.

Siepert, A., & Likert, R. (1973, February 27). The Likert School Profile Measurements of Human Organization. (Paper presented at the American Educational Research Association National Convention).

Stogdill, R. M. (1969). *Handbook of leadership.* Glenview, IL: Scott Foresman.

Taylor, F. W. (1911). The Principles of Scientific management. New York, Harper and Row.

Tingley, S. (1991, May). If we want true school reform, let's start by empowering principals. *The Executive Educator, 13*(5) 32.

Vroom, V.H. (1964). *Work and motivation.* New York: John Wiley.

Weber, M. (1957). *The theory of social and economic organization.* (A. M. Henderson & Talcott Parsons, Trans.). New York: The Free Press.

Willis, Charles L. (1988, Spring/Summer). Contributions to achievements of unusually successful schools: observations by superintendents and other central office personnel. *Record in Educational Administration and Supervision, 8*(2).

Yukl, G. (1994). *Leadership in organizations* (3rd ed.). Englewood

Chapter 2
School Supervision

Georgia J. Kosmoski

The Nature of Modern Supervision

The ultimate goal of all schools is student learning. An examination of most districts' vision or mission statements would support the contention that the American people expect and demand that the schools facilitate, foster, and promote student learning. Successful schools are often defined as those that demonstrate positive and increasing student academic achievement.

Students have the power to make the most basic choice about their own learning, because they may choose to engage or disengage. Educators want students to choose to learn. The goal of teachers is to inspire students to choose to engage, and the goal of supervisors is to support these teachers' efforts (Starnes & Paris, 2000).

The literature of the last decade has identified the process of supervision as a key for successful schools. Behind every successful school is an effective supervision program, although schools vary with respect to who carries out supervisory duties and responsibilities. Some schools assign supervisory tasks to department chairpersons, assistant principals, master teachers, and central office administrators. In these schools, the principal focuses not on supervision but rather on administrative functions such as budgeting, community relations, scheduling, and the physical plant. In other schools, the principal is chiefly responsible for all the supervisory tasks. Regardless of the organizational structure, all successful schools have one common property. In these schools, there is an individual or individuals who are assigned, responsible, and committed to the process of supervision (Glickman, Gordon, & Ross-Gordon, 1998).

If administrators wish to institute an effective supervision program in a district or school, they must understand and then apply the basic concepts and the best practices of supervision. The purpose of this chapter is to help the reader grasp the fundamental concepts and theories of effective supervision. It then provides suggestions for applying these basic tenets. To accomplish this goal, areas treated include definitions of supervision, identification of supervisors, the need for supervision, supervision models, types of supervision, and supervisory tasks. In short, the *what*, *who*, and *how* of supervision are discussed.

Supervision Defined

Supervision has long been recognized as an essential process executed by the educational leader, school administrator, or supervisor. In an attempt to improve the skills of the supervisor, educational administration specialists have defined this term in the context of their times, setting, philosophy, and research findings. It is not surprising that there are as many credible definitions for supervision as there are supervision experts. A chronological examination of some of these definitions will aid in the understanding of this essential process.

Jane Franseth (1961) reflects the human resource movement of the times and stresses the collegial nature of supervision. She emphasizes leadership, school effectiveness, and universality.

> *Today, supervision is generally seen as leadership that encourages a continuous involvement of all school personnel in a cooperative attempt to achieve the most effective school program.*

Simple and straightforward, the Campbell, Corbally, and Nystrand (1983) definition suggests that people are the focal point of supervision. The judgmental nature of supervision was underscored. They define supervision as the " . . .appraisal of personnel performance".

Sergiovanni and Starratt (1988) offer a pragmatic definition that recognizes that individuals often simultaneously perform multiple roles. They suggest that supervisory and administrative duties not only coexist but remain separate and distinct.

> *Supervision . . .can be viewed as a process component of a variety of administrative and supervisory roles or as a label to categorize roles the primary responsibility of which is the improvement of instruction.*

Robert Krey and Peter Burke (1989) equate supervision with instructional leadership, emphasizing that supervision encompasses a multitude of functions. They point out the wide scope of supervision.

> *Supervision is instructional leadership that relates perspectives to behavior, clarifies purposes, contributes to and supports organizational actions, coordinates interactions, provides for maintenance and improvement of the instructional program, and assesses goal achievements.*

Georgia Kosmoski (2000) draws from the common elements or threads found in the above definitions and reflects the principles found in human relations philosophy and the current research findings. Kosmoski's definition for supervision will be used as the definition of choice for the remainder of this chapter.

> *Supervision is that leadership process whose ultimate purpose is to improve instruction, and, thereby, facilitate and promote successful student learning.*

After examining these definitions of supervision, it becomes clear that the term *supervision* is elusive and convoluted. Each definition is predicated on the author's own personal perspective and educational philosophy.   With many philosophies existing simultaneously today, it is no wonder that there are so many diverse, cogent, and plausible definitions for educational supervision.

By extrapolating from the above definitions, it is possible to identify the main characteristics of supervision as we understand them today. For a brief synthesis, refer to Figure 2-1, Characteristics of Supervision.

Characteristics of Supervision

Supervision Specialists	Characteristics Identified by Definitions
Franseth	A continuous and cooperative process that involves all school personnel.
Campbell, Corbally, & Nystrand	Appraisal of personnel performance.
Sergiovanni & Starratt	The role with the primary responsibility to improve instruction.
Krey & Burke	Instructional leadership that focuses on purposes, actions, interactions, improvement, and assessment.
Kosmoski	Leadership that focuses on improvement of instruction to promote student learning.

Figure 2-1

School Supervisors

By accepting Kosmoski's definition of supervision as a process with the main purpose of improving teacher instruction, the definition of supervisor is also defined. Educators throughout the organizational hierarchy, engaged in the process of improving instruction, are supervisors. Typical supervisors include school principals, assistant or vice principals, department heads, chairpersons, master teachers, central office coordinators, and assistant superintendents.

What these educators have in common is their direct involvement in helping teachers as they improve their instructional practices. Since the titles of *supervisor* and *administrator* are often used indiscriminately by school districts, a person's function and responsibilities, rather than title, should be emphasized (Glickman, Gordon, & Ross-Gordon, 1998). For example, a central office employee whose chief responsibilities are grant writing, record keeping, and district-wide testing might hold the title *supervisor of social studies.* Whereas, a lead teacher with no supervisory title may be directly involved with assisting teachers to improve instruction. Obviously, the lead teacher, rather than the central office worker, is the true supervisor. Refer to Figure 2-2, Examples of Supervisors in Action, for additional illustrations of educators serving as supervisors.

Examples of Supervisors

The Educator	Example of a Supervisory Action
School principal	Participating in a clinical supervision cycle with a teacher
Master teacher	Serving as a mentor for a beginning teacher
Lead teacher	Using half of the working day to deliver professional development programs to colleagues
Experienced teacher	Participating as a member of a collegial-peer-coaching team
Assistant superintendent	Setting personal year-long goals with accompanying activities and assessment

Figure 2-2

Experts in school supervision have identified three common characteristics of the successful and effective school supervisor. The first is a strong knowledge base. The supervisor must understand what is required to move an individual teacher and an entire school faculty from the norm of mediocrity to the exception of excellence. Knowledge of accepted theory, paradigms, and best practices helps the supervisor initiate and maintain an effective program of supervision. Second, the supervisor has an interpersonal skills base. The effective supervisor demonstrates superior interpersonal skills when working with individual teachers, when facilitating groups, and when acting as a change agent. Finally, this supervisor has technical competence in observing, planning, and assessing instructional development (Glickman, Gordon, & Ross-Gordon, 1998; Kirkpatrick & Lewis, 1995; Kosmoski, 2000).

The Need for Supervision

There are at least four major reasons for the need for supervision:

1. Humans are natural learners. Teachers are human, and therefore, learners. All learners, including teachers, have the right to assistance in the pursuit of knowledge and understanding. Effective supervision provides teachers with the skillful assistance necessary to help them learn and grow. From the beginning teacher to the veteran on remediation, supervision should have a positive impact on all (Gorton, 1987). For the novice teacher, supervision serves as the vehicle to help the individual overcome insecurities, learn appropriate teacher roles, and practice specific behaviors. The competent or master teacher also needs appropriate supervision. For these teachers, supervision provides a process where they may expand their strategies and instructional techniques. It helps them solve problems, meet challenges, and face new situations. The

teacher on probationary status needs supervision, since the process provides the support the teacher needs to move from probation to a satisfactory state. Left alone, the probationary teacher might find the task of improvement impossible.

2. Sergiovanni and Starratt (1988) point out that supervision and teacher effectiveness are directly linked. A growing body of research clearly demonstrates that good supervision assists teachers to develop classroom skills proven to positively impact student achievement. Meaningful staff development programs and solid evaluation procedures are two supervisory activities proven to influence teacher effectiveness and, in turn, student achievement.

3. Supervision is frequently viewed as an avenue to motivate teachers and a method to allow them to attain satisfaction from their work (Hackman & Oldham, 1976). When the organization and the supervisor prioritize the improvement of instruction, it implies to the teacher that the work of instruction is highly valued, meaningful, and worthwhile. The teacher is more likely to feel accountable for classroom behaviors and more often assumes responsibility for his or her own actions. Supervision performed on a regular schedule affords the teacher an opportunity to analyze job performance and attain personal satisfaction.

4. Lastly, Lunnenberg and Ornstein (1991) argue the need for supervision from the professional development perspective. They suggest that supervision, particularly through professional development activities, fulfills school personnel's potential by giving them the opportunity to learn new skills and develop their abilities to the fullest. Supervision, by its very nature, allows teachers to do just that—learn new skills and develop abilities. Royal Van Horn (1999) points out the uneven quality of teacher education graduates whose abilities range from mediocre to excellent. No teacher preparation program thoroughly prepares beginners to effectively perform expected tasks. Both veteran and novice teachers need to upgrade and expand their knowledge and skills. A visual summation is found in Figure 2-3, The Need for Supervision.

The Need for Supervision

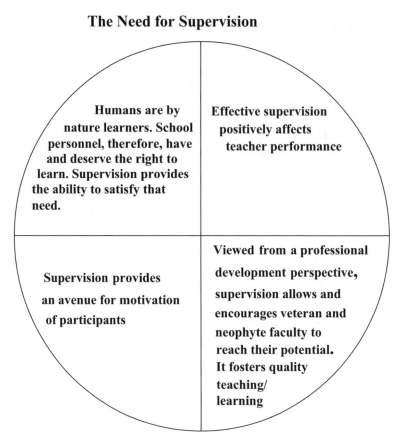

Humans are by nature learners. School personnel, therefore, have and deserve the right to learn. Supervision provides the ability to satisfy that need.

Effective supervision positively affects teacher performance

Supervision provides an avenue for motivation of participants

Viewed from a professional development perspective, supervision allows and encourages veteran and neophyte faculty to reach their potential. It fosters quality teaching/ learning

Figure 2-3

Supervision Models

Successful supervisors select and implement the appropriate supervision model that best fits their own orientation and philosophy, the situation, and the needs of the teachers. There are a number of specific models a supervisor might choose to implement a given perspective or supervisory task. Today, the most often utilized models are traditional, human resource, clinical, developmental, and collegial.

Traditional

The original supervision model used in American schools is the traditional, or bureaucratic model. This supervision model parallels the bureaucratic philosophy. Proponents view teachers as subordinates who need to be directed. This model is authoritative, directive, coercive, and punitive (Lunnenburg & Ornstein, 1991; Sergiovanni & Starratt, 1988). Supervision consists of monitoring and ordering. Teachers are told, not asked. They are punished for failure, not rewarded for success. Supervisors feel responsible for formulating standards and assuring compliance of the given standards. Experts report that, to some degree, the traditional model is still the most practiced form used in our schools.

Human Resources Supervision

The human resources model emerged in the 1960s. Also referred to as the human relations model, this model was the product of such specialists as Bennis, McGregor, and Argyris. The human resource model attempts to humanize the bureaucratic scientific management orientation. Sergiovanni and Starratt (1988) and Oliva (1993) point out that this model has three basic characteristics. Supervision should center on the human beings (teachers) involved in the process. The process is both personal as well as grounded within educational tradition. And supervision may only be exercised within the context of organizational dynamics.

Clinical Supervision

Originating in the 1970s, the clinical supervision model focuses on classroom behavior for the improvement of instruction. It postulates that, within a positive general supervisory climate, a strong and dynamic relationship exists between the teacher and the supervisor (Kaiser, 1993). Pioneers who shaped modern clinical supervision include Goldhammer, Cogan, and Acheson and Gall. Although these specialists disagreed upon the exact formula for obtaining effective results, they do agree upon three basic steps within the process. These steps are the Preobservation Conference, the Observation, and the Postobservation Conference.

The most commonly implemented clinical supervision models include the classic models by Goldhammer (1969), Cogan (1973), Mosher and Purpel (1972), and Acheson and Gall (1992). Other models grounded in the basic tenets of classical clinical supervision, yet possessing distinct variations, are the Russell and Hunter Model, which suggests that supervision should be based on the frequency a teacher engages in nine identifiable teaching activities and Eisner's Artistic Model, which urges the supervisor to rely on his or her own perception, sensitivity, and acquired knowledge when working with and evaluating teachers (Eisner, 1982;Russell & Hunter, 1980).

Developmental Supervision

In the 1980s, Glickman (1981) designed the Developmental Supervision Model. The developmental model views supervision as a supportive process, where the individual characteristics of teachers and the basic beliefs or orientations of the supervisor are key ingredients. The effectiveness of the supervision is predicated on how well the supervisor's orientation matches the teacher's characteristics.

Glickman (1990) suggests that teacher characteristics are the result of levels of abstraction (the ability of the teacher to think abstractly) and commitment (the level of dedication to the profession). These characteristics combine to produce four basic types of teacher: the Professional, who has high abstraction and high commitment; the Unfocused Worker, who has low abstraction and high commitment; the Analytical Observer, who has high abstraction and low commitment; and the Teacher Dropout, who has low abstraction and low commitment.

Glickman also posits that the identifiable orientations of supervisors include nondirective, collaborative, and directive. Finally, Glickman recommends that the supervisor select the orientation that best serves the type of teacher with whom he or she is working. For example, a nondirective supervisor would serve as a facilitator or guide to the teacher who would take responsibility for her or his own improvement. Observable behaviors of the nondirective supervisor would include listening, clarifying, encouraging, and presenting (i.e. ,expressing only a limited number of personal opinions to aid the teacher). This orientation is successful with the professional teacher and the unfocused worker. He suggests that a supervisor would use a collaborative style with the analytical observer but a direct orientation, which is telling, ordering, instructing, and demanding, with the teacher dropout.

Collegial Supervision

In the 1980s and 1990s, numerous forms of collegial or collaborative supervision were developed and implemented (Kosmoski, 1994; Glatthorn, 1984; Redfern, 1980). Generally, these are models with nontraditional supervisors who act within a supervisor/teacher partnership, encourage, guide, and facilitate. The focus of collegial supervision is the improvement of instruction. Supervisors do not necessarily have evaluation responsibilities. Some examples are mentoring, where an experienced master teacher assists a novice; peer coaching, where two or more experienced teachers share expertise; cohort groups, where tenured teachers with similar assignments jointly assume supervisory responsibilities for each other; and teacher rotation, where trained teachers take turns in the performance of supervisory tasks (Sacken, 1994). For an overview of these models, refer to Figure 2-4.

Models of Supervision

Model	Emerged	Pioneers	Main Characteristics
Traditional	1600-1800s	• Pilgrims • Horace Mann • Henry Barnard • Committee of 10	• Monitor/inspect • Authoritative Directive • Punitive
Human Resource	1960s	• McGregor • Benis • Argyris	• People centered • Responsive • Focus on growth
Clinical	1970s	• Goldhammer • Cogan • Acheson and Gall	• Collegial • Continuous • Observe classroom • Gather behavior data
Developmental	1980s	• Glickman	• Identify teacher type • Select supervision style • Match style to teacher's type
Collegial	1980-1990s	• Sergiovanni • Austin • Darling-Hammond	• Untraditional supervisor • Partnership • Absence of evaluation

Figure 2-4

Types of Supervision

In 1973, Cogan identified two major types or areas of supervision: general and clinical. Both types are interrelated, exist simultaneously, and are practiced by the school supervisor. General supervision refers to all tasks that the supervisor attends to outside of the classroom. These tasks are designed to indirectly provide the teacher and learner with an environment that promotes the learning process. General supervision supports the efforts of the teacher. Some activities included in general supervision are installing a safety alarm system, scheduling, and assigning classrooms and facilities. When a middle school principal insures a clean, safe building, insists upon on-time staff attendance, or replaces a disabled school bus, he or she is engaged in general supervision.

Clinical supervision is a more specific level of supervision where the supervisor works directly with the teacher. These tasks occur within the classroom, and their sole purpose is to improve instruction. Improvement is accomplished by active and direct modification of the instruction itself or through the promotion of the teacher's professional growth. For example, the elementary principal who regularly visits the classroom, actively observes, and then shares those observations with the teacher in order to help the teacher improve instruction is engaged in clinical supervision. Likewise, when a high school science department chairperson arranges for one of the science faculty to attend a workshop on integrated learning, the chairperson is practicing clinical supervision (see Figure 2-5).

Characteristics of General and Clinical Types of Supervision

Characteristics of General Supervision	Characteristics of Clinical Supervision
Indirectly affects instruction	Directly affects instruction
Occurs outside the classroom	Occurs inside the classroom
Goal is to provide best learning environment	Goal is to modify or increase teacher performance
Practiced simultaneously with clinical	Practiced simultaneously with general
Purpose is to improve instruction	Purpose is to improve instruction

Figure 2-5

Supervisory Tasks

One way to analyze supervision is to identify and examine the specific tasks or activities inherent in the leadership process of supervision. Starting with Burton in 1922, numerous supervision specialists compiled task lists. One of the most succinct yet thorough lists was formulated by Harris (1985), who identified 10 tasks that he grouped into the three classes of preliminary, developmental, and operational. Preliminary tasks are those performed prior to actual instruction by the teacher. Developmental tasks are those that should directly improve instruction. Operational tasks are those tasks that facilitate the ongoing operation.

Preliminary Tasks:

Preliminary tasks are activities ideally accomplished by the supervisor prior to teaching and learning. Before the start of the school year or term, the supervisor would have insured that these tasks were satisfactorily completed. The three preliminary tasks are:

1. Develop curriculum. This includes the design of what is to be taught.

2. Provide staff. This task provides adequate staff with appropriate qualifications and competencies.

3. Provide facilities. This task includes designing, remodeling, and equipping facilities to meet the needs and requirements of the particular type of instruction.

Developmental Tasks

Developmental tasks are specific activities the supervisor performs to directly improve the quality of instruction. These tasks directly impact the teacher and, therefore, indirectly affect the learner and the learning process. The two developmental tasks are:

4. Arrange for professional development. Harris (1985) refers to this task as arranging for inservice education, defining it further as providing instruction-related learning experiences for staff. Today, this definition is best labeled professional development opportunities, which (1) is much broader than the term inservice education, and (2) encompasses inservice education as but one of its manifested forms.

5. Evaluate instruction. This task includes the joint planning and implementation necessary for gathering meaningful data, analysis, interpretation, and decision-making for the purpose of improving instruction.

Operational Tasks:

Operational tasks are those duties and activities performed by the supervisor to facilitate the ongoing teaching/learning process. These tasks are continuous and occur during and throughout the instructional process. The five operational tasks include:

6. Organize for instruction. This task deals with day-to day order and logistics. The supervisor makes decisions and choices regarding the order of who, what, where, and when to best promote instruction. The supervisor engages in such processes as scheduling, grouping, distributing and storing materials, establishing timelines, and maintaining calendars.

7. Provide materials. The supervisor engages in selecting and securing the appropriate materials to insure proper instruction for the required curriculum. This includes written texts, computer hardware and software, manipulatives, and others.

8. Orienting new staff. This task entails providing staff with the basic information necessary to perform their duties and responsibilities. This includes acquainting and updating both beginning and new-to-the-building veterans with current facilities, procedures, and community and organizational developments.

9. Relate and provide special pupil services. This task addresses the coordination of special student services to best support appropriate learning opportunities.

10. Develop public relations. For this task, the supervisor's duties include promoting and providing the free flow of information between the school and the community, and enhancing community involvement in instructional matters.

An in-depth examination of these 10 tasks, activities, or areas of concentration will provide a clear understanding of the true breadth and nature of school supervision. This will clarify the scope of the primary supervisory responsibilities.

Develop Curriculum

Today, most curriculum development or instructional design is a collegial effort that occurs at the building level. The development team is composed of members that represent the faculty, student body, and school community. Although not necessary, most team chairpersons are the appropriate supervisors. Experts point out that curriculum developed by stakeholders who intimately understand the needs of the learner and school community will be more successful (Doll, 1992).

While engaged in curriculum development, the supervisor must successfully assume numerous roles. Three of these roles are guide, motivator for change, and expert. First and foremost, the supervisor oversees and guides the team as it works through the 6 stages in the development process. These are needs assessment, educational philosophy, goals and objectives, content, methodology, and evaluation (Tyler, 1949). Kosmoski (2000) suggests that the supervisor provides the team with leadership, organization, and structure. The supervisor facilitates the team as it makes decisions regarding the scope and sequence, guides, standards, evaluations, and timelines for units, courses, and programs.

Second, the supervisor serves as a motivator, change agent, or catalyst for the instructional design team. This is accomplished by helping the team identify curriculum problems or areas of need and then aiding them in the search for solutions. The supervisor stimulates the group to examine the existing curriculum and potential alternatives. He or she intentionally sparks dissatisfaction with the current so as to encourage the team members to embrace change.

Finally, the supervisor assumes the role of curriculum expert. The supervisor's expertise is not predicated on status alone, but rather upon the level of credibility perceived by fellow curriculum coworkers. Oliva (1993) posits that to achieve credibility, supervisors must be grounded in curriculum theory, knowledgeable about possible solutions, and cognizant of current national curricular developments and trends. Further, the supervisor should be facile in communication skills, group dynamics practices, and interpretation of research, social, and learning theory.

Provide Staff

The supervisor is responsible for providing qualified staff. Individuals who work directly with students must have the proper education and state-required certification or licensure. Professional staff should have a personal educational philosophy that enhances the school's mission and basic belief system. Teachers must be given specific assignments that best utilize their skills, knowledge, interests, and abilities. Further, the supervisor must adroitly match the teacher with the pupils and their needs. Classroom and specialist positions should be filled so as to properly serve the present student population. To retain the best teachers, the supervisor must encourage, challenge, and nurture these specialists (Cunningham & Cordeiro, 2000). Finally, the supervisor must monitor teacher performance. This is best accomplished by regular observations, review of lesson plans, and study of student progress.

This supervisory task also includes providing the best possible noncertified staff. Issues of school/student needs, work history, and daily performance of the noncertified workers are the concern of the supervisor.

Recruiting, hiring, assigning, retaining, and removing staff are examples of specific activities associated with this task or function. To successfully accomplish each of these activities, the supervisor must possess many skills (see Figure 2-6), The suggested list of skills is by no means inclusive; rather, the list is representative.

Supervisory Activities and Required Skills Necessary to Provide Staff

Activity	Skills
Recruiting	Communications, public relations, technological, legal, political, financial, etc.
Hiring	Interpersonal, communications, curricular, financial, social, legal, contractual, etc.
Assigning	Curricular, learning theory, decision-making, group dynamics, evaluation, financial, etc.
Retaining	Motivational, assessment, curricular, decision-making, communications, contractual, legal, etc.
Removing	Legal, contractual, communications, procedural, interpersonal, political, financial, public relations, group dynamics, etc.

Figure 2-6

Provide Facilities

The task of providing facilities implies acquiring, providing, maintaining, and improving the physical plant and educational setting. This includes the entire school campus, both the actual buildings and the grounds. The effective supervisor must approach this task seriously. Educational experts have demonstrated that the physical setting directly impacts the learning climate or environment (Sergiovanni, Burlingame, Coombs, & Thurston, 1999). A clean, well-lighted, and safe environment promotes both academic and social growth. Such an environment contributes to positive self-esteem, group productivity, and learning.

Some specific examples of activities associated with this task are:

- Maintaining existing classrooms, furniture, technology, and equipment.
- Adhering to regular replacement and repair schedules.
- Putting in place emergency procedures for unexpected maintenance or replacement.
- Updating and upgrading of the existing facility to meet the current needs and best practices.
- Allocating funds for new facilities to meet identified learning needs and teaching techniques.
- Implementing safety measures.
- Arranging for aesthetic additions.

Finally, it should be noted that the supervisor must follow established federal, state, and local guidelines when providing proper facilities. Compliance with the various regulations is mandatory.

Arrange for Professional Development

Since the developmental tasks directly affect the quality of instruction and, therefore, the quality of learning, arranging for professional development opportunities is a crucial supervisory task. For purposes of this discussion, professional or staff development is defined by Kosmoski (2000) as:

Staff development is a planned program of activities designed to promote personal and professional growth or remediation of staff members. Inservice education is one vehicle for accomplishing the goal or purpose of staff development (p. 297).

This definition views staff development as encompassing all avenues available for change, including programs that address staff members' personal and professional needs. This definition does not limit its scope to teachers, but recognizes the staff development needs of all staff members. Inservice education is identified as one of a number of possible methods or tools used to accomplish staff development (see Figure 2-7, Examples of Professional Development Activities).

Examples of Professional Development Activities

For Individuals	For Large and Small Groups
Teacher/supervisor partnership in clinical supervision cycles	All personnel inservice workshops held on district or school grounds
Beginning teacher mentoring	Department or grade level training sessions
Professional organization or agency-sponsored seminars, conferences, and outside workshops	Cohort groups for master teachers to develop new skills or knowledge
One-on-one peer coaching	Off-site training for trainers (where representative individuals are trained and then return to train others inhouse)
University coursework	Peer coaching models with three or more participants
Teacher/supervisor individual goal attainment plans	Teaching staff workshops

Figure 2-7

The effective supervisor understands that professional development activities benefit all employees within the organization. School supervisors and administrators, certified staff, support personnel, and clerical and custodial workers need these activities to upgrade efficiency, maintain skills, and dispel stagnation. Brown (1987) noted that to deny staff development opportunities to any group inevitably weakens the entire organization.

There are four reasons why all schools and school districts need these planned and organized activities. Staff development:

1. Serves as a vehicle for purposeful organizational change.
2. Supplements and expands the initial formal teacher training.
3. Insures staff maintenance and growth.
4. Combats complacency and satisfaction with the status quo.

Today's enlightened supervisors recognize that purposeful organizational change is a slow and difficult process for the school staff. Yet, school supervisors face mounting pressure to reshape or restructure the American schools (Guskey, 1985). Connor and Lake (1988) point out that organizational change is enhanced when leaders (1) identify the employees who have a great need for change, and (2) provide these employees with opportunities for growth. Staff development provides the supervisor with an apparatus to meet the organizational needs for change and growth.

Most college teacher preparation programs consist of a 4-year plan that includes approximately 25 courses dedicated to work in pedagogy or methodology, culminating with the *hands-on* experience of student teaching, which usually lasts from eight to 16 weeks. With all the knowledge and skill necessary to be a competent and successful teacher, it is obvious that the college training programs are only a starting point; hence, the need for continuing staff development programs throughout the career of the teacher.

Staff development programs focused on instruction provide opportunities for teachers to expand their knowledge and skills. Such staff development programs prepare teachers for their present teaching assignments and situations. Joyce (1990) makes a strong case for the need for staff development by reminding educational leaders that humans, like equipment, need maintenance and development or their value diminishes.

Finally, supervisors must be concerned with the status quo and staff apathy. Hunter (1990) notes that the final criterion of success in any profession is that its practitioners never stop learning better ways of providing service for their clients. She suggests that continuous examination and modification of practice is essential to professional growth. Staff development is necessary to combat complacency and satisfaction with the status quo (Kowalski & Reitzug, 1993). Professional development programs serve as a vehicle to motivate or provide avenues to rectify areas of dissatisfaction, allowing teachers to explore new or alternative options.

Staff development occurs in various forms that range from one-to-one mentoring to departmental training to entire staff informational sessions. It may occur internally or externally. Regardless of form or setting, staff development programs serve specific purposes. Those purposes, based on staff needs, include acquiring information, skills, competencies, and behavioral changes.

The competent supervisor has many professional development responsibilities. He or she serves as a guide, resource, and facilitator, rather than as a dictator. The effective supervisor acts as a role model and participant in all staff development. Recognizing the characteristics of effective programs, the supervisor works diligently to achieve these qualities.

Evaluate Instruction

Today's supervisor must understand that one of the most pervasive misconceptions in the area of school supervision is equating evaluation with supervision. Too many practicing veteran administrators still believe that supervision and evaluation are synonymous. This is not the case. Evaluation is but one of the 10 tasks of supervision. Evaluation, while a vital, pivotal supervisory task, is only a small part of the entire supervision process.

To be successful in the task of evaluation. the wise supervisor must understand three essential concepts: types of evaluation and their purposes, methods to minimize discomfort, and techniques to resolve conflict between supervision and evaluation. Understanding and applying these concepts will help the practicing supervisor become more effective.

Evaluation in education involves the assessment of programs, learning processes and outcomes, and personnel performance. There are two forms of evaluation, formative and summative, and both apply when evaluating instruction and teacher performance. Each has its own specific purpose and is a valuable tool for the supervisor and teacher alike. *Formative* evaluation may be equated to pertinent and appropriate feedback. It is individual oriented and nonjudgmental. It is primarily a continuous process that fosters skill improvement, professional growth, and overall improvement of instruction. Formative evaluation generally provides feedback concerning a limited area of concern or for a short time period. Oliva (1993) describes formative evaluation as *nonevaluative* and focusing on improvement of instruction through consultative feedback. That evaluation can be nonevaluative suggests only that no final decision has been made as yet. The literature describes the supervisor engaged in the formative process as a coach, developer of talent, trusted mentor and counselor, teacher-sponsor, and colleague (Gorton, 1983). The teacher and supervisor generally follow the following sequence during the formative process.

Together, the supervisor and teacher:

> Identify the teacher's strengths and weaknesses.
> Design a plan that includes an acceptable level of improvement.
> Implement the improvement plan.
> If acceptable improvement occurs, establish new objectives.
> If the acceptable level of improvement is not reached, develop new
> strategies or enter remediation that could terminate in dismissal
> (Murray, 2000).

Summative evaluation is judgmental and concerned with the purpose of the organization rather than the individual. Usually included are standardized performance criteria utilized to define that which is acceptable performance, plus a grading system for the perceived teacher performance. McGreal (1988) suggests the purpose of this form of evaluation is to provide documentation to support administrative decisions concerning career ladders and compensation programs as well as information required for decisions about renewal, transfer, or dismissal of personnel.

One obstacle to successful evaluation that the supervisor must face and overcome is the knowledge that many supervisors fear this activity. Many admit that they find evaluation a distasteful task, and numerous surveys by school administrators' organizations verify this fact. Why? Supervisors share that they are influenced by past thinking, feel unprepared to evaluate, and question the value of the evaluation process. One way to reduce and perhaps eliminate this problem is to encourage administrators to become more informed and skilled in the new evaluation techniques.

Finally, in most schools, conflict exists between supervisors and teachers because of the dual responsibilities of the supervisor. The prime directive and first duty of the supervisor is to improve instruction; yet another crucial responsibility is to make final decisions regarding retainment and dismissal. Schmidt (1990) states that teachers who know that their evaluators could eventually recommend their discharge are less likely to discuss the difficulties they are encountering in the classroom.

The supervisor should understand that the role conflict between serving as a supervisor, counselor, and coach and as an administrator, evaluator, and terminator does not have to occur. Experts have identified the leading causes for this conflict. They are lack of teacher trust, teacher personalities that make collaboration difficult, negative attitudes and selfish motives of either party, the misconception that supervision is equated to evaluation, and inept supervisors (Kosmoski, 2000). This conflict can be decreased, or virtually eliminated, with leadership practices that build trust, shape objectives, and encourage communication.

Organize for Instruction

This task provides the order necessary for the smooth and most effective delivery of instruction. For teaching and learning to be most productive, a reliable and prearranged order is essential. It is the supervisor's responsibility to organize the school operation. Although the original attempt to achieve order occurs prior to the start of the school year, the major tasks are continuous throughout the learning process. Some of the basic components of this task include student class scheduling, teacher assignments, use of facilities, curricular programs, and extracurricular events. Other considerations are selecting heterogeneous or homogenous student groupings to achieve the desired learner outcomes, the coordination of resources and events to insure accessibility and utilization, and the systematic and equitable distribution of materials and facilities. There are numerous duties and considerations necessary when performing the task of organizing for instruction. For examples, refer to Figure 2-8, Sample Duties and Considerations for the Task of Organizing for Instruction.

A savvy supervisor must understand that there are two existing factors that make the task of organizing for instruction difficult. These are *change* and *routine*. First, *change* is inevitable. Regardless of how efficient the supervisor is when organizing, unexpected changes will occur, rendering the organization less effective. Therefore, the supervisor can expect that organization will constantly require modification or complete revamping.

Sample Duties and Considerations
for the Task of Organizing for Instruction

Duties	Considerations
Student schedules	Student needs, state and district requirements, school and community philosophy, available staff, resources
Teacher assignments	Staff qualifications, teacher preferences, need to instigate change, student composition and needs
Teacher schedules	Individual and mutual planning time, regularly spaced, equity
Facility use	Student and content need, equity, maintenance, updating, safety, health, and governmental regulations
Curricular and noncurricular program calendars	Prioritizing, potential internal conflict, outside calendars (district and community events)
Student grouping	Special needs, faculty availability, school/district philosophy

Figure 2-8

A second concern is achieving a proper balance of *routine*. The lack of routine or too little routine produces chaos, instability, impermanence, and insecurity, whereas excessive routine stifles spontaneity, creativity, originality, and flexibility. The perfect balance of routine, implemented building-wide and encouraged within the classroom, impacts the learning process. Sarason (1996) addresses the effects of excessive routine on teachers and students:

> *If teaching becomes a routine, predictable experience, does this not have inevitable consequences for life in the classroom? The model classroom does not allow me other than to conclude that children and teachers show most of the effects of routinized thinking and living (p.200).*

Provide Materials

The supervisor engages in selecting and securing the appropriate materials to insure proper instruction for the required curriculum. This is not limited to texts, but includes whatever materials deemed appropriate and necessary to promote learning. Considerations the supervisor must make when engaging in this task are:

- Ensure that the materials provided match the approved curriculum. This implies that the supervisor is intimately familiar with the chosen curriculum and a wide variety of methodologies.
- Provide materials that utilize the new technologies so as to prepare students and teachers for learning now and in the future. Materials should include printed, audiovisual, and computer software materials.

- Procure materials with the best economic value. The supervisor must be concerned with getting the most possible within a given budget.

Orient New Staff

This task entails providing staff with the basic information necessary to perform their duties and responsibilities. This includes acquainting and updating both new and veteran teachers and all certified and noncertified personnel with current facilities and procedures, and with community and organizational developments. Staff members who require orientation may be categorized into returning but out-of-touch employees, veterans who are new to the setting, and beginning or neophyte staff.

The astute supervisor must remember that many changes occur while returning faculty are not on campus. While teachers are on vacation or break, policy, direction, and procedures may change or be newly adopted. One of the activities of orientation is to update returning staff.

Special consideration should be made for veteran teachers who are new to a given building. Effective supervisors recognize that each and every campus is unique and often operates with policies and procedures that differ from all other locations. With that understanding, the supervisor must be sensitive to the need for information and direction of the veteran "new to the building."

Finally, the effective supervisor must meet the needs of the beginning, novice, or neophyte teacher who requires special attention. Historically, supervisors have poorly aided the beginning teacher, providing inadequate induction to these novices. Unfortunately, many beginning teachers are faced with numerous and serious difficulties. These include inadequate resources, difficult work assignments, unclear expectations, a sink-or-swim mentality, and reality shock (Gordon, 1991). A short discussion of these five most widely acknowledged difficulties will clarify and underscore the plight of the neophyte teacher.

- Inadequate resources. Often prior to the close of a school year, returning teachers remove desirable supplies from vacated classrooms. Therefore, at the start of a new term, a neophyte teacher with the least experience often is assigned the physically least desirable classroom in a school (Glickman, Gordon, & Ross-Gordon, 1998).

- Difficult work assignments. Supervisors too often assign new teachers larger classes, extra duties, difficult courses, problem students, and low-achieving groups (Kurtz, 1983).

- Unclear expectations. Kurtz (1983) contends that novice teachers are often faced with conflicting expectations expressed by administrators, fellow teachers, parents, and students. Many are in a quandary about whose expectations should be addressed and met.

- Sink-or-swim mentality. Some administrators and experienced teachers feel that the beginning teacher's first year should be a *trial-by-fire* experience. They neither understand nor value the benefits of establishing collegial support groups or mentoring programs (Kosmoski, Pollack, & Schmidt, 1999; Sparks & Hirsh, 1997).

- Reality shock. Many novices enter teaching with an idealized vision of what they will encounter. Student learning difficulties, management problems, and environmental concerns quickly shatter the neophyte's ideals. This, coupled with the realization of their own inadequacies and unpreparedness, leads to reality shock. Veenman (1985) defines reality shock as "the collapse of the missionary ideals formed during student teacher training by the harsh and rude realities of classroom life" (p. 143).

For a visual summary of the difficulties encountered by beginning teachers, see Figure 2-9, Major Flaws in Beginning Teacher Induction Programs.

Major Flaws in Beginning Teacher Induction Programs

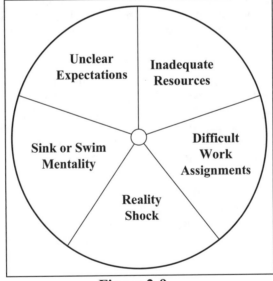

Figure 2-9

Relate and Provide Special Pupil Services

This task addresses the coordination of special student services to best support appropriate learning opportunities. Students who require the supervisor's attention include special education, environmentally deprived, endangered, legally entangled, and gifted students.

Some services the supervisor must provide include:

- Self-contained learning settings
- Inclusion into the regular classroom setting
- Individual, group, and family counseling
- Guidance sessions
- Social services
- Health services
- Speech, occupational , and physical therapy

Although most districts employ experts in special pupil services, the supervisor is often the responsible party, frequently serving as the building special service designee. Special pupil services involves developing and interpreting policies, determining priorities, defining relationships between service personnel, and monitoring individual student and school instructional goals.

To be effective in these duties, the supervisor must be skilled and current in a wide variety of areas. The supervisor must be familiar with the local, state, and federal guidelines, policies, and laws. He or she must understand and be able to implement the best practices identified by research. The supervisor must, without exception, adhere to due process procedures and legal constraints. Finally, the supervisor must firmly believe that his or her primary role is that of advocate for the given student.

In recent years, this task has been in constant flux, in part because new or changed policies and procedures are occurring at a rapid pace. The supervisor must pay special attention to his or her own professional development in this area. To remain effective, the supervisor must continually upgrade and expand her or his knowledge in the area of special pupil services.

Develop Public Relations

Bagin, Gallagher, and Kindred (1994) explain the traditionally accepted components of school public relations. They point out that public relations is a continuous dynamic process that combines the following practices.

"A way of life expressed daily by staff members in their personal relations with colleagues, pupils, parents, and people in the community.

A planned and continuing series of activities for communicating with both internal and external publics concerning the purposes, needs, programs, and accomplishments of the school.

A planned and continuing series of activities for determining what citizens think of the school and what aspirations they hold for the education of their children.

The active involvement of citizens in the decision-making process of the school so that essential improvement may be made in the educational program and adjustments brought about to meet the climate of social change" (p. 15).

To accomplish the above goals, a supervisor must be an effective communicator and connector. The task of developing good community relations demands a supervisor who is self-confident and skilled in relating to others. When working in this area, the supervisor creates a humane atmosphere, sets a positive work climate, and establishes an appropriate image to both the internal and external public. An astute supervisor understands that others react to how the supervisor talks, dresses, and works. He or she establishes the "feel" of the school by the image communicated.

To accomplish this task, the supervisor must demonstrate numerous human relations skills. Crucial among these skills is written and verbal communication. The supervisor must be an effective verbal communicator when working with individuals, small or large groups, and school and community members at committees or conferences .

Wiles and Bondi (2000) emphasize that the supervisor must successfully cope with the needs of today's constituents. Along with the traditional needs, several new challenges have emerged. They list several prominent challenges faced by the modern supervisor. These issues are:

- The need to motivate career teachers and appropriately handle the phenomenon of teacher burnout.

- The challenge to provide more help to students and teachers as they become a technological society.

- The additional newly acquired functions and services once provided by the family and other institutions.

- The outcry of public dissatisfaction with schools in general.

- The general reduction of economic resources available to the schools.

- The deteriorating social and economic conditions in large urban school districts.

- The increase of teacher and administrator stress.

- The push for a free-market choice system in education.

Hicks (2000) sadly demonstrates that the supervisory task of public relations is most difficult because public education is not highly supported by the public. He cites 14 indicators that support his conclusions. Among them are the lack of support and, in some cases, deliberate sabotage by the media, ultraconservatives, provincialists, nonprofessional educators, politicians, business, and governmental agencies.

Summary

There are numerous definitions of supervision that have merit. Kosmoski (2000) draws from the most widely accepted modern definitions and succinctly defines supervision as:

" . . . *that leadership process whose ultimate purpose is to improve instruction, and thereby, facilitate and promote successful student learning*" (p.14).

Educators want students to choose to learn. The goal of teachers is to inspire students to choose to engage and the goal of supervisors is to support these teacher efforts (Starnes & Paris, 2000).

Regardless of title, supervisors are educators who are directly engaged in helping teachers improve instruction. They can be found at all levels of the organizational hierarchy. They are only defined by function and duties. Typical supervisors include the school principal, assistant principals, lead teachers, department chairs, central office administrators, and master teachers.

All educators need supervision. There are four basic reasons for demanding quality supervision in our schools.

- Educators, like all humans, are natural learners. Their inherent nature demands the need to learn and grow. Supervision provides that need.

- Supervision is directly linked to teacher behaviors. Teacher behaviors are directly linked to student achievement. Therefore, indirectly supervision affects student academic achievement. Good supervision improves teacher performance. Good teacher performance improves student learning.

- Supervision motivates teachers and allows them to attain job satisfaction.

- No teacher, veteran or novice, is thoroughly prepared to perform all the tasks of quality teaching. Supervision, in particular professional development, provides for this lack.

Today, many supervision models exist simultaneously. Those most often utilized are traditional, human resource, clinical, developmental, and collegial. Although the traditional model is still most pervasive, the alternative models listed above are becoming more established.

Cogan (1973) identified two major types or areas of supervision, general and clinical. General supervision refers to all tasks that the supervisor attends to outside of the classroom. These tasks are designed to indirectly provide the teacher and learner with an environment that promotes the learning process. Clinical supervision is a more specific level of supervision where the supervisor works directly with the teacher. These tasks occur within the classroom. Their sole purpose is to improve instruction.

Supervision specialists have compiled lists that identify specific tasks associated with supervision. In 1985, Harris identified 10 tasks, which he grouped into the three classes of preliminary, developmental, and operational. Preliminary tasks are those performed prior to actual instruction by the teacher. Developmental tasks are those that should directly improve instruction. Operational tasks are those tasks that facilitate the ongoing operation.

Preliminary Tasks:
1. Develop curriculum.
2. Provide staff.
3. Provide facilities.

Developmental tasks:
4. Arrange for professional development.
5. Evaluate instruction.

Operational tasks:
6. Organize for instruction.
7. Provide materials.
8. Orient new staff.
9. Relate and provide special pupil services.
10. Develop public relations.

Supervision in the Future

In the future, we can expect that supervision will be given even greater attention, and there will be more nontraditional models from which to choose. Supervisors must continue to learn and grow themselves in order to perform their major function of supporting teachers and students. The supervisor's efforts will require much personal time and energy. He or she will have to overcome many obstacles, the most troubling of which is public education's tarnished image. The challenges that the supervisor will face in the future are numerous and enormous, but the potential rewards are far greater.

Case Study: A Need for Change

Dennis Foster shook his head as he left Mrs. Jane Steadfell's classroom. As Jane's supervisor, Dennis had been in her room many times over the last 4 years. In his mind, Jane was one of the best teachers in his school. She was always organized and knowledgeable. She used a great variety of instructional modes and was always full of enthusiasm. Dennis allowed Jane to take the lead in her own personal and professional development. This approach had been very successful.

However lately, something was different with Jane. Dennis realized that during his last two visits, Jane seemed unprepared and disorganized. She seemed listless and unfocused. Jane's students were still well behaved but appeared bored and uninvolved.

Dennis knew that recently Jane was experiencing difficulties in her personal life. Suffering from some form of cancer, Jane's mother had come to live with Jane and her family. Dennis suspected that this was probably the reason for Jane's lack of professionalism and classroom effectiveness, but he was unsure of how to help. What could Dennis do as Jane's supervisor? How would you advise Dennis Foster to proceed?

References

Acheson, K. A., & Gall, M. D. (1992). *Techniques in the clinical supervision of teacher,* (3rd ed.). New York: Longman.

Bagin, D., Gallagher, D., & Kindred, L. (1994). *The school and community relations* (5th ed.). Boston: Allyn & Bacon.

Brown, P. W. (1987). Inservice education: Cultivating professional growth at your school. *Perspectives for Teachers of the Learning Impaired, 5* (5), 16-18.

Burton, W. H. (1922). *Supervision and the improvement of teaching.* New York: D. Appleton-Century.

Cogan, M. (1973). *Clinical supervision.* Boston: Houghton Mifflin.

Connor, P. E., & Lake, L. K. (1988). *Managing organizational change.* New York: Praeger.

Cunningham, W. G., & Cordeiro, P. A. (2000). *Educational administration: A problem solving approach.* Boston: Allyn Bacon.

Doll, R. C. (1992). *Curriculum improvement: Decision making and process* (8th ed.). Boston: Allyn and Bacon.

Eisner, E. (1982). An artistic approach to supervision. In Thomas Sergiovanni (Ed.), *Supervision of teaching* (pp. 37-38). Alexandria, VA: Association of Supervision and Curriculum Development.

Franseth, J. (1961). *Supervision as leadership.* Evanston, IL: Row, Peterson.

Glatthorn, A. (1984). *Differentiated supervision.* Alexandria, VA: Association for Supervision and Curriculum Development.

Glickman, C. D. (1990). *Supervision of instruction: A developmental approach* (2nd ed.). Boston: Allyn and Bacon.

Glickman, C. D. (1981). *Developmental supervision: Alternative practices for helping teachers to improve.* Alexandria, VA: Association for Supervision and Curriculum Development.

Glickman, C. D., Gordon, S. P., & Ross-Gordon, J. M. (1998). *Supervision of instruction: A developmental approach* (4th ed.). Boston: Allyn and Bacon.

Goldhammer, R. (1969). *Clinical supervision.* New York: Holt, Rinehart, and Winston.

Gordon, S. P. (1991). *Helping beginning teachers to succeed.* Alexandria, VA: Association for Supervision and Curriculum Development.

Gorton, R. (1987). *School leadership and administration: important concepts, case studies, and simulations* (3rd ed.). Dubuque, IA: Wm. C. Brown Publishers.

Gorton, R. A. (1983). *School administration and supervision: Leadership challenges and opportunities.* Dubuque, IA: Wm. C. Brown Company Publishers.

Guskey, T. R. (1985). Staff development and teacher change. *Educational Leadership, 42* (7), 57-60.

Hackman, J. R., & Oldham, G. (1976). Motivation through the design of work: Test of a theory. *Organizational behavior and human performance 16*(2), 250-279.

Harris, B. M. (1985). *Supervisory behavior in education* (3rd ed.). Englewood Cliffs, NJ: Prentice-Hall.

Hunter, M. (1990). Preface. *Changing school culture through staff development: The 1990 ASCD yearbook.* Alexandria, VA: Association for Supervision and Curriculum Development.

Joyce, B. (1990). Prologue. *Changing school culture through staff development: The 1990 ASCD yearbook.* Alexandria, VA: Association for Supervision and Curriculum Development.

Kaiser, J. S. (1993). *Educational administration* (2nd ed.). Mequon, WI: Stylex Publishing Co., Inc.

Kirkpatrick, T. O., & Lewis, C. T. *Effective supervision: Preparing for the 21st century.* Fort Worth, TX: The Dryden Press.

Kosmoski, G. J. (1994). Initiation of the beginning administrators program at Governors State University. *Ad Prof:* The Illinois Counsel of Professors of Educational Administration, *5*(2), 9-13.

Kosmoski, G. J. (2000). *Supervision,* (2nd ed.). Mequon, WI: Stylex Publishing Company.

Kosmoski, G. J., Pollack, D. R., & Schmidt, L. J. (1999). Jekyll or Hyde: Changes in leadership styles and personalities of beginning school administrators. *Illinois Schools Journal, 79* (1), 23-35.

Kowalski, T. J., & Reitzug, U.C. (1993). *Contemporary school administration: An introduction.* New York: Longman.

Krey, R. & Burke. (1989). *A design for instructional supervision.* Springfield, IL: C.C. Thomas.

Kurtz, W. H. (1983). Identifying their needs: How the principal can help beginning teachers. *NASSP Bulletin, 67* (459), 42-45.

Lunnenburg, F. C., & Ornstein, A. C. (1991). *Educational administration: Concepts and practices.* Belmont, CA: Wadsworth.

McGreal, T. L. (1988). Evaluation for enhancing instruction: Linking teacher evaluation and staff development. In S. J. Stanley & W. J. Popham (Eds.), *Teacher evaluation: Six prescriptions for success* (pp. 1-29). Alexandria, VA: Association for Supervision and Curriculum Development.

Mosher, R. L., & Purpel, D. E. (1972). *Supervision: The reluctant profession.* Boston: Houghton Mifflin.

Murray, B. (2000). *People and supervision.* In G. Kosmoski. *Supervision (2nd ed).* Mequon, WI: Stylex Publishing Co.

Oliva, P. F. (1993). *Supervision for today's schools* (2nd ed.). New York: Longman.

Redfern, G. B. (1980). *Evaluating teachers and administrators: A performance objective model.* Boulder, CO: Westview.

Russell, D., & Hunter, M. (1980). *Planning for effective instruction.* Los Angeles: University Elementary School.

Sacken, D. (1994). No more principals! *Phi Delta Kappan, 75*(2), 664-670.

Sarason, S. B. (1996). *The culture of school and the problem of change.* New York: Teachers College Press.

Sergiovanni, T. J., Burlingame, M., Coombs, F. S., & Thurston, P. W. (1999). *Educational governance and administration* (4th ed.). Boston: Allyn & Bacon.

Sergiovanni, T. J., & Starratt, R. J. (1988*). Supervision: Human perspectives* (4th ed.). New York: McGraw Hill.

Sparks, D., & Hirsh, S. (1997*).* A new vision for staff development. Alexandria, VA: Association for Supervision and Curriculum Development.

Starnes, B. A., & Paris, C. (2000). Choosing to learn. *Phi Delta Kappan, 81*(5), 392-397.

Tyler, R. (1949). *Basic principles of curriculum and instruction.* Chicago: University of Chicago Press.

Van Horn, R. (1999). Inner-city schools: A multi-variable discussion. *Phi Delta Kappan, 81* (4), 291-297.

Veenman, S. (1985). Perceived problems of beginning teachers. *Review of Educational Research, 54*(20), 143-178.

Wiles, J., & Bondi, J. (2000). *Supervision: A guide to practice* (5th ed.). Upper Saddle River, NJ: Merrill, An Imprint of Prentice Hall.

Chapter 3
Legal and Financial Aspects of Public School Administration
Sandra Lowery and George Garrett

> This chapter presents the foundation of laws affecting schools and their students including the basis of special education law. The changing role of federal, state, and local government in the finance of public education is also presented.

Sources of Law

Constitutional Law

The Constitution of the United States and the constitutions of each of the states are sources of law under which public school systems operate. The Tenth Amendment to the Constitution specifies that all powers not delegated to the federal government are delegated to the states. Because education is not specifically delegated to the federal government by the Constitution of the United States, it is therefore a function of the states. Although education is a function of the states, interpretations of the Bill of Rights and the Fourteenth Amendment to the Constitution have served as foundations for claims of freedom of speech, religion, association, and other rights that have changed the operations of public schools across the nation. The Fourteenth Amendment to the Constitution has become the constitutional basis for special education through the concept of equal protection.

Every state has a constitution that provides the legal framework for governmental processes. All states have mandates regarding education in their constitutions, thereby providing authority for systems of public schools.

Statutory Law

Federal statutes based on provisions of the Constitution, including those dealing with civil rights, special education, and rights of the disabled, have had significant impact on public schools. Because establishing and operating schools is not a power delegated to the federal government, much of the legislation relating to education has been enacted through the power of the federal government to levy, collect taxes, and spend for the common good. With federal funds have come the multitude of federal laws and regulations that are tied to the funding. Schools must comply with these federal laws and regulations as conditions for receiving federal funds.

Since school districts have no inherent powers themselves, the authority to operate schools must come from state laws. State legislatures in each of the 50 states have enacted laws governing operations of the public schools in those states. These statutory laws are then interpreted by rules, regulations, and policies. These rules, regulations, and policies, written by governmental agencies, provide the specificity necessary for implementation of laws and have the force of laws themselves.

Judicial Law

The courts have created judicial law, or case law. When courts have interpreted statutes, regulations, and constitutional provisions, these interpretations and decisions have become judicial law. Judicial law began with the English "common law," which was based on decisions of juries and judges. When courts dealt with cases, they relied on earlier decisions that were similar. The English common-law practices were continued in colonial America and have been upheld. Courts today still follow decisions found in earlier cases, thereby adding to the body of judicial, or case, law.

Two sources of judicial power include horizontal and vertical power. Horizontal power includes decisions of the courts as they interpret the Constitution and a more limited form of horizontal power exercised by courts as they interpret laws created by the legislatures.

Vertical power is based on the hierarchy of the court systems. A typical hierarchy of trial court, appellate court, and the highest level, the court of last resort, is found in both federal and state court systems. The line of authority is specific within jurisdictions, but does not cross jurisdictional boundaries.

Legal Liability

Torts

A tort is a civil wrong, not involving contracts, for which a court will award damages. Intentional torts are those committed on purpose, with the intent to cause harm or injury, or reckless disregard for safety. Unintentional torts are those that result from negligence. School districts have usually been free from liability under the concept of general governmental immunity. School personnel and school board members, while acting in their official capacities, generally have a qualified, or conditional, immunity from liability.

Negligence

Negligence is conduct in which a reasonably prudent person would not engage under similar circumstances. A public school employee may be charged with negligence if he or she does not anticipate and take action to prevent an event that could reasonably have been foreseen as a potential threat to the safety or welfare of students.

School personnel who follow all reasonable rules, regulations, policies, and directives will be able to show in court that they were performing as a reasonable and prudent educator would. Regardless of all reasonable precautions, accidents do happen and students are injured, but the educator who is able to show that he or she did what any reasonable and prudent educator would have done in similar circumstances will be able to show that the injury did not result from negligence.

Federal Civil Rights Liability

Constitutional torts are civil causes of action, authorized by federal law, and brought by individuals whose civil rights have been violated. Since school employees usually have immunity from liability in common law tort actions, such as personal injury or negligence claims, many claims against school districts, school officials, and school employees are based on alleged violations of an individual's civil rights under the Civil Rights Act of 1983. The specific rights protected under this legislation include due process, equal protection, freedom of religion, freedom of speech, and freedom from unreasonable searches and seizures.

The defense of qualified immunity is available to school employees for actions taken in good faith and within the scope of their official responsibilities. In the context of qualified immunity, the courts first examine the school employee's conduct in the context of the law at the time the act occurred. Second, the court examines the deprivation of civil rights to determine if malicious intent on the part of the school employee existed. If a school employee showed a disregard for, or ignorance of, the existing law, or if he or she had acted maliciously, no qualified immunity could be considered.

Students

Sexual Harassment

Sexual harassment is defined as unwelcome sexual advances, requests for sexual favors, and/or other verbal or physical conduct of a sexual nature. Sexual harassment is a form of discrimination based on gender, which is made illegal by Title VII of the Civil Rights Act of 1964. Title IX of the Education Amendments of 1972 prohibits discrimination on the basis of sex in education programs and activities receiving federal financial assistance. Sexual harassment of students is a form of discrimination prohibited by Title IX (Department of Education, 1999).

Examples of some types of sexual harassment that occur in a school setting include: unwelcome verbal harassment or abuse; unwelcome letters, telephone calls, or other materials of a sexual nature; unwelcome and deliberate touching or other physical contact; unwelcome sexual teasing, jokes, or remarks, either verbal or written; and unwelcome pressure for sexual favors or activity.

The concept of "unwelcomeness" includes the interpretation that any sexual conduct between adult employees and students violates criminal law. Title IX has been interpreted to mean that any sexual conduct between any student and any school employee is impermissible. An underage student has no legal ability to consent. School districts should be particularly sensitive about the issue, since the harasser is frequently in a position of authority.

Quid pro quo sexual harassment occurs between a school district employee and a student when a school district employee explicitly or implicitly conditions a student's participation in an educational program or activity or bases an educational decision on the student's submission to sexual advances, requests for favors, or conduct. This description applies whether or not the student submits to the conduct.

Hostile environment harassment occurs when unwelcome sexual advancement, requests for sexual favors, or other verbal, nonverbal, or physical conduct of a sexual nature by another student or a school employee are sufficiently severe, persistent, or pervasive enough to limit the student's ability to participate in or benefit from an educational program or activity.

School districts are adopting policies of zero tolerance toward all sexual harassment, including employee-student sexual harassment and student-on-student sexual harassment. In order for a school district to be held liable for the acts of its employees, the violated or injured party must prove that the violation was caused by an unconstitutional policy or custom sanctioned by school district officials who have final policy-making authority. A school district must be found to show deliberate indifference to a student's welfare and rights before the school district will be held responsible. To be held liable, a school district must have permitted or furthered the illegal act through its policies or practices (Monell v. Department of Social Services, 1989).

The safest way to demonstrate that school districts are not deliberately indifferent to the rights of students is to take every report of sexual abuse or harassment seriously and to conduct a thorough investigation of every reported incident. To avoid liability, school districts should adopt policies and procedures that require every report of sexual abuse or harassment to be taken seriously and that conduct investigations of every reported incident.

Courts have recognized failure to train all employees as one area of liability (City of Canton v. Harris, 1989). School districts should design and implement programs to train employees in the reporting and investigation of sexual abuse and harassment. Students should be trained in the reporting of sexual abuse and harassment.

The legal standard for supervisory officials' liability has been established whereby a supervisor may be liable for the wrongful conduct of a subordinate (Doe v. Taylor Independent School District, 1994). When faced with an allegation of sexual harassment, school officials must take immediate and decisive action to stop it. School officials must also document all steps and actions taken toward stopping the sexual harassment. At the conclusion of the investigation, action must be taken in accordance with school district policy, administrative procedure, and the code of student conduct, and discussed with students and their parents in face-to-face meetings as soon as possible. Allowing for the passage of time before the school district acts is a significant factor in determining liability under the concept of "deliberate indifference." Any conference should be documented in writing, with copies maintained by the school district and given to all participants.

School districts may be held responsible for student-on-student sexual harassment if the school district is deliberately indifferent to sexual harassment that the school district has actual knowledge of and that is so severe, pervasive, and offensive that it deprives a student access to educational opportunities or benefits (Davis v. Monroe County, 1999). In this case, the U. S. Supreme Court established the duty of school districts not to allow student-on-student peer sexual harassment in school, during school hours, on school grounds, or at school-sponsored activities.

Gender Equity

Title IX of the Education Amendments of 1972 prohibits discrimination on the basis of gender in educational programs or activities that receive federal financial assistance. The Title IX regulations prohibit discrimination on the basis of gender in athletic programs and mandate that schools provide equal athletic opportunities to members of both genders.

Drug Testing

The U. S. Supreme Court has declined to disturb a court of appeals ruling that permits random urinalysis testing of students who participate in extracurricular activities (Todd v. Rush County Schools, 1998). In this case, a group of parents challenged an Indiana school district policy that prohibits students from participating in extracurricular activities or driving to and from school unless they consent to random, unannounced urinalysis exams. The court considered the school district's defense that the program was designed to deter drug use, not to catch and punish students who used drugs. Random testing has been upheld in another case based on the fact that students chose to participate in extracurricular activities (Veronia School District 47 J. v. Action, 1995).

School Safety Issues

Violence in our schools is a reality that necessitates strict control of weapons on school premises. The Gun-Free Schools Act of 1994 is designed to help school systems be free of drugs and violence and to provide a safe, disciplined environment conducive to learning. It encourages activities such as school safety reviews, conflict resolution, safe passage zones, counseling programs, and parental involvement. This act requires each state receiving federal funds to have in effect a law requiring local school districts to expel students for a period of not less than 1 year for bringing a weapon to school. The law allows the chief administrative officer of the local educational agency to modify the expulsion requirement on a case-by-case basis. Likewise, federal funds will not be available to any school district unless the district has a policy requiring referral to the criminal justice or juvenile delinquency system of a student who brings a firearm or other weapon to school.

Crisis Management

All schools are urged to develop school safety plans that address early warning signs and include sufficient counseling for students. The National School Board Association (1998) recommends that all schools and school districts develop "safe school" plans that address early warning signs and include sufficient counseling for students. Schools should implement the following procedures:

- Establish reporting procedures for safety and security concerns
- Take proactive risk-reduction measures, including consistent enforcement of security-related policies
- Institute comprehensive staff training; conduct periodic emergency drills
- Schedule regular assessment by community-based collaborative groups (school security professionals, parents, students, local government agencies, and administrators.

Indicators of safe schools include supervision of access to buildings and grounds, a closed school campus during lunch, and staggered lunch periods and dismissal times. Also recommended are supervision at key times when students are outside classrooms; adjusted schedules and hallway traffic patterns to limit potential conflicts; and monitoring of grounds, parking lots, and bus stops. Increased adult presence, including visiting parents, throughout the buildings and grounds is also stressed as a preventative measure (National Commission on Safe Schools, 1998).

Search and Seizure

The Fourth Amendment to the U. S. Constitution guarantees the right of the people to be secure in their persons, houses, papers, and effects against unreasonable searches and seizures by government officials. While public school students do have a reasonable expectation of privacy while attending school or school-sponsored activities, they have a lesser expectation of privacy than members of the general population. Searches in school settings are subject to less stringent standards than those that apply to law enforcement officials. The police search is subject to a probable cause standard, whereas school officials must comply with the lesser reasonable suspicion standard. Under the standard of reasonable suspicion, the closer the search is to the person, the more evidence the school official must have. For example, a student's expectation of privacy in a locker is not as substantial as the privacy associated with a backpack. Likewise, a backpack is not as private as touching a student in a patdown search.

In a landmark decision, the U. S. Supreme Court addressed the search of students on school grounds and established that students do have constitutional rights (New Jersey v. T.L.O., 1985). In that case, a teacher found a student smoking a tobacco cigarette in the school restroom. A search of the student's purse revealed marijuana. The U. S. Supreme Court ruled the search was reasonable. The principles established in that case were:

Actions that are a search:

- Drug screening by urinalysis or blood
- Breath test
- Looking into pockets; examining purses, backpacks, bookbags
- Patting down a person's clothing or person
- Dog's sniff of a person, especially if the dog actually touches the person
- Actual searches of a person

Actions that are not a search:

- Observing what is in open view
- Dog's sniff of cars, lockers, belongings
- Questioning a person
- Sniffing the air inside a car or other area
- Examination of abandoned items thrown out or into trash

Any search by school officials must be reasonable. That is, there must be reasonable grounds for suspecting that the search will result in evidence that the student has violated a school rule, policy or the law. The search must also reasonable in scope, and search measures must be related to the object being searched for and not excessively intrusive, given the student's age and nature of the infraction.

School lockers are the property of the school, and many courts have ruled that schools have a right to control and search them if necessary. It is recommended that school districts adopt policies clearly stating that lockers are school property and may be searched at any time by school officials.

The use of metal detectors in public schools is another school safety issue. The courts have allowed the use of such devices because there is a compelling need to deter violence or harm and provide a safe learning environment. Searches with metal detectors are usually considered reasonable because they are minimally intrusive. When the need is great, intrusiveness is kept to reasonable minimums, and safeguards are in place to protect a reasonable expectation of privacy, such searches have passed constitutional standards (People v. Dukes, 1992).

The concept of individualized suspicion in the New Jersey v. T.L.O. case has been interpreted to prevent a search of a group of students because school officials think one student in the group is guilty. In light of recent school violence, there is precedent for conducting reasonable searches without individualized suspicion (DesRoches v. City of Norfolk School Board, 1998).

Many school districts use dogs that have been specially trained to sniff out drugs and other prohibited substances present on school premises. Dogs may be used to sniff lockers or cars on school property because this is not considered to be a search. No reasonable suspicion is required. However, students have a high expectation of the privacy of their bodies. Using a dog to sniff an individual student is a search and requires reasonable expectation.

The trained dogs are usually reliable in indicating the presence or recent presence of drugs, weapons, and other prohibited substances; a dog alert of a locker or automobile may provide reasonable suspicion. Once this reasonable suspicion has been established, the backpack, purse, or automobile may be searched.

Student Discipline

Due Process

Student due process issues usually include three questions: (1) Did the school take action? (2) Did the school deprive the student of "life, liberty, or property"? (3) Did the school provide the process that is due if deprivation did take place? The concept of due process was applied to students when the U. S. Supreme Court ruled that short-term suspension was a deprivation of educational services and must involve due process (Goss v. Lopez, 1975). Students must be given either written or oral notice of the charges and the intended punishment, given an explanation of any evidence that school authorities have, and be provided opportunity to present their side of the story. In general, as the degree of loss suffered by the student increases, the degree of due process also increases.

Student Code of Conduct

The student code of conduct is a familiar concept in school law. It is a basic concept of due process that students can only be held accountable for rules of which they were advised. Most schools develop and distribute a student handbook containing all rules and regulations that students will be expected to follow.

While dress codes are legally permissible, school officials must be careful not to intrude on students' rights of expression. The First Amendment rights of students were established in Tinker v. Des Moines Independent Community School District (1969), but courts have upheld student dress codes. In one case, the purpose of the student dress code was to discourage gang activity, and the dress code was upheld (Jeglin v. San Jacinto Unified School District, 1993).

Reasonable student dress codes may prohibit attire that might lead to disruptions or interferes with the rights of others. Student speech that is indecent, lewd, or profane is not entitled to any constitutional protection (Bethel School District No. 403 v. Fraser, 1986).

Suspension

Suspensions are short-term removals that are used to punish students for violating school rules. The Goss v. Lopez ruling has been translated into policies that require informal due process procedures for both suspensions that remove students from school premises and in-school suspensions or isolations. Minor forms of classroom discipline, such as time-out, do not usually necessitate the level of due process required by suspensions from school or in-school suspension assignments.

Expulsion

Expulsion is the removal of a student from school for a lengthy period of time, usually more than 10 days. Offenses such as violence, stealing or vandalizing school property, causing physical harm to others, possessing a weapon, possessing or using drugs or alcohol, and criminal activity frequently result in expulsion. The Gun-Free Schools Act of 1994 requires expulsion of at least 1 year for bringing a firearm to school. State laws include specifications of student expulsions. Except for possession of weapons, expulsions generally do not exceed the end of the current academic year. Due process requirements for expulsion are more stringent because the student is being deprived of educational services.

Effective Student Discipline

Because student discipline is based in part on effective rules, rules should have a rational purpose. Students are more likely to follow rules that make sense for providing a safe and orderly environment. Rules should be clearly stated and enforced consistently and fairly.

Special Education

Statutes, regulations, and court decisions from both federal and state levels govern special education. In addition, Congress and state legislatures have passed statutes or laws on special education. Regulations and policies, written at both federal and state levels, provide guidelines for implementing the statutes. Some of these are displayed in Table 3-1.

Special education is defined in the statutory language as "specifically designed instruction, at no charge to the parents or guardians, to meet the unique needs of a child with a disability" [Individuals with Disabilities Education Act (IDEA) of 1997]. Public schools must provide special education, and related services such as transportation, counseling, occupational therapy, physical therapy, medical services, orientation/mobility services, rehabilitation counseling, speech pathology, and psychological services to eligible disabled students at no cost (Yell, 1998).

Special Education Cases, Legislation, and Requirements		
Event	Year	Requirements
Brown v. Board of Education	1954	Civil rights Equal Protection
PARC v. Commonwealth of Pennsylvania	1972	Free, appropriate public education
Section 504, Rehabilitation Act	1973	Protected rights of handicapped
P.L. 94-142		Free, appropriate public education Procedural safeguards Least restrictive environment Individualized education program Nondiscriminatory evaluation
P.L. 99-372	1986	Allowed recovery of attorneys' fees
P.L. 101-476	1990	Added autism and traumatic brain injury as handicapping conditions Transition plans required
P.L. 105-17, Individuals with Disabilities Education Act	1997	Restructured the law Changes in IEP team Mediation introduced Changes in discipline of handicapped students

Figure 3-1

The civil rights movement, which sought equality of opportunity for minorities in the 1950s and 1960s, had a major victory in Brown v. Board of Education (Brown v. Board of Education, 1954). The Brown decision has not only served as the basis for civil rights actions but has also affected many areas of school law and procedure. The Brown case has also resulted in historical changes in the education of handicapped students due to the concept that states may not deny any citizen equal protection under the law. If states provide education for any citizens, then they must provide education for all citizens (Turnbull & Turnbull, 1997).

In 1971, the Pennsylvania Association for Retarded Children (PARC) brought a class action suit against the Commonwealth of Pennsylvania. The suit was resolved by consent agreement, with the stipulation that all children with "mental retardation", ages 6 through 21, be provided a free public education in the least restrictive environment (Levine & Wexler, 1981).

The Rehabilitation Act of 1973 was the first federal legislation enacted to protect the rights of individuals with disabilities. Under Section 504 of that act, an individual with a disability is one who has a physical or mental impairment that substantially limits one or more major life activity, has a record of such impairment, or is regarded as having one (Vocational Rehabilitation Act of 1973). School districts are responsible for identifying and evaluating students who are suspected of having a disability and an educational need for services under

Section 504 (Zirkel & Kincaid, 1995). The district must then provide these students with a free, appropriate public education with appropriate modifications, if needed. These protected students are therefore entitled to many services similar to those provided disabled students under Public Law 94-142 and Public Law 105-17, Individuals with Disabilities Education Act Amendments of 1997. The Americans with Disabilities Act of 1990, follows Section 504 in defining individuals protected by law and prohibiting discrimination against persons with disabilities. Employment, public services, accessibility, monetary damages, and telecommunications are all addressed in ADA (Wenkart, 1993).

In 1975, Public Law 94-142, the Education for All Handicapped Children Act, was enacted. This legislation, requiring a free, appropriate education for disabled children, procedural safeguards, least restrictive environment, nondiscriminatory evaluation, and an individualized education program for every disabled child, has changed the public schools of the nation (Education for All Handicapped Children Act of 1975). Legislation since 1975 has clarified and expanded the original statutes.

Public Law 99-372, the Handicapped Children's Protection Act of 1986, provided for recovery of attorneys' fees and costs to parents who prevail in lawsuits. Further expansion occurred in 1990 with the requirement of transition plans and the addition of autism and traumatic brain injury as handicapping conditions (Education for the Handicapped Amendments of 1986) Figure 3-1 summarizes all of these laws and lawsuits.

The Individuals with Disabilities Act was enacted to assure that all children with disabilities have a free, appropriate public education that emphasizes special education and related services designed to meet their individual needs (Individuals with Disabilities Education Act (IDEA) of 1997). Figure 3-2 lists these categories of handicaps. The categories are discussed in greater detail in the subsequent sections.

Categories of Disabilities Covered Under IDEA, 1997

Autism
Deaf-blindness
Deafness
Hearing impairment
Mental retardation
Multiple disabilities
Orthopedic impairment
Other health impairment
Emotional disturbance
Learning disabilities
Speech or language impairment
Traumatic brain injury
Visual impairment

Figure 3-2:

Other legal concepts regarding special education include:

Zero Rejects – Every disabled child, regardless of the severity of disability, will be provided a free, appropriate public education. Each state has responsibility for providing this individualized education program, unconditionally and without exception (Timothy W. v. Rochester, New Hampshire School District, 1989)

Age Requirements – Eligible students, between the ages of 3 and 21 and with disabilities, must be provided services. Infants and toddlers, birth through age 2, may receive services for handicapping conditions such as developmental delays, deafness, hearing impairment, and visual impairment.

Identification – School districts are responsible for taking affirmative action to locate, identify, and evaluate eligible students. Referrals can be made by parents, teachers, health care professionals, state public service agencies, and other individuals familiar with the needs of a disabled child. School districts must evaluate those children who live within school district boundaries who are thought to be in need of special education services.

Assessment – Data compiled in the assessment process includes health, vision, hearing, social and emotional status, intelligence, academic functioning, communication, motor abilities, language development, and language proficiency. A multidisciplinary team, with no single criterion or procedure used to determine eligibility for special education services, performs this multifactored evaluation. Assessment procedures must be conducted in the child's native language and with measurement instruments that are not racially or culturally biased. A complete reevaluation must be conducted at least every 3 years.

Individualized Education Plan – Members of the Individualized Education Program (IEP) team are responsible for developing an individualized education plan and appropriate placement for each eligible student. Team members must include a representative of school district administration, a regular education teacher, a special education teacher, the parents, the student (if age appropriate), and a representative of the multidisciplinary team who can interpret evaluation results. Other personnel representing career and vocational education, related services personnel, and other agencies may be included if necessary. The IEP is a legal procedure that commits the services of the school district to provide handicapped students with a free, appropriate public education.

Each IEP must include:

- Present levels of educational performance
- Measurable annual goals
- Related services, supplementary aids, or technology-assisted instruction required
- Placement in least restrictive environment

- Modifications to the state or district assessment of student achievement
- Dates of services
- Transition plan, beginning at age 14
- Statement of how student progress on annual goals will be communicated to parents

Least Restrictive Environment – Handicapped students must be educated with their nonhandicapped peers to the maximum extent possible. The concept that the handicapped student be educated in the regular setting if possible underlies the requirement of least restrictive environment. If the regular setting does not meet the needs of the handicapped student, modifications, supplementary services, and related services may be required. A more restrictive environment is permitted only to the extent that the student's needs cannot be met in the regular program.

Procedural Safeguards – Detailed notice and consent requirements specify that parental consent must be given before any evaluation. Law requires parental access to records. Timelines, notification procedures, and parental rights are elements of IDEA that assure procedural safeguards. Schools must provide written notice to parents prior to IEP team meetings, thereby affording parents the opportunity to participate in any meeting where their child's program will be planned or changed. Due process requirements, mediation, administrative hearings, judicial reviews, and provisions for remedies and attorneys' fees are also mandated.

Related Services – Related services are those that may be required to assist the disabled child to benefit from special education. Transportation, speech pathology, audiology, physical therapy, occupational therapy, music therapy, art therapy, counseling, social work services, transition services, medical services, orientation and mobility services, and school health services have been specified by IEP teams as related services. The Tatro Test, developed by the U. S. Supreme Court, is used to identify qualified related services. First, the student must be an eligible special education student. Second, the service must be necessary for the student to benefit from special education. Third, the service must be performed by a nonphysician (Irving Independent School District v. Tatro, 1984).

Extended Year Services – The courts have found that Extended Year Services, beyond the number of days of a traditional school year, must be provided if students will be harmed by an interruption of special education services. Extended Year Services are required only when regression will be severe enough to keep the student from regaining lost skills within a reasonable length of time. Extended Year Services must be a part of the student's Individualized Education Plan.

Unilateral Placements – School districts have been required to fund unilateral placements in private school settings (School Committee of Burlington v. Department of Education (1985). The courts have found in these cases that parents must present a heavy burden of proof that the education offered by the school district is inappropriate and that the private school placement is the only appropriate solution. School districts have avoided fiscal responsibility in unilateral placements by providing documentation that the school district can provide a free, appropriate public education.

Discipline of Handicapped Children – Students with disabilities are not exempt from school discipline rules (Gorn, 1996). There are, however, special rules that apply to disabled students. A Functional Behavioral Assessment may be required prior to any change of placement. The general purpose of functional assessment of behavior is to provide the IEP team with additional information, analysis, and strategies for dealing with undesirable behavior (Joseph M. v. ISD No. 2310, 1998). After the Functional Behavioral Assessment has been completed, the IEP team may write a Behavior Intervention Plan. This Behavior Intervention Plan includes the strategies, interventions, and supports that the school will provide for the student. Courts have approved a range of discipline measures, including time out, assignment to restrictive settings, and restriction of privileges. If the misconduct is related to the student's handicapping condition, special consideration must be given. Short-term disciplinary consequences can usually be applied as long as the handicapping condition is found not to be a decisive factor by the IEP team.

Religious Issues

Separation of Church and State

The First Amendment of the United States Constitution prohibits Congress from making laws that either respect the establishment of religion or prohibit the free exercise of religion. The establishment clause is generally interpreted to mean that neither a state nor the federal government can set up a church. This wall of separation philosophy has been used since it was stated in Everson v. Board of Education, (1947). Although the First Amendment speaks specifically about Congress, courts have found it to apply to local and state governments, including school boards.

The test used for many years to determine the constitutionality of practices challenged as religious activities is the Lemon Test. An activity of a governmental entity, which is challenged as being in violation of the Establishment Clause, will be found to be constitutional if it complies with the three-pronged test.

- There is a legitimate, secular, nonreligious purpose for the activity;

- The primary effect of the activity neither advances nor hinders religious belief or practice; and
- The activity does not foster excessive entanglement between the governmental entity and religious concerns (Lemon v. Kurtzman, 1971).

The Coercion Test asks whether the practice in question involves state-sponsored activities that coerce participation by objectors. Coercion has been interpreted to mean psychological or social pressure to conform.

The Free Exercise Clause prohibits the government from burdening an individual's exercise of religion. The Free Exercise Clause has been interpreted to guarantee parents the right to control their child's religious education. It does not, however, require public schools to establish and implement curriculum based on religious sensibilities.

State-Sponsored School Prayer, Silent Meditation

A public school student has a right to individually, voluntarily, and silently pray or meditate in school in a manner that does not disrupt the instructional or other activities of the school. A person may not require, encourage, or coerce a student to engage in or refrain from such prayer or meditation during any school activity. Both student-led and adult-led prayers have been ruled by the courts to be inherently religious activity and, therefore, not constitutionally admissible (Engle v. Vitale, 1963).

Schools may not sponsor prayer, and school personnel may not allow voluntary, student-initiated, student-led prayers over the public address system. Teachers may not lead prayers or allow student volunteers to lead a class in prayer, even if objecting students are permitted to leave the class. The state may not set aside a time for silent meditation or prayer.

In another case on school prayer, the U. S. Supreme Court struck down a Rhode Island school district's practice of allowing its middle and high school principals to select a member of the clergy to give a nonsectarian, nonproselytizing invocation at graduation ceremonies (Lee v. Weisman, 1992).

A few courts have found that using prayer to solemnify an event is a permissible secular purpose. The Fifth Circuit ruled that student-initiated, student-led, nonsectarian, nonproselytizing prayer is permissible at such events as graduation. Under this thinking, graduation is a singular and unique event, probably once each school year, as opposed to sports activities that take place with a high level of frequency (Jones v. Clear Creek ISD, 1992).

Religious Literature

The courts have ruled that any use of the Bible or other religious writings must be clearly secular. Religious writings may be used in history courses, literature courses, or classes on comparative religions. The Bible may be contained in a school library, provided that Christianity, or any other religion, is not favored by the library over other religions.

Several courts have dealt with the issue of secular humanism, noting that even if books and curriculum materials do seem to promote a secular humanistic point of view, the use of those books and materials is not unconstitutional (Grove v. Mead School District, 1985). These courts also cautioned school officials to not attempt to balance the secular materials with Bible-oriented instruction.

Religious Displays and Holiday Observances

Courts have ruled that school policies permitting observance of holidays, including Christmas, Easter, Passover, Hanukkah, and St. Patrick's Day, are acceptable since these holidays have both religious and secular connotations. The inclusion of Christmas and Chanukah on school calendars is acceptable as long as particular faiths are not being promoted.

Religious Symbols

Whether a religious symbol, such as a cross or nativity scene, may be displayed in public schools depends on the circumstances of the case. The U. S. Supreme Court ruled that a nativity scene, a Santa Claus house, and a Christmas tree at a courthouse did not violate the Constitution. The U. S. Supreme Court also ruled that a nativity scene, displayed by itself on a courthouse lawn, did violate the Establishment Clause, but a menorah, standing outside the courthouse next to a Christmas tree and a sign about liberty, did not violate the Constitution (County of Allegheny v. American Civil Liberties Union, 1989).

School districts must also pay attention to other religious displays. The U. S. Supreme Court ruled that a school could not require posting of the Ten Commandments in every classroom because the display did not have a secular purpose (Stone v. Graham, 1980). In addition, lower courts have ruled that permanent religious displays of any kind violate the Establishment Clause.

The courts have considered the content and context of the alleged religious display to determine whether a reasonable person would feel that the primary effect of the display is to advance or inhibit religion. For example, the use of "Blue Devil" as school mascot was found to have a secular purpose and was allowed (Kunselman v. Western Reserve Local School District, 1995).

The wearing of religious symbols has been addressed in a case in Texas. Students successfully challenged the district's gang-related apparel rule when a federal district court ruled that wearing rosary beads outside their shirts did not constitute significant disruption to justify infringing on the students' religiously motivated speech (Chalifoux v. New Caney ISD, 1997).

Use of School Facilities by Religious Groups

Schools often receive requests from student groups who wish to conduct Bible study meetings before or after school, and church groups frequently ask permission to use school facilities for religious activities. Courts have generally ruled that public schools are not traditional public forums and that the schools have the right to refuse access to all individuals and groups during noninstructional hours. A limited open forum is created when a school allows one or more noncurriculum-related student groups to use school facilities during noninstructional time. The U. S. Supreme Court ruled that allowing one noncurricular group to use school facilities thereby involved the Equal Access Act, and thus other groups should be admitted (Board of Education of Westside Community Schools v.Mergens, 1990).

Creation Science

The U. S. Supreme Court struck down an Arkansas law that prohibited the teaching of evolution in Arkansas public schools. The Court did not find a secular purpose in the Arkansas law (Epperson v. Arkansas, 1968).

In 1987, the U. S. Supreme Court ruled that a statute passed by the Louisiana Legislature requiring Louisiana public schools to teach creation and evolution equally was unconstitutional because the state's primary purpose was to teach the Christian perspective. The Court did not rule out the teaching of creation science as part of the science curriculum if it is presented with other theories and the material is taught objectively. This case holds with lower court decisions rejecting the mandatory teaching of creation science in public schools (Edwards v. Aguillard, 1987).

Religious Exemptions

In a landmark case on religion in public schools, the U. S. Supreme Court ruled that Jehovah's Witness students should not be forced to salute the flag. This case provides a basis for the practice that government should not compel a person to profess a belief (West Virginia State Board of Education v. Barnette, 1943).

In another case dealing with religious objections, the U. S. Supreme Court ruled that Amish parents could take their children out of school after the eighth grade (Wisconsin v. Yoder, 1972). The Old Order Amish objected to the Wisconsin compulsory attendance law, and the court ruled that those parents need not comply, since the compulsory attendance law was in conflict with their religious beliefs.

A number of states have laws granting exemptions if a school activity conflicts with the parents' religious beliefs. Excusal for participation at religious training and observances is practiced in many states. The growth of conservation organizations that stress a parent's right to direct the educational program of his or her child has increased the practice of granting exemptions for religious purposes.

Rights of Parents

The Right to Direct a Child's Education

In 1923, the constitutional right of parents to direct the education of their children was identified by the U. S. Supreme Court (Meyer v. Nebraska, 1923). The Court found that the liberty to direct the upbringing and education of their children was a constitutionally protected right under the Fourteenth Amendment. In these early cases, the power of the state to prescribe a curriculum for state-supported schools, exert reasonable regulation, and require attendance were upheld. Through the years, the courts have considered the right of parents to control their children's education in several different areas:

Religious objections – Parental and religious rights of Amish parents prevailed over the state's interest in compulsory attendance (Wisconsin v. Yoder, 1972).

Student discipline – Parental right to control a child's education does not exceed the necessity faced by schools to maintain and provide a safe learning environment (Jensen ex rel. C.J. v. Reeves, 1999)

Curriculum issues – Parents do not have fundamental rights to dictate school curricula (Cornwell v. State Bd. of Education, 1969).

Parental access to public classrooms – The parental constitutional right to direct a child's education does not obligate schools to permit parents to attend classes of their children (Ryans v. Gresham, 1998).

Standards for home schools and testing of home-schooled students – Courts have generally ruled that parents must comply with home schooling regulations (Battles v. Anne Arundel County Board of Education, 1995).

School Accountability: Meeting Accountability Demands

Beginning with the release of "A Nation at Risk" (National Commission on Excellence in Education 1983), accountability has been a significant part of education reform efforts nationwide. Accountability components within reform and restructuring became a part of state legislative initiatives. Most states have addressed educational accountability issues (King & Mathers, 1997).

Currently, 26 states have high school exit examinations in place or in the planning stage. Although some educators have voiced concerns about judging a school staff's success on the performance of that school's students on standardized achievement tests, about 20 states publicly identify failing schools (Popham, 1999). Almost all of the 49 states that have adopted performance standards assess progress toward those standards yearly with a standardized exam (Natt, 1999).

In requiring that students pass competency tests in order to graduate, states have established new criteria based on academic judgment. These subjective decisions, including graduation criteria, level of test scores, type of questions, and the difficulty of items, have been upheld. Courts have traditionally upheld the right of schools to determine academic requirements. A U. S. District Court upheld the Texas Assessment of Academic Skills test, ruling that although the test does adversely affect minority students in significant numbers, the state has demonstrated an educational necessity for the test, students' civil rights were not violated, and the test is not discriminatory to minority students (MALDEF v. Texas Education Agency, 2000).

The School Finance Process

Funding public education is an enormous undertaking in the United States. It is the largest portion of most state and local governmental budgets (Odden & Picus, 2000), and the cost of financing the fifty state school systems now approaches $200 billion annually (Burrup, Brimley & Garfield, 1999). A system of public schools that educates all the children of all the people is big business.

Traditionally, school finance issues have largely been equity issues. Although there are differences among the state finance systems, too much reliance on property taxes and significant variances in the funding available to school districts within each of the states have led to fiscal disparities (Walker & Casey, 1992). School districts with lower property values, or property-poor districts, have traditionally had less to spend on a per-pupil basis than their wealthier neighbors. Most public schools find it impossible to escape the financial circumstances in which they find themselves, largely due to location. In the 1970s, construction of a nuclear reactor within a public school district might mean that a school could go from poverty conditions to suddenly being able to finance a very adequate educational program. However, the reality was more likely to be that school districts once located in affluent industrial areas gradually found themselves in poverty as older industry disappeared to be replaced by high technology corridors.

School Finance Equalization

The equalization formulas adopted by many states have been designed to equalize or level funding. There are four basic models of school finance equalization:

- Foundation program
- Percentage equalizing
- Guaranteed tax base
- Power equalization

All these models are built on such factors as property wealth, district needs, district tax effort, district tax yield, and inclusivity of state funding (Clark & England, 1996). Attempts in some states to equalize funding now include weighted pupil formulas that include more funding for students in special education, bilingual education, and career and technology programs. Other equalization strategies include additional state funds for levels of taxation approved by local taxpayers that are over and above minimum levels and adjustments for cost differences among school districts.

Sources of Public School Financing

The earliest known attempt to finance the education of all children on a statewide level through the use of public taxation was adopted by the Commonwealth of Massachusetts in 1642. This Compulsory Education Law required each family to teach the children of the household to read, but the problem was that many parents could not read themselves. The Massachusetts Legislature resolved the problem 5 years later by passing the "Old Delude Satan Act of 1647." This act simply and eloquently laid the groundwork for development of tax supported education (Odden & Picus, 2000, pp.8-9).

Because the majority of citizens capable of supporting the commonwealth through taxes were small landowners, the property tax evolved in New England as the primary source of taxable income for public schools. However, the property tax would later lead to enormous problems of inequity. In a critical analysis of public education in 1943, Henry C. Morrison referred to the property tax structure as "late New England colonial" and described the school district as "a little republic at every crossroads" (as cited in Swanson & King, 1997). This focus on decentralization has been noted as both a strength and a weakness of the American public education system (Swanson & King, 1997).

From its earliest beginnings, education has been recognized as a responsibility of the states and not the federal government. Centralized control in the early years was practically impossible due to lack of communication and difficulty of travel. As a result, each state developed school districts to serve students at local levels. Only one state, Hawaii, has a state system of administration, thereby avoiding the problem of taxable inequity among several hundred school districts within the state.

School Finance Equity

The nation has developed from an agrarian society based on small farms to a highly industrialized society to a technology society. This development has exacerbated the disparity between rich and poor school districts based largely on local property taxes. Elements of school finance equity usually include both pupil equity and taxpayer equity. Pupil equity may be considered through the dimensions of horizontal pupil equity, vertical pupil equity, and equal opportunity. Discussions of taxpayer equity usually include fiscal neutrality, in which equal tax rates generate equal revenues per pupil.

In the late 1960s, a growing number of court cases appeared attacking the inequity of school financing based on district taxable wealth. It was during this period that the California Supreme Court handed down its decision in Serrano v. Priest, 1976. The court noted that even though the basic state aid program tended to equalize school districts, there were great disparities in school revenues and the system as a whole generated school revenue proportional to the wealth of an individual school. After concluding that education was a fundamental interest, the court found the state's system of financing schools unconstitutional (Alexander & Alexander, 1997).

The state of California was forced to raise additional tax revenue to equalize school financing without unduly penalizing wealthier school districts. The resulting taxpayer revolt in California led to the hammer blow of Proposition 13, which severely affected the tax system. This case also set the stage for reforms in school finance in other states (Alexander & Alexander, 1997).

In another school finance case, San Antonio Independent School District v. Rodriguez, 1973, a federal district court ruled that the Texas system discriminated against people who happened to reside in poor school districts. This case was eventually reversed by the United States Supreme Court in 1973. Federal court challenges to the constitutionality of state school finance plans were dealt a blow when the Supreme Court ruled that while the Texas system of financing education was unjust and discriminatory, it was not unconstitutional.

A series of lawsuits in Texas courts finally led to significant change to the Texas system of financing education. As a result of the Rodriguez case, about one-half of the states have reformed their finance systems to provide more equitable educations for their children. The states that have experienced the most difficulty in reforming their finance systems have been the highly industrialized states, such as Illinois. In Illinois, the presence of taxable wealth based on industry provided most school districts with adequate to large amounts of taxable wealth. The large amount of tax layout required to minimally equalize school district funding, while holding the extremely wealthy districts harmless, found neither major political party anxious to tackle the problem.

Between 1971 and 1994, 38 states were involved in school finance litigation (Clark & England, 1996, p. 5). School finance cases are usually tried on issues of equal protection provisions in state constitutions and/or efficiency clauses in state constitutions. Frequently cited causes of school finance inequities that resulted in court cases include:

- Disparities in taxable wealth among school districts, causing significant differences in levels of expenditures;

- Differences in local efforts to support the schools; and

- State finance plans that do not equalize the differences between wealthy and poor school districts;

- Too much reliance on local property taxes (Clark & England, 1996, p. 5).

The Role of the Federal Government

The "let alone" policy of the federal government that may be traced back to Continental Congress is still an issue (Burrup, Brimley & Garfield, 1999). The increasing complexity of social institutions, the economic order and the political structure has resulted in increased governmental services. Observations about the role of federal aid to education include:

- The widespread and complex involvement of the federal government in helping to finance public education is likely to fluctuate. There is evidence that specific programs may change considerably, as they are influenced by changing philosophies and changing leadership in the three branches of the federal government.

- The United States Department of Education is the logical agency to administer most, if not all, of the federal programs directly related to education.

- Additional federal programs need not greatly increase the degree of control over education at the national level. There is, however, a need to give national purpose to education. Funds for education, regardless of their source, should be directed toward achieving specified goals.

- Establishment of federal, state, and local partnerships would provide assistance in solving many educational problems.

Although categorical and block grants contribute greatly to educational programs, some form of general aid would also be advantageous (Burrup, Brimley & Garfield, 1999).

School Finances and Decision-Making

The extent to which schools are able to succeed in the mission of educating the next generation is inextricably tied to sound decision-making in the schools themselves, and to the adequacy of funding provided by their patrons. Among their patrons may be those citizens who are committed to sending their children to parochial schools. Their commitment is demonstrated by their willingness to pay tuition and other private school costs in addition to taxes required to support public schools. While those citizens who send their children to public schools benefit from the large outlay of the taxes used to support public schools, they often complain about inefficient operations and the supposed lack of sound decision-making within the schools.

Some school management theorists have proposed decision-making models based on the concept that school budgets could be developed based on need and the funding then somehow acquired to finance an adequate educational program. The idea was to start with a needs assessment of the entire district and each school within the district. The needs assessment was based on the goals and objectives required to deliver the educational program desired. The goals and objectives were then translated into the dollar amounts required to finance the total school program. The problem with this approach is that most public schools operate within a narrow range of school funding, based on local property taxes and a fairly rigid state formula for financial support. Educational goals and objectives must fit the level of financial support generally available, rather than adequate financing appearing after educational wishes and desires have been translated into goals and objectives. Such models may, however, provide the basis for excellent long-range plans to work toward in developing a more adequate educational program.

Lunnenburg defines decision-making as "a process of making a choice from a number of alternatives to achieve a desired result" (Lunnenburg, 1995). The key point in this definition is that a number of options are available, one of which will produce efficient and educationally sound results. Good decision-making in school finances has sometimes been referred to as "getting the biggest bang for the buck." In school construction, should the contractor who produces a lower bid by proposing cheaper materials always be preferred simply because more room can be afforded? Such decisions often result in buildings that do not perform well either in the short run or the long run.

The principles of sound decision-making may be effectively applied at all levels of the educational system. For example, an elementary school with a significant number of students of migrant families may face unique challenges. Migrant workers will often take children from school a month before the end of the school year to help the family boost income. As these migrant families move north during the harvest season, they will eventually return to school one or two months after school begins. A reading program relying on basal readers was problematic for these students. To attack this problem, one school began by establishing a reading committee composed of parents, teachers, a social worker, and the principal. By applying the principles of sound decision-making, they arrived at a multilevel reading series for each grade level, grades one through three. As a result, if a migrant child finished levels one and two before his family left to follow the harvest in the spring, he simply began reading at level three of the first grade on returning the following fall. The principles of sound decision-making that were followed by this reading committee can be applied to almost any educational problem. The principles are:

1. Clearly define the problem. In the example, the problem was not a lack of ability on the part of the children. The problem was that the children were never able to finish the first grade basal readers before they were expected to begin grade two. The solution was to divide each grade into multiple reading levels and acquire appropriate materials. Parental involvement helped gain approval for the new approach.

2. Gather information. The critical information necessary was to determine, through a careful study of leaving and arrival times of the migrant families, approximately how many reading levels were needed in each grade. After all issues were addressed, the final problem was to locate a publisher with appropriate reading materials.

3. Analyze the problem. Analysis of the problem is not simply gathering the relevant information. It also involves correctly understanding what the information means. Knowing that the migrant children were behind other children, knowing that they were missing a significant amount of the school year, and knowing that they had average or above average potential were of little help as the reading committee planned the best solution for the problem.

4. Develop alternative solutions. Among the alternative solutions to this problem might have been retaining the migrant students until they mastered the basal readers at each level. This might have been better than promoting the students to the next grade level unprepared. However, a better solution was to allow the student to work at the second grade level while finishing the first grade reading.

5. Test the solution. The solution was tested with the migrant children. An unexpected benefit was that, after testing for a year with the migrant students, this plan was also used to bring other students to higher reading skills through a step-by-step process.

6. Apply the plan. The testing of this plan eventually led to the adoption of the plan, not only for migrant students and students experiencing reading problems but for the entire reading program in this elementary school.

The principles of sound decision-making as described in this example can be effectively applied to almost any school, or district wide problem.

The Future of School Finance

The new century is likely to see a higher level of continuing cooperation between the federal, state, and local levels of government in meeting educational needs. Regardless of its problems, public education will likely continue to be the primary hope of rescuing the urban poor, immigrants, and the vast majority of American children from the condemnation of lives spent in poverty and ignorance. While schools may not be able to solve all the social, economic, and spiritual ills of our society, they will continue to play a large role. Burrup, Brimley and Garfield (1999) have identified several future finance issues:

School choice issues, including charter schools, vouchers, and other options, will continue to be of interest to Americans. They are discussed in greater detail in another chapter of this textbook. Despite increased flexibility, some school leaders continue to express frustration with the effects of certain state and federal mandates.

- Improving instruction is the ultimate purpose of school reform. Successful reform agendas must include strategies for providing effective professional development for current teachers and improved preparation programs for prospective teachers.

- Policymakers and educational leaders are seeking effective ways to attract and maintain the best new teachers, to assist teachers with implementation of standards-based reforms, and to make coherent reform in the whole enterprise of teacher preparation and professional development.

- There is an emerging consensus that school reform must be a community-wide enterprise of partnerships composed of parents, businesses, social service agencies, and other community institutions.

- Restoring public confidence in public education is a major challenge in an era when a majority of the voting public does not have children in school and more parents are looking to private schools and alternative choices for quality education.

- Although many citizens support education reform in general, they may disagree on the specifics or may be unprepared to accept the costs, discomforts, and time required to make significant changes.

- Demographic and social changes are creating new governance, financial, and management challenges for education. Different children may require different methods of instruction to achieve at high levels.

- Social problems such as poverty, drugs, and crime are affecting the health of children. Their safety and readiness to learn are creating new demands for human services. Schools will be asked to do many things that require additional time, energy, and resources in order to achieve their main mission: educating children.

Case Problem: Searching With Magnetometers

With the increased concern about violence in schools, some school officials use metal detectors to maintain a safe school environment

A high school has been experiencing a series of incidents involving weapons at school, triggered in large part by increased gang activity. The superintendent directed the high school principal to install magnetometers—door frame size metal detectors through which students pass—at the building's main entrance. The magnetometers are used daily to screen students for weapons as they enter the building. While metal detectors are standard equipment in airports and many public buildings, to what extent does use of such devices constitute a search?

Cases

Battles v. Anne Arundel County Board of Education, 904 F. Supp. 471 (1995)

Bethel School District No. 403 v. Fraser, 106 S. Ct. 359 (1986).

Board of Education of Westside Community Schools v. Mergens, 496 U.S. 226, 110 S. Ct. 2356 (1990).

Brown v. Board of Education, 347 U. S. 483 (1954).

Chalifoux v. New Caney ISD, 976 F. Supp. 659 (1997).

City of Canton v. Harris, 489 U. S. 378 (1989).

Cornwell v. State Bd. of Education, 312 F. Supp. 340, 344 (D.C. Md. 1969).

County of Allegheny v. American Civil Liberties Union, 492 U. S. 573 (1989).

Davis v. Monroe County Board of Education, 111 Ed. Law Rep. 1107, 91 F.3d 1418, U. S. Court of Appeals, Eleventh Circuit, 1996

DesRoches v. City of Norfolk School Board, 156 F. 3d 571 (4th Cir. 1998).

Doe v. Taylor Independent School District, 15 F. 3d 443 (1994).

Edwards v. Aguillard, 107 S. Ct. 2573 (1987).

Engle v. Vitale, 370 U.S. 421, 424-25, 82 S. Ct. 1261 (1963).

Epperson v. Arkansas, 393 U. S. 97 (1968).

Everson v. Board of Education, 330 U. S. 1 (1947).

Goss v. Lopez, 419 U. S. 565 (1975).

Grove v. Mead School District, 753 F. 2d 1528 (9th Cir. 1985).

Irving Independent School District v. Tatro, 104 S. Ct. 3371 (1984).

Jeglin v. San Jacinto Unified School District, 827 F. Supp. 1459 (C.D. Cal. 1993)

Jensen ex rel. C.J. v. Reeves, 45 F. Supp. 2d 1265 (1999).

Jones v. Clear Creek ISD, 977 F. 2nd 963 (5th Cir. 1992).

Joseph M. v. ISD No. 2310, (Minnesota Hearing Officer; 29 IDELR 330 (1998).

Kunselman v. Western Reserve Local School District, 70 F. 3d 931 (1995).

Lee v. Weisman, 112 S. Ct. 2649 (1992).

Lemon v. Kurtzman, 403 U.S. 602, 91S. Ct. 2105 (1971).

MALDEF v. Texas Education Agency (W. D. Texas 2000).

Meyer v. Nebraska, 262 U. S. 390 (1923).

Monell v. Department of Social Services, 436 U. S. (1989)

New Jersey v. T.L.O., 105 S. Ct. 733 (1985).

People v. Dukes, 580 N.Y. 2d 850 (N.Y.City Crim. Ct., 1992).

Ryans v. Gresham, 6F. Supp. 2d 595 (E.D. Texas 1998).

San Antonio Independent School District v. Rodriguez, 411 U. S. (1973).

School Committee of Burlington v. Department of Education, 105 S. Ct. 1996 (1985).

Serrano v. Priest, 18 Cal. 3rd 728, 557 P. 2d 929 (1976).

Stone v. Graham, 101 S. Ct. 192 (1980)

Timothy W. v. Rochester, New Hampshire School District, U. S. 875 F.2d 954 (1989).

Tinker v. Des Moines Independent Community District, 393 U. S. 503 (1969).

Todd v. Rush County Schools, 133 F. 3d. 984 (7th Cir.1998).

Veronia School District 47 J. v. Action, 115 S. Ct. 2386 (1995).

West Virginia State Board of Education v. Barnette, 319 U. S. 624 (1943).

Wisconsin v. Yoder, 406 U. S. 205 (1972).

References

Alexander, K., & Alexander, M. D. (1998). *American public school law* (2nd ed.). Belmont, CA: West/Wadsworth.

Americans with Disabilities Act of 1990, 42 U.S.C.A.

Burrup, P., Brimley, V., & Garfield, R. (1999*). Financing education in a climate of change* (7th ed.). Boston: Allyn and Bacon.

Clark, C. & England, C. (1996). *Educational finance briefing paper: Texas public school finance and related issues.* Austin: Texas Center for Educational Research.

Department of Education. Office of Civil Rights. (1999). *Sexual harassment guidance: Harassment of students by school employees, other students, or third parties.* Washington, D.C: Department of Education. Retrieved 2001 from http://www.ed.gov/offices/OCR/sexhar00.html.

Education for All Handicapped Children Act of 1975, 20 U.S.C.

Education for the Handicapped Amendments of 1986, 20 U.S.C.

Gorn, S. (1996). *What do I do when: The answer book on special education law.* Horsham, PA: LRP Publications.

Handicapped Children's Protection Act of 1986, 20 U.S.C.

Harvey, I. W. (1989). *A history of educational finance in Alabama.* Auburn, AL: Auburn University.

Individuals with Disabilities Education Act of 1990, 20 U.S.C.

Individuals with Disabilities Education Act Amendments of 1997, Pub.L.No. 105-17, 105th Cong., 1st sess

King, R.A., & Mathers, J.K. (1997). Improving schools through performance-based accountability and financial rewards. *Journal of Educational Finance.* 23 147-176.

Levine, E. L., & Wexler, E. M. (1981). *P. L. 94-142: An act of Congress.* New York: Macmillan.

Lunnenburg, F. (1995). *The principalship: Concepts, and applications.* Englewood Cliffs, NJ: Prentice-Hall.

National Commission on Excellence in Education. (1983). *A nation at risk* (LC8405556). Washington, DC: U. S. Government Printing Office.

National Commission on Safe Schools. (1998). *Safe schools.* Washington, D.C. U. S. Government Printing Office.

National Schools Boards Association (1998*). Keep schools safe: A collection of resources to help make schools safer.* National School Boards Association. .Retrieved 2001 from http://www.keepschoolssafe.org/.

Natt, Jane, (1999) *Backlash against high-stakes testing growing.* American Association of School Administrators Online Leadership News. Retrieved 2001 from http://www.aasa.org/publications/ln/12_99/12_22_99standards.htm

Odden, A. & Picus, L. (2000*). School finance: A policy perspective.* Boston: McGraw-Hill.

Popham, W. James. (1999). *Your school should not be evaluated by standardized test scores.* American Association of School Administrators Online Leadership News. Retrieved 2001 from http://www.aasa.org/issues_and_insights/assessment/8_26_98_Popham_standardized.htm.

Rehabilitation Act of 1973, Section 504, 29 U.S.C.

Swanson, A. & King, R. (1997*). School finance: its economics and politics* (2nd ed.). New York: Longman Publishers.

Turnbull, A. P., & Turnbull, H. R. (1997*). Families, professionals, and exceptionality: A special partnership* (3rd ed.). Upper Saddle River, NJ: Merrill Prentice Hall.

Vocational Rehabilitation Act of 1973, 29 U. S. C. 794 (Section 504).

Walker, B. & Casey, D.T. (1992). *The basics of Texas public school finance* (5th ed.). Austin: Texas Association of School Boards.

Wenkart, R. D. (1993). The Americans with Disabilities Act and its impact on public education. *Education Law Reporter*, 82, 291-302.

Yell, M. (1998). *The law and special education.* Upper Saddle River, NJ: Prentice-Hall, Inc.

Zirkel, P. A., & Kincaid, J. M. (1995*). Section 504, the ADA and the schools.* Horsham, PA: LRP Publications.

Chapter 4
Community Relations
Sondra Estep

This chapter defines community relations; its history, power structures, values, partnerships, and methods of communication. The chapter also contains a special section on gangs policy and on crises planning..

Introduction

Community Relations Defined

Community or public relations is defined by Holliday (1988) as a "function on all levels of a school system, established as a program to improve and maintain optimal levels of student achievement, and to build and maintain public support" (p. 12).

Pawlas (1995) suggests that there is a distinct difference between public relations (PR) and community relations. PR is an attempt to influence public opinion about schools through a one-way communication process. The public is merely kept informed. Pawlas states that community relations "involves the community in a process of two-way communications with the school and emphasizes increasing understanding between the schools and its community, not increasing the community's understanding of the school" (p. 2).

Each of these definitions points to the key concepts of a community relations program:

- Building public support for schools
- Involving all responsible parties in the process
- Improving student achievement
- Developing two-way communication

Holliday (1998) also offers this succinct summary of the reason for having a formal community relations program in a school district:

Education must be viewed in terms of a school-community setting, which includes students and teachers, administrators and support staff, board members, parents and other citizens.

Whether a school system is excellent or mediocre depends on how those people work together –how they communicate, relate, are involved, participate and share. A public/community relations program is aimed at focusing on the relationships of all those people with an overall goal of improving student achievement (p. 12).

Although a good public relations program is a part of a good community relations program, it cannot be the entire community plan. Administrators who mistakenly confused PR as community relations end-up with ill-conceived plans and less-than-desirable results.

Orientation

During the one-room school house era (1647-1900), school buildings were constructed by a local group of residents having a common need to educate their children. The group hired the teacher, which meant that the teacher generally reflected the values and beliefs of this group. Parents purchased the books that they wanted their children to study and sent their children to school with those books. The teacher was responsible for teaching the books that were sent. Governance of the school was absolutely under local control during this era.

By 1909, compulsory education had become a reality in most states. Along with the system of common schooling in America came the right of government to tax citizens to support the schools. Americans willingly began to support the public school system with their tax dollars.

By 1950, schools had become corporations serving children in towns and cities. School boards were elected. Citizens were now expected to channel their opinions and desires through the elected or appointed school boars. Parents no longer had direct control over a specific school.

However, this era heralded the onset of a strict separation between parents, community members and school officials. Educators proclaimed that they were experts in the field and the citizenry should bow to their expertise. Certainly, teachers had gone through teacher preparation programs to learn how to be teachers. What could a common citizen possibly know about the intricacies of educating a child? School corporations saw little value in listening to what their stakeholders had to say. Educators would preach to parents and community members but seldom listen to them. Communications became one-way – from the school to the home. Schools virtually closed-out input from their external constituents.

In 1983, the U.S. Secretary of Education released an alarming report on the state of American education. *A Nation at Risk: The Imperative for Educational Reform* lambasted schools for the decline in student test scores. It asserted that we had particularly lost our international ranking, with many countries surpassing American students in numerous areas. Regardless of the validity of the claims within the document, the perception was created that American students were no longer the best and brightest.

The perception created in a *Nation at Risk* still permeates the attitudes of parents, community members, and most importantly, legislatures. This report marked the end of state and federal dollars being thrown at education and marked the beginning of the educational reform movement.

About the same time that the report became public, Americans were beginning to grow intolerant of union-led teacher strikes. Year after year, schools opened late, while the teachers pounded the pavement for an equitable pay scale. The argument became circular – test scores were declining, teachers wanted more money, yet more money had only resulted in further declines in test scores. Public awareness and concern about the state of their schools was starting to take hold across the nation.

In 1994, the United States Department of Education (DOE) emphasized the need for school reform as a means of increasing student achievement through the release of the Goals 2000 (also called America 2000) program (U.S. Department of Education (1991). The program was designed to assist districts with their school reform efforts. One of the publications that they made available to assist schools is *Goals 2000: An Invitation to Your Community*, a publication offering guidance on how to include the community in developing a school's comprehensive action plan. The federal government was sending the message that it was time to involve the community in the educational process.

Just how did the federal government get involved in education? The U.S. Constitution does not mention free or public education; however, the Tenth Amendment assures that all rights that are not mentioned or prohibited in the Constitution are a responsibility of the states. Thus, states became responsible for educating their youth through the Tenth Amendment. Most states delegated that responsibility to local districts – at least the daily operations and management of schools.

Prior to 1985, few politicians ran under an education platform, particularly those running for federal office. Today, however, it would be considered negligent if a politician did not take a major position on education. For example, in the 1990s President Clinton popularized the idea that: it takes a village to educate a child. In 2000, President G. W. Bush's educational platform was "no child will be left behind."

The reform movement also marked the beginning of the current era of accountability. As legislators have taken the politically correct role of active involvement in educational issues, there has been increased pressure to raise test scores. All but two states have mandated state wide testing programs, and most have a high school exit exam in place. Politicians have clearly sent a message that allocating more money to education has not resulted in any impressive gains in test scores. Now states are linking test score improvement to grants, incentives and rewards that come from both the state and federal coffers. Politicians seem to need hard evidence in order to justify increases in educational spending.

In brief, schools moved from the local control of a one-room schoolhouse to the current corporate configuration of schools. When corporate bureaucracy pushed parents and community members out of the educational process, disenfranchised stakeholders caused schools to rethink their relationship with the communities they serve. Educational reform has resurrected the inclusion of parents and community members. That requires a broad base of input from all stakeholders in the community. As a result, education seems to have come full-circle. Schools now place a high value on involving the local community in school decisions, and accountability has prompted even more involvement of the responsible parties in a community.

Power Structures

Who are "responsible parties," and what influence do they have? Responsible parties is an alternative name for stakeholders. It suggests the notion that all members of a community are responsible for the education of the youth in that community (Joyce, Calhoun, Hopkins, 1999).

Bagin and Gallager (2001) define *power structures* as "an interrelationship among individuals with a vested interests who have the ability or authority to control other people, to obtain their conformity, or to command their services (p. 22)." There are groups within a community that an administrator needs to understand. Power structures can be organized into three models: the power elite model, the pluralist model, and amorphous or inert moidel. A school leader should know how to identify each group, the scope influence of each group, and how to best work with each.

Knowing who holds the power in a community helps administrators define their own roles. Ignoring a community's politics will catch the naive administrator off guard and could have devastating effects on the administrator's tenure with the district and on the school district itself.

Power Elite

In every community, there are people with considerable influence and power. They usually have control over political, social, and economic decisions. The power elite model views power and control as being held by a very small, very influential group(s) or individual(s). They control or have power over the financial, industrial, and commercial interests of the community (Bagin & Gallager, 2001.) Their power often comes from their position in the community or from personal or corporate wealth. They dominate a community through the power of their position. They can be members of a clergy, politicians, leaders of racial groups, or others who hold power positions. Those who advocate the power elite model believe that elitists usually have control over political, social and economic decisions in a community. Their power and control may or may not be known to the general populous, since they can wield their influence through others. For example, a substantial contribution to a politician may result in the politician carrying the banner for the elitist's wishes.

The power elite model comes from sociological research. As Figure 4-1 shows, a community can be viewed as pyramidal. Those with the power are at the apex of the pyramid, where power is concentrated and held by a few. The influence of the elite flows downward through a community impacting the masses at the base of the pyramid.

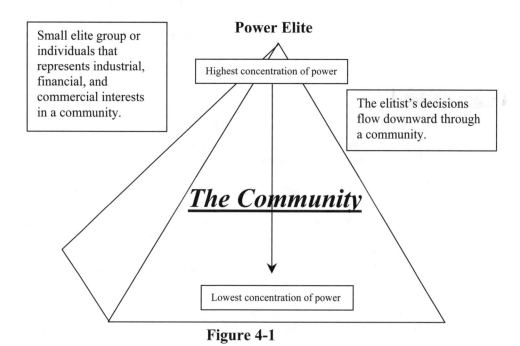

Elite Power Model

Power Elite

Small elite group or individuals that represents industrial, financial, and commercial interests in a community.

Highest concentration of power

The elitist's decisions flow downward through a community.

The Community

Lowest concentration of power

Figure 4-1

Elitists are often long-established members of the community, spanning many generations. They have a vested interest in the community, and understand that the schools are often key as to how the community is viewed. A negative reputation can have a terrible impact on a community. Companies do not want to locate (or remain located) in a community that cannot provide them with an educated citizenry. Young families do not want to buy new home in a district that has declining test scores.

The power elite in a community can be identified through the *reputational technique* (Polsby, 1985). To identify the power elite, first, assemble the names of community leaders, business and finance leaders, political leaders (e.g., League of Women Voters), society leaders (e.g., newspaper editors), leaders in civic organizations (Chamber of Commerce, Kiwanis,

Rotary, etc.), and others holding positions of power. Second, ask each member to identify the most influential member of the community. This can be done formally by creating a panel or informally through conversations with each person. Next, ask this newly identified group to name the community members who have the most influence on decisions made in the community. This process narrows the list in each round. It can be repeated until an elitist hierarchy is developed. Savvy administrators would then have the knowledge to know to whom they need pay particular attention when making major school decisions affecting the community. For example, building a new high school could have a significant tax impact on the citizens and require their approval through a referendum. Without the support of the power elite from the initial phases of the decision-making process, an administrator might be hard pressed to muster community approval.

Pluralist Model

The pluralist model of power structures is followed by political scientists who believe that there is no central power elite. Rather, they believe that power in a community is diffused. This model claims that there are multiple centers of power.

The pluralist model holds that various members of a community occupy positions of power related to specific issues. Each of these groups is very influential in its areas of interest and activism. No one group is in full control. For example, there may be parent groups in a community representing age-group athletics, such as soccer and Little League. These groups may have tremendous influence over local park boards in determining the development of playing fields but have little or no influence on police department decisions. These groups are often silent until an issue rises that effects them.

It is important for an administrator to identify group leaders prior to an issue surfacing. Savvy administrators will be prepared to work with these groups if they have studied past issues and have identified the groups most actively involved in resolving those issues. Administrators can provide a proactive framework by including these groups from the very initial phases of the decision-making process.

Administrators also need to be aware that there can be rapid and unexpected shifts in power among these groups. Therefore, it is in the administration's best interest to avoid alienating any faction, even those viewed as having the weakest levels of influence. Due to power shifts, the weakest groups could suddenly emerge as the ones with the most power and support.

Amorphous or Inert Model

The last power structure model is the inert, or amorphous group. In 1971, McCarty reported on the absence of an identifiable power structure in some communities. Power is either absent, or, even worse, it is latent. An inert structure is found in communities where there is little interaction among residents. People in these areas lack a sense of feeling that they are part of a community. This is most commonly found in rural settings, high-rise condominiums, apartment buildings, new communities, or mobile parks. High mobility rates, isolation from one another, or living in a newly developed community renders these groups inert.

These residents not actively involved in school or political issues. They support and maintain the status quo. In districts where this is the dominant power structure, there is very little movement toward educational reform activities or the introduction of experimental programs. The school board itself is often the actual power structure, and the community defers power to the board to keep things on an even keel. These groups also look to the superintendent to make decisions for them.

It is definitely challenging for an administrator to communicate with this type of configuration. The messenger needs to go to them rather than expecting them to come to him or her. Even when they are invited to participate in the decision-making process, the response will be low. Meetings are held at apartment buildings or at community centers. Sending a mass mailings may be the only way to mobilize such a group.

Regardless of the model one ascribes to, it is important for an administrator to know who has power and influence in a community. An educational leader must have a proactive approach for dealing with a community's movers-and-shakers and must involve them early on in the decision-making process. Ignoring power structures can result in the undermining of school improvement. The goal is to create dynamic partnerships with representatives from a community's power structure.

Understanding Power Structures

In order to provide a better understanding of power structures, four research studies of the elitist and pluralist models are offered below:

1. Kanawha County, West Virginia (Pluralist Power Study). This example of pluralist power is often referred to as the *battle of the books* controversy. To understand the controversy, you must first understand the history of people. People of this region are commonly referred to as Appalachians. They have a history of hardship, struggle and of receiving welfare.

In the seventeenth century, England was pressed to feed and house a growing population, so they sent their undesirables to America as indentured servants. Some worked-off their servitude, while others just ran away to the Appalachian Mountains. Those who eventually worked-off their indentured servant status followed the runaways to the mountains. Through this experience, these people developed a deep disdain for authority.

They came from a variety of religious backgrounds in England. So, when they came together in the mountains, they never developed one predominant religious affiliation. To this day, they do not have large numbers in an organized religion. Missionaries attempted to bring religion to them, but the mountainous terrain made this nearly impossible. The missionaries were the primary literacy providers of the times, but they could not reach the people, literacy disappeared and poverty prevailed.

Historically, Appalachians have demonstrated violence as a way of life. It has been thought that when they fought against the Indians, they were the ones who taught the Indians how to scalp. Appalachians fought with distinction in the War of 1812, and fought on both sides of the Civil War. After that war, they could not let go of their North or South allegiances. Those allegiances lead to feuds, such as the feud between the Hatfields and the McCoys. During Prohibition, Appalachians fought violently over illicit whiskey stills. They fought with federal agents and with each other over the trade of moonshine (Goode, 1983).

Although poor, the Appalachians nurtured and passed down their values of rugged individualism. They hold one deep belief that a person must spend great energy in this world preparing for the next world, where good things would finally happen. To this day, they still live close to one another along the creeks and hollows.

In 1974, the schools staff of the Kanawha County School District, recommended new books for adoption by the school board. One board member objected to some of the books claiming that they contained white racism, poor use of English, and unacceptable political opinions. A second out of the five school board member joined the first. By a vote of 3-2, the controversial textbooks were adopted.

The Appalachians objected to the use of ebonics, values clarifications, and what they thought was an un-American slant to the books. The values education in these books were in discord with the Appalachians' belief that it is the responsibility of adults to direct children when they misbehave. Children should not be allowed to make their own decisions about right and wrong. This stems from the Appalachians' belief that doing things right in this world guarantees a better after life.

As the controversy progressed, the groups who supported the textbooks clashed with those who opposed the adoption. Compromises were rejected time after time. Violence and chaos became rampant. Schools were bombed. When those responsible were apprehended and convicted, the controversy final came to an end (Goode, 1983).

2. Middletown (Muncie), Indiana – Power Elite Study. The study of the Ball family's power was a landmark study of American communities (Lynd & Lynd, 1929 and 1937). The family owned a business that made canning jars that are used to preserve fruits and vegetables.

It was, and is, the central business of the community. Ball State University in Muncie, Indiana, was named after the family. Goode (1993) offers this summary of the study:

> *The Lynds' investigation revealed that the dominant interests in the community were the business interests, the center of which was the X [Ball] family. This group derived its power from the tremendous influence of capitalism, which of course pervaded many aspects of community life. This was not an organized group with a high profile, but, nonetheless, their influence was enormous. Professional politicians were not ordinarily a part of this group, yet their political futures depended very much on working with this group.* (p. 112).

Middletown is a landmark study, because it was the first to identify a ruling power elite group in a community. It proved that the elite are a very influential component of a community power structure. Although this was not a study of school systems, the study did reveal that the Ball family had a tremendous influence over the local community college. The Ball family held membership on the local community college board of directors and were allegedly able to censor books and determine who spoke at the college (Goode, 1993).

3. Yankee City and Regional City. (Power Elite Studies) The Yankee City study was conducted in 1941 by Warner and Lunt. This study revealed that those with the highest socioeconomic status in the community had the greatest power and influence. Most are familiar with the terms upper class, upper middle class, middle class, lower middle class, and lower class, which emerged from this study. This study concluded that when there is conflict, the upper class will hold the upper hand.

In 1953, Floyd Hunter reported the results of his study of *Regional City* (Atlanta, Georgia). His sociological study concluded that the city "was run by a small group of powerful men who determined policy informally and behind the scenes. This group was identified by Hunter as the *power elite.*" (Goode, 1993). The study developed the *reputational technique* and used it to determine who constituted the power elite in Regional City. The *reputational technique* was discussed earlier in this chapter.

4. New Haven (Pluralist Power Study). Robert Dahl is the name most often associated with the pluralist approach to studying power structures (Polsby, 1980). Pluralists believe that power is dispersed amongst many people or groups who only come forward when an issue directly effects them. This is in contrast to districts where power is held by a few very influential members of a community. "In contrast to sociological Hunter-elitist concepts of the power elite as a single power structure in a community, the Dahl's political science approach is that power is decentralized in communities and that individuals seek power positions on those issues that are of importance to them" (Goode, 1993, p. 115).

Dahl (1961) studied particular issues such as urban development, public education, and political nominations. The method that he developed to focus on specific issues is referred to by pluralists as *issue analysis*. "Dahl determined that decisions on all issues were not made by a single elite group, but that decision making and influence by individuals clustered around specific issues" (Goode, 1993, p. 115).

When dealing with power structures, an administrators can apply what was learn from these studies. The lessons learned include:

- Identify all power structure groups in your community.
- Conduct a needs and values assessment to know what is important to members of your community.
- Involve representatives from all responsible groups in the decision-making process.
- Learn how to involve your community by attending professional development workshops or seminars.
- Be a proactive leader.
- Be flexible and avoid treading on tightly held dogma. Flexibility does not equate to weakness. It can be a sign of secure and responsible leadership.
- Decentralize the decision-making process.
- Delegate responsibility to subordinates in order to make decisions that reflect the desires of those closest to the issue.
- Be prepared to respond quickly to specific problems or issues.
- Learn to be an active listener! Ask questions and then just listen.
- Become a member of service organizations in the community. This is an excellent way to build relationships with many power brokers.
- Use informal situations to gather information.
- Keep an ear to the ground and find out what the word on the street is. Do not hesitate to ask that question directly. Many citizens will be flattered that their opinion is valued.
- Learn who is a reliable source of information and be able to differentiate that from gossip. Some sources may be self-serving and tend to attribute the sentiment to the entire community when it may only be of importance to them.
- Share the synthesized information with other administrators to check out the assessment of who holds power in the community.
- Use common sense along with the information about the power structure of the community.
- Never lose sight of the reason for doing all of this: Increased opportunities for success for all students.
- Know that a proactive approach to forming school-community alliances can thwart negative pressures brought to bear on schools by some power wielders.

Values and School-Community Relations

The purpose of American schools is to provide a literate citizenry that can up hold the values of our democracy. This is critical to the survival of democratic institutions. Through tax dollars, American invest in the future by providing children free and public education.

There are many arguments and legal complaints regarding the equity of the educational opportunities provided in one community compared to another. In return for that investment, citizens have certain rights and expectations from the educational institutions. Wealthier communities believe that they have the right to contribute to their schools at a rate that is commensurate with their expectations. On the other hand, poor communities complain that they do not have the tax base to provide basic needs, let alone the high-tech experiences.

Schools have resorted to community fundraisers to try to bring an equitable solution to sorely needed resources. Parent groups have been mobilized to sell holiday wrapping paper, donuts, entertainment discount booklets, candy, baked goods, or concession stand products. A successful program that reaches out to alumni and the general community is the sidewalk-paver program. For a cost, a brick is inscribed with the contributor's name and then cemented into the main sidewalk leading into the school. This is a visible show of community support for all who enter the school.

Other monies come through state and federal grant programs. Many grants have a poverty-level component that is usually based on the number of students in the school or district who participate in the free lunch program. The federal guidelines for free lunch give an indication of the local poverty level by the number of students participating.

One area that has received national attention is know as the *digital divide*. Students in very poor school districts do not have the same technology advantages as students in wealthier districts. The predominant view is not that children will learn better through technology but rather that they will not be prepared to successfully participate in a world that is technology based. The enriching experience of being taught with technology will not be afforded to them. To bridge the gap, the federal government began assessing a tax on telephone bills via the Telecommunication Act of 1966. Those monies are dedicated to providing schools with the infrastructure needed to create a computer network. The program, known as *E-Rate*, pays for everything up to the back of the computer, and funding is distributed to the poorest schools first. If a school is at an 85% poverty level, that is the rate at which the federal government will fund the grant. The result has been that the gap has closed slightly, with both poor and wealthy districts increasing their level of connectivity.

How accumulated resources are distributed sets a priority agenda for a school district. This can be a source of controversy. Controversies can arise over which factions are entitled to what portion of those resources. How resources are distributed has been extensively written about by Rescher (1996). Goode (1993), summarizes the notion of *distributive justice* as follows:

> *Distributive justice questions who is entitled to what amount of a public institution's resources. Rescher has promulgated a principle of utility that asserts that goods and services should be distributed according to the greatest good for the greatest number. Community members have a diverse and disparate number of claims on public institutions.*

School administrators must recognize the existence of these claims and evaluate each of them before making decisions on the distribution of a school's resources.

Peter Blau (1967) has described this phenomenon of people expecting certain benefits from their institutions as fair exchange. He has suggested that satisfaction with the benefits people receive depends not so much on the quantity of those benefits, but on the fact that their expectations are not totally disappoint. Simply stated, individuals do not want to feel ignored by institutions they support. Administrators of public schools who ignore the expectations of segments of their communities may ultimately pay a dear price for doing so (p.103).

These principles influence educators at all levels when they make decisions on what is best for the majority. Teachers select teaching materials based on what they think is best for most of their students. Principals attempt to create professional development opportunities that meet the needs of most of the teachers. School boards set drug abuse policies, such as zero tolerance, because it is good to remove the abuser from the majority of the students.

Only in the area of special education do we set policies on what is good for the individual student's educational program rather than the majority. The law states that children should be educated in the least restrictive environment, a concept that is often misunderstood or misinterpreted. For example, a child who is reading at a third-grade level may be included in tenth-grade English, but only for the purpose of socialization. Teachers have had a hard time understanding that a child in their class may not be doing grade-level work and question the appropriateness of the placement.

PL 94-142, The Education for All Handicapped Children Act of 1975, ensured that a free and appropriate education would be available for all handicapped children between the age of three and eighteen. Section 504 of the Rehabilitation Act of 1973, PL. 93-112, is designed to eliminate discrimination on the basis of handicap in any program or activity receiving federal financial assistance. In other words, if your district receives any federal funds, it must abide by this act and are required to submit assurances (a board policy) that the program is in compliance with the act.

Schools have had to shift resources that would impact the many to meet the needs of a few disabled students. These highly specialized services for a few puts an enormous strain on school funds that might be spent for the many. The priority of the expenditures for these services can be the source of controversy.

A very wise principal once told a young and naive teacher that if you are going to distribute apples to teachers, students, parents, or any school group, always be sure that the apples are exactly the same size or someone will surely complain. If a large apple is good for most students, then why shouldn't my child have a big one, too? This analogy brings the concepts of distributive justice into an easy and clear lesson for administrators to follow. It should be kept in mind when prioritizing the distribution of resources.

Crisis Planning

The term *lock down* once was associated only with securing prisons during times of prisoner turmoil. Now, it is a term that schools commonly use when they go into a high-security mode. Once, metal detectors were most commonly associated with passing through airport security. Now, it is common for schools, particularly high schools, to have them at building entry points.

National events have caused schools to review their readiness to deal with security and safety situations. After the carnage at Columbine High School in 1999 (Raywid & Oshiyama, 2000), schools across the nation were pressured to find ways to prevent school shootings. The terrorist events of September 11, 2001, in New York City prompted many schools to immediately go into a lock-down mode.

Unfortunately, some schools continue to operate with the attitude that those kinds of thing happen elsewhere. The *not my school syndrome,* can result in people making reactive decisions during highly charged times rather than being proactive so that all students and staff know exactly what they need to do. It was impossible for anyone to have predicted that two commercial airliners would be flown into the Twin Towers in New York City causing both towers to collapse into a super-heated pile of rumble. Although nearly 4,000 people perished that morning in New York, there were thousands of people who escaped through the emergency stairways by following procedures for an orderly evacuation.

Safety is the pivotal component of crisis management. The most important consideration for a school district is the health, safety, and welfare of students and staff. A crisis management plan details how to "identify, confront and resolve the crisis, restore equilibrium, and support appropriate adaptive responses" (Virginia Department of Education, 1999, p.1).

Schools must develop procedures for dealing with existing and potential student and school crises by preparing a comprehensive plan. An important component of any plan is a set of interagency agreements with various local agencies to aid timely communications, coordinate services, and affirm responsibilities. A comprehensive crisis management plan includes three sets of procedures: a) intervention, b) crisis response, and c) critical incident procedures. The following is adapted from The Virginia Department of Education. It clearly defines each of these as follows:

> **Intervention Procedures** provide a systematic process for identifying, referring, and assessing students who may be suicidal or represent a potential threat to others. Crisis teams established in each school can provide immediate intervention with referred students. Team members should be trained to assess the seriousness of the situation

and respond according to specific guidelines. Teams gathers information from other sources, choose team members to interview the referred student, develop a plans, direct students and families to appropriate help, appoint case managers, and provide follow-up. Additionally, schools should regularly provide inservice training to faculty and staff about recognizing students in crisis and on referral procedures.

Crisis Response Procedures guide staff in responding to more frequently occurring crises such as the deaths of students or teachers and other traumatic events that can affect the school community for days. These procedures are intended to be time-limited, problem-focused interventions designed to identify and resolve the crisis, restore equilibrium, and support productive responses. The crisis team uses crisis response procedures to help administrators:

- gather information;
- establish communication with the family;
- disseminate accurate information to faculty and students;
- intervene directly with students most likely to be affected;
- increase the available supportive counseling for students and staff; and
- guide students in helpful ways to remember the deceased.

Critical Incident Procedures help school personnel handle potentially dangerous events such as an armed intruder in a school and other life-threatening events. Code words such as *Code Blue* can be established in all school buildings to provide a uniform method of warning staff and students of high risk situations involving imminent danger to life or limb (pp. 8-9).

The Virginia plan calls for establishing a coded alert system that defines a coded message that teachers and students clearly understand to be a critical situation. Some school districts have a multicoded system that designates the urgency of the situation. That is, a *code red* may refer to immediate danger, and a *code green* to an unarmed intruder. Confidential codes can be used to alert teachers without alarming students. For example, "Please resend today's attendance to the office immediately" may mean that we are evacuating the building due to a bomb threat.

Types of Crisis

Although it is impossible to predict every type of crisis that might occur, a comprehensive plan should at least address commonly identified threats to the safety and welfare of students and staff. A comprehensive plan might include:

- Armed intruders
- Bomb threats
- Suicide

- Severe weather: tornado, hurricane, earthquake
- Death of a student or staff member
- Loss of power or phone service
- Child abuse
- Sexual assault
- Fire
- Hostage situation
- Serious physical fighting
- Lethal violence
- Possession or use of firearms or other weapons
- Chemical, gas, or biological contamination
- Terrorist activities

Creating a Crisis Plan

A school that develops a crisis plan demonstrates that it is prepared to keep the school a safe place for children and staff. Being a proactive leader should bolster community confidence in a district's readiness to deal with a serious situation. Creating a crisis plan communicates the importance placed on the health, safety, and welfare of students and staff.

A school board generally initiates the process of developing a crisis plan by adopting a district policy. Implementing board policy is a superintendent's responsibility. A superintendent can personally take charge of creating a crisis plan or delegate the leadership to another administrator.

A plan must have a designated leader who has the authority, organizational competence, and human relations skills to facilitate interagency agreements. Developing a comprehensive plan can be a hefty commitment of time, approximately a year to complete a well-developed plan.

Development of the crisis plan offers an opportunity for a school district to create a close, working relationship with many local community agencies such as fire departments, police, hospitals, merchant associations, and social service agencies. Those organizations and agencies will provide invaluable input into the planning process. The interaction between the school and its community agencies will strengthen school-community relations.

Because creating a crisis plan is a process, not an event, designing a plan for creating the crisis plan is essential. Simply put, create a plan for planning. Too often it is said that the plan failed when, in reality, we failed to plan. The pedagogy and paradigms of strategic planning can be used to create a framework for the process. Developing a crisis plan framework will provide a guide for the leader. A strategy for creating a crisis plan offered in the twelve steps below:

12 Steps For Creating A Comprehensive Crisis Plan

1. *Form a broad-based committee that involves all the people and agencies who might be called upon during an emergency.* Cooperation of law enforcement agencies, fire, mental health providers, HAZMAT (Hazardous Material Action Team), civil defense, media representatives, evacuation site representatives, hospital personnel, parents, community leaders, politicians, and local clerical leaders results in a creditable planning team. School-side members of the team would include administrators, counselors, school psychologist, transportation director, technology director, school union representative, teachers, students (where appropriate), custodians, and school board representatives. Schools can develop a sense of ownership in a plan through the active involvement of those who might be first responders in a crisis situation. Involving interagency leaders in the process, demonstrates a unified approach.

2. *Define the kind of the crisis that you will include in your plan.* The list of crises provided above, is a good beginning. Districts need to include items that may be specific to the uniqueness of their local community as well as those that are state specific or national issues. For example, Florida would include a section on hurricanes, whereas North Dakota would not.

3. *Conduct an internal and external assessment of the current safety level of the schools in the district.* By assessing the current reality of safety within the schools, three things happen: First, information regarding what is or is not in place is gathered. Second, information regarding perceptions and important issues is identified. It broadens the base of involvement in the planning process. Last, analysis of the data can provide the planning team with valuable information to guide them in creating the plan.

4. *Create a plan* that includes a district policy; identifies the crisis response team; includes response procedures and medical protocols; and delineates roles, responsibilities, training, practice, and an ongoing assessment process. The plan should include a short, concise checklist of the types of crises, the response, who is responsible, and who is the spokesperson(s). A crisis management leader must be appointed prior to a crisis. If a crisis counseling team needs to be summoned into action or an area needs to be readied for media briefings, someone who is an expert on the crisis plan must be ready to hit the ground running. During a crisis, the last thing a district needs is the appearance of being unorganized or unprepared to handle the event. Any appearance of incompetency or unreadiness will not bode well with the community and could endanger students and staff. A crisis management leader needs to be appointed as soon as the plan is formally adopted. This gives the leader time to bring members of the response team together. The size of the team will vary from five to twelve people (Bagin & Gallager, 2001). The district team leader should meet regularly with the crisis management team, as

should building-level team leaders. These meeting should focus on bringing clarity to the individual roles and responsibilities of each member of the team. Meeting regularly reinforces the readiness of the team to respond.

5. *Secure board approval* of the plan. Before a crisis plan is activated, it must be reviewed and formally approved by the school board. Board approval makes the plan official and gives a legal protection for employees who follow the emergency response procedures.

6. *Have the plan at your fingertips* -- administrators should organize information to have readily available during a crisis. Some things to include in your fingertip files are:
    - checklist pages from the crisis plan
    - cell phone
    - a copy of important phone numbers: district and building level administrators, interagencies, key parents, and media.
    - staff and student directories
    - media guide or fact sheet about your school
    - daily attendance record
    - evacuation site contact numbers
    - how to disconnect internet and television leads.
    - phone trees

Administrators should also create an at-home packet for themselves, because a crisis can happen in off-school hours. For example, a principal is notified of an malicious school break-in where, among other things, the phone system has been destroyed. That principal need to immediately reach for phone directories, beginning with a call to the superintendent at home.

7. *Distribute the plan widely.* All members of the planning team, school board, and district and building level administrators, and all school personnel should have a copy of the plan. Key communicators should spread the good news throughout the community that a comprehensive plan for crisis management has been completed and has been adopted by the school board. Using planning team members to communicate the plan to the groups they represent is an effective way to get the word out. A police chief who makes a report at a town council meeting regarding the police department's role in creating the school crisis plan and the interagency agreement, will surely garner media attention. The support of the planning team in making the plan publicly known is profound.

8. *Select the spokesperson and the crisis team leader.* During a crisis, one person, and only one person, should have the responsibility to speak for the district. In the absence of an official community or public relations person, superintendents normally assume this role. Superintendents feel that they are ultimately responsible

and that the community would expect to hear the news directly from them.

9. *Train the staff at both the district and building level.* If you do not communicate and practice the plan, you might as well not have one. Too often, the plan becomes a dusty binder sitting on a shelf. In the event of a crisis, the crisis may be that nobody knows what to do. To avoid a crisis within a crisis, it is imperative to provide the entire staff with training.

   Reviewing the crisis plan is often welcomed by faculty and staff with a yawn. Principals have been known to distribute the plan and then just tell the staff to read it. A comprehensive crisis plan can be over 150 pages long. It is not likely that the principal will get 100% compliance.

   Even worse, principals often forgets that new teachers were not there when the plan was adopted and did not get the advantage of the initial training. Again, the new teachers are handed a thick binder and told to read it when you get time. The section on fire drills is usually read because they know they will be held accountable for the monthly drill. An important part of new teacher orientation is to carefully review the entire crisis plan. Districts that have a new teachers mentoring program should include crisis training within their schedule of services.

10. *Annually retrain the staff.* During a crisis, all staff and students must know their roles and responsibilities. A staff that annually revisits their crisis plan will be prepared to care for the safety and security of the students and their colleagues. Teachers can get excited about exploring new teaching methods, whereas practicing for a crisis can be viewed as a waste of valuable teaching time. The odds of a crisis happening are low, which makes it even less of a priority.

    During a crisis, responses need to be rote. A staff must train and rehearse to be able to respond without hesitation. It is an administrative responsibility to facilitate that training. Surviving a crisis may depend on how a staff is trained.

11. *Annually revisit the plan.* Members of the planning team should convene yearly, if not more often, for the purpose of reviewing, revising, or making drastic modification to the plan. After every crisis, the crisis team should assess how well they responded to determine if there are areas that need to be improved. Their suggestions should be forwarded to the planning team for review and action. Assessing the effectiveness of how the crisis team responded is an essential component. Taking time to reflect will lead to improvement of the plan.

12. *Loop back to STEP 1.* Schools need to reevaluate their plan to keep it up to date. A feedback loop is an essential requirement of good planning.

Rapidly changing events in our global society can present schools with devastating situations that are presently unknown. A student using deadly force at school was unimaginable in 1950; now it is part of every comprehensive crisis plan. In 2001, schools turned their attention to dealing with how to explain the terrorist attack on the World Trade Center in New York City and how to deal with the associated psychological problems students were experiencing from witnessing mass destruction. Crisis teams began meeting to determine how to address this missing part of the plan. This new level of security was an unknown when the plan was developed and now needed to be addressed.

Planning teams will change over time. The police chief will retire, the school board will change, but student and staff safety will remain a priority. Therefore, annually bringing the plan team together provides an opportunity for new and old members to reacquaint. Bringing together the entire planning team to review and/or revise the plan allows for:

- recommitting
- building ownership in new members
- communicating revisions
- reestablishing bonds between plan team members
- providing a channel for the input of new ideas and concerns
- evaluating the advances in technology used for crisis management

Crisis Communications

Although the first rule of communicating information during a crisis is to tell the truth, spokespersons can indeed control the media without telling lies. If a child has died at school, tell them. However, you would not release the name, address or other personal information about the child. If the circumstances surrounding the death are unclear, then it would be appropriate to state that the matter is under investigation.

During a crisis, only the designated spokesperson should be communicating information. Others should not respond with, "I don't know," or "No comment." A more appropriate response might be, "Let me refer you to Mrs. Smith." "No comment" gives the appearance that you are ignorant about what has happened. The sound bite on the six o'clock news may be, "Can you confirm that there was a gas leak in your school today?" with the principal responding, "No comment." Viewers may infer that the administrator did not have enough knowledge about the incident to make a comment. Having a single spokesperson is a protective luxury for both teachers and administrators. During a crisis, emotions run high, and it is easy to respond to a reporter with words that do not communicate the intent of what you are trying to say. Unintentionally, you could make yourself and the district look ineffective.

School secretaries are key players during a crisis. They are the ones who answer the telephone and greet guests in school offices. Depending on the scope of the crisis, either the principal or a district administrator should quickly craft a written statement for the school secretaries so that the information that is distributed is uniform, accurate, and reassuring. For example, a parent calls the school and the secretary tells her that the school will not be evacuated. The parent follows-up with a call to the district office, where the secretary responds that they are determining the seriousness of the situation and possible evacuation of the school is being considered. Conflicting statements do not promote trust and confidence.

The media can be relentless. They want to know the who, what, where, when, why, and how. Schools must be very careful, since releasing information about minors or school personnel has legal limitations and implications. If members of the media want statements from teachers and students, do not let them randomly roam the school to select interviewees. Rather, arrange for a teacher(s) and student(s) to provide their perspective of the event. This way you control the scope of the information. It is appropriate to tell the media that selected teachers and students will be available for questions.

Generally, the media appreciate an organized method of releasing information. The spokesperson should let them know when and where they can get information. Provide the media with the time and location of where press releases will be made. At the end of the sessions, tell them when you expect to have more information to share with them. It is also acceptable to release a written statement. A district that attempts to conceal information gives the appearance of "not knowing," which is what will be reported. Controlling the flow of information does not mean concealing information.

Incidents happen during the school day that can range from critical to hoax. Either way, gossip about the incident will get passed along. The message will get inadvertently altered as it is repeated. A hoax can turn into an urban legend overnight. It is best to send a written message home with the students explaining the reality of the situation, what measures were taken, and what else is planned to insure student safety. Principals may create various forms of backpack letters that they can quickly revise to send home with students at the end of the day.

Public Relations or Community Relations

The National School Public Relations Association (NASPRA, 1985) offers the following definition of *public relations*:

> *Educational public relations is a planned and systematic management function to help improve programs and services of an educational organization. It relies on a comprehensive two-way communication process involving both internal and external publics, with a goal of stimulating a better understand of the role, objective, accomplishments, and needs of the organization. Educational public relation programs assist in interpreting public attitudes, identify and help shape policies and procedures in the public interest, and carry on involvement and information activities which earn public understanding and support* (p. 48).

There are two major differences between the definition of school public relations and school community relations. Community relations definitions tend to emphasize that the purpose of building relationships is to foster improvements in student achievement and to build a community base of support that will translate into financial support. Public relations definitions appear to omit these purposes and focus on creating a positive image of the school or on influencing public opinion. A school's community relations program should combine both definitions. A community relations program that is viewed as being entirely self-serving, that is, only there to shed a positive light on school activities, will be short lived.

Schools are reluctant to hire a PR person. If they do, the title of the position will seldom be Director of Public Relations. More common titles include: Public Information Director, Community Relations Coordinator, Partnership Chair, or Crisis Management Director. The reason why schools avoid the PR title is that it can be viewed negatively by the public. First, there may be suspicion that the school is trying to put a positive spin on information or trying to sanitize it. Public relations is sometimes associated with putting a positive spin on unpleasant news. The public may begin to wonder what the schools are trying to conceal. Second, when schools lament the lack of funds to properly educate students, expenditures on public relations can be viewed by some people as unnecessary. During contract negations, unions would be the first to point out that the district can afford a "spin doctor" but does not have the money to fund a raise for teachers. Understanding the important role that school community leadership can provide and justifying the expense to the public can be stressful for even the best administrator. This is why the position seldom exists with a PR title.

Many districts do not have any one job title indicative of the responsibility. The responsibility is usually given to another position, such as, Director of Grants or Special Service. Most often, the responsibility falls to the administrative team. District and building level administrators bear most of the responsibility for building relationships with their stakeholders.

Typical is the experience of Bill Smith (2001). Bill is a retired superintendent with over thirty years' experience. Under his leadership, five out of five funding referenda passed. He did not have community relations person in his employ. He proudly relates that it was through the many relationships he and the entire administrative team formed with the community that he was able to rally community support. Every administrator was required to be an active member of a service organization. The two-way communication that is achieved during informal situations lets the community know that the schools want to play an active role in supporting community activities.

Bill Smith's platoon approach, with himself as the key communicator, worked well in his district primarily because he had a plan. School districts that have not delegated the responsibility to a single person and do not have a back-up plan leave their building-level administrators to fend for themselves. Some principals have been successful in building relationships, but unfortunately, others do not have the time, skill, or training to reap the benefits of working with community groups.

Partnerships

In the late 1970s, businesses and schools began to formalize their relationship through partnerships. Partnerships were pursued by school districts to secure funds or equipment. According to Lankard (1995), ". . . the conditions in the United States in the early 1980s-the education crisis in public schools, the low skill level of entry-level workers, and the demands of an evolving economy accelerated the development of partnership" (Lankard, 1995). This continues today.

The two most common types of partnership are: a) school-to career or career awareness programs, and b) corporate sponsorship programs such as, adopt-a-school (Clearing House on Educational Management, 2000). Partnerships that are linked to school improvement goals are most successful (Epstein, 2001).

Partnerships that go beyond being a one-way, one-shot donation to schools and move into two-way partnerships tend to build long-lasting relationships between the school and the business. Two-way partnerships are those where the school offers something to the business in return for what the business provides to the school. For example, Community Hospital in Munster, Indiana, provided an outdoor fitness center for one of the elementary schools in town. In return, the school allowed the hospital to use the school hallways before and after schools for rehabilitation patients to walk laps. The faculty and students went a step further by providing decorations, books, placemats, and notes for the pediatrics departments during holidays. This resulted in an ongoing relationship with the hospital. When the hospital had funds or programs that fit nicely with a school, their partner school was the one they turned to first.

Partnerships also focus on parent and family involvement and outreach programs. Research suggests that the most accurate predictor of student achievement is the extent to which a student's family is involved in the child's education (National PTA, 2000). Federal government-supported research indicates that family involvement, not income, social status, or parent material status, has a positive correlation with increased educational achievement. The federal government passed Goals 2000 Educate America Act which states " By the year 2000, every school will promote partnerships that will increase parental involvement and participation in promoting the social, emotional, and academic growth of children" (National Education Goals Panel, 1998, p. 6).

Outreach programs focus on "collaboration and cooperation between schools and community, rather than simply on an *adding to* the schools *from* the community" (Crowson, 1998, p. 237). The school becomes the facilitator of health and welfare services for students. Some of those services include vision and hearing screening, inoculations, and school breakfast/lunch programs. Social service agencies might be given space in schools to provide a convenient meeting place for parents who might need their help.

Businesses have become highly visible partners with schools. Morrison (1990) notes that businesses are "taking the lead in long-term revolution to save public education" (p. 8). Dumaine (1990) added "Leading the field are such companies as IBM, Exxon, Coca-Cola, RJR, Nabisco, and Citicorp, which have mounted a virtual crusade to save the public schools" (p. 12). However, working with business in order to improve the educational capacity of schools across the nation must be tempered by the commercial influence these business can have on schools, programs, and students.

Communications

Communicating requires both the sending and receiving of information. That means that one must be as good at listening as at speaking. Because communications are both written and oral, one can also send a message through body language, gestures, and tone of voice. School administrators need to understand that good communications do not just happen, they are planned. Since school principals spend as much as seventy-five percent of their day in one-on-one communications, they need to understand how to plan for effective communications (Dolan, 1995).

Technology as a Communications Tool

Because technology has the power to provide instant communications between the school and home, administrators need the highest level of communication skills to craft instant web messages. Without a compelling message to communicate, technology is impotent (Kowalski, 2000). This implies that the 21st century administrator needs to be tech savvy and understand the uses and abuses that can result from the use of technology-based communications. The power for a school to communicate through the use of technology is limited only by the administrator's technology knowledge and ability.

The end of the 21st Century witnessed the build out of infrastructures that support the information age. People want information that is short, to the point, easily understood, reliable, accessible, and instantly available. Technology offers ways for instant communications through email, faxes, videoconferencing, and Web-accessed databases. School districts not taking advantage of technology lose a necessary aspect of their community relations efforts.

It is not uncommon for a school or district to have a Web site. On the site, they communicate general information about themselves along with specific information. General information would include the name, address, telephone numbers for the districts; the mission; and strategic links to information that the school wants to share, such as information announcing school-closings, meetings, fees, calendars, staff, awards, ——— everything from book fees to prom tickets. Some schools have sites so sophisticated that parents can use a credit card to add money to a lunch card, pay book rental fees, pay for a field trip, or buy a yearbook for their child. Schools can link their electronic grade books to the Web so parents (password protected) can access a weekly grade report for their child.

For example, Homework Hotline is a widely used telephone system. The school can leave a general message, such as announcing that the school office is closed for the holidays and classes will resume on some date. The caller can link to a specific teacher's mailbox to hear what homework is due, the following day's lunch menu, or a reminder to wear warm clothes for the wilderness field trip tomorrow. Teachers must update their voice box daily for the system to be effective. Homework Hotline also allows for two-way communications. Parents can leave a message for a teacher stating a concern or a question. No longer can children fool their parents into believing that they have no homework for tomorrow!

The Hotline also has outward-bound calling features. The system can be set to send a message to a class or the entire school. The time that calling begins and ends can be set to avoid sending calls at unreasonable hours. That is, a message announcing a school closing emergency can be set to be sent to all students and faculty until 10:00 p.m. and then resume calling the list at 6:00 a.m. The system is smart enough to do call backs for busy signals or no answers, and it can be directed to leave the message on an answering machine or not. School principals and teachers can access all of these features (within system rights) from school or home.

Elements of a Communications Model

Bagin and Gallager (2001) identify five elements of a common communications model. The elements are: source, encoder, channel, decoder, and receiver.

First, the source of information conceptualizes the message that the individual or school needs to send.

Second, the message encoder is the form the message will take. Keep in mind that the message needs to be understandable and have common meaning for both the sender and the receiver of the message. It is a waste of time to send a message that has no meaning to the receiver.

Third, the channel is the device or signal used to send the message. One needs to determine if this is a message that needs to be delivered in person, by newsletter, or through the mass media. Select the channel that best fits the message. If it is a written message, make it clear, clean, and attractive to the reader.

Fourth, the decoder must be able to decode the message accurately. Schools with a large Hispanic population usually send written messages in both Spanish and English. If the receiver cannot translate the message, why bother sending it?

Fifth, the receiver, who is usually the decoder, will translate the words into meaning. If the encoder has done a good job, the receiver will understand the message and decide what the response is to be. There are some things that the sender cannot control, such as the health, mental state, or disposition of the receiver. That is why a message may evoke different reactions from different receivers.

The action that the receiver takes provides feedback to the encoder. Did the message get home? Was it read? Was it understood? Will it evoke a positive action? How do you know? The person who sends the message (encoder) can determine the effectiveness of the communication through feedback that answers those questions. The encoder can then decide if further action is necessary.

The Art of Persuasion

Persuading others to accept new ideas and innovations involves five stages: awareness, interest, evaluation, trial, and adoption (Bagin & Gallagher 2001). Persuasion begins by raising the level of awareness to the new idea. Awareness will peak the individual's interest so that they will try to obtain more information about the idea. After they have learned more about the idea they will evaluate how the idea impact them. Since schools do not have products to send out as samples, the trial stage could become a pilot program. The last stage is full-scale adoption of the plan.

Persuasion works best when contact is made in person. The neighbor who hangs over the fence to discuss a school issue with the person next door has more influence than any written communication. During school campaigns or referenda, community members are often asked to host small, informal sessions in their homes to facilitate face-to-face conversation.

Many factors can influence the acceptance of an idea. In a large group situation, peer pressure causes some to remain silent on the issue rather than show disagreement with the group's sentiment. When written communications are used to persuade, people can read their own meaning into the message.

A forum can be used to present one or both sides on an issue. When using a public forum to persuade others, there are some rules: a) Do not talk down to the audience. b) Be objective when presented with a hostile audience. c) Present both sides of the issue if the audience is of high intellect and good educational background. It does not matter if the pro or con presenter goes first. d) Present one side of the issue if the audience is apt to support the idea. e) Do not withhold information. Start with the weak side of the argument and build to the strong points.

None of the points listed above will persuade the audience unless the speaker is viewed as a person who has position power, expertise, and is a good oral communicator. Research has dispelled the stereotype that women are more easily persuaded than men. However, women inspire more confidence than men when trying to effect attitudinal change (Bagin & Gallager, 2001).

Written Communications

To be an effective communicator, administrators must be a master of both the oral and written language (Hughes & Hooper, 2000). It takes time to write, proof, edit, and rewrite. However, an administrator's day seldom allows for a block of uninterrupted time to concentrate on writing a message. Before the advent of computers, a secretary might be called into the principal's office for quick dictation. Today, many principals word process their own written work. However, principals should use the school secretary to proof and edit their work. People receiving messages from educators will be highly critical of spelling or grammatical errors. Proof, proof, and proof again before the message is sent. While email can be very effective, grammar and spelling rules hold just as true for electronic messages as they do for other types of written or oral communications.

The use of a communications specialist is suggested for school districts that have the money to pay for consulting services, particularly for works that have broad distribution. Communication specialists can offer more than editorial advice. They help with layout, readability, and the general appearance of the publication. Schools are competing for readership with many other publications, so, an effort should be made to construct a document that screams, "Read me first!"

Hughes and Hooper (2000) summarize Bates' essential elements for written communications:

- Be concise. Keep sentences and paragraphs short.
- State your purpose clearly.
- Get straight to the point.
- Be specific; avoid abstractions.
- Know your audience.
- Write to be understood, no to impress.
- Prefer the active voice. Put action in your verbs.
- Weed out unnecessary word, phrases, and ideas (p.143).

In sum, administrators should not embarrass themselves or the district by appearing less than knowledgeable or not having a grasp of basic grammar. Being the leader of a school suggests that one has the education and intellect to be able to communicate through coherent written communications. Written faux pas will not be tolerated and will have an adverse effect on the administrator.

Media Relations

Creating a Relationship with the Media

Conrad (2001) states that school or program advocacy is "the most important non-instructional responsibility of every educator" (http://www.manteno.k12.il.us/fineanrts/magic/). "This means that administrators must actively promote their school. Administrators can begin by cultivating a positive relationship with the media (Dolan, 1995)." Taking a proactive stance on spreading the good news about successful endeavors at a school contributes to a community's opinion about the school, students, teachers, and principal. Promoting the good things that happen in schools can be maximized by building a working relationship with the media. If media representatives have been included as members of district or building plan teams, the relationship building has already begun.

Usually, a teacher who is doing an outstanding job in the classroom with appropriate relationships with students does not get press coverage, but a teacher who has an inappropriate relationship with a student will make headlines (Dolan, 1995). The press will actively pursue covering this type of story because it is unexpected and out of the ordinary. That makes it news! To get the good news out in the media takes time and hard work by a very insightful administrator. However, it is well worth the time investment. Administrators should know that "Learning how to deal with the press is a survival skill" (Black and English, 1986, p.92).

The first step an administrator should takes is to develop a *media directory* which should include all local media agencies, the names of those assigned to covering education, addresses, telephone and fax numbers, and email addresses. Newspapers, radio, and television contacts should be included in the directory.

A new administrator will attract the attention of the press. When they call to conduct an interview, this is an excellent opportunity to secure the information necessary for the media directory. It is also a time to begin to build a relationship with the education reporters. If they do not call you, contact them. Explain the importance that you place on promoting student achievement and that you want to know how they would want you to communicate your stories to them.

Reporters are busy, hard-working people. They are in the business of reporting news, but they do not have time to cover every local event. Administrators should express a willingness to help them out. Tell the press that they will be supplied with news stories and photographs about activities at the school. Ask the reporters questions. Do they prefer email attachments, or are faxes the best way to send the story? Are there any special formatting requirements? How much lead time do they need? Expressing interest in the process of becoming a "junior reporter" will convey sincerity and help build the relationship.

The benefits of having a good relationship with the local media has its rewards. For example, in the fall, the media always reports on children returning to school. Across the nation, we see front page pictures of children charging through the front doors of schools. When a photographer or television crew is dispatched to get the pictures, the administrator with a good relationship with the media might be the first school that comes to mind. Administrators who have taken the time to cultivate a relationship tend to have more positive press coverage about their schools than the surrounding schools.

Working effectively with the media has an accidental payoff. When administrators promote their school or district, they also promote themselves as leaders. Be warned, though, if promoting oneself is the primary reason for being a media advocate for the school, it will more than likely backfire. Self-serving values are transparent. On the other hand, "if you don't promote yourself, who else will?" (Conrad, 2001).

Press Releases

Well-meaning educators will write and send news releases that announce upcoming events that they would like to see the press cover. Or they call and leave the information on voice mail. When nobody shows up they do not understand why they did not get coverage. Educators should assume that nobody will show and be prepared to cover the story themselves.

Newspapers, in particular, like to get a well-written article that is ready for publication. Those who take the approach of using a press release to send an article, rather than an up-coming event announcement, report that they get considerably more coverage for their school. If the district has a public relations director, you can still take this approach. Public relations directors are more apt to release an article when all the work has been done for them.

A news story needs to answer the basic journalistic questions: who, what, where, when, why, and how. Quotations lend an air of professionalism and should be included. If you cannot remember exactly what the person said, write what you remember and then read the quote to that person. Often, most will not remember exactly what they said and will approve a quote that captures the essence of the idea.

Figure 4-2 is a typical news release. It is clean, crisp and includes all vital information. The press release should:

- be printed on white 8 ½ " x 11"paper
- use a clean font, such as Courier, Times New Roman, or Helvetica
- have 12-15 size font
- be double spaced
- have 1" margins
- have the words PRESS RELEASE centered at the top of the first page in bold print
- have the the words PHOTOS ATTACHED at the end of the article when appropriat.
  - use the printers marks of "-30-" or "###" to indicate the end of the article.
  - be factual. This is not a time for opinions
  - use the rules stated previously in this chapter for written communications

These are the standard rules for creating a press release and they must be followed. Conrad (2001) suggest that educators can save time by using these rules to create a computer template for press releases for their school (see Figure 4-2).

Working with Reporters

Dolan (1996) suggests that administrators need to be positive whenever dealing with reporters. He offers the following do's and don'ts for working with media representatives:

1. Don't ever tell a lie.
2. Be open to answering questions.
3. Don't talk off the record. Nothing is ever considered "off the record."
4. Take time to furnish details.
5. Avoid using education jargon.
6. Know what is public property and what is not. The privacy of students and staff are protected by law.
7. Return calls.
8. Stay calm regarding errors. It's generally unwise to make an issue of a minor infraction.
9. Don't ask to see a story before it is printed or aired. Asking to approve the story may be interpreted as an attempt to suppress unfavorable news.
10. Don't be overly concerned about detail accuracy.
11. Feel free to compliment a reporter.
12. For substantive inquiries, contact the superintendent. If a journalists are investigating a controversial issue and interviewing school-site personnel about the issue, they should inform the district office about the interviews (pp. 260-262).

Happy Days Elementary School
123 ABC Lane, Happy Days, State 46111
888.555.1212
www.happydaysschool.org

PRESS RELEASE – FOR IMMEDIATE RELEASE

To: Mary Smith, Education Editor

Contact: Dr. Sandi Estep, Principal
     O: 888.555.1212 or H: 888.555.2121
     s-estep@happydaysschool.edu

Date: January 10, 2010

Mission: The mission of Happy Days Elementary School is to provide a safe and nurturing atmosphere where all children will learn to be responsible citizens and demonstrate the highest levels of academic achievement.

Happy Days Elementary School Hosts a Town Meeting With the President of the USA

Print the body of your story here using a clean font such as Courier, Times New Roman or Helvetica; use a 12-15 size font.

Use 1" margins and double space.

Number each page of the news release with a "Page x of x" format.

PHOTOS ATTACHED

-30-
[Note: -30- or ### indicates the end of the story.]

Page 1 of 1

Figure 4-2

Preparing a Media Packet

A media packet is a written document that contains all the pertinent information that a journalist might need when writing a story about the school district. The purpose of creating a media packet is that it is gives a journalist the facts about a school or a district. Reporters appreciate information that makes their job easier. The media packet also makes an administrator's job easier. Rather than responding to repetitive questions from various journalists, the media packet will have the answers to their inquiries.

A media packet might typically include:
- Attractive cover page.
- Table of contents.
- School or district mission.
- List of school board members.
- *About the school,* one page that describes the age of the building, the population it serves, awards (such as National Blue Ribbon School), unique teaching modalities (ungraded school), etc.
- Directory of all buildings in the district.
- Directory of building and district administrators.
- *About the administrators*, a short narrative resume that outlines education, experience, and awards.
- List of the staff by curricular and extracurricular responsibility.
- School demographics: location, enrollment, number of teachers, special services, etc.
- Summary of school test scores–the school's report card.
- Recent accomplishments
- Short summary about the town or city where the school is located.
- History of the school.
- Full year calendar of major events–the events might draw media coverage.
- Directory of media with education coverage contact information.
- Quotes–what others have said about your school. Did the governor visit your school and say something complimentary? Put the quote here.

The above items are a guide that should be adapted to showcase the uniqueness of the school or district. Depending on the size of the school or district, the packet might be three to 20 pages in length. The quality of printing, dependent on the budget, can be as simple as making copies on the school copy machine or as elaborate as sending it out to a professional printer to create a color brochure.

The media packet is also recommended for departments within a school. The athletic department would profile each coach, championships, and schedules; the performing arts department would profile the directors, show groups, championships, and calendar.

The media packet can be distributed to the media and local realtors. Realtors can become ambassadors for the school, since many of their clients want information about the school their child might attend. Just as administrators carry business cards with them, they should carry a media packet with them. You never know when a journalist might approach you for a story. How impressed will that journalist be when you hand over a media packet to supplement the interview?

In sum, proactive administrators will have edges over those in other schools in capturing press time or space. The good news of the schools of proactive administrators will be well known in the community, which helps form positive perceptions about the school, staff, students, and the administrator.

Public Sentiment

Policies on Gangs

Since 1979, a general increase in juvenile gang membership and activity has been reported. In 1960, 58 U.S. cities reported that they had a gang presence. In 1992, that number had grown to 769 (Huff & Trump, 1996). Public concern about gang-related activity has grown because gangs have been involved in higher rates of adolescent violence, crime, and drugs use (Evans, Fitzgerald, Weigal, Chvilicek, 1999).

Contrary to common belief, gangs are not just a big-city problem (Evans, Fitzgerald, Weigal, Chvilicek, 1999). Gang activity has spread to suburban and even rural communities. In fact, there has been no significant difference in gang membership between rural and urban schools. Therefore, the school safety issues related to gang activity must be addressed by *all* schools across the nation.

Gangs have formed a culture of their own. The language, music, tattoos, and clothing of gangs has grown to become a part of the youth pop culture throughout the country, which makes identifying gang members more difficult for school administrators (Evans, Fitzgerald, Weigal, Chvilicek, 1999). The culture includes group norms to which conformity is not only expected, but required.

The major source of early identification of emerging gangs has been school administrators. This lead to cooperative efforts between schools and law enforcement agencies. Two prevention and intervention programs that have brought schools and community agencies together are Drug Abuse Resistance Education (D.A.R.E.) and Gang Resistance Education and Training (G.R.E.A.T.). The G.R.E.A.T. program was first piloted with the Cleveland Office of the Bureau of Alcohol, Tobacco, and Firearms and the YMCA. The interagency linkages between the police, school staff, and other community agencies improved the intervention and prevention of potential problems (Huff & Trump, 1996).

Street gangs have developed innovative ways of acquiring power in a community. "Street gangs are hierarchical and in may ways similar to other community power structures, but their power may be considered innovative in that it is derived from their ability to gain resources and influence through means not usually associated with established social and political institutions" (Goode 1993, p. 120). Goode (1993) offers the following description of street gangs:

Street gangs ARE terrorist organizations and, although there have been some attempts, particularly during the 1970s, to characterize them as groups with the potential to foster and operate positive community activities, when the veil of respectability has been stripped away, the face of terror still stares back. A classic example of this can be found in the case of the Blackstone Rangers (now know as the El Rukins), one of the fiercest of Chicago's south side gangs. During the 1970s, this group sought and obtained funds from corporate, federal and private sources under the guise of promoting community activities...Like many gangs, these funds enabled the El Rukins to escalate their activities from isolated felonies to major organized criminal activities including drug trafficking, gambling, and prostitution. To protect these activities, they have acquired veritable arsenals of high powered weapons (p. 120).

Gang members recruit students as young as elementary age, and affiliation to the gang can last through adulthood. Affiliation to a group has strong sociological motivators, such as rewards, recognition, a sense of belonging, and tremendous financial rewards.

A graduate student from the Chicago Public Schools, shared his experience teaching in a gang infested community. He described "Corner Willie" as a youth who is a dropout, gang member, and drug dealer who uses a street corner near the school as his place of business. Not only does "Corner Willie" influence students to use drugs, but he conveys a mindset that you can be abundantly wealthy by not going to school. It becomes very difficult to convince students to stay in school when they can make thousands of dollars a week by joining a gang and claiming a street corner as their turf.

Implications for administrators include establishing policies and alliances with appropriate community agencies. First, the school board must adopt a policy regarding gang activities. The policy should include a statement that gangs pose a substantial disruption to school activities and how the board will prohibit the existence of gang activity. The board policy should specify other activities that are prohibited, such as gestures, hand signs, hand shakes, colors, insignia, jewelry, hats, clothing, or anything that suggests gang affiliation. The code should also state the penalties and severe consequences for violations of the policy. Schools that have adopted dress code policies have been upheld in the courts when the code is connected to protecting the schools from disruptions caused by gang activities. This sends a clear message to the community that their school is aware and is taking action to keep the school a safe place.

Schools need to eliminate everything that has a gang affiliation, which begins by identifying local gangs and rivalries. Administrators need to collect as much information as possible about the gangs in the community. The school site should be strictly monitored and measures taken to prevent entry of unauthorized visitors. Last, graffiti should be removed immediately, since it marks a gang's turf and can escalate gang rivalries (Goode, 1993).

Coping with gang activities requires the cooperation of schools and the community – neither can do it alone. Proactive programs that are aimed at prevention and intervention need to be cooperatively developed with law enforcement agencies, community service organizations, church organizations, and parents. School administrators should take the lead in bringing these organizations together. Failure to understand gangs and their culture and to take measures to make the school safe for students could result in deadly situations at a school.

Not-My-School Syndrome

Since 1985, when *A Nation At Risk* (United States Department of Education) was released, the American system of education has been openly criticized in the press. Because the report created a mass perception that Johnny cannot read, write, or do arithmetic, the reaction of state legislators was to begin statewide testing programs. The notion was that schools could use the results to assess their strengths and weakness to make data-driven improvements. The reality is that test scores have become a frenzy for media analysis. Results of testing programs, by school, not by student, are public information. Understanding that extraordinary events are what makes news, those communities with an abundance of under-performing schools are publicly held accountable by the media.

The negative news surrounding low test scores across the nation has created the perception that schools are not properly educating our youth. The 32nd Gallup Poll (Rose & Gallop, 2000) asked parents to grade schools. Eighty percent gave the nation's schools a grade of C or lower. However, when the same group was asked to grade their own schooln 47% gave their school a grade of A or B. People have a very high opinion of their own schools yet believe that schools across the nation are doing very poorly. Therein is the prevailing attitude: *Not my school–those bad schools are somewhere else!* This is one of the factors that contributes to the reluctance to move into more current models of instruction.

Safe Schools

The not-my-school syndrome seeps into other educational issues, such as school safety. School shootings and other deadly attacks on teachers and students do not happen in my upper-class, suburban neighborhood. That is an urban, inner-city issue. On May 20, 1988, the residents of Winnetka, Illinois, an upscale community, found out differently. The Violence in Our Schools Web site states (http://www.columbine-angels.com/other_shootings.htm):

Laurie Wasserman Dann, 30, started the day off as an arsonist and ended it a murderer. She set a fire at Ravina Elementary School in Highland Park about 9 a.m., but no injuries were reported. She drove home and started another fire, then she drove to Hubbard Woods. Laurie invaded a boys restroom and shot one boy, she then went into a classroom and told the teacher that a boy had been shot in the restroom. She went into another room, this time full of second graders. She forced several children into a line against the wall and saying, "I'll teach you about life," she opened fire with her .32-caliber handgun. Laurie killed Nicholas B. Corwin and wounded 5 other children. She left the school, and entered a nearby home where she wounded Phillip Andrew, then killed herself.

Violence in Our Schools chronicles another relevant example that occurred on November 12, 2001, in Caro, Michigan:

Chris Buschbacher, 17, was upset over a breakup with his girlfriend two days earlier. He went to his alternative high school early today, then left and returned about 3 p.m. with a .22-caliber rifle and a 20-guage shot gun. His ex-girlfriend was in the science room when returned with the guns, however, Chris only took Joseph Gottler, the teacher, and a 15-year-old girl, Audrea Jackson, hostage. He did fire a shot at principal Earl Nordstrom while inside the school, however, the shot missed the principal. Chris negotiated with police to free Audrea for a pack of cigarettes and a light. He freed Joseph 90 minutes later. Chris then shot himself in the head at 6:16 p.m. with the shotgun as a state police team was preparing to enter the building. The school, of roughly 110, does not have metal detectors, security checkpoints or guards.

The profile of a school shooter and the types of school communities involved in violent crimes provides a much different reality. The shooter is usually white, male, and goes to a suburban, predominately white, middle-class school. One need only look at Columbine High School to see the difference between reality and perception. Columbine, Colorado, is an affluent suburban community where 15 students and teachers were murdered and 23 were injured on April 20. 1999 (http://www.columbine-angels.com/other_shootings.htm)

Where perception does match reality, there appears to be a reluctance to take overt measures to deal with safety. Installing metal detectors, for example, might send a message that there is a weapons problem at the school. What schools consider preventative measures may be misinterpreted by the public. Most, but not all, high schools in metropolitan Chicago, Illinois have some sort of security at the main entrance to the school, but most of the elementary schools have taken minimal or no security measures. Generally, the front door is unlocked and there is only a sign that asks visitors to report to the office. Those schools that have taken action may have metal detectors, buzzers to get into the school, or security guards at each entrance

Technology has impacted how administrators attempt to keep their schools safe. Rather than walking through a free-standing metal detector, school doors are now being manufactured with the detector imbedded in the door frame. Those entering the school would not know that they are going through a detection device.

Video and audio systems that are commonly found in commercial businesses are now found in high schools. From a central point, on multiple screens, one person can monitor halls, exits, and gathering places. This system also gives the school a media record of an event for evidentiary purposes. Audio systems that link administrators to one another and to key personnel are likewise used to monitor security.

Vouchers, Private Schools, and Charter Schools

Private schools have always understood the importance of school-community relations. The reputation of the school is what attracts parents to pay tuition to send their children to privatized educational centers. These schools understand the importance of marketing and public relations for keeping their school enrollment at a level of financial feasibility.

Critics suggests that vouchers and charter schools have become an insidious method of siphoning off public school dollars in the name of school reform. Charter schools are wavered from adhering to state rules and regulations so that they may have the freedom to explore new models of teaching. They are also wavered from the accountability measures that states have laid on public schools.

Vouchers have been introduced in some states to provide parents with public grants to send their children to public or private schools. Of all the school choice alternatives, vouchers are the most controversial. Vouchers are constitutional in some states, but not in others. During the 1990s, the United States Supreme Court appeared to have become more willing to let state aid flow to sectarian schools (Hadderman, 2000) and in 2002, a 5-4 decision, the U.S. Supreme Court approved the use of vouchers for private and parochial schools (see Chapter 13 in this textbook). It remains to be seen how states will reconcile separation of church and state.

For the school administrator, school choice has created pressure to compete for average daily attendance dollars. Advocates for school choice believe that competition is healthy and will motivate the public schools to do better. Robertson (1999) summarizes:

> *But just when education has adopted maketese and globalspeak as its vernacular, the privatization alliance has begun to couch its school reform agenda in the argot of equity and opportunity. The clamor for greater public funding for private schools is positioned as a battle over "choice" and "equity," not as a contest between private and public interests. Demands for charter and voucher systems are treated as bold but apolitical calls to reinvent schools, not as incremental privatization (p. 732).*

For an indepth look at the school choice movement, see Chapter 13.

Summary

School community relations focus on both public relations and community relations. Although this chapter offers many guidelines for administrators to follow, remember that they need to be adapted to meet the unique needs of each community. Whether a district hires a person charged with the responsibilities of community relations or distributes the job among the administrative team, the main objective remains the same: creating optimal circumstances for student success.

Administrators can best promote their schools by being the foremost advocate, because spreading the good news about a school has a powerful impact on how the school is viewed by the community. Administrators must hone their oral and written communications skills as well as their ability to use technology.

Research has shown that power structures in a community are identifiable. The power elite model runs contrary to the American principles of democracy and for that reason, it is too quickly and very naively dismissed by some administrators. It is very important for an administrator to understand who holds the power over major decisions and work at building relationships with those individuals.

Community relations is only one of the many hats that an administrator wears. When various responsibilities of the position compete for an administrator's time, community relations activities are too often put off. Yet nothing an administrator does will have a bigger payback for a school and its students.

> *Community relations can be simply put in the terms of the Monroe Doctrine:*
> *Alliances with all, entanglements with none!*

Case Problem: Crisis Management Update

The superintendent has informed you that the district will be updating a comprehensive crisis management plan and you have been selected to chair the process. He explains that the world has changed since the last time the district updated the plan. The district has one high school, one middle school, and three elementary schools. You have been the principal of one of the elementary schools for three months. The superintendent has handed you a list of people that have been invited to the initial meeting. The list includes students from the high school, teachers, all the principals, a counselor, the school psychologist, the police chief, the fire chief, the director of civil defense, parents, a hospital liaison, a reporter, three clerics, a school board member, and three business owners. Detail exactly what you would do. Pay particular attention to how you will bring a group of strangers together into a position of ownership over the crisis management plan.

References

Bagin, D. & Gallagher, D. R. (2001). *The school and community relations (7th ed.)*. Boston, MA: Allyn and Bacon.

Black, J. A. & English, F. W. (1986). *What they don't tell you in schools of education about school administration*. Philadelphia, PA: Technomic.

Blau, P.M. (1967). *Exchange and power in social life*. New York: John Wiley & Sons, Inc.

Bovet, S. R. (Ed.) (1992). Discovering databases: On-line services put research at practitioner's finger tips. *Public Relations Journal, 45*(11), 2-4.

Columbine-angels.com (2002) http://www.columbine-angels.com.

Conrad, D. (2001). *Telling your story*. Presentation at a symposium held at Governors State University, University Park, IL.

Crowson, R. L. (1998). *School-community relations under reform* (2nd ed.). Berkeley, CA:McCutchan Publishing Corporation.

Dahl, R.A. (1961). *Who governs?* New Haven: Yale University Press.

Dumaine B. (1990). Making education work. *Fortune 121*(12), 12-22.

Dolan, K. (1995). *Communications: A practical guide to school and community relations*. New York: Wadsworth.

Epstein, J.L. (2001). Building bridges of home, school, and community: The importance of design. *Journal of Education for Students Placed at Risk 6*(1/2), 161-168.

Clearinghouse on Educational Management (2000). *School-Business Partnerships*. Retrieved November 18, 2001from
http://eric.uoregon.edu/publications/policy_reports/business_partnerships/partnerships.html

Evans, W. P., Fitzgerald, S., Weigel, C., Chvilicek, D. (1999). Are rural gang members similar to their urban peers?: Implications for rural communities. *Youth & Society 30* (3), 267-282.

Goode, D. J. (1983). *A study of values and attitudes in a textbook controversy in Kanawha County, West Virginia: An overt act of opposition to schools*. Unpublished doctoral dissertation, Michigan State University, East Lansing. Accession Number AAI8415221

Goode, D. J. (1993). *The community.* In Kaiser, J. (1992) *Educational administration (2nd ed.),* p. 101-128. Mequon, WI: Stylex Publishing Co., Inc.

Hadderman, M. (2000). Educational vouchers, ERIC digest. number 137. ERIC # ED442194. ERIC *Clearinghouse on Educational Management. Number 137.*

Holliday, A. E. (1988). In search of an answer: What is school public relations?" *Journal of Educational Public Relation 11*(2), 12-16.

Huff C. R. & Trump, K. S. (1996). Youth violence and gangs: School safety initiatives in urban and suburban school districts. *Education and Urban Society 28*(4) 492-503.

Hughes, L.W. & Hooper, D.W. (2000). *Public relations for school leaders.* MA: Allyn and Bacon.

Joyce, B., Calhoun, E. & Hopkins, D. (1999) *The new structure of school improvement.* Philadelphia: Open Press.

Kowalski, T. J. (2000). *Public relations in schools* (2nd ed.). New Jersey: Prentice Hall.

Lankard, B. A. (1995). Business/industry partnerships. *ERIC Clearing House on Adult, Career and Vocational Education.* Retrieved on November 18, 2001: http://icdl.uncg.edu/ft/071700-01.html

Lynd, R. S. & Lynd, H. M. (1929 and 1937). *Middletown.* New York: Harcourt, Brace and World.

McCarty, D. J. (1971). Community school relations: Community power structure. In *The encyclopedia of education* (pp.347-351). New York: Crowell-Collier.
Morrison, A. (1990). *Saving our schools. Fortune 121*(12), 8.

National School Public Relations Association (1985). *Evaluating your school PR investment.* Arlington, VA: NSPRA..

National PTA (2000). *Building successful partnerships.* Bloomington, IN: National Education Service.

Pawlas, G. E. (1995). *The administrator's guide to school-community relations.* New York: Eye on Education.

Polsby, W.P. (1980). *Community power and political theory (2nd ed.).* New Haven: Yale University Press.

Polsby, N.W. (1985). Prospects for pluralism. *Society 22*(2), 30-34.

Raywid, M.A. & Oshiyama, L. (2000). Musing in the wake of Columbine: What can schools do? *Phi Delta Kappan, 81*(5), 444-449.

Rescher, N. (1996). *Distributive justice.* New York: Bobbs Merrill.

Robertson, H.J. (1999). Shall we dance? *Phi Delta Kappan, 81*(10). 729-736.

Rose, L.C. & Gallup, A.M. (2000). The 32nd annual Phi Delta Kappa/Gallop poll on the public's attitudes toward the public schools. *Phi Delta Kappan 82*(1), 41-57.

Smith, W. (April, 2002). *Spreading the good news.* Presentation paper at symposium at Governors State University, University Park Illinois.

United State Department of Education. (1991). *America 2000: An Education Strategy.* Washington, D.C.: Author

United State Department of Education. (1991). *Goals 2000: An Invitation to Your Community.* Washington, D.C.: Author

United State Department of Education (1983). *A nation at risk: The imperative for educational reform.* # ED-99-CO-0032. Report EDO-TM-99-02. Washington, D.C.: U.S. Government Printing Office.

Virginia Department of Education (1999). *Model school crisis plan.* Retrieved March 3, 2001 from the Web site: http://www.pen.k12.va.us/VDOE/Instruction/model.html.

United States Government. (1996). *E-Rate* Telecommunications Act of 1996.

Warner, W. & Lunt, P. (1941). *The social life of a modern community* (Vol 1, Yankee City series). New Haven, CT: Yale University Press

Chapter 5
The Role of the Administrator in Curriculum

David I Blood

The role of the administrator in curriculum varies greatly among school systems and changes according to the administrator's position in a school's hierarchy. This chapter will examine the various roles that administrators perform in the area of curriculum. Some administrative roles examined will be those of curriculum supervisor, curriculum developer, curriculum evaluator, and curriculum leader. These roles will be examined in relationship to the building principal, assistant superintendent for curriculum, business manager, and superintendent. Additionally this chapter will offer definitions of curriculum and a general framework for working with curriculum. Figure 5-1 presents an outline of administrative roles in curriculum.

Curriculum Defined

Curriculum has many different meanings and is used in different ways, even by curriculum specialists. Some definitions of curriculum are:

- What is taught in school

- A set of subjects

- Program content

- A program of studies

- A set of materials

- A sequence of courses

- A course of study

- A series of school experiences

- Everything that takes place under the supervision of the school (Oliva, 1988)

For the purposes of understanding the administrator's role, curriculum shall be defined as *a course of study or a sequence of courses*. Within this definition are the necessary components of a course of study, such as goals, objectives, content, and other components.

Curriculum may also be viewed from the micro and macro points of view. Macro refers to the total curriculum of a school system or the total sequence of courses in a content area such as reading or math. Micro refers to a section of the macro curriculum, such as one course or one grade level in a content area.

ROLES OF ADMINISTRATORS IN CURRICULUM	
ROLE	GENERAL IMPLICATIONS
Curriculum Supervision	- Ensure that the content and processes of each content area are being implemented. - Monitor and record specific needs and problems for use later in curriculum review. - Monitor pilot programs. - Develop inservice programs to support curriculum implementation.
Curriculum Development	- Provide leadership for curriculum committees. - Communicate needs and general philosophy of education to curriculum committees. - Provide a structure for committees to function within. - Ensure that all steps in the development process are completed. - Obtain board approval for final curriculum and curriculum document.
Curriculum Review and Evaluation	- Determine if the curriculum review & evaluation is meeting the purposes for which it was designed. - Use a variety of assessments, not just standard tests. - Work with committees to see that evaluation is an on-going process.
Curriculum Leadership	- Motivate teachers and other curriculum committee workers. - Provide assistance and resources to help others achieve curriculum goals. - Specialize in group process, interpersonal relations, decision-making, and communication.

Figure 5-1

Curriculum Processes

To function effectively as a curriculum supervisor, curriculum leader, or curriculum evaluator, an administrator must conceptualize the general processes involved in curriculum, curriculum development, and curriculum review. These processes involve one's philosophy of education, needs assessment, development of goals and objectives, content selection and organization, methodology, and assessment or evaluation. Not only does the school administrator need a complete understanding of these processes but also a concept of the sequence in which these processes are developed and how each process fits with the others. The relationship of these processes to each other is shown in Figure 5-2.

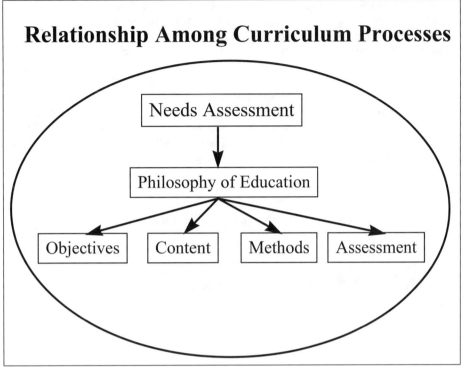

Figure 5-2

Needs Assessments

Needs assessment refers to any procedures for identifying and validating the needs of the school's constituency. The prioritizing of needs is an important part of needs assessment (Pratt, 1980). Curriculum development and curriculum review usually begin with a general assessment of the needs of the constituency that are to be met by the curriculum being reviewed or developed. From the micro perspective, the classroom teacher often examines what can be done to improve student achievement in a specific subject or what content should be taught in a specific subject. From the macro perspective, the school's administration examines a wide range of needs and capabilities. Whether needs assessment is at the macro or micro level, the result should be content and methodology designed for the specific population served by the school.

> *What a wise parent would desire for his own children, that too a nation, insofar as it is wise, must desire for all its children.*
>
> - R. H. Tawney -

A study by the Rand Corporation revealed that most curriculum developed in schools is reported and shelved and has little effect on what actually happens in the classroom. Unruh and Unruh (1984) cite two probable reasons for this problem, the lack of direct faculty involvement in the development of the new curriculum and the lack of sufficient local needs assessment.

Pratt (1980) recommends that school districts ask their communities what is considered important to be taught in schools. To some administrators, the question of what needs are to be met may seem simple. Needs assessments are, however, becoming more important as society becomes more complex. Consider the differences in needs between school systems with any of the following characteristics:

- A significant dropout rate

- Several students whose parents work at the local scientific lab

- A community with several oil refineries that employ its graduates

- An all-girls or all-boys school

- A low-income blue-collar community

- A rural school

- A school with a mix of several different minorities

- A school with a high percent of college-bound students

- A high student mobility rate

To meet the needs of any constituency, those needs must be identified. Making that identification involves the collection of both opinion and factual data. It must go beyond the traditional armchair assessment and requires obtaining data from all the school's main constituents.

Sources of data and opinion include parents, taxpayers, students, pressure groups, politically influential individuals, teachers, academic specialists, employers, recent graduates, dropouts, and community agencies. These sources and others provide important information about what needs the school's curriculum should address.

With the sources identified, the method of gathering data must be determined. Needs assessment information is gathered in several ways, including questionnaires, interviews, public meetings, observation, brainstorming sessions, and reading local newspapers. Of these methods, the most common are questionnaires and public meetings.

Questionnaires

When developing a needs assessment questionnaire, consider the following:

1. Ask questions that those being surveyed have the experience to answer. "What degree of difficulty is your child having with math?" will produce more useful information than "How well is the school teaching math?" If necessary, give respondents details of the existing instruction before asking them to make a judgment about that instruction (Pratt, 1980).

2. Read information on measurement of attitudes (Henerson, 1978) or on design of needs assessment tools (Witkin, 1976).

3. Consider ready-made needs assessment packages.

4. Use questionnaires as one of several data-gathering instruments, and crosscheck the results with those of interviews, and other tools (Pratt, 1980).

Public Meetings

Public meetings or community forums are used for the collection of information in a short period. The following information should be helpful when considering a public meeting as a needs assessment tool.

1. Advance notification and a public invitation to attend should be given to the local media.

2. Hearings should be informal, to enable participants to explore and build on one another's ideas.

3. Keep in mind that the most influential and eloquent participants tend to dominate the proceedings.

4. The opinions expressed have a low validity because some people will not attend or express their opinion.

However the needs of the public are assessed, be sure to use the information in curriculum development and curriculum review.

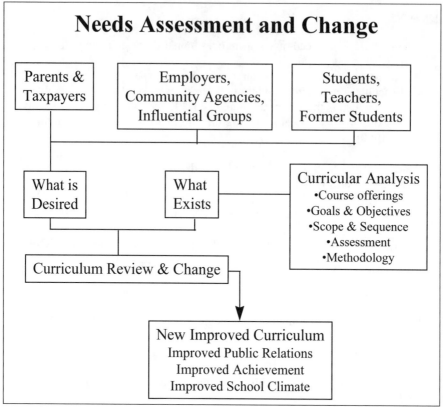

Figure 5-3

Developing a Philosophy

A second consideration of curriculum process is philosophy of education. The word philosophy, to many administrators, evokes theory and complicated, impractical ways of dealing with schools. This need not be the case. Think of philosophy as a general view or belief about education. All administrators have a philosophy of education. Most educators have basic beliefs about schools. In fact, many conflicts in schools result from differences in basic philosophy.

Administrators' philosophies of education reflect the way they think and feel about every aspect of schooling. Some of these areas are:

- the role of the teacher

- the type of methodology used in the classroom

- the way content is selected

- the method of discipline used

- the amount of input parents have in the student's education

- the way academic gains are assessed

- the way the administrators run the school

- the balance of academics and the affective domain

Philosophy affects every area of schooling. In curriculum, the role of philosophy of education is that of a screen. All practices and policies must pass through this screen before being accepted in the school. While room is left for some individual differences, practices and policies that are contrary to the philosophy of the school are usually not adopted. Normally, practices and policies fit the general guidelines adopted by the board of education. The philosophies of American schools are based to a large extent on the views and needs of the local community.

The administrators at each level of district administration monitor curriculum and curriculum practices to assure that the school district's general theory of education is being implemented. Superintendents monitor district policies, district curriculum, and the success of building principals in implementing the board policies built from the district-wide philosophy of education. At the building level, the principal monitors building policies and practices. If the district philosophy in science is that students will experience hands-on process science as opposed to lecture and discussion, then it is the building administrators' role to monitor the science curriculum to make sure that happens.

Administrators, boards of education, teachers, and community constituents should establish a written philosophy for the district and for each curricular area. To develop a written philosophy, the administration and board should provide the leadership to help these groups work together in its development. The Philosophy Survey at the end of this chapter is useful in gathering the different views and ways of thinking about education.

It is very unlikely that a community, faculty, administration, and student body will all agree on a philosophy of life or a philosophy of education. Figure 5-4 describes some classic philosophies and how they affect one's view of education. Some definitions have been adapted from Zais's *Curriculum Principles and Foundations*, (1976).

Classic Philosophy and Education	
Philosophical Label	**Role in Education**
The Idealist	- Believes there is one best or correct way to teach, to behave, and to function.
	- The teacher/administrator should be a model of what is expected.
	- The emphasis is on theory. Absolute knowledge is received.
The Pragmatist	- Believes in using whatever works to achieve the goal.
	- Emphasis is on the practical.
	- Relative knowledge is constructed.
The Realist	- Selection of methodology is based on data.
	- Emphasis is on factual information and feedback.
	- Uses proven methods.
	- Absolute knowledge is discovered.
The Existentialist	- What is needed, what is to be learned, and how it is best learned is different for all persons based on their experiences.
	- Relative knowledge is constructed from experiences.
	- Only the learners know what is best for themselves.
The Perennialist	- The discipline and doctrine of a subject is what is important.
	- Drill is the favored method.
	- Academic excellence, mental discipline, and liberal arts are key.
	- The mind should be elevated above the biological universe.

Figure 5-4

Whittle Communications has now contracted with 8,216 schools for its satellite-beamed Channel One. The controversy is over the philosophy of allowing a private entrepreneur into the curriculum with 2 minutes of commercials for every 12 minutes of news to a captive audience of teenagers (Healy, Jones, Kelly, 1991).

Determining Goals and Objectives

Goals and objectives are the guideposts of curriculum implementation. They are beacons that keep implementation headed in one general direction. Goals and objectives provide continuity to the curriculum even when it is being implemented by several different teachers in several locations.

While goals and objectives are similar, they do serve slightly different purposes. A goal is a more general statement of the direction in which learners should move as a result of curriculum implementation. Goals are usually not immediately measurable. An objective is a statement of what the student will be able to do because of the curriculum. When written out, an objective contains one verb that indicates how achievement can be measured. Remember, goals are more general statements of direction and objectives are more specific statements of what the learner will be able to do in a shorter run. The samples below are chosen from the Illinois Goal Assessment Plan (Blood, 1985). They describe a goal and suggested objectives for each goal.

GOAL: As a result of their schooling, students should be able to apply skills and knowledge gained in the social sciences to decision making in real-life situations.

Objective: Students should be able to predict the outcome of a social program that aims to satisfy a need expressed by a group.

Objective: Students should be able to rate sources of information about products and programs according to bias, accuracy, completeness, and interest.

GOAL: As a result of their schooling, students should have a working knowledge of the social and environmental implications and limitations of technological development.

Objective: Students should be able to identify hazards in common household products.

Objective: Students should be able to identify changes in natural ecosystems resulting from human behavior.

GOAL: As a result of their schooling, students should be able to plan a personal physical fitness and health program.

Objective: Students should be able to list daily practices that contribute to good health.

Objective: Students should be able to differentiate between exercises that contribute to muscle strength as compared to those that contribute to muscle endurance.

Goals and objectives serve as a basis for the selection of curriculum content and for learner assessment. Continuity must exist between goals, objectives, content selected, and assessment. Curriculum committees must take care to develop goals and objectives that reflect the needs of the students, the philosophy of the school, and the important achievements that are expected of learners.

When writing objectives, curriculum committees should use a hierarchy or taxonomy to separate different levels of difficulty. Bloom's (1956) taxonomy divides the cognitive domain into six levels.

1. *Knowledge*: the simple recall of specifics, methods, structures, etc.

2. *Comprehension*: understanding of a type that does not include the ability to see its fullest implications.

3. *Application*: the ability to use generalizations or rules in specific situations.

4. *Analysis*: The ability to divide a communication into a hierarchically arranged organization of its component ideas.

5. *Synthesis*: the ability to arrange and combine unstructured elements into an organized whole.

6. *Evaluation*: the assessment of material, methods, etc., using selected criteria.

The use of a taxonomy such as this will help add structure and sequence to the development of objectives.

Administrators should see that committees develop goals and objectives that are consistent with the needs of the students and the philosophy of the school. Once the goals and objectives are in place, it is the administrator's responsibility to see that they are implemented by the faculty.

Selection and Organization of Content

Content in the curriculum should be selected based on the goals and objectives that have been developed. Whether the content comes from a textbook or another source, it must help students achieve the objectives written in the curriculum document. Content is not an end in itself but a means to achieve the objectives and goals.

A *scope and sequence chart* is often developed to get a quick idea of the content in a curriculum. *Scope* refers to the content being taught and the depth and breadth to which it is taught. *Sequence* refers to the order in which it is taught.

Developing a scope and sequence chart of the content contributes to the continuity, balance, and integration of content in the curriculum. Continuity is established by teachers at each grade level following the sequence of content specified in the chart. Balance in the curriculum can be quickly analyzed through use of the scope and sequence chart, and the integration of one subject with another can be more easily accomplished if the chart is used as a reference point.

Scope, determined by the goals and objectives of the curriculum, is often influenced by traditional content offered at the specified grade level. The depth and breadth to which a subject is taught at a particular grade level will vary from school to school based on the needs of those particular students. However, to achieve continuity within a school system, teachers should teach all the content slated for their grade level.

Administrators should ensure that teachers are familiar with the scope and sequence chart and that they are using the chart to guide their instructional planning. Curriculum supervision ensures that teachers are preparing students for the next course or grade.

Content in a scope and sequence chart may be sequenced in many different ways. Figure 5-5 lists Doll's (1988) seven methods of establishing sequence.

Sequencing Methods

- Chronological order of events, from simple to complex
- Based on prerequisite skills
- Part to whole or whole to part
- Present to past
- Ever-widening circles of understanding
- From concrete to conceptual

Figure 5-5

Curriculum Mapping, Curriculum Alignment, and Textbook Selection

Curriculum mapping, curriculum alignment, and textbook selection are three areas in which curriculum developers and curriculum supervisors are often involved. Curriculum mapping refers to documenting the content and objectives that are taught, when they are taught, and in what course or grade level they are taught. Curriculum alignment is the process of aligning the content and objectives of the curriculum to a chosen set of standards. Textbook selection is self-explanatory but is often done poorly, without regard to the curriculum guide, curriculum map, or curriculum alignment.

Curriculum Mapping

Curriculum mapping refers to documenting the content and objectives that are taught, when they are taught, and in what course or grade they are taught. School administrators often have a difficult time knowing what is taught in different disciplines, courses, or grade levels. Sometimes the same skill or content is repeated or taught in a contradictory fashion in different courses. Needless to say, this destroys sequence and continuity in the curriculum. Curriculum mapping can give administrators and teachers visual evidence of what is happening, and curriculum decisions can then be made based upon the curriculum map.

The curriculum mapping process may be slightly different based on the style of the administrator, but it should include the following.

- A committee, comprised of teachers, that represents the course or grade level

- Materials, textbooks, lesson plans, and any curriculum guides for the course or grade level

- Identification of major content and objectives

- Identification of when the content or objectives are taught

- A finished product format, such as an outline, flowchart, scope and sequence chart, or grid

- Review and discussion of the curriculum map

- A thorough search for overlap, gaps, continuity, and balance.

Other steps as needed:

- Production of a new curriculum map as needed after major changes

- Linking of content for integration with other subjects

- Inclusion of appropriate uses of technology

- Checks for spiral curriculum development

- Dates for the next curriculum mapping cycle

Effective curriculum mapping should lead to a better scope and sequence. The curriculum should become more efficient and insure continuity, balance, and integration.

Curriculum Alignment

Curriculum alignment is the process of aligning or matching the content and objectives of the curriculum to a set of standards. Some school systems align their curriculum to national standards, some to state standards, and other to the objectives published by norm referenced testing companies. Curriculum alignment has become a very desirable process in states that have statewide testing programs. Other schools have tried to improve their achievement test scores by making sure that the curriculum that is tested is the same as the curriculum that is taught. Curriculum alignment is sometimes controversial. Teachers, administrators, and boards of education sometimes cringe at having someone else dictate what the local school system should teach.

Curriculum alignment can begin with the standards or with the curriculum map. The process of alignment is very similar to that of mapping, but with the standards in place to guide decision making.

The curriculum alignment process will be slightly different based on the style of the administrator, but it should include the following.

- Copies of the standards for those involved

- A committee, comprised of teachers, that represents the course or grade level

- Materials, textbooks, lesson plans, and any curriculum guides for the course or grade level

- A curriculum map of what is currently being taught

- Matching, additions, or deletions of content based on the standards

- Alignment of testing and assessment to the standards

- A finished product format to follow, such as an outline, flowchart, chart, or grid

- Review and discussion of the curriculum alignment chart, etc.

- Dates for the next curriculum alignment cycle

Curriculum alignment will help ensure that the curriculum matches the desired national or state standards.

Textbook Selection

The textbook(s) selected for any grade or course has become extremely important. Many teachers use the textbook as the main source of content. New teachers sometimes follow the textbook page for page throughout the whole year. Extreme reliance on the textbook is also common in schools that do not have a written curriculum guide. Textbook selection is not to be taken lightly. Textbooks are expensive, and most schools only purchase books every five or six years.

Administrators should lead the textbook selection process. Depending on school philosophy and administrative style, the process might include the following:

- Selection of a committee that is representative of all teachers that will use the textbook

- Development a form to use when evaluating various texts (suggestions for the form are listed below)

- Determination of the role of the committee and how much weight its decision will have

- Ordering of textbook copies and sample materials for review

- Review of the textbooks individually by committee members, using the form for evaluation

- A committee meeting to share information and rate the textbooks as a whole

- Presentations from textbook representatives from the top-rated texts for all who are interested, keeping in mind that they are there to make the sale

- A committee meeting to make the final decision.

- Preparation of two or three proposals for the board of education, including a bare-bones text adoption, a middle-of-the-road plan, and a plan that includes all the materials available to support the textbook

- A recommendation to the board of education, with an available defense of the decisions and reasons for the selection, as well as available rating forms, as the board of education is responsible for the final budget decision and is unlikely to take that responsibility lightly.

The textbook evaluation form should be easy to use and have both numerical ratings and a place for comments. The following should be considered when designing the items on a textbook evaluation form.

- Does the textbook match the curriculum guide, the standards, or other alignment documents?

- Is the reading level appropriate?

- Are there remedial and advanced activities for students?

- Does the text lend itself to the types of teaching methods and assessments preferred by the teachers?

- Is it better than the current text? How?

- What collateral materials are available?

- How good is the teachers' edition?

- What type of ongoing support does the company provide?

- Is this textbook better than the others that are being reviewed? Why?

Selecting a textbook that matches the curriculum and the standards is very important. Do not rely on the textbook company to provide the correlation of the textbook to the standards or norm-referenced test. The committee should examine this area itself. Most schools only purchase new texts every five or six years. Once a decision is made, the teachers will have to live with it for a long time.

Choosing Methodology

Methodology is an area of education that is often viewed as a separate entity from curriculum, yet it has extensive effects on the achievement of objectives by students. Methodology must be addressed within the structure of curriculum. The method of instruction chosen by the teacher should be based on the type of objective to be achieved, the teacher's view of educational psychology, and the content to be taught. When a specific method is preferred by the curriculum developers, the curriculum guide should state that fact.

Some curriculum revolves around the use of a specific method or approach. Some examples are the whole language approach to language arts, the Madeline Hunter approach to instruction, and process-oriented science instruction.

A school's philosophy may also

> *What is a good man but a bad man's teacher?*
> *What is a bad man but a good man's job?*
> *If you don't understand this, you will get lost, however intelligent you are. It is the great secret.*
>
> -Lao-Tsu-

influence teaching methods. If a school favors individualized instruction or mastery learning, then methodology must be altered to be consistent. Administrators should supervise curriculum implementation while supervising instruction. The best curriculum is of no value if not taught effectively by the classroom teacher.

Assessing and Evaluating

Assessment and evaluation of instruction and of the curriculum are very important processes. Administrators, teachers, and students must be evaluated to obtain feedback on how well actual performance matches planned performance. Assessment and evaluation of students help the administration, teachers, and students know if the students are achieving the goals of the curriculum and if the curriculum in general is meeting the purpose for which it was designed. Teacher-made tests, observational checklists, and criterion-referenced tests are among the devices that provide teachers and administrators with formative assessment data to determine if students are successful. Norm-referenced achievement tests give teachers and administrators data that allow them to compare their students and curriculum to students in other schools in the nation.

Whether the assessment is at the classroom level or at the school level, it is of little value if it is not consistent with the curriculum. Administrators should work with teachers to ensure that students' progress is appropriately assessed. Administrators also should review achievement test data carefully to determine if the tests are consistent with the school's curriculum. Norm-referenced tests comparing students' scores with students throughout the school, the local geographic region, the country, and the world give students, faculty, administrators, and community constituents a clear understanding of how their students stand compared with others.

Specific Administrative Roles in Curriculum

The curriculum process needs leadership at all levels of district administration. This section will discuss the administrative roles of curriculum supervisor, curriculum evaluator, curriculum leader, and curriculum developer.

Curriculum Supervisor

Curriculum supervision is a very critical role. Building level and central office level administrators are responsible for seeing that the district's and school's curriculum is the one implemented. Unruh and Unruh (1984) describe the following roles of supervision.

Administration of supervision. An assistant superintendent or principal of a large school may perform this role. In curriculum implementation, this person works with the superintendent of schools in preparing recommendations to the board of education for changes in curricula, usually because of committee work. Once approved, support for implementation is the responsibility of the designated administrator, including gathering the financial resources, employing new staff or consultants, overseeing supervisory operations at the school sites, and evaluating the quality of site supervision in the implementation of the new program (Unruh and Unruh, 1984).

General supervision. Principals, assistant principals, curriculum specialists, or coordinators perform this role. In the implementation of new programs, this area of supervision is centrally concerned with preparing new curriculum guides, selecting materials, developing in-service programs, and coordinating auxiliary services, such as hiring substitute teachers to release teachers for training, or hiring secretaries to type and distribute outlines, guides, and other written materials. (Unruh and Unruh, 1984).

Clinical supervision. Direct assistance in the classroom is the focus of clinical supervision. The term may be a misnomer, as it describes a team effort to implement a new program, skill, or curriculum content rather than any type of evaluative function. The clinical domain is the interaction between a specialist, consultant, or coordinator and a specific teacher or it may be peer interaction within a team of teachers. It involves a process of planning, observing, and analyzing what the teacher and students are doing during the instructional period in which the new curriculum is being presented. Clinical supervision assumes a sincere effort by all parties, with openness of communication (Unruh and Unruh, 1984).

Curriculum Developer

Administrators are often called upon to develop or redevelop curricula. The most common structure for curriculum development is that of a teacher committee led by an administrator. The administrator's role in this process is to provide leadership and structure for the committee. The purpose for developing or redeveloping the curriculum, the needs of the constituency, and the school's general philosophy should be shared with the committee. Administrators should ensure that the steps or processes outlined previously in the chapter are all completed and that there is consistency among those steps. Additionally, administrators should see that a curriculum document is produced and that it is an accurate reflection of the committee's work. Finally, the administrator should obtain board approval for the final curriculum plans and the start of curriculum implementation.

Curriculum Evaluator

Curriculum evaluation models have been analyzed extensively by Unruh and Unruh (1984); Saylor, Alexander, and Lewis (1981); and Tyler (1949).

Curriculum evaluation, according to Saylor, Alexander, and Lewis (1981), is the process used in judging the appropriateness of curriculum choices. They pose the following questions as significant for curriculum evaluation:

- Is the curriculum fulfilling the purposes for which it was designed? Are these purposes themselves valid?

- Is the curriculum appropriate to the particular students involved?

- Are the selected activities the best choices, considering the goals that are sought?

- Is the content the best possible?

- Are the assessment procedures consistent with the rest of the curriculum?

Unruh and Unruh (1984) add:

- Are the materials used for instructional purposes appropriate and the best available for the envisioned goals?

Curriculum evaluation is a process for searching out ways to improve the substance of the curriculum, the implementation procedures, the instructional methods, and the effects on students' learning and behavior.

Tyler (1949) views evaluation as a checking process that should be applied at four different stages in curriculum development.

- The first stage is when choosing between goals or ideas that are proposed for developing a curriculum program, a set of materials, or an instructional device. At this point, Tyler recommends reviewing evidence from others' experiences and experiments that may indicate the probable effectiveness of the idea before energy is wasted on an approach that did not work elsewhere.

- The second stage for evaluation is in the process of implementation. Once the plan is thought to be in operation, a check of the entire situation should be made to see whether it actually is in operation or whether certain conditions essential to success of the program are missing. At the point of implementation, alternate procedures could be discovered that would be more effective than those outlined in the original plan.

- A third stage at which evaluation can contribute to the effectiveness of the curriculum is during actual operation; that is, following the early trials, it will be necessary to monitor the ongoing curriculum. Various evaluative procedures can keep students and teachers in touch with the necessary elements of the curriculum implementation process and can furnish information to guide them.

- The fourth stage occurs when a program has been carried out and it is desirable to decide whether the results are good enough to continue with it, undertake modifications, or drop the program

Also according to Tyler (1949), evaluation becomes a process for finding out how far the learning experiences, as organized and developed, are actually producing the desired results. This evaluation process would include identifying the strengths and weaknesses of the plans. In turn this approach helps to check the validity of the basic premises from which the instructional program was developed. As a result of evaluation, it should be possible to pinpoint in what respects the curriculum is effective or needs improvement.

Additionally the administrator should decide if the evaluation at hand is *formative* or *summative*. The purpose of formative evaluation is to revise an ongoing curriculum. Summative evaluation, used to make a statement about the value of a specific curriculum, is often used to decide if a specific curriculum will continue in operation. The type and amount of information gathered will differ according to the purpose of evaluation. Administrators with curriculum evaluation as a major area of responsibility are well advised to familiarize themselves with Unruh and Unruh's (1981) description of goal-attainment models of evaluation, judgment evaluation models, decision-facilitative models of evaluation, descriptive evaluation models, and status-assessment models of evaluation.

Curriculum Leader

The role of curriculum leader involves the administrator's ability to work with group process and committees. As a curriculum leader, an administrator should work toward teacher empowerment and ownership of the curriculum. Only through teacher ownership will implementation, development, and evaluation result in processes that have real meaning (see Chapters 1, 2, and 8 for further elaboration of the organizational and personal benefits of empowerment). The attitude and motivations of the administrator toward curriculum will have a dramatic effect, negative or positive, on teachers' views of curriculum.

Levels Of Curriculum

Curriculum development and other curriculum work occurs at a minimum of five major organizational levels: a) national, b) state or regional, c) local, d) individual institution, and e) individual classroom.   There are important differences in curriculum-development activity at each level (Armstrong, 1989).

The National Level

National curriculum work can be directed toward many ends. Beginning in the mid-1950s and continuing throughout much of the 1960s, there was an effort to bring subject area professionals together to develop comprehensive programs for the schools. These went beyond statements of goals and identification of content elements. Several of these programs developed classroom-ready materials and specific instructional guidelines for teachers. Among these projects were the Biological Science Curriculum Study, the Georgia Anthropology Project, the High School Mathematics Study Group, and Project English (Armstrong, 1989).

More recent work at the national level has been less comprehensive, with less emphasis on developing complete programs providing specific suggestions for instructors. Developers have taken the view that general guidelines formulated nationally can be filled in with more specific information as they are adapted to state and local settings (Armstrong, 1989).

National curriculum projects often engage the talents of experts in academic areas and experts in curriculum development. The involvement of these people often attracts the attention of state and local authorities. Therefore, guidelines developed at the national level do exert an important influence on state and local educational programming (Armstrong, 1989).

The State Level

State boards of education and state departments of education set down many guidelines affecting school curricula. These agencies are charged with implementing broad policies outlined by legislators. They also monitor schools' compliance with state regulations. Often these authorities have the power to make policy in areas that have not been addressed directly by legislation (Armstrong, 1989).

In the past, state-level curriculum reform efforts were often directed toward winning legislators' support for certain programs or courses. Sometimes narrow interest groups lobby for the inclusion of special topics into the existing curriculum. For example, in some states, drug education and consumer education were mandated by law (Armstrong, 1989). Sometimes legislators were influenced to change basic components of the required program, such as adding a required course in state history or changing the number of years of English required for high school graduation.

Historically, curriculum work at the state level involved decisions going little beyond specification of particular courses or specialized units of study to be included in educational programs. In recent years, however, some states have begun to exert much more influence over specific elements of content treated within the authorized array of school courses. Texas and Illinois are examples. Texas has a list of "essential elements" for every subject taught in grades K to 12. These specify content elements that, by law, must be treated in each school subject. Illinois has mandated goals in seven content areas (Blood, 1985).

Alhough this pattern is by no means universal, there is a tendency for curriculum activity at the state level to result in program decisions that, formerly, were left to state departments of education, local school districts, and teachers. While curriculum specialists may play some role at the state level, decisions are often heavily influenced by the opinions of legislators. Since legislators react to what they hear from their voting constituents, the judgments of nonpolitical, but informed curriculum leaders and educators may carry less weight than at the local and institutional levels (Armstrong, 1989).

Not all curriculum development at the state level involves political decision-making by legislators. State organizations of educators, for example state English and mathematics associations, sometimes establish guidelines for instruction in their respective subjects. Often, these guidelines suggest general patterns and leave more specific implementation decisions to curriculum specialists and educators at the local, institutional, and classroom levels (Armstrong, 1989).

The Local Level

Much curriculum work continues to occur locally, where curriculum leaders play very important roles. It is here that master plans guiding instructional programs are developed and steps are initiated that result in more specific building-level and individual classroom-level plans.

Curriculum leaders and administrators at the local level oversee curriculum development at the school-system level, the building level, and the individual-classroom level. These specialists aim for programs that encourage instructional practices in individual classrooms consistent with goals adopted at the school-district level.

The work of the individual curriculum leader can vary with the size of the local setting. In a large school district, a curriculum director may supervise a staff of curriculum specialists. In smaller operations, one curriculum specialist may be responsible for all curriculum development work. Additionally, various lines of communication also exist depending on size and administrative philosophy. Figure 5-6, taken from Armstrong (1989), shows common local-level administrative structures.

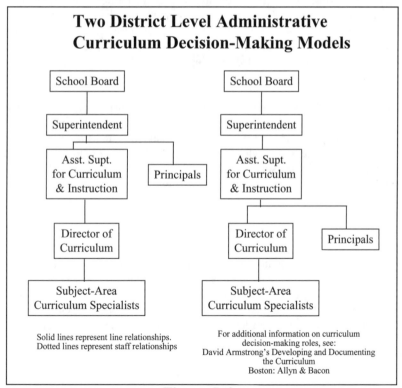

Figure 5-6

The School Level

Curriculum work at this level involves planning, developing, and implementing instructional programs for use in the individual building. Typically, district-level curriculum leaders work closely with building administrators and with teacher representatives in curriculum-development projects.

Special attention is given to providing for the instructional needs of both building administrators and classroom teachers (Armstrong, 1989).

Curriculum work at the level of the individual school often ties planning to more general guidelines developed at the local school district level. Administrators, particularly school principals, play a role together with some teachers to produce guidelines that can be refined and made more specific by classroom teachers and instructors.

The Classroom Level

Curriculum work at this level requires the direct participation of many people. It focuses on careful planning of instructional units that are "classroom ready." Curriculum development in this setting has a very practical orientation, directed at providing teachers with highly specific information regarding what is to be taught, practical suggestions for introducing content, testing ideas, sources of needed learning materials, and other issues of importance to teachers and instructors.

Curriculum leaders and administrators play an important information-dissemination role at the individual classroom level. They provide information regarding general guidelines that may have been developed at the local or divisional level and the individual institutional level. They may suggest general models for teachers and instructors to follow as they prepare instructional units. Curriculum specialists' roles here are, largely, directed to overseeing the development of instructional units that will be consistent with more general institution-level and division-level guidelines.

Summary

The role of the administrator in curriculum varies greatly from school system to school system, changing according to the administrator's position in the school's hierarchy. This chapter has examined the various roles that administrators perform in the area of curriculum. Some administrative roles examined were curriculum supervisor, curriculum developer, curriculum evaluator, and curriculum leader. These roles were examined in relationship to the positions of principal, assistant superintendent for curriculum, business manager, and superintendent.

Philosophy Survey

I. EDUCATION

A. Education should emphasize verified truths and the means by which truth is obtained. It should aid students in adjustment to adult life and its new experience.

B. Education should preserve and transmit our social and cultural heritage. It should be a means toward human happiness and prepare one for unity with God and future life.

C. Education should assist people who are young in acquiring skills and techniques that are used in effective functioning within their environment.

D. Education should aim toward the development of a cultivated personality. It should be a process of self-realization.

II. THE ADMINISTRATOR

A. Administrators should try to keep in close contact with their community, but not concern themselves with far-reached theory about the universe.

B. Administrators should expect everyone to make the best of themselves. Administrators should look for vigorous cooperative personalities in return.

C. Administrators' decisions should be dictated by the impersonal results of objective experimentation. However, they should be ready to modify procedures as more efficient methods are established.

D. Administrators should be conscious of the school's duty to instruct in the administrators' religion's virtues. Administrators should oppose vocational preparation in secondary education and should formulate policies upon the concept of a general education for all.

III. THE TEACHER

A. The teacher should be the voice of science: clear, objective and factual.

B. The teacher should instruct students in my religion's virtues and through a study of authoritative written works, reveal a synthesis of human relationships and scientific thought.

C. The teacher should occupy the central position and should develop each student's potential self, self-reliance, and self-direction.

D. The teacher should suggest problems that will stimulate students to find for themselves solutions that are effective in everyday life.

IV. THE LEARNER

A. The student should be viewed as endowed with certain potentialities that are the responsibility of the school to develop fully.

B. The student should be viewed as having the ability to reason. Students are indebted with duties to themselves, their fellow humans, and their God. This spiritual nature is viewed as superior to the organic.

C. Students should be viewed as Physio-chemical combinations adjusting to the environment in which they find themselves.
D. The student should be viewed as a bio-social being in need of guidance to become an effective functioning member of our modern world community.

V. PROGRAM BUILDING

A. The program should be based upon authenticated knowledge and established skills because they provide a basis for new experiences.

B. The curriculum should reflect changing national, economic, and religious emphasis.

C. Essentially, it occupies position of secondary educational importance.

D. The traditional curriculum should be perpetuated because of the challenge provided each individual. An emphasis should be placed upon activities that bring out the best effort in students and thereby develop their personalities.

VI. PROGRAM CONTENT

A. The program should reflect the needs, interests and abilities of students and should reflect an emphasis on hygienic principles and carry-over skills that are of value in everyday life.

B. The program should contain certain activities that will prepare students for life. Conscious attempts should be made to develop the program on a scientific basis.

C. The curriculum should emphasize skills that provide a challenge to everyone. Activities should be selected based on their contribution to the development of the person.

D. The program should emphasize skills that have been a part of Man's heritage. Attention should be directed toward moral and ethical development.

VII. LEARNING

A. Learning is a process of acquiring objective knowledge by the scientific method.

B. Learning is a process of overcoming the deficiencies of immaturity. It attempts to make understandable the truths that provide human happiness.

C. Learning takes place through mental processes. Humans seek an intellectual explanation of things.

D. Learning is a process of social interaction and is concerned with the experiences that constitute life.

VIII. TEACHING METHODS

A. The teacher should approach the activity area from the standpoint of student interest and conduct the class as a cooperative enterprise. Emphasis is placed upon the process rather than the product of experimentation.

B. The teacher should make an analysis of the skills to be learned, breaking them down into their elements and interrelations.

C. The teacher should instruct by analogy so that students may interpret and generalize the values essential for human happiness.

D. The teacher should enlist the loyalty of students through example and emotional motivation, always with a view toward developing personality.

IX. EVALUATION

A. Students should be evaluated based on their aspirations as well as their achievements.

B. Students should be evaluated on social development and the practical carry-over skills that will aid them in the solution of problems.

C. Students should be evaluated on their development of moral character and the degree to which their efforts approach capacity.

D. Students should be tested in an attempt to determine their standing with other similar groups.

X. THE UNIVERSE

A. The universe is God-Centered and exhibits certain related universal and unchanging laws.

B. Ours is an ever-changing and evolving universe.

C. The universe and reality are mental creations and are explained though ideas or persons.

D. The universe is exactly as it appears. External objects constitute reality.

XI. HUMANS

A. Humans are the creatures of instinct and habit. They exist and have significance within an impersonal and objective world.

B. Humans are viewed as an integral part of their related universe, kin to the Divine, and possessed of body and soul. They are capable of immortality.

C. Humans are the center of the universe. They are spiritual unities, expressing purposes of the mind. Humans are viewed as products of social and cultural forces. As the future holds no certainty for humans, they strive to promote the greatest good for the greatest number.

XII. VALUES

A. Value rests in the fulfillment of satisfaction that contribute to a personal well being. For the most part these personal satisfactions coincide with a larger pattern of behavior that has lasting value.

B. Values exist in the mind of God, independent of humanity. They are objective and absolute. These values tend to parallel intelligent, rational conduct.

C. Value is that which motivates humanity. Value is inherent in that which motivated humanity in the successful adjustment to surroundings.

D. Values are human made to serve man's own needs. They are derived from experience and represent instruments that make possible effective functioning within our environment.

Answer Key for Philosophy Survey

1. A.R B.A C.P D.I   2. A.P B.I C.R D.A
3. A.R B.A C.I D.P   4. A.I B.A C.R D.P
5. A.R B.P C.A D.I   6. A.P B.R C.I D.A
7. A.R B.A C.I D.P   8. A.P B.R C.A D.I
9. A.I B.P C.A D.R   10. A.A B.P C.I D.R
11. A.R B.A C.I D.P   12. A.I B.A C.R D.P

Key: I = Idealist   P = Pragmatist   R = Realist   A = Religious Idealist

Case Problem: New Science Goals

Tess Tyler, a principal in a school system that has four other schools, has just learned that the State Department of Education has issued new goals in science education. Tess's superintendent has appointed her to evaluate, review, and revise the science curriculum in light of the new goals. Tess has been asked to consider the following in her role as leader, supervisor, evaluator, and developer: committee work, curriculum processes, initial and continuing implementation, ownership, and procedure. How should she proceed?

References

Armstrong, D. (1989). *Developing and documenting the curriculum*. Boston: Allyn and Bacon.

Blood, D. (1985). *Standards and assessment*. Springfield, IL: Illinois State Board of Education, Standards and Assessment Division

Bloom, B., Krathwohl, D., & Maisa, B. (1956). *Taxonomy of educational objectives*. New York: McKay.

Doll, R. (1988). *Curriculum improvement*. Boston: Allyn and Bacon.

Healy, M., Jones, D., & Kelly, (1991, April 30). Channel one beams to 8,216 schools. *USA Today*, 8D.

Henerson, M. E. (1978). *How to measure attitudes*. Beverly Hills, California: Sage.

Lao-tsu (1988) (origin c. 479 B.C.E.). *Tao Te Ching* (S. Mitchell, Trans.) New York: Harper & Row, Publishers, Inc.

Oliva, P. (1988). *Developing the curriculum*. Glenview, IL: Scott Foresman.

Pratt, D. (1980). *Curriculum design and development*. New York: Harcourt Brace.

Saylor, J. G. Alexander, W. M., Lewis, A. J. (1981). *Curriculum planning for better teaching and learning.* New York: Holt, Rinehart, & Winston.

Tyler, R. W. (1949). *Basic principals of curriculum and instruction.* Chicago: University of Chicago.

Unruh, G. and Unruh, A.. (1984*). Curriculum development, problems, processes, and progress.* Berkeley: McCuthan.

Witkin, B. R. (1976). *Needs assessment models: a critical analysis.* Paper presented at the American Educational Research Association Annual Conference, San Francisco, CA.

Zais. (1976). Curriculum Principles and Foundations. Toronto: Harper And Row.

Chapter 6
Strategic Planning and Program Evaluation
Marcus Ahmed and John Borsa

This chapter addresses an expanded concept of planning, which includes change and quality management. The reader will be exposed to planning, the process of developing a change paradigm, and implementation of a quality management program. Issues related to program evaluation will be discussed.

Introduction

To understand the planning issues and the planning process in this chapter, read each of the following hypotheticals and determine what should have been done to alleviate the problem as stated in the situation.

Hypothetical 1

School District A: This K-12 district is rural, with a school enrollment of 1500 students. The administration is composed of a superintendent, a high school/middle school principal, and an elementary principal. Though not financially stressed, the district does not have a large amount of discretionary funds. Farming is the main source of income for this and other local districts. At the last board of education meeting, four of the district's patrons asked that the district incorporate technology, especially satellite technology, into the agriculture curriculum. With the advent of technology, farmers have been able to better manage their farms. Satellites have assisted them in planting, crop rotation, and irrigation. Unfortunately, the board had planned to use the available funds to implement an English as a Second Language (ESL) program for migrant farm workers.

Hypothetical 2

School District B: This K-12 district is urban, with a school enrollment of 150,000 students. There is a superintendent, multiple assistant superintendents and directors, and many principals and assistant principals. The district is on the state's financial watch list. Last week, the superintendent was informed that the district was not in compliance with the deadline to incorporate Reauthorization–IDEA 97 into the district's programming.

Hypothetical 3

School District C: This K-12 district is suburban, with a school enrollment of 2,000 students. There is a superintendent, an associate superintendent, two assistant superintendents, seven principals, and two directors. The school district has an excellent tax base. Very little change has taken place due to the compliancy. For the past five years, the district has had an increasing number of parents become disgruntled with the program for gifted students, for students with disabilities, and for minority students.

Discussion

Reactive or proactive, how would a typical district deal with the problems depicted in the situations described above? The nature of planning in educational settings has been developmental in nature. Every school district plans, but it is the nature and depth of the planning that must be analyzed. Too often, districts have entered the strategic planning mode without understanding the dynamics of quality and change. If a true planning paradigm is to become part of a school district culture, a broader definition needs to be implemented. In each of the situations, the school districts are faced with decisions that will alter their direction.

If, for example, School District A decides to fund the technology plan rather than the ESL program, language problems will arise within the classroom. School District B has not fulfilled its obligation to meet the standards established under the reauthorized IDEA in 1997. The district could face the curtailment of federal and state funding if the standards are not met. In the case of District C, parents are unhappy with the educational programming for the gifted, special needs, and minority students. Planning for any group of students other than the programming currently offered will take a great deal of study. The planning for these special groups may affect the entire district.

It does not matter if a district is considered poor or wealthy; the end can be the same. Without strategic planning, the potential for concern is just a problem away.

Planning as a useful tool for all school districts has been magnified as the 21st century has unfolded. The hypothetical situations listed above represent only a few of the increasing number of issues that face school districts. In each of the hypotheticals, the districts faced problems that encompass more than planning. Each organization needed a quality management process, a propensity for change, and a strategic planning process. Strategic planning without a foundation based on quality and change has a tendency to loose its potential effectiveness, because the school culture was not prepared to deal with the planning effort.

Strategic planning is an intense process that must be developed in light of a philosophy of quality and change. Figure 6.1 depicts such a coordinated process. In it, an organization establishes the foundation for quality, integrates it with an understanding of change, and implements the final process through strategic planning. However, school districts often implement strategic planning without establishing a foundation. Because of the intense nature of strategic planning, it often fails to produce the expected results. Once a district has implemented a quality philosophy and established the organization's ability to accept change as a way of life, it is a much easier task to begin the strategic planning process.

The Process of Strategic Planning

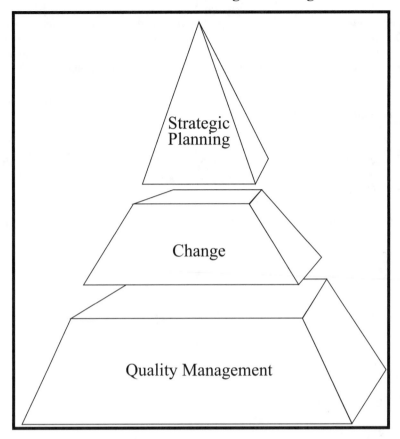

Figure 6-1

Quality Management

What is quality? Generally, quality is thought of as a predefined standard against which products and services are measured. In a quality management philosophy, the customer defines the quality. In a quality program, the organization meets the customer's needs and requirements on a consistent basis (Hodge-Williams, Wynn, & Godsey, 1998). Quality management is a strategic, integrated management system for achieving customer satisfaction. It involves everyone employed by the organization and uses quantitative methods to continuously improve processes.

Senge (1999) defines the quality process in the following manner:

"The roots of the quality movement lie in assumptions about people, organizations, and management that have one unifying theme: to make continual learning a way of organizational life, especially improving the performance of the organization as a total system. This can only be achieved by breaking with the traditional authoritarian command-and-control hierarchy—where the top thinks and the local acts—and by merging thinking and acting at all levels."

The concept of *Total Quality Management* (TQM) was developed by A. Edward Deming to meet the needs of industry. Deming developed the following 14-point process that summarizes TQM (1986).

1.   Create constancy of purpose for improvement of product and service.

2.   Adopt the new philosophy.

3.   Cease dependence on mass inspection.

4.   End the practice of doing business on price tag alone.

5.   Improve constantly and forever the system of production and service.

6.   Institute programs of training.

7.   Institute leadership.

8.   Drive out fear.

9.   Break down barriers between staff areas.

10. Eliminate slogans, exhortations, and targets for the workforce.

11. Eliminate numerical quotas.

12. Remove barriers to the pride and joy of workmanship.

13. Institute a vigorous program of education and retraining.

14. Take action to accomplish the transformation.

The principles that Deming developed are applicable to education. Bonstingl (1992) applied Deming's principles to the school setting in the following manner. A summary of four of the 14 is presented here.

1. Create constancy of purpose for improvement of product and purpose:
   Schools must focus on helping students to maximize their own potentials through continuous improvement of teachers and students working together. Maximization of test scores and assessment symbols is less important than the progress inherent in the continuous learning process of each student.

2. Adopt the new philosophy:
   School leaders must adopt and fully support the new philosophy of continuous improvement through greater empowerment of teacher-student teams. Cynical application of the new philosophy, with the sole intent of improving district-wide test scores, destroys interpersonal trust, which is essential to success.

3. Improve constantly and forever the system of production and service:
   School administrators must create and maintain the context in which teachers are empowered to make continuous progress in the quality of their learning and other aspects of personal development, while they learn valuable lessons from (temporary) failures.

4. Institute a vigorous program of education and retraining:
   All of the school's people benefit from encouragement to enrich their education by exploring ideas and interests beyond the boundaries of their professional and personal worlds.

At the heart of the quality process is the PDCA cycle (Plan-Do-Check-Act). The PDCA cycle is a never-ending cycle of experimentation. The Japanese design pilot tests so that the pilot is repeated many times with many people involved. Each time the cycle is repeated, new knowledge is gained. When it is time to implement the changes organizationally, people adopt the practice rapidly because of the large-scale involvement.

Senge (1999) believes that there are four important tools that need to be implemented into the organization's thinking:

1. *Building shared vision.* There is no substitute for organizational resolve, conviction, commitment, and clarity of intent. They create the need for learning and the collective will to learn. Without shared vision, significant learning occurs only when there are crises.

2. *Personal mastery*. An organization that is continually learning how to create its future must be made up of individuals who are continually learning how to create more of what truly matters to them.

3. *Working with mental models*. Organizations become frozen in inaccurate and disempowering views of reality because they lack the capability to see their assumptions and to continually challenge and improve them.

4. *Team learning*. Ultimately, the learning that matters is the learning of groups of people who need one another to act, which is the real meaning of "team". The only problem is that people have lost the ability to talk with one another. Most of the time, they are limited to discussion. What is also needed is dialogue, which comes from the Greek *dia-logos*, meaning that when a group of people talk with one another, the meaning (logos) moves through (dia) them.

Obisesan (1999) studied the effect that *Quality Management* (QM) had on three suburban school districts. The findings suggested that QM influenced administrators' motivations for change in key areas of academics, improved discipline, improved budget utilization, improved communications, enhanced collaboration, and increased emphasis on human resources development.

Peters and Waterman (1982) studied excellence in the workplace, determining that there are eight attributes that characterize outstanding companies. These attributes are:

1. *A bias for action* – The organization is proactive. It does not allow itself to be stifled by inaction, but gets on with solving the problem.

2. *Close to the customer* – Quality, service, and reliability are the hallmarks of these organizations. They listen to the customer and make adjustments when necessary.

3. *Autonomy and entrepreneurship* – The organization fosters innovation through leadership development; everyone has something to contribute.

4. *Productivity through people* – The organization fosters respect for the individual; everyone is a source of ideas that help to promote a better company.

5. *Hands-on, value-driven* – The organization has a basic philosophy that everyone understands and fosters. Management tests the philosophy by meeting with and visiting each of the organizations' subunits.

6. *Stick to the knitting* – The organization stays close to the business that it knows. It does not stray from the organizations mission.

7. *Simple form, lean staff* – The organization's top-level management is lean, allowing for communications flow.

8. *Simultaneous loose-tight properties* – The organization believes in autonomy to the lowest level and at the same time strives for specific rules that everyone must follow.

James Law (1993) indicates that TQM is not a program or a short-term solution. He gives six elements that are critical in making TQM successful. The six steps are: envision, audit, plan, train, implement, and monitor.

Change

The general format that districts have followed to initiate change usually begins with strategic planning, but as Fullan (1993) states, "Vision and Strategic Planning come later—Premature visions are planning blind. "

With critical attention by the media and political entities, and with parental needs and perceptions, it was inevitable that many cures would be offered to "fix" the ills of the public school system. Business and the media have tried to make parents critics of their children's schools by helping them exercise choices, ask questions, and make demands that insure their children's futures (Grace 1995). Organizations like the Conference Board of Canada (1991) envision the work place as high-tech, with employees highly skilled in communication and cooperation, and having the ability to take the initiative to solve problems. To do this, the Conference Board believes that schools must drastically change the way they educate their students.

Caldwell and Spinks (1992) point to an educational market that is occupied with image, public relations, and competition. Figure 6.2 indicates a sample of issues facing schools in the beginning of the 21st century. Each one of the issues carries with it the potential to create chaos in the leadership and management of a school district. Districts and individual schools face the dynamic of change in the same manner. Saranson (1990) and Schargel (1994) share the view that it is difficult for an individual school to change, and that even if a change is made by an individual school, it does not last. Individual school change does not last because of a lack of change to the overall organization.

Issues Affecting School Districts

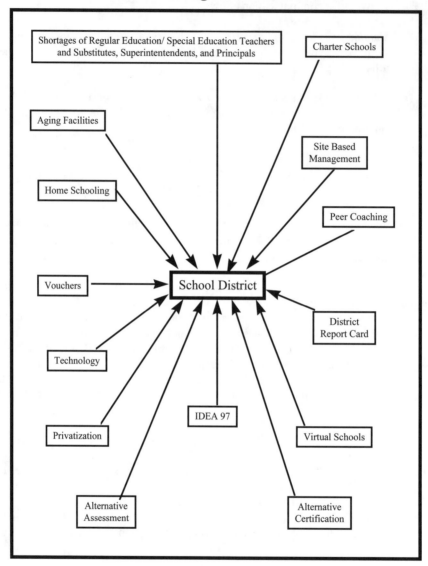

Figure 6-2

Issues Affecting School Districts

In the very near future, school districts will be faced with some or all of the following problems depicted in Figure 6-2.

- Shortages – It is estimated that toward the end of the first decade of the new millenium, there will be a need for 2,000,000 teachers, 350,000 special education teachers, and a shortfall in the area of substitute teachers. It is further estimated that a majority of superintendents are of retirement age. A shortfall in principals is also being projected.

- Charter schools – Is the local district legally responsible for the potential issues that may face charter schools?

- Lack of training – site-based management's weakness revolves around a lack of training on the part of administrators and faculty.

- Peer coaching – As the profession approaches losing large numbers because of retirement, there will be too few mentors to fulfill the demand established by negotiated agreements.

- District report cards – In the area of special education, many districts will struggle with the accommodations necessary to fulfill the mandates of federal law.

- Virtual schools – Will schools have the flexibility to meet the growing use of instruction via the Internet?

- Alternative certification – Can/will states utilize alternate certification to meet the growing demand for teachers and administrators?

- IDEA 97 – Can school districts offer the changes necessary to meet the requirements of this law?

- Alternative assessment – Do districts have the ability to offer alternative assessment to meet the varied needs of their students?

- Privatization – What will the effect of private enterprise be on public schools?

- Technology – Is technology being used to its fullest potential in the public schools? If not, how can a district justify the expense?

- Vouchers – Political parties are pressing the use of vouchers. What will be the effect on the receiving school and the sending school?

- Home schooling – A rapidly growing trend, home schooling may offer legal tests to the local school district.

- Aging facilities – School facilities are aging. What will the effect of the aging facilities be on school budgets?

Planning

Higher education and K-12 districts began to take notice of planning when the Program Evaluation and Review Technique became popular in the late 60s. PERT, as it became known, was used to "fast-track" the building of atomic-powered submarines. The process defined each aspect of a program, designating a time for completion and the personnel responsible for the particular part of the program. This and other planning initiatives, however, were short lived for most of the school districts in the U.S.

In 1983, with the publication of *A Nation At Risk* (National Commission of Excellence in Education), school districts began to feel pressure to improve. The constant focus upon school improvement from the media, political entities, and business forced school districts to begin programs to improve academic standards. Thus was born the strategic planning movement.

Simerly (1998) reviewed the literature on planning and determined that there are four types of planning. He describes them in the following manner:

➢ Turnaround Emergency Planning (crisis planning) – This is typically used in emergency situations.

➢ Contemplative/Philosophical Planning – This is often referred to as "blue sky" planning, where participants are asked to contemplate the past, present, and future. This is often used as a brainstorming activity.

➢ Futuristic Scenario Planning (Visioning) – This type of planning asks the participants to peer into the future by looking at various scenarios.

➢ Strategic Long-Range Planning – This type of planning is the most action-oriented type of planning. It calls for specific accountability measures. Specific objectives are developed around large, generalized goals.

Although school districts had always planned, the planning usually consisted of the type of planning that Simerly (1998) referred to as "Turnaround Emergency Planning," also referred to as "reactive planning". An emergency would occur, and the district prepared a plan to alleviate the issue. Some school districts went farther and established committees to contemplate the future and make plans to meet that future. With this emphasis on planning came a series of potential processes that included Management by Objectives (MBO), Planning Programming Budgeting Systems (PPBS), and Strategic Planning. School districts were searching for a process that would provide a framework for decision-making and managing an effective organization. Of these planning initiatives, strategic planning offered the most effective proactive design.

Most strategic planning programs have four general phases: the design phase, the implementation phase, the monitoring phase, and the measurement phase. Cook (1988) went a step farther by presenting a plan that he defines as:

> *"...an effective combination of both a process and discipline which, if faithfully adhered to, produces a plan characterized by originality, vision, and realism. This discipline includes the vital ingredients of the plan itself; the process is the organizational dynamic through which the vital ingredients are derived"* (p.93).

What are the components of a strategic plan? Although there are variations on the theme, the general format depicted in Figure 6-3 is consistent across processes. The process begins after the district has developed a foundation of quality management and has put into practice the aspects of change necessary to allow strategic planning to be successful.

The process develops as follows:

1. The process begins with an overview of strategic planning to the board of education by the superintendent. It is essential that both the board and the superintendent take ownership of the process.

2. A very important step when considering the longevity of the process is the approval of a policy on strategic planning.

3. It is important to appoint a facilitator to organize and manage the development and implementation of the planning process. A district should consider hiring an organization that specializes in the strategic planning process or have district personnel trained to be facilitators.

4. It is imperative that the initial core strategic planning committee include the board of education, the superintendent, parent leaders, teacher leaders, and community leaders. Although the initial meeting calls for a great deal of dedicated time over

three or more days, this is important to the development of the end product. Although there will be parent, teacher, and community involvement, it is important to communicate with parents, teachers, and community leaders who are not members of the planning committee. Mason and Mitroff (1981) believe that before strategic planning can begin, it is necessary for the organization to agree on a set of assumptions.

Following is a list of assumptions typically incorporated as a guide for the strategic planning committee:

- Strategic planning is a continuous planning process; it is not an event.

- It is essential that tasks be assigned to individuals within the organization. This will decentralize problem solving, an important part of the strategic planning process.

- Conflict within the organization must be expected as problem solving is decentralized.

- Staff development is an important part of the process as one means of preparing faculty and staff to implement the strategic plan.

5. The first, and sometimes the most, exasperating part of the process is the development of a vision, beliefs, and a mission statement. This can be exasperating in that the development of the vision, beliefs, and mission statement depends on focus and a large amount of time.

   a. *Vision* – The strategic planning committee determines what should and could be. Where does the planning committee believe the district should be in 3 to 5 years?

   Example: The Shenandoah Valley School District's vision is for the district to operate as a cohesive unit, following the philosophy of quality, change, and strategic management, in the next 3 to 5 years.

   b. *Beliefs* – The belief statements are indicative of the values of the school district.

Example: We, the members of the Shenandoah Valley School District, believe that parents have the inherent right to be a partner in district decisions and in measuring the results of these decisions.

    c. *Mission Statement* – The mission statement is a shared vision of the students, community, staff, administration, and board of education about the ultimate meaning of education in the district.

        Example: The mission of the Shenandoah Valley School District is to prepare students to become ethically responsible citizens and to provide them with the skills necessary to meet the challenges of the 21st century.

6. Assessment of the strengths and areas of growth is a critical part of the process. Each of the following areas should be assessed for strengths and areas of growth:

- Special Programs

- Curriculum

- Instructional Support

- Human Resources

- Business Services

- Support Services

Example: Special Programs would include the special education program, gifted and talented program, special reading program, alternative learning program, and adult continuing education program. A template would be developed for each area and would include a status report and long-range plans for the program that would include date-sensitive requirements, and potential costs.

7. When the strengths and areas of growth have been determined, a district profile is developed.

8. From the district profile, a set of priority goals is determined. This is an area that often causes problems in the strategic planning process. Vested interest groups and internal power struggles can disrupt the process at this point by allowing for a

large number of priorities to be considered significant. In Step 6, a general overview of each program, along with long-range plans, was developed. It is in Step 8 that the district must determine what takes priority.

9. The evaluation plan helps to determine if the goal has been achieved. It also helps to determine if the specific goal should be continued in a revised strategic plan.

10. In this step, the operational plan is developed from the list of priorities. This is the master plan for the district, which includes dates for review and revision.

11. At a time specified in the operational plan, an update meeting is held for the strategic planning committee and the general public. Some of the main agenda items for this meeting are updates to the community on:

    - Achievement of goals/if achieved, should the goal be carried forward to the revised strategic plan?

    - Goals that were not achieved/reasons for not achieving the goal/what can be done to eliminate the issue of not achieving the particular goal?

12. At the conclusion of the update assessment meeting, a new district profile is developed and prepared for the board of education and the general public.

13. The strategic plan is now into its first year. This is an important milestone. At this meeting, it is essential to summarize the entire strategic planning process for the board and the general public.

14. To complete the cycle and to insure the longevity of the planning policy and the process itself, it is crucial to train new board members, district personnel, and community members in strategic planning.

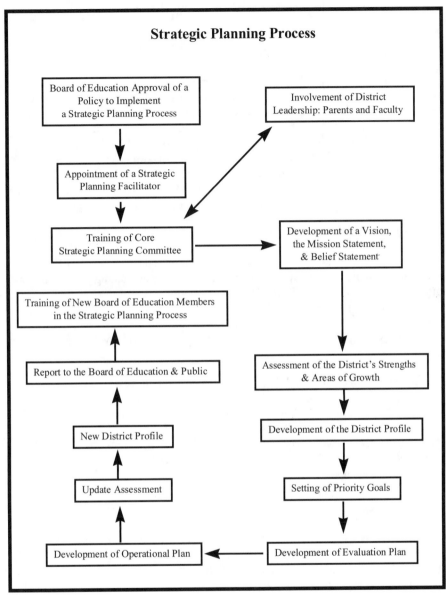

Figure 6-3

Strategic planning and total quality management (or total quality or TQM) are tools that are complementary to the change process. The reader should take a moment to review the hypotheticals that introduced this chapter and to use the concepts discussed in this chapter to determine how to respond to the scenarios. Note any difference resulting from the ideas presented here.

Program Evaluation

The final segment of this chapter examines the issue of program evaluation and provides the practicing administrator with a selection of processes that may be utilized at the district or site level to assess the extent to which programs are meeting expectations. In the words of Michael Scriven, "Evaluation is the process of determining the merit, worth, and value of things and evaluations are the products of that process" (1991). If the planning process discussed earlier is to meet with success, there is a need to take the view of Scriven and other proponents of program evaluation into account. In the context offered by those cited here, program evaluation is utilized as a decision-making tool. Evaluations provide data that will allow administrators to decide whether programs will be continued as is, altered, or eliminated.

Popham (1993) advances the idea that "There are different, defensible ways to carry out educational evaluations" (p. 22). Among the ways discussed here will be those advocated by Ralph Tyler, Elliot Eisner, Michael Scriven, Robert Stake, Daniel Stufflebeam, James Sanders, and Egon Guba. The foundation of Tyler's scheme of evaluating educational programs is an outgrowth of the *Eight-Year Study*. It has as its major goal the desire to develop, review, and revise curricula so as to reach a higher level of efficacy in instruction. His approach begins with the development of educational goals that should emerge from an analysis of three goal sources (students, society, and subject matter) and two goal screens (psychology of learning and philosophy of education).

His approach to evaluation followed the steps listed below:

- Establish broad goals or objectives.
- Classify the goals or objectives.
- Define the objectives in behavioral terms.
- Find solutions in which the achievement of objectives can be shown.
- Develop or select measurement techniques.
- Collect performance data.
- Compare performance data with behaviorally stated objectives.

When there is a negative difference between performance and expectations, there is a need to modify the program to address the deficiency; then the evaluation cycle is repeated. For Tyler (1989), "The process of evaluation is essentially the process of determining to what extent the educational objectives are actually being realized by the program of curriculum and instruction" (p. 105-106). In essence, he would have educators look at what they want to accomplish and then evaluate how close they came to their objective via the instructional program.

A present-day adaptation of the Tylerian approach would call for educators to:

- Identify the major purpose for education established by stakeholders.
- Select academic standards from subject area specialist.
- Organize these standards into instructional experiences that benefit the student population.
- Evaluate the instructional program to determine the extent to which the articulated purposes and standards have been met.
- Revise the program and begin again.

The concepts for evaluation offered by Tyler are reinforced, in essence, by Elliot Eisner in *The Educational Imagination: On the Design and Evaluation of School Programs* (3rd ed, 1994). Specifically, his process advocates the following: a) diagnosis, b) revision, c) comparison, d) anticipation of educational needs, and e) determination if objectives have been met. This five-step process is based on the concept that *". . . evaluations are used in education to provide a wide variety of functions"* (p. 171, 1994). The sources of the educational objectives for Eisner again mirrors Tyler in that outcomes are student and subject-area specific. The third dimension of Eisner is teacher-specific or program-specific outcomes.

Stufflebeam's Systematic Evaluation

In the 1970s Daniel Stufflebeam introduced the CIPP model for the evaluation of educational and social agency programs. The process utilized by Stufflebeam and his associates called for evaluators to determine the congruency between organizational goals and performance. CIPP defines evaluation as the process of delineating, obtaining, and providing useful information for judging decision alternatives. The acronym CIPP represents four types of evaluation:

1) **Context evaluation**: Its purpose is to identify the strengths and weaknesses of a program to provide direction for improvement.

2) **Input evaluation**: This element is designed to prescribe a program by which to bring about necessary change and to consider alternative programs that will assist in meeting the program's direction.

3) **Process evaluation**: This component calls for the ongoing monitoring of the plan of implementation.

4) **Product evaluation**: The last step calls for the evaluator "to measure, interpret, and judge the attainments of a program" (p. 176).

CIPP was designed to foster an improvement orientation to program evaluation. The CIPP model is characterized as having a "systems view" of education; that is, it is concerned with "providing ongoing evaluation services to decision makers in an institution" (p. 165). The purpose of this approach is to help programs work better toward the intended purposes of such programs. Within this context, the implementation of the CIPP strategy provides for institutional growth. and it helps those responsible for leading the organization to obtain feedback that may be used in a systematic fashion to help the organization meet it goals and objectives.

Stufflebeam provides an outline of the items to be addressed when designing an evaluation. The major components of that plan are listed in the Figure 6-4 below.

Outline for Designing an Evaluation	
Review of the Charge	1. Definition of the object of the evaluation 2. Identification of the client and audiences 3. Purposes of the evaluation 4. Type of evaluation 5. Principles of sound evaluation
Plan for Obtaining Information	1. The general strategy 2. Working assumptions to guide measurement, analysis, and interpretation 3. Collection of information 4. Organization of information 5. Analysis of information 6. Interpretation of findings
Plan for Reporting the Results	1. Preparation of reports 2. Dissemination of reports 3. Provision for follow-up activities
Plan for Administering the Study	1. Summarization of the evaluation schedule 2. Plan for meeting staff and resource requirements 3. Provisions of metaevaluation 4. Provisions for periodical updating of the evaluation design 5. Budget 6. Memorandum of agreement or contract

Figure 6-4

Institutional Self-Study

In *Evaluating Educational Program: The Need and the Response* (1976) Robert Stake analyzed the institutional self-study technique suggested by the National Study of School Evaluation (NSSE). His findings indicate that this technique had as its purpose a desire by staff to increase their effectiveness in the educational arena. This method asked faculty and staff to work in teams to set standards, benchmarks, etc., that would lead to improved performance and increased professionalism. The NSSE's 1997 and 1998 publications, *Indicators of School of Quality – Volume I: Schoolwide Indicators of Quality* and *Volume II*, which addresses program evaluation, continue the practice cited by Stake. The indicators of quality examined by the NSSE tool include:

1. Focusing on the quality work of students.

2. Focusing on the quality work of the school.

3. Putting the Indicators of School Quality to work on behalf of school improvement. Listed below are the Principles of Organizational Effectiveness of Schools of Quality as seen by NSSE:

Educational Agenda: Values, Beliefs, Mission, and Goals

- The school facilitates a collaborative process in developing its vision, beliefs, mission. and goals. The process engages the school community in an in-depth study and assessment of important information sources (e.g., student assessment data, demographic data, environmental scanning, future trend information, workplace expectations, etc.).

- The school develops a shared vision, beliefs, and mission that define a compelling purpose and direction for the school.

- The school defines measurable goals, focused on improving student learning.

Leadership for School Improvement

- The school promotes quality instruction by fostering an academic learning climate and actively supporting teaching and learning.

- The school develops schoolwide plans for improvement focused on student performance.

- The school employs effective decision making that is data driven, researched based, and collaborative.

- The school monitors progress in improving student achievement and instructional effectiveness through a comprehensive assessment system and continuous reflection.

- The school provides skillful stewardship by ensuring management of the organization, operations, and resources of the school for a safe, efficient, and effective learning environment.

Community-building

- The school fosters community-building conditions and working relationships with the school.

- The school extends the school community through collaborative networks of support for student learning.

Culture of Continuous Improvement and Learning

- The school builds skills and capacity for improvement through comprehensive and ongoing professional development programs focused on the school's goals for improvement.

- The school creates the conditions that support productive change and continuous improvement (NSSE, p. 149).

The evaluation component of this method allows the administration, faculty, staff, and stakeholders to assess the extent to which the principles, goals, standards, etc., established by the school have been met. NSSE utilizes a variety of Likert-type scales to gather input from interested parties, including administration, students, teachers, parents, and community members. These computer-graded assessment instruments are tabulated and returned quickly so that the results may be used to make decisions about the programs and practices in place.

The National Study of School Evaluation would provide its clients with an instrument similar to the one in Figure 6-5.

Other means of support are available from numerous sources. The Center for Prevention Research & Development and The Association of Illinois Middle-Level Schools (1998), for example, provide their partners with the opportunity to conduct a self-study utilizing input from students, administrators, teachers, parents, and other stakeholders. The comprehensive process has as its major focus the improvement of the middle school program and all of its components. The chart in Figure 6-6 demonstrates some of the elements addressed in the self-study.

Evaluation Instrument Designed by the National Study of School Evaluation

Community Opinion Inventory	SA	A	N	D	SD	NA
School Program Awareness The community receives the information it needs about the school's programs.						
Responsiveness to the Community 1. School board members represent our community well.						
2. Schools are appropriately available for community functions.						
Quality of the Instructional Program 1. Students receive adequate instruction in the basic skills.						
2. Our school's programs help students to understand and get along with other people.						

SA = Strongly Agree   A = Agree   N = Neutral   D = Disagree   SD = Strongly Disagree   NA = Does Not Apply or Do Not Know

Figure 6-5

Elements of a Self-Study of Classroom Activities and Methods

In my classes:	Never	Several Times a Year	Monthly	Several Times a Month	Weekly	Several Times a Week	Daily
1. Students read and discuss newspaper articles.							
2. Students revise their reports and papers.							
3. Students participate in cooperative learning.							
4. Students work on group projects.							
5. Students work on development of materials/projects for portfolios.							
6. Students search the World Wide Web for information for class.							
7. Students complete their homework using computers.							

Figure 6-6

Conclusion

This chapter examined the issues related to educational planning and program evaluation. The role of strategic planning in the life of an educational institution is considered paramount to the success of a school district. The systematic nature of the planning, as advocated by Senge, Cook, and others, provided the school administrator with a template that would permit the goals and strategies of the district to permeate the entire organization.

The quality of the school programs is also of concern to the school administrator. Total Quality Management, as proposed by Deming and others, provides the educational administrator with a mindset that is predisposed to improving the quality of school programs. This will allow directors of educational programs to maintain consistently high levels of quality throughout the organization.

The items addressed above, coupled with evaluation techniques, will assist the school organization in meeting its goals. The prudent administrator takes into account strategic planning, total quality management, the change process, and program evaluation in the planning and improvement cycle and utilizes these techniques to improve the school organization.

Exercise

Educational Issues and Concerns

Playing the role of members of the following groups, identify major issues and concerns you have with the educational program as executed in your school/school district. Using brainstorming techniques, work with colleagues to list as many of the issues and concerns as possible. After the designated time period, rank the issues and concerns in priority order. Select the top five to address in extended discussion. In the extended discussion, speak to the following:

- What is the primary issue; whom does it affect primarily and secondarily?
- What is/are the most immediate solution?
- What is/are the long term solutions?
- What are there financial considerations?
- Who can change the situation?
- What other issues are associated with the issue or concern?

Stakeholders:

Parents

Community

Teachers

Career Service

School Administrators

District Administrators

School Board Members

Business Community

Competing Schools and Districts

Politicians

Other Stakeholders Not Identified

References

Bonstingl, J. J., (1992). *Schools of quality*. Alexandria, VA: Association for Supervision and Curriculum Development.

Caldwell, B., Spinks, J. (1992). *Leading the self-managing school*. Philadelphia: Farmer Press.

Cook W.J. (1988). *Strategic planning for America's schools*. Montgomery, AL: Cambridge Management Group, Inc.

Conference Board of Canada (1991). *Employability skills profile* Ottawa, Ontario, Canada: National Bureau and Education Center.

Center for Prevention Research and Development and Association of Illinois Middle-Level Schools (1998). *1998/1999 school improvement self-study staff survey*. Urbana, IL: University of Illinois.

Deming, W.E. (1986). *Out of the crisis*. Cambridge, MA: Massachusetts Institute of Technology Center for Advanced Engineering Study.

Eisner, E. W. (1994). *The educational imagination: On the design and evaluation of school programs* (3rd ed.). New York: MacMillan.

Fitzpatrick, K. A. (1997). *Indicators of schools of quality*. Schaumburg, IL: National Study of School Evaluation.

Fullan, M. (1993). *Change forces*. London, U.K.: Falmer Press.

Grace, G. (1995, April). *The changing culture of educational leadership in England*. Paper presented to the annual meeting of the American Educational Research Association, San Francisco, CA.

Gredler, M. E. (1996). *Program evaluation*. Englewood Cliffs, NJ: Prentice-Hall.

Guba, E. G. & Lincoln, Y. S. (1981). *Effective evaluation*. San Francisco: Jossey-Bass.

Hodge-Williams, J., Wynn, J. F., Godsey C.M. (1998*). Quality-centered/team- focused management.* Washington, DC: Child Welfare League of America.

Joint Committee on Standards for Educational Reform. *The program evaluation standards: How to assess evaluations of educational programs* (2nd ed.). Thousand Oaks, CA: Sage.

Law, J.E. (1993, October) How to make total quality management work for you. *School Business Affairs*, *59*(10) p.48-51.

Mason, R. O., & Mitroff, I. I. (1981). *Challenging strategic planning assumptions*. New York: John Wiley and Sons.

National Commission on Excellence (1993). *A Nation at Risk*.

National Study of School Evaluation (1997). *Indicators of Schools of Quality: Vol. 1 – Schoolwide Indicators of Quality*. Schaumburg, IL: K. Fitzpatrick, Project Director.

National Study of School Evaluation (1998). *Indicators of Schools of Quality: Vol. 2 – Program Level Evaluation*. Schaumburg, IL: K. Fitzpatrick, Project Director.

Fitzpatrick, K. A. (1997). *Indicators of school quality*. Schaumburg, IL: National Study of School Evaluation.

Obisesan, A. A. (1999, April). *Management and system change in three suburban public school districts*. Paper presented at the Annual Meeting of the American Educational Research Association, Montreal, Canada.

Peters, T.J. and Waterman, R.H. (1982). *In search of excellence*. New York: Harper Row:

Popham, W. J. (1993). *Educational evaluation* (3rd.ed.) Boston: Allyn and Bacon.

Popham, W. J. (1993). *Classroom assessment: What teachers need to know*. (2nd. ed.) Boston, MA: Allyn and Bacon.

Sarason, S.B. (1990). *The predictable failure of educational reform*. San Francisco, CA: Jossey-Bass.

Schargel, P.F. (1994). *Transforming education through total quality manage management*. Princeton Junction, NJ: Eye on Education.

Scriven, M. (1991). *Evaluation thesaurus* (4th ed.) Newbury Park, CA: Sage

Senge, P. (1999, November/December) It's the learning: The real lesson of the quality movement. *The Journal for Quality and Participation*.

Shore, C.A. (1981, Fall) PERT philosophy and the curriculum supervisor. *Education*.

Simerly, R.G. (1998, Winter) An easy-to-implement strategic long-range planning model. *The journal of continuing higher education* .

Stilian, G. N. (1962). *PERT: A new management planning and control technique*. New York: American Management Association.

Stake, R. E. (1976). *Evaluating educational programs: The need and response: a collection of resource materials*. Paris, France: Organization for Economic Co-operation and Development. (Washington, D.C.: OECD Publication Center.

Stufflebeam, D. L. & Shinkfield, A. J. (1985). *Systematic evaluation: A self-instructional guide to theory and practice*. Boston: Kluwer-Nijhoff Publishing.

Tyler, R. W. (1949). *Basic principles of curriculum and instruction*. Chicago, IL: The University of Chicago Press.

Tyler, R. W. (1989). *Educational evaluation: classic works of Ralph Tyler*(G. F. Madaus and D. Stufflebeam, eds) Boston: Kluwer Academic.

Worthen, B. R., Sanders, J. R., & Fitzpatrick, J. L. (1997). *Program evaluation: Alternative approaches and practical guides*. (2nd ed.) White Plains, NY: Longman

Chapter 7
Administrative Assessment

Jack Klotz

This chapter reviews the roles and functions of school principals and methods used for assessing their successes.

Roles and Functions of the School Principal

Preparation programs for the training of future educational administrators have existed for a considerable period of time. Yet the question remains today as it has throughout the years: are such graduate programs specializing in the area of educational administration really preparing future school site administrators to assume their place within the field as functioning educational leaders, capable of not only leading teachers and others in delivering quality educational endeavors for students, but also of functioning as true instructional leaders? In the early days of school leadership, principals tended to be selected from the ranks of teachers who were perceived to possess leadership skills within the classroom that were thought to be transferable to the principal's office. Whether justified or not, in some instances, local school policy makers reflecting the values and mores of their communities selected individuals to become school principals who were perceived as exemplifying those same held values and mores.

With the publication of the report *A Nation at Risk* (1983), demands for reform in the preparation of educational leaders heightened across the United States. Indeed, the report brought into focus the need to recognize the vital role school principals play in improving student academic performance (Heck, 1996). Certainly within and outside the field of educational administration, the study of leadership and its associated traits or characteristics has existed for some time. As is exemplified by the *Management Process Study* begun in 1956 by AT&T, and which attempted to identify those variables most closely associated with effective leadership in the business field, those characteristics that were desegregated from analyzed data were the following:

- General effectiveness: overall staff perception of decision-making, organization and planning, creativity, and human relations skills
- Administrative skills: skill in organizing, planning, and decision-making
- Interpersonal skills: human relations skills, behavior flexibility, and personal impact
- Control of feelings: tolerance of uncertainty and resistance to stress
- Intellectual ability: scholastic aptitude and range of interest
- Work-oriented motivation: primacy of work and inner work standards
- Passivity: ability of delay gratification, delay need for security, and delay need for advancement
- Dependency: need for superior approval, need for peer approval and goal flexibility.

According to Byham (1970), the AT&T study became the basis for most, if not all, of the subsequent efforts to identify data leading to the support for the concept of "assessment centers" within both the business and educational arenas. In 1974, Stogdill reviewed 163 trait studies and identified the following eight traits as being associated with organizational leaders:

Strogdills 8 Traits of Organizational Leaders

- Self-confidence and personal identity
- Strong drive for responsibility and task completion
- Persistence in the pursuit of goals
- Adventurous attitude and originality in problem-solving
- Initiative in social situations
- Acceptance of consequences for decisions and actions
- Ability to influence the behavior of others
- Ability to structure interaction to the purpose at hand.

Figure 7-1

Yet when specific attention is given to the role and function of school principals, additional considerations/responsibilities surface as role demands. Gottfredson and Hybl (1987) explored the role function expectations for school principals and identified 14 specific tasks/functions. Their findings were drawn from input from over 1,100 functioning school principals working in urban, rural, and suburban settings. The role functions perceived by the respondents as key expectations held for them by their superiors, teachers, and community are:

Gottfredson and Hybl's 14 Role Functions

1. Observation and providing feedback
2. Providing staff direction
3. Planning and action
4. Interacting with students
5. Keeping current
6. Instructional management
7. Parent and community relations
8. Personnel management
9. Policy development
10. Attending to school system interaction
11. Coping with disorder
12. Co-curricular activities
13. Budget management
14. Union negotiations

Figure 7-2

Of these 14 role functions for school principals, the first three were identified as very important, while numbers four through eight were listed as of average importance, and items nine through 14 were seen as being below average in perceived level of importance.

According to Haller, Brent, and McNamara (1997), during the 1980s, a number of reports addressed the notion of "excellence" in education. All of these reports concluded that American schools suffered from numerous ills, although the remedies proposed differed somewhat. Nevertheless, perhaps the most common recommendation was that if schools were to be improved, principals would have to become effective instructional leaders (p. 222).

By 1994, 45 states required prospective school leaders to obtain at least a master's degree in educational administration prior to assuming the role responsibilities of a school administrator (ibid). Additionally, during this time, many professional associations began to call for significant increases in the preparation required of future school leaders (principals).

In an attempt to validate the quality of future school principals to meet the role responsibilities and expectations subscribed for school principals, the NASSP (National Association of Secondary School Principals) developed its "Principals Assessment Center Program." This process has existed for nearly 3 decades and has assessed, during that time, thousands of school personnel for selection and placement in principalships nationally. As the name implies, "assessment centers" were designed to measure skills that were related to the principal's world of work and how to identify those individuals perceived capable of performing effectively in that role (McCleary and Ogawa, 1989). Engel (1989) noted that research at that time also indicated that principal preparation programs were often viewed as falling short of teaching the skills identified as important to effective principal performance and also listed within the parameters of the NASSP assessment center model. As the concept of the viability of assessment centers expanded, numerous such assessment centers became scattered across the United States, reaching from Maine to California. Indeed, by 1989, 25 such centers were operating under the auspices of the NASSP.

As the model evolved, the assessment center process was comprised of six exercises: two leaderless group exercises, two in-basket simulations, a fact-finding exercise, and a personal interview (ibid). During the assessment process, 6 trained assessors observed 12 participants as they completed the various exercises over a 2-day period. Simulation situations were designed to measure and validate specified skill levels based on a phenomenological model, i.e., measurement of performance in simulated situations that becomes the basis for predicting leadership behavior in an actual work setting, such as a principalship. Following the completion of the process, the team of assessors reviewed the performance of each participant and then drafted a written report on each candidate. Each candidate was rated on 12 performance skill dimensions, as well as his/her overall performance. Performance profiles were written for each candidate containing ratings and descriptions of the evidence considered by the assessment team in reaching their conclusions (ratings).

Twelve specific performance dimensions were designed to evaluate and predict candidate performance as a potential school principal and were dispersed among four specified skill areas, namely: 1) administrative skills, 2) interpersonal skills, 3) communications skills, and 4) personal dimensions. The following represents a brief description of these performance dimensions and is taken from the NASSP's Assessor's Manual:

NASSP Performance Dimensions			
Administrative Skills	**Interpersonal Skills**	**Communications**	**Personal Dimension**
Problem analysis—the ability to seek out relevant data and analyze complex information to determine the important elements of a problem situation; searching for information with a purpose.	**Leadership**—the ability to get others involved in solving problems; the ability to recognize when a group requires direction and to interact effectively with that group to guide it toward accomplishing a task.	**Oral communications**—the ability to make a clear oral presentation of facts and ideas.	**Range of interest**—competence to discuss a variety of subjects—educational, political, current events, economic, etc.; desire to actively participate in events.
Judgment—the ability to reach logical conclusions and make high quality decisions based on available information; skill in identifying educational needs and setting priorities; the ability to critically evaluate written communications.	**Sensitivity**—the ability to perceive the needs, concerns, and personal problems of others; skill in resolving conflicts; tact in dealing with persons from different backgrounds; the ability to deal effectively with people concerning emotional issues; knowing what information to communicate and to whom.	**Written Communications**—the ability to express ideas clearly in writing; to write appropriately for different audiences - students, teachers, parents, et al.	**Personal motivation**—the need to achieve in all activities attempted; evidence that work is important in personal satisfaction; the ability to be self-policing.
Organizational ability—the ability to plan, schedule, and control the work of others; skill in using resources in an optimal fashion; the ability to deal with a volume of paperwork and heavy demands on one's time.	**Stress tolerance** —the ability to perform under pressure and against opposition; the ability to think on one's feet.		**Educational values**—possession of well-reasoned educational philosophy; receptiveness to new ideas and change.
Decisiveness—the ability to recognize when a decision is required (disregarding the quality of the decision) and to act quickly on that decision.			

Figure 7-3

It has been argued that the NASSP Assessment Center offers two related advantages to school districts in the selection of principals, namely, a source of objective data on candidates and a basis for selection on the merit of individuals for the position of school principal. However, McCleary and Ogawa point out that

> "...*more is involved in the assignment of principals than whether or not candidates possess particular skills . . . [second], 'merit' involves the point in the selection process at which the assessment center is employed . . . school districts employ conventional formal and informal processes to select individuals for participation in the assessment center. Thus, the extent to which merit, even as narrowly defined by the assessment center, determines selection and appointment to a principalship is greatly compromised"*. (pp. 111-112)

Yet, in its defense, it must be stated that the assessment center model did provide a more useful source of data that could be utilized in the selection and ultimate assignment of school administrators than was previously available to school districts.

As Fletcher and Anderson (1998) pointed out, in the concept of assessment centers and their close relatives, development centers, viability has not been without its detractors. Indeed, as late as 1998, it was reported that 50 percent or more of major employers within the business community were still using this vehicle to screen and select management personnel. In the article *The Superficial Assessment*, Fletcher and Anderson state, *"Organizations might ask themselves whether they really need something that looks like an assessment center. If the demand or the resources are limited, the alternative is to use competency-based interview and psychometric tests. These can be nearly as good at predicting performance and if used properly, will probably be far cheaper and certainly more effective"* (p. 46). Fletcher and Anderson identified a number of factors that they found to be negatively associated with what they identified as the superficiality of some assessment centers. Fletcher and Anderson present the following negative influencing factors that are signs of superficial assessment:

Fletcher and Anderson's Signs of Superficial Assessment

- Lack of assessor training
- Plenty of glossy documentation, but little real written background or guidance from assessors
- Claims that they are assessing an all-encompassing range of competencies
- No clear rationale for the links between the exercises and the dimensions that are being assessed
- Short courses, usually lasting between a half day and a full day
- Perfunctory consideration of the candidates during the assessors' conference
- Absence of any validation or monitoring of ongoing effectiveness

---

Figure 7-4

Given the continued call for quality candidates to enter the dwindling ranks of educational site administrators, it is not hard to understand why many researchers and policy-makers have called for a reformation in how future principals are trained. As early as 1988, it was predicted that half of all current U.S. principals would retire within four or five years

(Klauke, 1988). Klotz and Daniel (1998) stated that as society and its schools change, if maximum educational outcomes are to be realized, methods for teaching students and for leading those who teach students must also change. Each generation of schooling offers its own challenges to school leaders. Wilson (1993) further exemplified this concern when he said, *"The preparation of school leaders for the 1990's and beyond must deal with the changing demographic and economic context of schooling, as well as the enduring problems of education for a democratic society"* (pp. 220-221).

To further emphasize the need for changes in the preparation of future school leaders, Merseth (1997) noted that educational administrators intending to practice in the 21st century need professional preparation that helps them work effectively in a world characterized by accelerating change, exploding knowledge, growing diversity, galloping technology, and increasing uncertainty. Such demands require preparation that not only equips administrators with cutting-edge knowledge but also with the capacity and appetite to continually improve their practice (p. 1). In the estimation of some (e.g. , Griffiths, Stout & Forsyth, 1988), the need for reform of administrator preparation programs was not only a good idea, but a critical one. In fact, some (e.g., Haller, Brent, & McNamara, 1997) even question the usefulness of administrative preparation as was currently being practiced. Murphy (1992) noted that it is "difficult" to assess and analyze the current state of administrative programs, for in doing so, one becomes "despondent." Thus, he asserts that the focus should be on radical change in an attempt to redirect the present course of practice.

The call for change in the preparation of future school leaders can be traced to such reports as the 1988 publication by the University Council for Educational Administration (UCEA) 's, a report entitled *Leaders for America's Schools* (Griffiths, Stout & Forsyth, 1988). Drawing on the recommendations of earlier movements, this report raised important questions about educational administrators and their role in managing reform efforts in school improvement. Specifically, the report questioned, " . . . whether the preparation of future school leaders needs to be redesigned, and what the roles of federal, state, and local policymakers, teacher organizations, and particularly institutions of higher education should be in these changes" (Jacobson & Conway, 1990, p. x).

Leaders for America's Schools contained seven chapters detailing the National Council on Education of Educational Administrators's (NCEEA) report on the condition of educational administration in the United States, and an additional 26 chapters presenting papers on related topics by various scholars in the field. In discussing the aim of the book, the editors noted:

> *The original idea was that these papers would present to the commissioners new ideas and alternatives to current American practice. In large part, this goal was achieved. The papers address the present critique of educational administration, theory and research in educational administration, practice, preparation programs, and international perspectives . . . An effort was made . . . to present viewpoints that might lead the Commissioners to question deeply held attitudes, opinions, and ideologies . . . . No doubt, some will view these*

proposals as radical while others will see them as a part of a continuum of change already occurring. The Commission appeals for an understanding of the seriousness of changes being asked of schools and their leaders. Policymakers and influentials throughout the country are asked for resolve and great urgency in meeting the task of reform in educational administration. (Griffiths et al., 1998, pp. xiv-xv)

When a decade had elapsed from the publication of *Leaders for America's Schools* (Griffiths et al., 1998), there had still been no shortage of attention to the reform of educational administrator preparation programs. For example, at least five professional associations have prepared full-length volumes expressing their policy statements regarding the preparation of school administrators (e.g. American Association of Colleges of Teachers Education, 1988; Ashbaugh & Kasten, 1992; Council of Chief School Officers, 1996; National Association of Elementary School Principals, (NAESP) 1991; National Policy Board for Educational Administration, 1993). Indeed, three additional full-length volumes have been written on the general topic: Daresh and Playko (1992) proposed a career-long model for education of school administrators, Murphy (1992) developed a philosophical basis for building preparation programs, and Jacobson and Conway (1990), in an edited work, presented views of a number of authors on the topic of administrator preparation.

Many other scholarly works on the topic of preparation of educational administrators exist. In 1998, Daniel and Southerland offered a categorized review of 98 works spanning the period of time from 1988 to 1998. According to the Daniel-Southerland categorizations, readings ranged in themes from documentations of innovative practices to calls for radical and systemic changes in programs for preparing administrators. The extant scholarly works represented a collective wisdom on the topic of administrator preparation, with focus placed on the continuation of a strong knowledge base for administrator training, a heightened focus on problem-centered learning and field-based experiences, and a renewed emphasis on the affective development of administrators.

To say the least, the many calls for reform have not fallen on deaf ears. In several states (e.g., North Carolina, Missouri, Mississippi, and Louisiana), efforts designed to reform administrator preparation programs have been mandated externally at the state level. In the state of Mississippi, for example, state standards (i.e., professional competencies) for school administrators were developed (Mississippi Department of Education, 1997) that closely mirrored the administrator standards developed by several of the national organizations (e.g., Council of Chief School Officers, 1996; National Policy Board for Educational Administration, 1993). In Mississippi, the state further mandated that all programs within its borders develop reconceptualized administrator preparation programs based on the recommendations of a statewide study group (Mississippi Administrator Preparation and Certification Task Force, 1994). These study group recommendations addressed a variety of program issues, including selection of candidates for programs, curricular guidelines, and development of assessments to rate student competencies during and upon exit from programs. Based on these statewide initiatives, six Mississippi institutions now have been given approval by the state to operate their reformatted administrator preparation programs.

Principals for the New Millennium

What, then, should reformatted instructional programs at universities look like in order to effectively prepare future school principals to lead others in the quest for improved school environments that enable students to achieve their potential? According to Behar-Horenstein (1995), models of training programs at the university level are exhibiting a "movement away from the . . . managerial, authoritarian, and top-down leadership styles that are typically associated with the science of administration" (p. 18). Others agree (Lumsden,1993; Milstein, 1993; Thompson, 1991; Thomson, 1992, 1993). Today, there is an observable transition toward collegial and empowering forms of leadership, which, according to Behar-Horenstein (1995), has been catalyzed by a reconceptualization of the principal's role to such an extent as to seek congruence between theory and what happens in "real world" school-based practice. Efforts to bring university programs into alignment with actual practice has been reflected in the development of group processing skills (Worner, 1994), participatory decision-making and consensus-building skills (Thurston, Cleft, & Schacht, 1993), reflective thinking (Gordon & Moles, 1994), and monitoring of principal candidates and newly appointed principals (Grand, 1991; Stakenas, 1994; Snyder, 1994, & Worner, 1994).

Transitions in the professional preparation of future school principals have coincided with significant programmatic changes at many different levels. First, according to Behar-Horenstein (1995) " . . . many post-secondary educational administration programs previously accentuated planning, facilities, buses, and budgets. Second, newly reconstituted departments have been renamed as departments of educational leadership or educational leadership and policy" (p. 19). Many of these newly configured programs have been designed to promote a "holistic" approach to preparing building principals. Such programs are attempting to train future principals to have the skills and abilities to empower local schools and their publics to come together for the purpose of having a strong impact on student academic accomplishment (Heck 1992; Krug, 1993; Rosenholtz, 1989). Current candidates for the principalship must be skilled in the school-based management model, which has significant implications relative to school principal accountability, supervision, and efforts to improve student achievement. Future principals are expected to have the ability to voice and lead others to a vision of what effective schools look like.

Further, principals must be able to function in disparate population settings. They must also possess the skills and abilities to provide leadership for teaching diverse age student populations and facilitating instructional change that accompanies inclusion efforts, and also be capable of overseeing the functioning of full-service school settings. Added to this list of expectations, Thurston et al. (1993) recommend that " . . . professional preparation programs should prepare leaders who are knowledgeable about child development and cultural and linguistic diversity, as well as the social and academic aspects of schooling . . . they further suggested that prospective principals participate in administrative internships and work with stakeholders, including teachers, teacher educators, community leaders, and politicians who are engaged in school improvement efforts" (p. 93). They further suggest that such individuals be skilled in writing, listening, speaking, and thinking, and that they possess the ability to be understood by their audiences.

Finally, when exploring the concept of the principal as an instructional leader, Whitaker (1997) observes that a review of the literature on effective schools was abundantly clear in its contention that, for such schools to exist, it was necessary for there to be an "effective principal." Accordingly, for such to be present, the principal has to be an individual that the instructional staff (teachers) look to for leadership. This orientation of the principal as an instructional leader has been the focus of educational research for over 20 years, according to Whitaker. The research is clear on the fact that part of being an instructional leader is for the principal to be highly visible. Niece (1983) found three major themes within a review of the qualitative research on effective instructional leaders, namely that such individuals were:

- people-oriented and interactive,
- able to function within a network of other principals, and
- found to have administrative practitioners who acted as mentors for them.

To add the previous findings, Smith and Andrews (1989) identified four areas of strategic interaction that were conducted by instructional leaders that lead to higher student achievement levels. In all cases, the instructional leaders were:

- a resource provider,
- an instructional resource,
- a communicator, and
- a visible presence.

As reported by Klotz and Daniel (1998), principals for the new millennium " . . . must be especially well-skilled in mobilizing teams of varied people and players to accomplish collaboratively the school's goals" (p. 9). *"Furthermore, the "pluralism of students, staff, and community requires school leadership appreciative of and capable of working with others from diverse cultures, ethnicities, and perspectives with particular understanding, sensitivity, and commitment to a concept of inclusivity for meeting the cognitive, social, emotional, and physical needs of an increasingly diverse student and external population. Indeed, today's school leader must be committed to moral, ethical leadership that sets the tone for establishing school as a "community of learners" (p. 9), wherein mutual respect, trust, and concern for each other characterizes the climate and culture of the school and community".* To achieve this, the leader for the next millennium must be skilled in reflective practice earmarked by decision-making and problem-solving, based on a well-examined belief system. By this, what is meant is an acquired, readily referenced core of values, which Steven Covey calls a state of *"centeredness"* that can guide one through difficult decision-making and crises. Finally, as referred to previously, today's leaders must be knowledgeable about child growth and development, including cognitive and affective dimensions, guiding principles, and best practices of teaching and learning. Furthermore, they must embrace a much broader concept of what constitutes human intelligence than schools have traditionally acknowledged.

Assessing the Product

Based on a review of the research literature on the preparation of school leaders, Daniel, Gupton, and Southerland (1998) conclude that, " . . . *the reform wave had moved beyond the 'quality education' and quality teacher' loci . . . and was now focusing on the inadequacies of educational leaders, the deficiencies of the programs that prepared these leaders, and the means for achieving renewal of such training programs"* (p. 3). The literature, as has been noted, was well buttressed with calls for changing the focus and quality of training programs for future school administrators. Again, Daniel, Gupton, and Southerland (1998) found that, as an example, the literature was calling for shifts in the preparation of future educational leaders from .a managerial to a human-centered focus, and from the macro-level of a smooth-running organization to the micro-level of the learning needs of the individual student. They found that most of the calls also featured at least three other features: a) a continued focus on the importance of a "knowledge base" that is best learned via traditional academic preparation (i.e., college or university courses) b) a strengthening of focus on learning by doing (via problem-centered and problem-based learning, simulations, and enhanced field experiences), and c) a renewed focus on the importance of personal and professional characteristics of the administrator (e.g. emphasis on the affective qualities of leaders, calling for a return to "moral" or "ethical" leadership. (pp. 7-8)

Thus, many preparatory programs for educational leaders began to adjust, modify, and/or refocus their efforts/program designs to more accurately reflect the literature's call for change.

Indeed, many preparatory programs are moving to train future school administrators toward leadership orientations. These are arranged along the lines of skill development in such areas as instructional leadership, collegial and empowering forms of leadership, group processing skills, consensus decision-making, reflective thinking, mentoring, and other actions associated with school leadership. They bring about a congruence between theory and practice, with efforts to link candidate training experiences with school-based practices. While movement toward such an instructional foci was viewed as refreshing and appropriate, the question remains as to how to ensure and validate that future educational leaders possessed the envisioned skills, knowledge, and abilities to perform their duties in a manner that reflected the calls for a different administrative operational orientation, style, and capability.

To that end, the National Council for Accreditation of Teacher Education (NCATE) initially utilized 21 standards to assess the quality of college programs preparing school leaders. The number of NCATE standards currently being proposed for review of such training programs has been modified to reflect only 6 key standards. This move is more reflective and congruent with the standards that have been developed by the Interstate School Leaders Licensure Consortium (ISLLC) an organization that has as its members over 22 states (see Appendix 1 for a comparison of the NCATE standards and the existing ISLLC established standards).

Early on in its efforts to identify performance standards for administrative candidates, ISLLC recognized the need to develop a methodology for assessment with a degree of assurance that individuals desiring to become school administrators possess the basic skills, knowledge, and disposition necessary to function appropriately in the field as school leaders. To this end, early on, six member states (the District of Columbia, Illinois, Kentucky, Mississippi, Missouri, and North Carolina) provided the financial support and guidance necessary for the Educational Testing Service to develop a new assessment paradigm for validating perspective school leaders skills, knowledge, and dispositions.

Currently, 4 ISLLC member states (Maryland, Mississippi, Missouri, and North Carolina) require newly graduated future school leaders to pass the *School Leaders Licensure Assessment* (SLLA) prior to receipt of their official licensure to hold a position as a school principal. This was developed and administered by Educational Testing Service (ETS). Alaska is currently considering the addition of the SLLA to its certification/licensure expectation. This assessment process is felt to reflect the most current research, professional judgment, and experiences of educators across the country and is further predicated on a national job analysis study of school leaders, with correlation to the established ISLLC Standards. While there is no nationally established passing score or level for the SLLA, each state that currently utilizes this vehicle has established its own level of score acceptability for passage.

Figure 7-5 reflects the design structure for *the School Leaders Licensure Assessment*" instrument as reported in the *1999-2000 Registration Bulletin*. The actual assessment process is completed in a 1-day session and requires each candidate to present their individually amassed skills, knowledge, and dispositions relative to school leadership over a 6-hour period. The actual results of the assessment are scored by selected school leaders who have been carefully trained relative to the established ISLLC Standards and the content specifications for assessment.

School Leader Licensure Assessment Design Format

Number of Time-Scored Responses	
Evaluation of Actions 1 1 hour	10 vignettes
Evaluation of Actions 2 1 hour	6 case studies
Synthesis of Information and Problem Solving 2 hours	2 case studies (1 elementary oriented and 1 middle or high school oriented)
Analysis of Information and Decision Making 2 hours	2 questions based on 7 presented documents

Figure 7-5

Closer examination of the SLLA format contained in the booklet *"Test at a Glance: School Leadership Series- School Leader License Assessment"* discloses the following information on each test module:

- Evaluation of Actions 1: contains 10 vignettes, each describing a situation that a principal might encounter and requiring the individual to explain his action/response based on focused questions as to how a principal might respond, factors that would be considered in the response, and possible consequences of proposed response.

- Evaluation of Actions 2: contains 6 somewhat longer vignettes that present dilemmas based on issues related to teaching and learning. All individuals are expected to focus their responses based on their analysis of the data presented.

- The vignettes require the individuals to deal with competing requests for resources, prioritize their planned actions, articulate the instructional issues, explain instructional and curricular strategies appropriate to their response, and discuss the implications instructionally as presented in the vignette.

- Synthesis of Information and Problem Solving: this module is designed around 2 lengthy case study situations that also provide the individual with several appropriate documents.

- The test taker is expected to examine the documents, select appropriate information, and then respond to questions that have been posed relative to possible administrative actions that address the problem presented.

- Analysis of Information and Decision Making: here, the test taker is presented with 7 specific documents, which might typically be available to a school leader. Generally, 6 of the 7 documents will be related to teaching and learning.

- Given the information provided, the individual is asked to respond to 2 questions that will require action to be taken supported by the information available in the provided data.

Typically, the following types of documents would be provided: assessment data, portions of school improvement plans, budget information, class schedules, resource distribution data, staff evaluations, and curricular information.

Final assessment of the candidates' responses to the overall assessment modules is based on pre-established scoring rubrics that are highly correlated to the established six ISLLC standards. (See Appendix I for these standards).

Sample Vignettes, Case Studies

What follows are several examples of vignettes and case studies to help prepare students to think and react to ISLLC and NCATE standards. For each vignette and case study, sample reflective questions are provided to help identify the type of considerations that should be made .

Vignette 1: (ISLLC Standard 2).

You are approached by three of your staff members, the head football coach, the band director, and the speech teacher, all with the same concern: Billy Smith. It seems that Billy has made the depth chart on the football team as the starting tight end, according to Coach Jones. However, Mr. Tone, the band director, informs you that Billy is the lead French horn player in the band and is required to be at all performances. Mrs. English, the speech teacher, advises you that Billy is a star performer with potential for college speech scholarship and that he will need to attend three contests during the fall that are scheduled for Fridays and Saturdays. You are being asked to decide who has the right to expect Billy's attendance at which extracurricular activities. At this point, the three staff members have admitted they cannot find a solution to the problem.

Questions to Consider:

1) What is your decision? 2) What data, if any, do you need to make a decision and why? 3) Do you need to talk with any other individuals, and, if so, who, and regarding what? 4) When you reach your decision, on what will you base your action/decision?

Vignette 2: (ISLLC Standard 3 and 5)

In the wake of the recent number of school violence incidences on other school campuses, your Board of Education recently adopted a policy of "zero tolerance" toward students bringing guns or other weapons onto school grounds. Your school safety officer approaches you shortly after the school day has begun and shares with you that while he was checking a car in the student parking lot, he noticed what looked like a rifle on the floor behind the driver's seat. He gives you the license number of the vehicle and also the student parking permit number. On going to the office and checking the files, you learn that the vehicle belongs to James Earl, the Senior Class President, a straight "A" student and the son of a newly elected board member. You call James to the office, and when you question him about the rifle, he says that his father borrowed his truck to go deer hunting with a friend from work over the weekend and must have forgotten to take it out of the truck when he returned late last night.

Questions to Consider:

1) What is your decision? 2) What data, if any, do you need to make a decision and why? 3) Do you need to talk with any other individuals, and, if so, who, and regarding what? 4) When you reach your decision, on what will you base your action/decision?

Case Study 1 (ISSLC Standard 3)

It had been a calm, yet productive, week at Advanced High School. Mrs. South was looking forward to the extended weekend. The last bell for the day had already rung, and only a few teachers and the custodian remained as she worked to complete the remaining paperwork. The angry entrance of Mr. Washington, a veteran social studies teacher, broke the quiet of the office.

In a calm voice, Mrs. South asked Mr. Washington what the problem seemed to be. "I have had it with all of these special education students," he said. Mr. Washington proceeded to tell her about the latest incident in his classroom.

A special education student had disrupted the class to the point that teaching and learning could not take place. When the student was confronted about the problem, he cursed at the instructor and refused to leave the classroom stating, "I have an IEP and you can't do anything to me."

Following the description of the incident in the classroom, Mr. Washington stated, "Either they go or I do. Either way, I will not have to deal with special education students again," at which point he stormed out of the office.

Questions to Consider
1) What are the areas of conflict in this situation?
2) Are there underlying legal issues that impact Mrs. South's response?
3) In light of the situation, what should Mrs. South do next?
4) Do you see any conflict resolution skills that could be used?
5) What are some possible ways of dealing with the student involved?

(Case provided by permission of Dr. Michael Arnold, Southwest Baptist University Bolivar, Missouri)

Case Study 2: (ISLLC Standards 2,3,5, and 6)

Mr. Brolin, Principal of Drake Elementary School, walked into the superintendent's office and immediately felt uneasy. Dr. Overton's secretary said to go into the office and that Dr. Overton and Dr. Harris, special education administrator, were waiting for him. Mr. Brolin had been a principal for 20 years, and he knew that there was an important concern as he was not actually summoned to the superintendent's office.

Mr. Brolin sat across from Dr. Overton and next to Dr. Harris. Dr. Overton began the conversation.

"Mr. Brolin, we have a special problem we'd like to discuss with you. We have a family who just moved into our district, the Stevens, who have a 12-year-old son, Jake. Jake is

placed in a private day treatment facility for students with behavior disorders. Mr. and Mrs. Stevens and personnel from the private day treatment facility have contacted me and requested that Jake be returned to the regular school setting, and your school would be his home school. Dr. Harris, could you tell Mr. Brolin more about Jake?"

"Sure," said Dr. Harris, "This is an unusual case, and we need your input to decide how we will proceed, Mr. Brolin. Jake, as Dr. Overton said, is t12 years old. He's a rather large boy for his age, about 150 pounds. Jake had gifted potential until the age of five, when he contracted a case of encephalitis. He suffered a long-term fever and had several grand mal seizures, which damaged his brain. At this point, he is labeled 'traumatic brain injury.' His level of intellectual functioning at the present time is mild retardation, with an IQ of about 68. For the past year, he has been placed in the private day treatment facility. His parents have also had difficulty with him at home and they have been attending family counseling at the day treatment facility".

"Prior to this placement, Jake was moved from one special education program to another. I talked to the special education administrator where Jake resided previously, and he was totally frustrated with Jake and his family. Jake was in a program for mild mentally disabled children, but his behavior was too severe for this placement to be successful. He was then transferred to a self-contained behavior disorders program in the public school, and even this placement was unsuccessful. Prior to the day treatment placement, he verbally threatened to attack his teachers and threatened to kill other students".

"During the year at the day treatment facility, Jake was physically restrained many times, especially during the first semester. When Jake was confronted by authority figures, he responded by cursing, throwing furniture, and verbally threatening others. On two occasions during Jake's first semester at the day treatment facility, Jake's actions resulted in minor injuries to three staff members. During Jake's second semester at the day treatment facility, Jake's behavior dramatically improved. He had only one act of violence directed toward a peer and only had to be physically restrained one time. The day treatment facility recommended that Jake be returned to the public school this year because he has improved. They also recommended trial placement in the regular classroom because they think Jake will respond to positive peer role models. As Dr. Overton said, we have just received the request for an IEP meeting to return Jake to the regular school setting, possibly a regular 6th grade classroom with support services."

Mr. Brolin said slowly as the color drained from his face, *"You mean the parents want us to place this child in **my** school?"*

Dr. Overton said, *"Yes, I'm afraid so. The day treatment staff are supportive because they think a normal learning environment will help Jake behaviorally. They think a personal assistant would be necessary. My feeling is that we should at least attempt this placement."*

Mr. Brolin stood up as he said, *"I will not under any circumstance take this child into my building. I am responsible for the education and well being of 400 students and many staff members. I refuse to take this child."*

Dr. Overton also stood up and said, *"Listen, Mr. Brolin, this may be temporary, but I think we owe it to the child and his family to try to make this placement work. In fact, I insist that we meet with the parents."*

Mr. Brolin stated emphatically, *"After 20 years, you are going to insist that I take a child into my building who has the potential to hurt people. I simply won't do it!"*

Mr. Brolin walked out of the superintendent's office and went back to his building. He was worried about his behavior with the superintendent. He had never refused to do anything in the past. He always tried to do the best he could even though he didn't agree with all requests. However, he thought, this was different. He would feel terrible if he agreed to this placement and someone got hurt.

Back in the superintendent's office, Dr. Harris and Dr. Overton talked.

Dr. Harris said, *"Wow, I didn't expect this type of reaction from Mr. Brolin. However, with time, he'll come around and support us."*

Dr. Overton said, *"He'd better, or he may not be principal of that building or any building in the district. Dr. Harris, go ahead and arrange for the IEP meeting. Schedule it at Mr. Brolin's building and invite the regular education teacher for 6th grade and any special education teachers you feel might be involved."*

Jake was ultimately placed in Mr. Brolin's building and assigned to the regular education 6th grade teacher. A one-to-one assistant was assigned to Jake. A nonaversive behavior management program was implemented using direct treatment strategies, positive programming, and reactive procedures. A highly structured program was designed to take into account Jake's cognitive abilities, instructional needs, and behavior. Jake's program included several school jobs and was implemented in a variety of school settings throughout the day. The majority of his time was spent away from his regular sixth grade peers.

The initial implementation of the program was difficult. The first one-to-one assistant resigned within 3 months. Two one-to-one assistants, one in the morning and one in the afternoon, were hired. Jake also received the direct services of a behavior specialist, inclusion facilitator, social worker, speech therapist, and physical therapist. Because Jake could not eat breakfast prior to leaving home in the morning due to medication issues, his first hour of school was spent preparing and eating breakfast.

Under the current condititons, Jake's behavior improved. He had not engaged in any physical altercations in the past 6 weeks. However, his program was constantly updated and reviewed to address behavior and academic challenges.

Questions to Consider

1. If a similar student transferred to your building tomorrow, how would you, as building administrator, prepare for the student? 2. Was Mr. Brolin's behavior acceptable in the superintendent's office? Why or why not? 3. Did the program, as implemented, provide a free and appropriate public education? Was the program in the least restrictive environment? How do you know?

Case study drawn with permission from Weishaar and Borsa (2001)

Future Assessment Directions

Beyond ISLLC and the School Leaders Licensure Assessment, what does the future hold for assessing graduates of school leader's preparatory programs? Already, both some ISLLC member states and NCATE are discussing the use of authentic portfolio assessment as an additional source of data to be considered in the granting of a first administrative license, as well as for recertification extensions. Some administrative preparation programs, e.g. the University of Southern Mississippi's Department of Educational Leadership and Research requires all of its Master's Degree students to create and present a portfolio of their learnings, skills, and abilities at the conclusion of each of the degree's three, 12-credit-hour instructional blocks, their two semesters of internship experience, and, finally, a culminating portfolio with selected artifacts from all segments of their degree program.

Another example of the conceptualized use of portfolios is the program developed by Catherine Eggeston Hackney of Kent State University and Michel Gaski, Director of Curriculum and Instructional Technology of Summit County Educational Service Center. This work is present here with the permission of the authors and is based on material shared at the 1999 American Association of Educational Service Agencies annual Conference held in Marco Island, Florida. They developed a strategy for employing portfolios for the evaluation of practicing school administrators. A Reflective Practice and Evaluation Model for use with portfolio assessment is presented in Figure 7-6. The program is designed around three models which address first-year principals in *Model One: The Standards Based Model* (see figure 7-7), experienced principals in *Model Two: The Targeted Competing Based Model* (see Figure 7-8) and *Model Three: The Inquiry Based Model* (see Figure 7-9)

Model One is designed around the ISLLC Standards. Model Two might be viewed as a modified form *of Management by Objectives* portfolio approach. Model Three is more of a portfolio assessment strategy that is configured to resemble an action-research-based approach to administrative assessment.

What Is Ahead in Administrative Assessment

The nature of administrator assessment has passed through numerous phases, the last being one designed around the concept/model of assessment centers. This has been replaced by an orientation directed toward validating candidate competencies viewed as essential for successful administrative functioning in the "real-world" setting. Where the field will progress from here is yet to be determined; however, it seems safe to project that use of assessment procedures, such as the developed by SLLA and portfolio-oriented efforts, will continue to expand as valid means of assessing and insuring that future administrators have adequate skills, knowledge, and dispositions essential to successful infusion into the ranks of practicing educational leaders.

Reflective Practice and Evaluation
(for use with portfolio assessment)

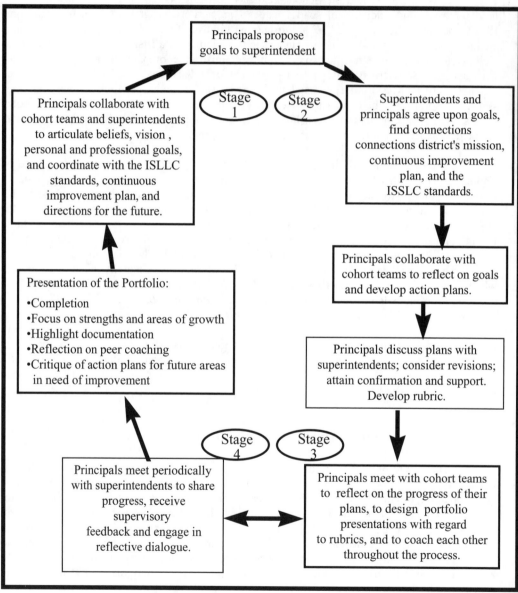

Figure 7-6

Three Models for Using Portfolios for Evaluation of Administration Performance

Model One: *The Standards Based* Model

Stage One: The Personal Vision	Stage Two: *The Exploration of Administrative Competencies*	Stage Three: *The Action Plan*	Stage Four: *The Presentation of the Portfolio*
Principals collaborate with their cohort teams to explore their own set of beliefs and values.	Principals meet with cohorts to review ISLLC Standards for Administrative Performance Evaluation.	Principals work with cohorts for help developing the action plan, which includes: Administrative activities *Artifact collection Portfolio composition Relationship to ISLLC Standards*	Principals complete portfolios and submit to the superintendents.
Principals compose their own personal visions by which they will guide their schools strategically and day-to-day.	Principals meet to discuss possible professional goals as they relate to the six ISLLC Standards and personal visions.	Principals and superintendents meet regularly to discuss action plans, share progress, offer supervisory feedback, and engage in reflective dialogue.	Composition revolves around the six ISLLC Standards with documentation supporting achievement of each standard.
Principals collaborate with cohort teams to discuss personal visions and their relationships with building and district philosophies.	Principals and superintendents decide on specific goals that address the six ISLLC Standards for administrative performance assessment.	Artifact collection centers on the six ISSLC Standards and their achievement.	Principals present the portfolios to the superintendents. Focus is on strengths, areas of growth, reflections on the process, and plans for improvement activity, with respect to the ISLLC Standards.
			Principals and superintendents review beliefs, missions, and goals for personal, building and district development.
			Principals and superintendents set directions for the future through: Professional growth *School improvement Inquiry Evaluation models*

Figure 7-7

Model Two: The Targeted Competency –Based Model			
Stage One **The Personal** **Vision**	**Stage Two** **The Exploration of** **Administrative Competencies**	**Stage Three** **The Action Plan**	**Stage Four** **The Presentation of the** **Portfolio**
Principals collaborate with their cohort teams to explore their own sets of beliefs and values.	Principals meet with cohorts and superintendents; review ISLLC Standards and the traditional areas of administrative performance: Vision development Curriculum & Instruction Professional development Supervision of learning Organization & management Technology Parent & community relations	Principals work with cohorts for help developing the action plan, which includes: Administrative activities Artifact collection Portfolio composition Relationship to ISLLC Standards	Principals complete portfolios and submit to the superintendents.
Principals compose their own personal visions by which they will guide their schools strategically and day-to-day.	Principals and superintendents will agree upon goals and begin work on action plans.	Principals and superintendents meet regularly to discuss action plans, share progress, offer supervisory feedback, and engage in reflective dialogue.	Composition resolves around the areas of administrative performance chosen as goals by the principals and superintendents.
Principals collaborate with cohort teams to discuss personal visions and their relationships with building and district philosophies.		Artifact collection centers on the traditional areas of administrative performance determined by principals and superintendents earlier in the process.	Documentation supports achievement of goals in collaboratively selected areas and their connection with the ISLLC Standards.
		Principals create linkages from the areas of administrative performance to focus on the ISLLC Standards.	Principals and superintendents review beliefs, missions, and goals for personal, building and district development.
			Principals and superintendents set directions for the future through: Professional growth School improvement Inquiry Evaluation models

Figure 7-8

Model Three: The Inquiry Based Model			
Stage One: The Personal Vision	*Stage Two: The Exploration of Administrative Competencies*	**Stage Three: The Action Plan**	*Stage Four: The Presentation of the Portfolio*
Principals collaborate with their cohort teams to explore their own sets of beliefs and values.	Principals will selects area of interest and inquiry around which they might develop personal goals for the purpose of school improvement and professional growth.	Principals work with cohorts for help developing the action plan, which includes: Administrative activities *Artifact collection Portfolio composition Relationship to ISLLC Standards*	Principals complete portfolios and submit to the superintendents.
Principals compose their own personal visions by which they will guide their schools strategically and day-to-day.	Principals and superintendents will agree upon the goals, frame the questions, and decide upon an action plan.	Principals and superintendents meet regularly to discuss action plans, share progress, offer supervisory feedback, and engage in reflective dialogue.	Composition revolves around the collection of artifacts, which supports achievement of goals representative of the areas of inquiry pursued by the principals.
Principals collaborate with cohort teams to discuss personal visions and their relationships with building and district philosophies.		Artifact collection centers on the traditional areas of administrative performance determined by principals and superintendents earlier in the process.	Principals make connection with the ILLSC standards, which correspond to their areas of inquiry.
		Principals create linkages from the areas of administrative performance to focus on the ISLLC Standards.	Principals and superintendents review beliefs, missions, and goals for personal, building and district development.
			Principals and superintendents set directions for the future through: Professional growth *School improvement Inquiry Evaluation models*

Figure 7-9

Appendix 1

NCATE (2000)* and ISLLC** Standards Matrix	
NCATE Standards	**ISLLC Standards**
Standard 1. Candidate Knowledge, Skills, and Dispositions: Candidates preparing to work in schools as teachers or other school personnel know and demonstrate the content, pedagogical, and professional knowledge, skills, and dispositions necessary to help all students learn. Assessments indicate that candidates meet professional, state, and institutional standards.	**Standard 1:** ,A school administrator is an educational leader who promotes !he success of all students by facilitating the development, articulation, implementation, and stewardship of a vision of learning that is shared and supported by the school community.
Standard 2 Assessment System and Unit Evaluation: The unit has an assessment system that collects data on the applicant qualifications, candidate and graduate performance, and unit operations to evaluate and improve the unit and its programs.	**Standard 2:** A school administrator is an educational leader who promotes the success of all students by advocating nurturing and sustaining a school culture and instruction program conducive to student learning and staff professional development.
Standard 3 Field Experiences and Clinical Practice: The unit and Its school partners design, implement and evaluate field experiences and clinical practice so that teacher candidates and other school personnel develop and demonstrate the knowledge skills, and dispositions necessary to help all students learn.	**Standard 3:** A school administrator is an educational leader who promotes the success of all students by ensuring management of the organization, operations, and resources for a safe, efficient, and effective learning environment.
Standard 4 Diversity: The unit designs, implements and evaluates curriculum and experiences for candidates to acquire the knowledge, skills and dispositions necessary to help all students learn These experience include working with diverse higher education and school faculty, diverse candidates, and diverse students in P-12 schools.	**Standard 4:** A school administration is an educational leader who promotes the success of all students by collaborating with families and community members, responding to diverse community interest and needs, and mobilizing community resources.
Standard 5 Faculty Qualifications, Performance and Development: Faculty are qualified and model best professional practices in scholarship, service, and teaching, including the assessment of their effectiveness as related to candidate performance. They also collaborate with colleagues in the disciplines and schools. The unity systematically evaluates faculty performance and facilities professional development.	**Standard 5:** A school administrator is an educational leader who promotes the success of all students by acting with integrity, fairness, and in an ethical manner.
Standard 6 Unit Governance and Resources: The unit has the leadership, authority, budget personnel, facilities, and resources including information technology resources, for the preparation of candidates to meet professional, state, and institutional standards.	**Standard 6:** A school administrator is an educational leader who promotes the success of all students by understanding, responding to, and influencing the larger political, social, economic, legal, and cultural context.

*NCATE Standards come from *Professional Standards for the Accreditation of Schools, Colleges, and Departments of Education.* (2002) Washington DC: The National Council for Accreditation of Teacher Education. http://www.ncate.org/2000/unit_stnds_2002.pdf

**ISLLC Standards may be found at http://www.ohioprincipals.org/isllc_standards.htm with workshops available from NAESP at http://www.naesp.org/npa/isllc.htm

References

American Association of Colleges for Teachers Education. (AACTE) (1996). Washington, DC: Author

Arnold, M. (2000) *Case contribution*. Bolivar, Missouri: Southwest Baptist University

Asbaugh, C.R., & Kasten, K.L. (1992). *The licensure of school administration: Policy and practice*. Washington, DC: American Association of College for Teacher Education.

Behar-Horenstein, L.S. (1995). Promoting effective school leadership: A change-oriented models for the preparation of principals. *Peabody Journal of Education, 70* (3), 18-40.

Byham, W.C., (1970). Assessment center for spotting future managers. *Harvard Business Review, 48,* 150-160.

Council of Chief State Officers. (1996). *Interstate school leaders licensure consortium: Standards for school leaders*. Washington, DC: Author.

Daniel, L.G., Gupton, S.L., & Southerland, A.R. (1998). *Approaches for reforming the preparation of school leaders: A literature review and a proposed model.* Paper presented at the annual meeting of the Southwest Educational Research Association, Houston, TX.

Daniel, L. G., & Southerland. (1998). *New wisdom or misguided judgment?; A critical view of a decade of reform literature on the preparation of school leaders.* Paper presented at the annual meeting of the American Educational Research Association, San Diego, CA.

Daresh, J.C., & Playko, M.A. (1992). *The professional development of school administrators: Preservice, induction, and inservice applications.* Boston: Allyn and Bacon.

Educational Testing Service (1999). *School leaders licensure assessment: 1999-2000 registration bulletin.*

Engle, T.E. (1989). *An analysis of content and methods of instruction at Michigan institutions the prepare principals.* Doctoral dissertation, Western Michigan University.

Fletcher, C. & Anderson, N. (1988). A superficial assessment. *People management, 4,* 44-47.

Gordon, D., and Moles, M. (1974). Mentoring becomes staff development: A case of serendipidity. *NAASP Bulletin. 78* (559), 66-70.

Griffiths, D.E., Stout, R. T., & Forsyth, P.B. (1998). *Leaders for America's schools: The report of the National Commission in Excellence in Educational Administration*. Berkeley, CA: McCutchan.

Hackney, C.E, & Gaski, M. (1999). *Using portfolios for evaluating principals*. Charts and tables presented at the AASA conference, Marco Island, FL.

Haller, E.J., Brent, B.O., & McNamara, J.H. (1997). Does graduate training in educational administration improve America's schools? *Phi Delta Kappa, 79*, 222-227.

Heck, R.H. (1992). Principals' instructional leadership and school performance: Implications for policy development. *Educational Evaluation and Policy Analysis, 14* (1), 21-24.

Heck, R.H.& Marconlide, G.A. (1996). The assessment of principal performance: A multilevel evaluation approach. *Journal of Personnel Evaluation in Education, 10,* 11-28.

Jacobson, S.L., & Conway, J.A. (1990). *Educational leadership in an age of reform.* New York: Longman.

Klotz, J., & Daniel, L. (1998). *Formatting a proactive principal preparation program in response to the national reform movement in education administration preparation.* Paper presented at the annual meeting of the Mid-South Educational Research Association, New Orleans, Louisiana, November 4-6, 1998.

Klauke, A.(1988). Recruiting and selecting principals. ERIC Clearinghouse on Educational Management (ED297481).

Krug, S.E. (1993). Leadership craft and the crafting of school leaders. *Phi Delta Kappan, 75,* 240-244.

Lumsden, L. (1993). *The new face of principal preparation.* Alexandria, VA: National Association of Elementary School Principals.

McCleary, L.E. & Ogawa, R. (1989). The assessment center process for selecting school leaders. *School Organization, 9,* 103-133.

Milstein, M. (1993). *Changing the way we prepare educational leaders: The Dansforth experience.* Newbury Park, CA: Corwin Press.

Mississippi Administrator Preparation and Certification Task Force. (1994). *Improving the preparation of Mississippi school leaders; The final report of the Mississippi Administrator Preparation and Certification Task Force.* Jackson, MS: Author.

Mississippi Department of Education. (1997). *Mississippi standards for school leaders.* Jackson, MS: Author.

Murphy, J.F. (1992). *The landscape of leadership preparation: Reframing the education of school administrators.* Newbury Park, CA: Corwin.

National Association of Elementary School Principals. (1941). *Elementary and middle schools: Proficiencies for principals* (Revised). Alexandria, VA: Author.

National Council for Accreditation of Teacher Education, *Proposed NCATE 2000 Unit Standards*. (2000). February Draft.

National Policy Board for Educational Administration. (1993*). Principals for our changing schools: knowledge and skill base.* Lancaster, PA: Technomic.

Niece, R. (1993). The principal as instructional leader: Past influences and current resources. *NASSP Bulletin, 77* (553), 12-18.

Rosenholtz, S.J. (1989). *Teachers workplace.* New York: Longman.

Snyder, W.R. (1994). A very special specialist degree for school leaders, *NASSP Bulletin, 78,* 23-27.

Stakenas, R. G. (1994). Program reform in administrator preparation. *NASSP Bulletin, 78 (559),* 28-33.

Stogdill, R. H. (1974). *Handbook of leadership.* New York: Free Press.

Thompson, S.D. (1991). Principals for America 2000. *Journal of School Leadership, 1 (4),* 294-304.

Thomson, S.D. (1993). Professionalizing the principalship. *International Journal of Educational Reform, 2,* 296-299.

Thurston, P., Clift, R. & Schacht, M. (1993). Preparing leaders for change oriented schools. *Phi Delta Kappan, 75, 259-265.*

Weishaar, M. and Borsa, J. (2001) *Inclusive Educational Administration: A case study approach.* St. Louis, MO: McGraw Hill

Whitaker, B. (1997). Instructional leadership and principal visibility. *Clearing House, 70,* 155-156.

Worner, W. (1994). The national alliance at Virginia Tech: Making a difference. *NASSP Bulletin, 78,* (559), 57-61.

Chapter 8
Personnel Administration and Empowerment
Peter Strodl

A comprehensive description of personnel administration encompasses all aspects of the employment of professional and nonprofessional employees. The mission includes hiring and firing, compensation, benefits, maintenance of records, oversight of evaluations of work, and maintenance of procedures according to legal requirements. Personnel administration enhances public support for schools and internal support from faculty and staff when these constituencies are involved in personnel selection and policy development.

The role of personnel administration has grown to include policy initiation and implementation; this has generated greater employee productivity and work satisfaction, increasing responsibility for designing and carrying out service processes, and coordination of personnel and procedures with viable perspectives of the school district. (Castetter, 1986).

Because of the complexity of personnel administration issues, the personnel administrator must have tact, courtesy, consideration, sensitivity, compassion, conflict management skills and skills, for working with others. The complexity of personnel administration is illustrated in Figure 8-1, disclosing many areas of interest and many sources of stress for the personnel administrator.

Constituencies in the school community include those interested in promoting economic, political, and social issues in the community. Local school district constituencies include teachers, paraprofessional employees, school board members and community groups they represent, taxpaying citizens, parents of private and parochial school children, older citizens, those who are retired and on fixed incomes, minority and majority groups, various cultural and socioeconomic groups.

School and Central Office Personnel Administration

At the school building level, the principal confers with the personnel administrator at central office on unusual matters to assure correct procedures are being followed. In large school systems, detailed policy manuals with extensive personnel policies contain correct procedures, based on legal decisions, for most circumstances. In smaller systems, shorter commentaries are counter-balanced with consultations with the superintendent or personnel director whenever a matter is out of the ordinary.

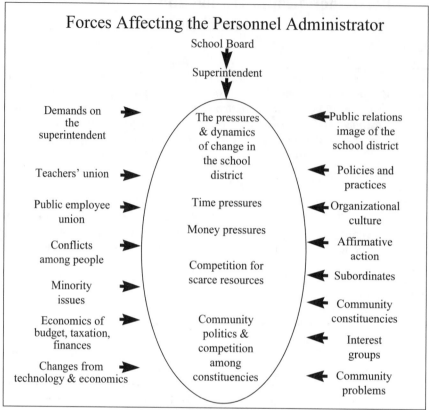

Forces Affecting the Personnel Administrator

School Board

Superintendent

Demands on the superintendent →

Teachers' union →

Public employee union →

Conflicts among people →

Minority issues →

Economics of budget, taxation, finances →

Changes from technology & economics →

The pressures & dynamics of change in the school district

Time pressures

Money pressures

Competition for scarce resources

Community politics & competition among constituencies

← Public relations image of the school district

← Policies and practices

← Organizational culture

← Affirmative action

← Subordinates

← Community constituencies

← Interest groups

← Community problems

Figure 8-1

At the district level, personnel administration is a network of interactions among school board pressures and fiscal circumstances, community pressures, professional needs, legal requirements, and the need to adapt to a changing world. Working through conflicting pressures requires tact, courtesy and the ability to negotiate with all sides. This puts much pressure upon the superintendent, personnel director, and others dealing with personnel administration.

Figure 8-2 illustrates the various functions of personnel administration, using a house as a model for central office personnel administration. The bottom half of the house shows the traditional conceptualization of personnel administration as a hiring and firing entity. The upper half shows the many responsibilities in the more recent conceptualization of personnel administration as a function of human resource development. Staff development, organizational development, and educational effectiveness research expand the efficiency of the school district by applying resources to benefit the children, and by being responsive to the needs of the community.

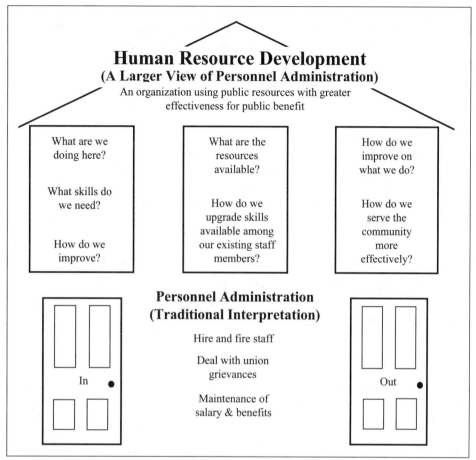

Figure 8-2

Human Resource Development: A Broader View of Personnel

As Figure 8-2 indicates, human resource administration is an expanded concept of personnel administration. Human resource development has the added expectation that staff are resources, and as such, they must be cared for and developed to maintain and increase performance throughout their life in the organization. Although *personnel administration* is often the term used in schools, the scope of the job more often includes *human resource development* (Castetter, 1986, Nadler, 1984).

A central task of local school administration is to motivate voluntary cooperation of employees. Personnel administration takes a broader view of this to insure that appropriate people are in appropriate positions and that they are ready to work to achieve the goals of the school district. Staff development energizes employees to adapt to new social and curriculum pressures and to fulfill instructional responsibilities (Castetter, 1986).

Teacher Duties

On a symbolic level, teacher roles are well developed. A deeper understanding of these roles is fundamental in teacher development programs. Teacher roles differ according to grade levels, developmental differences of students, and differences in subject matter, thus demanding differences in teacher disposition. Teachers may be asked to perform certain duties outside the classroom related to work with students. This includes nonacademic duties such as student-related clerical duties, loading of school buses, supervision at athletic events, selling tickets for student events, collecting school pictures money, student business supervision, etc.

These activities are incidental to classroom teaching. In contrast, teachers may not be asked to perform duties not implied in the teachers' contract such as janitorial duties, bus driving, and traffic duty. Teaching is changing with our society. Teachers need to relate to the "heart and soul as well as the mind" (Sergiovanni, 1990, p. 63, Alexander & Alexander, 1985) to be free to relate fully to their students.

Teacher Freedoms

Key issues under teacher freedoms are speech and expression, religion, loyalty, self-incrimination, discrimination, and due process. Public employment is perceived as a privilege and not a right, but teachers are not expected to cast off their rights upon entering the school.

As respected community members, teachers are trusted with the safety, security, and development of the young people of the community. Teachers must be treated with respect, because they are leaders in the community. To treat teachers as less than professionals means giving up the edge of loyalty and commitment that teachers have toward the community's children. Communities need to defend the right of teachers to express points of view and to share a broad basis of information for the growth of students (Alexander & Alexander, 1985).

Freedom of Speech, Expression, and Behavior

Teachers, people who speak much the time and who express themselves on a variety of subjects, are protected by the constitutional freedoms of speech and association. Teachers must be held accountable for promoting the interests of the school by maintaining order, maintaining the learning environment of the school, and providing the personal appearance necessary for leadership of a community's youth.

It is generally seen as unconstitutional to limit teacher expression on matters of politics. However, students are seen as a *captive audience* because of mandatory attendance laws. Teachers are advised to limit expression to personal opinions eliminating efforts at persuading others to their own point of view, especially on such things as religion. Sometimes, the out-of-school activities of teachers, such as alcoholism, sexual misconduct, and gambling, reflect on the school and affect the ability of the teachers to perform their public function. (Alexander & Alexander, 1985).

Freedom of Religion

All of us in the United States have the right to free expression of religious liberty. This does not mean that teachers can behave in whatever way they want to in the classroom. The religious freedom of teachers is protected if they fulfill their responsibilities, conduct themselves appropriately, and do not infringe on the rights of students. Discussion of religious issues should be limited to comparisons among religions or sharing the cultural aspects of religion and its literature. Teachers whose religious beliefs do not include the pledge of allegiance to the flag must understand they legally must lead the pledge to the flag as an assigned teaching responsibility. It is illegal to refuse to employ anyone "on the basis race, color, religion, sex, or national origin" (Civil Rights Act of 1964, Title VII, 1972 Amendments, Alexander & Alexander, 1985).

Staff Development

Teachers often have a way of viewing their classrooms as territorial realms. Change of any kind may be viewed by the teacher as impinging upon teacher authority which often has effects on social relationships and instructional procedures. Changing a procedure often results in a perfunctory teacher response, giving the appearance of having made the change while little change occurs behind the closed classroom door. The source of resistance to this change may be a conflict between the necessary change and a teacher's sense of a need to foster stability and traditional values. Inservice programs as part of staff development often provide the knowledge necessary for illumination and, therefore, for countering resistance to change. In-class mentoring programs also can help.

Teacher *empowerment* includes teacher participation in staff development planning. Participative local management and participative policy decision making also result in a sense of ownership and a deeper level of commitment (also see Chapters 1 and 10). To encourage teachers to adjust successfully to the many changes thrust upon them, staff development programs should involve teachers in setting the agenda. Broader-based decision making will enlighten teachers about the school needs and increase willful cooperation. Empower teachers to share a vision for the school enables them to share more of themselves, and in turn, motivate pupils to participate more fully in the learning process (Sergiovanni, 1990).

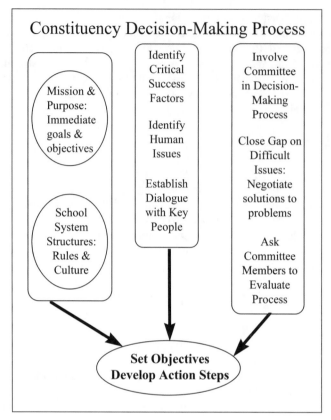

Figure 8-3

Figure 8-3 illustrates how teachers can be involved in developing a philosophy and mission for a school and in solving educational problems. As this occurs, teachers will be more deeply committed to accomplishing necessary change.

Establishing Communication Links among Employees

Many schools suffer from communication problems among employees. Lieberman and Miller (1984) describe these challenges in terms of teachers' actions in an isolated world, with large blocks of work interaction limited to children. Teachers are largely without the presence of other adults when they are in their classrooms, usually teaching alone, without the benefit of close working peers. The relationship of teacher to principal is often a question of obtaining privilege; consequently teachers are not always forthright with their building administrators. Teachers feeling lonely and isolated often willingly pay the price to avoid the uncertainties of publicity or intrusions upon the "territory" of their classroom (Lieberman and Miller, 1984).

Lieberman and Miller suggest that overcoming the difficulties in communication in schools requires staff development activities in faculty meetings and many other situations. To solve communication problems in schools, staff development days should develop teachers' assertiveness skills and other skills to facilitate participative decision making. Similarly, principals need to learn how to encourage teachers to express concerns and how to encourage their involvement in the decision-making process.

Another problem with communication stems from the fact that teachers are accustomed to being in charge of the territory of their classrooms, whereas principals are accustomed to being in charge of the territory of their school buildings. Direct communication is necessary between school administrators and teachers to prevent any potential territorial conflict.

Assertiveness skills help people to verbalize their problems when difficult situations arise, and teachers can develop assertiveness skills to prevent intimidation from the authoritarian behavior of others. As more assertive teachers venture forth to talk more about their problems among staff members of the school, the more willing others will be to become involved in more direct communications with the administrators and others.

An important aspect of personnel administration is recognizing when a once-enthusiastic employee has become stagnant. This can happen to anyone who has been devoted to students by wearing an optimistic face in the classroom when real life is troubling. Years of emotional stress, alcohol abuse, and social demands may rob otherwise wonderful teachers of their exuberance (also see Chapter 14).

Often personnel administrators just need to bring up the subject and listen, but they should also know of helpful resources for employees who need additional help. Often straight talk is needed to help an employee begin to deal with years of painful emotions. The result can be that the employee who might have spent many years being sarcastic and miserable with children will again find the joy of teaching and dealing with people.

Adults, too, go through developmental stages just as children do. Personnale administrators should understand the stage of adult development so they can help their teachers effectively communicate with and motivate students. For example, personnel administrators cannot deal with tenured teachers in the same way that they would deal with new employees. When nearing retirement, some teachers focus on things that went wrong over the years. These negative feelings can cause anxiety about what their future in retirement holds for them. Because of this unfortunate pitfall, teachers need help planning for their retirement and some may even require serious employee counseling.

Procurement of Staff

Rights to privacy, due process, and confidentiality are issues, that, although legally supported, are sufficiently sensitive that they often cause administrators difficulty. Choice of the wrong word during an interview can cause serious legal or political difficulties for the administrator and school district. Such difficulties can continue for years before a solution is found in or out of court. An example is in the case at the end of this chapter.

A healthy respect for the laws involving personnel matters is mandatory. The wrong word during the interview of a potential employee can result in several years of data collection for federal and state investigations with a department of human rights. Many school districts prepare lists of interview questions to be asked of every interviewee. Using the same carefully prepared interview questions asked of all interviewees lowers the probability of litigation. Uncomfortable situations can be avoided by the careful choice of words, with a general awareness of the laws, and, at times, with the wisdom to seek advice from a more experienced advisor.

Certification

Certification is usually a state document indicating that the teacher has met the minimum qualifications for teaching in a particular area. This does not mean that the teacher is entitled to employment, or that the teacher has met the qualifications of the local school district. State regulatory agencies such as state departments of education may have higher qualifications than those established by state legislatures. Additional requirements may be made by the local school district according to the needs of the district for the specific position. In times of teacher shortage, however, school districts, depending on state law and state regulations, may make some temporary arrangements to hire teachers who are not certified. Criteria for hiring such temporary staff often include the applicant's ability to work with children. (Alexander & Alexander, 1985, p. 529-30).

Teacher Residency Requirements

Some municipalities and school districts require that teachers live in the school district where they teach. The courts have decided this issue both ways. Districts have the right to make such a rule, even if the rule applies to new teachers and not to previously hired teachers. Municipalities are more likely to require employees to reside within their boundaries when there is a surplus market of employees (Wardewell v. Board of Education of the City School District of the City of Cincinannati, et. al US Court of Ap, Sixth Circuit, 1976, 529 F. 2nd 528 Alexander & Alexander, 1985).

Hiring a Teacher

Hiring a teacher is not simply a question of filling an open position. There are many things to be considered in the selection process. Teachers are not babysitters, nor are they police. They are representatives of the adults in the community who will lead and nurture children to become responsible adults. Figure 8-4 lists district considerations for selecting a new teacher.

**Considerations For
Selecting a New Teacher**
- Concerns of the community
- Needs of existing teachers
- Curriculum requirements
- Budgeting constraints
- Cultural composition of the community and staff
- Formal credentials
- Training
- Experience

Figure 8-4

Teachers have always served as role models for their students. In hiring teachers, many districts consider issues beyond credentials and educational qualifications. There is the thought that teachers should provide excellent role models for students. Often this includes high moral and ethical standards, standards for work ethics, and model values. Such requirements should be addressed prior to hiring. It is also important to remember that differing personalities belong with differing age groups and that some people do not have the personality to teach well or relate well to children at all levels. Experiences, including volunteer work with children or being a camp counselor, Sunday school teacher, and babysitter while not essential, are useful additions to the applicant's track record and often predict high potential for rapport with students.

The Selection Committee: Avoiding Controversies in Procurement

In deciding to hire a new person, it is essential to consider what kind of professional qualities need to be considered for the position and what kind of personality fits in with present staff.

Not only should a new teacher have desirable qualifications, and work well with children, but it is essential the new person be accepted by other teachers and community members. Appropriate appointments on a selection committee will serve well the need to adjust the hiring process to community demands and to anticipating political controversies in the selection process. Although an administrator will likely have the final say in recommending a candidate to the board of education for employment, a selection committee can help to eliminate all but a few finalists.

Community representatives and teachers need to be involved in the selection process to insure the new hire's acceptance. A selection committee of seven to ten people should be formed. The committee should include:

   1) a personnel administrator or appropriate administrator
   2) the principal of the school to which the successful candidate will be appointed
   3) representatives from among the faculty who would work most closely with the successful candidate
   4) parents who represent school constituencies
   5) parents who represent children with whom the new teacher will work

This committee will raise important issues and sensitivities that the administration, acting alone, might miss.

The selection committee will recommend a list of desirable criteria to the personnel department or appropriate administrator. The criteria must meet legal requirements of affirmative action as well as considerations listed in Figure 8-4. After working with the committee to prioritize selection criteria, it is the job of the personnel administrator to advertise the position and mail out application forms in response to queries. Some districts may choose to include committee members in this part of the process.

> *If I were on a selection committee to choose a leader for a non-profit organization and there were a roster of men and women as candidates, what would I look for? First, I would look at what the individuals have done, what their strengths are. Most selection committees I know are too concerned with how "poor" the candidate is.*
>
> -Peter F. Drucker-

The larger the original pool of applicants, the greater the chances of reducing the pool to approximately twelve outstanding candidates. However, writing criteria is similar to writing bid specifications; the tighter the specifications, the fewer bids will be received. The looser the criteria, the greater the number of nuisance applications.

When screening applications, the committee may want to use a grid system. This is a chart with the names of candidates on the vertical axis and the approved criteria on the horizontal axis. Each line represents each applicant's credentials according to the criteria categories. The advantage of such a system is that it allows an objective comparison of candidates. This is particularly useful when screening many applications simultaneously.

The job of the committee then becomes one of interviewing the candidates whose credentials best meet the stated criteria. The other applicants' credentials are held to the side until the entire selection and hiring process is completed. Those applicants eliminated early during the process of reviewing credentials should not be informed of their status until a candidate has been hired. This will save the committee and the district some embarrassment if the committee must go back to the entire pool of applicants, as is often the case, when the successful applicant turns down the job offer.

After screening folders and credentials, a group of approximately twelve semifinalists may be selected. Each semifinalist's references must be called. It is highly advisable to use the same list of questions when calling each semifinalist's references. This will allow for more objective decision making and prevent the need to call anyone's references more than once. One method for rating candidates on their references response to questions is to use a *valence chain.* Positive recommendations are listed as "+," negative recommendations are listed as "-" and neutral recommendations are listed as "±." Generally, recommendations given over the telephone are more frank than written recommendations. Neutral, unenthusiastic or noncommittal recommendations might indicate negative reference information if the candidate is well known to the person giving the recommendation. Or, there might be some implicit meanings underlying neutral recommendations that can be explored by telephone. Fear of litigation prevents many references from placing specifics in writing.

It is often unreasonable to expect anyone or any committee to interview all twelve semifinalists for the same job. Therefore, of the twelve semifinalists, often all but the top five may be eliminated. The exact number of final candidates often depends on the time the district has available for interviews and on any budget constraints regarding committee member release time, and interviewing expenses. The committee may have a structured interview sheet where each person asks one question in turn while others write down reactions or answers to the questions and discussion. Care must be taken not to violate the civil rights of applicants. Finalists also may be asked to react to case problems and pre-approved tests of their knowledge of pedagogy and subject matter. Some districts incorporate the observation of finalists in real teaching situations.

The names of the interviewed finalists may be presented to the superintendent in prioritized order of desirability, with pros and cons next to each finalist's name, or according to other district policy. The name presented by the superintendent to the board of education for hiring approval will likely be the superintendent's choice of the finalists presented. In all but the very largest of school districts, the superintendent will have also interviewed the finalists. Therefore, the superintendent's recommendation to the board of education will be from a very small pool of finalists selected by the selection committee, interviewed by the selection committee, and selected and interviewed by the superintendent. Throughout the process, the superintendent, personnel director, and entire selection committee would do well to keep in constant communication. Position requirements often change drastically as enrollments and teacher assignments become clearer at the year's end.

Discrimination in Employment

The Equal Protection Clause of the U.S. Constitution bears upon race, sex, age, and handicap discrimination in the workplace. Emanating from this clause, the Civil Rights Act of 1964, the Equal Pay Act, the Age Discrimination in Employment Act, the Pregnancy

Discrimination Act, and the Rehabilitation Act have all addressed issues of employment discrimination.

To support claims of discrimination, plaintiffs must provide evidence of historical developments, the exact sequence of experiences leading to discrimination, and departure from accepted norms and practices. Similarly, the district must document fair procedures, and the adherence to necessary criteria in selecting a teacher with needed skills. (Alexander & Alexander, 1985) (also see Chapter 3).

Job Analysis

Before a job analysis, it is important to have an overview of the total arrangement of departments, school and work units, and jobs within the school district. An organizational chart indicates who reports to whom, what specialized functions exist within the school district, and the presence of overlapping functions or conflicting areas of decision making.

A *process chart* is more specific than an organization chart. It displays how jobs are connected to each other in the process of a project over time. It shows the flow of work to and from lower-level employees and a breakdown of jobs into specific tasks. More sophisticated program evaluation and review techniques using *critical path methods* are used in industry as part of *statistical process quality control* to move a process toward peak efficiency.

Job analysis involves an examination of the duties and responsibilities of jobs and how they fit together in the mission of the school district. Each school district expects that the work being done by its employees is according to the stated objectives and goals of the school district.

Job analysis, illustrated in Figure 8-5, involves examining the mission of the school district, work presently being done by employees, the extent of the coordination of these tasks, data collected on worthwhile and dysfunctional aspects of work, job descriptions, job specifications, and how employees perform within related task units (Ivancevich & Glueck1986). The term *job evaluation* is used to describe a process for determining the correct amount of pay for a specific job or job category.

Job analysis examines the priority devoted to completing important job tasks, the grouping of tasks into jobs, the structure of jobs for increasing performance, the behaviors needed to perform the work, the human qualifications necessary for particular jobs, and the relationship between job specifications and the needs of students.

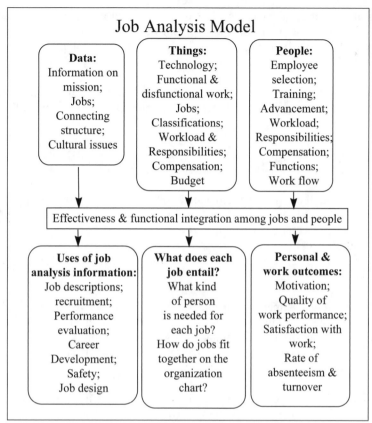

Figure 8-5

Job analysis information supports administrative guidelines for employee selection, standards for performance, payment of overtime, defense against unfair discrimination charges, and the physical requirements needed to perform a job. Job analysis is devoted to preparation of job descriptions, job specifications, recruitment, selection, performance evaluation, and training, staff development, career advancement programs, compensation, safety, and job design. Many personnel managers now believe that job analysis is essential for satisfying federal requirements under the Fair Labor Standards Act, the Civil Rights Act, and the Equal Pay Act, as well as to maintain the standards established with several landmark cases (Ivancevich & Glueck,.1986). Job analysis information also can be used to justify essential positions in the school district and recommended personnel expenditures during budget hearings, or under austerity conditions.

Direct observation, as a technique in job analysis, is used for positions involving work with children. The technique examines complex behaviors involved in dealing with large or small groups of students, with students who are handicapped and require much attention, and with tasks varying in social and emotional requirements. This observation is not for evaluating teachers; rather, it is for examining the tasks necessary for job completion and for defining work flow.

Interviews of people currently holding positions are often used with observations to permit a fuller understanding of what the person is doing and feeling and about the stresses and strains of work.

Functional job analysis divides jobs up into three areas: data, things, and people (see Figure 8-5).

- The *data* dimension might include information on the relationship between the job and the district's mission, the formal relationships between the job and other jobs in the district, and any cultural issues.

- The *things* dimension includes technical essentials and the equipment that facilitates work.

- The *people* dimension includes socially interactive situations such as the requirements in the job for leadership, negotiating ability, instructing ability, supervising ability, persuading ability, speaking ability, serving ability, and the ability to take instructions. These are the people skills necessary in the job under analysis.

Additional knowledge to be included in the job analysis includes information received by the position holder; the mental processes required for reasoning, decision making, and planning the relationships with other people required to perform the job; the physical activities and tools needed to perform the job; and the social and physical context where the job is to be performed. (Ivancevich & Gueck, 1986).

Job analysis of the position of *teacher* in school districts is particularly difficult because the job is socially interactive, requiring artistic and cultivated interpersonal skills, the ability to deal with the emotional pressure of changing behaviors, and consistent management of the tasks and actions of many young people at one time. Job analysis also should address *class size* and the number of different subjects taught by each job incumbent.

The U.S. Department of Labor publishes the *Dictionary of Occupational Titles*, which may help in the initial stages of a job analysis. Obviously, sizable differences exist among the work requirements of different kinds of teachers, bus drivers, cafeteria workers, secretaries, and school administrators.

Job Descriptions

One of the products provided by a systematic job analysis, a job description, provides a description of what the job involves. A job description usually includes: (Ivancevich & Gueck, 1986)

- Job title
- Job summary
- Job activities
- Working conditions
- Physical environment
- Social environment
- Illustrative responsibilities
- Organizational relationships between the employee and important others including to whom the job incumbent reports
- Decision making and discretionary authority
- Systems of communications for disseminating information to others
- General supervision activities
- Initiative and independent judgment required in performance of assigned tasks.

A list of job activities can include information regarding participation in decision making, participation in school management, leadership responsibilities, those with whom the employee confers, functions maintained independently, employee evaluation, employees supervised, and a contingency description such as "other related work as assigned."

Affirmative Action

Rebore (1991) presents an excellent historical analysis of orders and legislation affecting the present state of affirmative action. One of the first official acknowledgments of what is now known as *affirmative action* can be traced through the following:

- President Franklin D. Roosevelt's Executive Order 8802 issued in 1941. This established a policy of equal employment opportunity in companies holding defense contracts.

- In 1961, President John F. Kennedy issued Executive Order 10925 establishing the President's Committee on Equal Employment Opportunity, the first committee having the power to make and enforce its own rules by penalizing noncomplying contractors.

- In 1965, President Lyndon Baines Johnson's Executive Order 11246 gave the Secretary of Labor jurisdiction over government contract compliance and established the Office of Federal Contract Compliance, replacing the Committee on Equal Employment Opportunity. Every employer was thereby required to agree not to discriminate against anyone in hiring or during employment because of race, color, creed, or national origin.

- President Johnson's Executive Order 11375 amended Executive Order 11246 by adding sex and religion to the list of protected categories.

- The Equal Employment Opportunity Commission (EEOC) was established by Title VII of the Civil Rights Act of 1964 and strengthened by the 1972 Equal Employment Opportunity Act. It extended coverage to private employers of 15 or more persons, all educational institutions, all state and local governments, public and private employment agencies, labor unions with fifteen or more members, and joint labor-management committees for apprenticeships and training.

The following eight steps provide a framework for school district compliance with EEOC guidelines:

1) Each school district should have a written policy, to be enforced by the superintendent.
2) The superintendent should appoint a top-level official to implement the program. This official's usual title would be *Director of Affirmative Action*.
3) The district should publicize the program internally and externally.
4) The district must survey itself for minority and female employees by job classification. The percentage of minorities and females in each major job classification should approximate the percentage in the relevant geographic labor market. This will identify any *underutilization* or *concentration* of minorities and females.
5) The district must develop measurable and remedial goals on a timetable, with targets for the employment of minority employees.
6) The district must develop specific programs to eliminate any discriminatory barriers.
7) The district must establish internal auditing and reporting systems to monitor and evaluate progress toward the goals of affirmative action.
8) The district must develop supportive programs such as those that a) encourage current employees to further their education to qualify for promotions and b) aid in the recruitment of minorities and females.

Developing a Philosophy of Affirmative Action

Affirmative action assures that professional employees represent the broadly based community, minorities included. A written philosophy of affirmative action assures community communications, public relations, and community support.

In public schools, and many private schools as well, many perceive as critical the school's relationship to the community, with its social and economic support. Changes in the social, cultural, and ethnic composition of the residential areas of the community determine changes in the enrollment of schools. Often, new teachers reflect changes in the ethnic composition of the community, while older teachers reflect the historical social basis of the community. While schools can help the community adjust to social stress, more often, schools become the focal point of cultural and social tensions (Castetter, 1986).

It is essential for school districts to develop increased awareness among employees. All employees perceive and interpret the present in terms of prior experiences, "sifting" their expectations through their cultural traditions, habits, and background experiences. An ombudsman may help overcome misunderstandings and problems. For many minorities, prejudice is very close to the surface of their experiences with nonminorities. Sensitivities may be high, especially during times of scarcity of economic resources, such as the availability of jobs, promotions, and security.

Because employees must believe in the fairness of the administration of rewards and criticism, establishing acceptance and trust should be part of the work relationship for everyone. An extra measure of care should be devoted to encouraging, guiding and supporting equitable administrative behavior despite race, religion, gender, or ethnic background.

Extra care also needs to be extended toward the goal of improving communication between minority and nonminority employees. Special programs on cross-cultural communications, problem solving, and conflict management among employees will extend the ability of the school district to function effectively. Once a successful affirmative action program is in place, the school district will be better able to communicate more effectively with all the constituencies within the school district. Students are also very sensitive to any perceived inequities in hiring, promotion, and tenure of faculty and staff.

Providing minority employment is not enough. Employers should feel a sense of responsibility toward new employees and should try to help them fit into the faculty or staff. Employees who feel a part of the team will be more willing to act as team players.

Finally, personnel administrators must be aware of human sensitivities, be calm and understanding of human imperfections, and be fair and faithful to the challenge of teamwork.

Problem-Solving Affirmative Action Issues

Affirmative action goes far beyond minority issues. It also involves community relationships, overcoming problems of bureaucratic isolation, and avoiding authoritarianism. To work successfully with a workforce of people from many backgrounds and cultures, it can be helpful to follow a few suggestions for educational administrators that may keep things running smoothly.

- Be mindful of personnel stress and dissatisfaction. Those employees who appear dissatisfied should know that they can talk to their principal, a personnel administrator, or the superintendent.
- Speak and act in an affirmative manner, asserting positive efforts to benefit all groups in the community.
- Explain personnel policies before tensions surface.
- Publicize the job advancements of paraprofessionals to professional teaching positions and of teachers to administrative positions. Career advancement is a matter of pride for all employees, in particular those in the community who identify most closely with those promoted. Figure 8-6 illustrates how community constituencies may be included in selecting personnel for hiring and advancement. Care should be taken to follow board-approved guidelines for affirmative action.
- Use public relations work to emphasize these efforts at affirmative action so that the entire community can understand the district's interest in equity.
- Have "top management" participate in any meetings involving community concern about affirmative action. This is an excellent time to take advantage of the situation and show interest in minority issues through presentations on the latest efforts to help minority interests advance.
- Avoid compromising contract issues that will impede contract negotiations. While it is important to respond fully to a grieving group, it is also important to insist on respect for all people. Emotions will be expressed at such meetings. This is understandable and should be handled by administrators in a calm and accepting way. Agree to discuss individual problems in a confidential situation. Listen actively. (Refer to Chapter 12 for methods of conflict resolution.)
- Be willing to make symbolic gestures that communicate meaningfully the interest in all the community's constituencies. Administrators need to follow through on agreements. Symbolic gestures indicate more credible cooperative relations for the future.
- Follow up on agreements with attention to details and the relationship that has been or is being established. Maintain dialogue even when it is difficult to do so. Asking the aggrieved for their opinions can establish an initial climate of respect, but follow-through will develop the actual trust necessary for further growth.

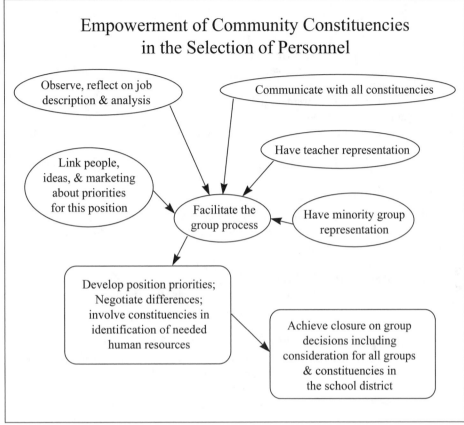

Empowerment of Community Constituencies in the Selection of Personnel

Observe, reflect on job description & analysis

Communicate with all constituencies

Have teacher representation

Link people, ideas, & marketing about priorities for this position

Facilitate the group process

Have minority group representation

Develop position priorities; Negotiate differences; involve constituencies in identification of needed human resources

Achieve closure on group decisions including consideration for all groups & constituencies in the school district

Figure 8-6

Employee Charges of Discrimination

The EEOC receives thousands of charges from employees alleging discrimination each year. State-level agencies are usually involved. The following is the process that must generally begin within 180 days of the alleged discrimination (Rebore, 1991).

1) *Investigation*, including the supoena of employer records.
2) *Determination of reasonable cause* or *no cause*.
3) *Conciliation*, whereby both parties come to an agreement or whereby the EEOC gives the charging party a right-to-sue notice granting the charging party 90 days to bring legal action against the employer.
4) *Litigation*, wherein the EEOC sues the alleged discriminating employer.

Maintenance

Maintenance of employees includes all the terms and conditions of employment. Compensation and benefits, employee evaluations, supervisory procedures, grievance procedures, dismissal procedures, due process procedures, workers compensation, safety and health issues, insurance plans, retirement policies, health benefits, life insurance, annuities, and collective bargaining all contribute to the environment within which employees work. How carefully these are dealt with can mean the difference between motivated employees and angry employees.

Collective Bargaining

Labor laws, which govern many aspects of employment, affect the conduct of collective bargaining, strikes, wages, hours, and working conditions. Four separate acts of Congress affecting collective bargaining are:

- *Norris-Laguardia Act of 1932*

  Concept: Workers have the right to organize. Management cannot require employees to promise nonaffiliation with unions ("yellow dog" contracts)

- *National Labor Relations Act of 1935 (The Wagner Act)*

  Concept: Workers have the right to organize. This act prevents employers from any discrimination against union members and requires employers to bargain with representatives of their employees ' union. The National Labor Relations Board (NLRB) was established to conduct union elections.

- *Labor-Management Relations Act of 1947 (Taft-Hartley Act)*

  Concept: Protects an employee's right not to join a union, outlaws closed shops, allows federal government to seek injunctions to postpone strikes injurious to national welfare, prohibits unions from refusing to bargain. These and other prohibitions of the Taft-Hartley Act imposed many restrictions on unions.

- *The Labor-Management Reporting and Disclosure Act of 1959 (Landrum-Griffin Act)*

  Concept: Union members have the freedom to speak at union meetings and have a secret ballot on proposed dues increases.

Over 75% of the states also have permissive or mandatory statutes concerning the rights of public school employees to organize.

Contracts

**Five Basic Elements
of Valid Contracts**

- Offer & acceptance
- Competent Persons
- Consideration
- Legal subject matter
- Proper form

Contracts in the United States are protected by the constitution. This basic element of the constitution guarantees the viability of agreements made between people so that government cannot invalidate them. (U.S. Constitution, Article I, Section 10). In the famous Dartmouth College case, the Supreme Court interpreted the Constitution as saying that states could not enact laws that impair responsibilities of contracts.

In 1927, the Indiana legislature passed a law repealing tenure for teachers. The Supreme Court of Indiana overruled a lower court, saying that particular attention should be given to laws such as tenure and retirement statutes that create a contract between an individual and the state. Contracts by school districts must conform to general contract law, but they must be defined as an agreement between two or more competent persons and must include the five basic elements of valid contracts: (State ex rel. Anderson v. Brand, 303 US 95, 58 S.Ct. 433 1938 Alexander & Alexander, p. 553-7). In the illustration above, *consideration* refers to the trade of something of value for something else of value.

Terms and Conditions of Employment

Terms and conditions of employment concern collective bargaining agreements and related labor rules, the work environment, and supervisory behavior. Contracts specify aspects of employment, protecting the rights of employer and employee, the rules and procedures for grievances, notice of termination, appointment to tenure, and just about anything else both parties agree to put in writing.

Contracts deal with issues agreed to by employees and management to overcome problems and address issues not covered in state laws. Items agreed to may include work procedures, administrative procedures as they apply to employees, the length of time teachers may teach, the length and number of faculty meetings they must attend, grievance procedures, dismissal procedures, employment procedures, and empowerment issues. Class size may be negotiated; however, boards of education are usually not required to do so. Although teachers argue that class size is a condition of employment, boards often argue that class size is strictly a management decision.

Terms and conditions of employment also may include aspects of employment as they relate to the later years of a tenured teacher's life. The age for retirement has been set by federal law at age 70. Thus, the contract must indicate when and under what conditions employees may retire before age 70. It also must specify due process procedures to insure the fair treatment of employees. The contract also may grant temporary leaves with and without pay for detoxification stays at clinics for alcoholism and drug abuse. The contract also may resolve issues of due process for determining when a tenured employee is no longer competent.

Mediation, Arbitration, and Strikes

Three possibilities exist when contract negotiations reach an impasse. A mediator may be called in to listen to both sides of the impasse and makes suggestions for resolving it. The suggestion arrived at through *mediation* is not binding on either the union or the board of education.

Outside arbitrators also may be called upon to listen and examine each side of the problem. In *arbitration,* however, the arbitrator's decision is binding and becomes part of the contract.

Public school employees may organize unions, and negotiate agreements, but they may not *strike* in most states. They often strike anyway. Without authorization from a state statute, school boards may not submit to binding arbitration. Distinction between public and private sector employees is insignificant, although the laws of the state may treat them differently. Strikes by private employees may be at least as crippling as strikes by public employees, and the same rights guaranteed by the constitution apply to public employees (Alexander & Alexander).

Teacher Appraisals

Decisions must be made about teacher reemployment and tenure. Appraisals must be written, usually annually, depending on state law and local contact. Formal decisions about the future work of the teacher must be substantiated and must be fair. *Fairness* incorporates complete records, investigation of questionable events, due process procedures, and a positive interpretation to the fullest extent possible but with interest in the community's values and interests for its children.

As concerns become more serious, records should be kept of discussions held and efforts to remediate problems. It is important to keep records on any serious personnel question. Discussions in the hallways with teachers, easily forgotten, need to be written down. Significant encounters in the school administrator's office should be written down to create a *track record* and *documentation* that may be used in difficult decisions down the line.

As a practical issue, the administrator may keep a file folder with scraps of paper as reminders about concerns, questions, and discussions throughout the year. Copies of accomplishments, notes on unusual efforts and praise from parents, formal reports, written letters, and written observations should be given to the teacher. Leading up to the writing of annual evaluations, the informal scraps of paper may be saved for the preparations of these evaluations, including notes from the teacher. Notes of informal discussions may be used in formal performance appraisals and then thrown out. Among the more successful schools, principals go to greater lengths to write letters of praise to teachers for their accomplishments and extraordinary efforts on behalf of the children.

In the most successful schools, teachers' personnel folders are thought of as portfolios of teaching accomplishments. Copies of special projects, pictures of outstanding bulletin boards, pictures of assembly presentations, and copies of outstanding worksheets and student works may be archived here as testimonials to teachers' achievements. This positive outlook on teacher efforts and accomplishments encourages more of the same, and saving the recollections of these accomplishments increases their positive value as inspiration and motivation. Thus saved and occasionally shared, these accomplishments become symbols of work that is valued by the school and the community.

Tenure

Usually, before teachers are granted tenure, teachers may be dismissed for almost any reason at all. Once tenure has been granted, the teacher must be reemployed in that school district while there is an appropriate teaching position until death, resignation, or retirement. Only in the case of formal charges and due process can a tenured teacher be fired. Some refer to the three "I's" as reasons for firing a tenured teacher: incompetence, immorality, and insubordination.

Tenure allows the teacher relative freedom from the disruptive professional fluctuations that occur when administrators change, or school populations change and teaching methods must adapt to societal transformations. Tenure guarantees full due process procedures. Although tenured teachers may be reassigned to other teaching duties as needed, the courts dislike "undesirable reassignments" used to get rid of a tenured teacher. If the teacher is qualified to teach in the new assignment area, it is permissible for the school to reassign the teacher to the new area. If a tenured teacher is to be found unable to teach, the case must be clear and the teacher must be dealt with fairly at every point (Supreme Court of Pennsylvania, 1959, 397 Pa. 601, 156 A.2d 830 Alexander & Alexander, 1985).

Stability is important to schools as maintainers of social mores and civil responsibilities among the younger community members. Tenure for teachers helps maintain stability for schools and communities, and tenure is often seen as an advantage given instead of higher wages. But it has never been accepted as an excuse for underpaying teachers. In many school districts, longevity agreements in teacher contracts assure that the most experienced teachers continue in the positions they have held and are qualified for. Often, new positions are opened to tenured teachers on the basis of seniority. Similarly, "excessed" positions may eliminate the least senior employees first.

Teacher Dismissal

A distinction is made between nonrenewal and dismissal. When a teacher is not tenured, contracts tend to be year-to-year. If at the end of the year the contract is not renewed, the teacher is in effect out of a job but has not been dismissed for cause. State laws usually specify the date by which a teacher must be notified of nonrenewal unless there is some question of constitutional freedom or right. Dismissal, on the other hand, requires full procedural due process.

When teachers have tenure, they are entitled to hearings before termination of employment. Incompetency means that a teacher is not physically or mentally fit to perform effectively. Insubordination indicates a willful disregard for implied and explicit directions of the employer as does recurring refusals to obey reasonable regulations. (Alexander & Alexander, 1985).

Nontenured teachers are most often given written probationary agreements of a year or more. Teachers are rarely dismissed during the school year, because when this occurs there are serious concerns for the safety and well-being of the students. Dismissal during the school year is an extreme action. The recruitment and hiring of a replacement teacher has a disruptive influence on the flow of the school year for the students.

Procedural Due Process

Due process means all parties have had the opportunity to express themselves fully on any issues of disagreement. As issues become more important, requirements become more complicated. Usually, issues are dealt with first informally and become more formal as the issues become more serious. When constitutional rights are at stake, it is expected that some kind of prior hearing has been held (Supreme Court of the United States, 1972 408 US 564, 92 S.Ct. 2701).

Grievance Procedures

Grievance procedures are formal due process procedures usually mentioned in the teacher contract. If the parties have had opportunities to express themselves in informal situations, assuming a degree of responsiveness on both sides, formal procedures may not be necessary. Once fair and informal approaches to the problem have been exhausted, the personnel administrator can anticipate formal grievance procedures.

Generally, it is considered a better idea to settle problems informally than to get into formal hearings and charges. People who speak to one another face to face usually can work things out in the most efficient manner. On the other hand, it is a common practice for teachers' unions to seek legal remedies. Often, the union representative should be called in as a part of the procedural due process hearing to simplify issues that may arise later. Records should be kept concerning all meetings for which there may be formal implications later (Alexander & Alexander, 1985). The more formal the proceedings, the more difficult it may be to compromise in future proceedings.

Compensation and Benefits

Salary and benefits are critical issues for most teachers, who must rely on their salary for support of their families. These issues in personnel must be treated as basic human survival issues. It is essential that paychecks get to employees on expected paydays with "robotic" predictability (Castetter, 1986).

The Equal Pay Act was intended to eliminate salary discrimination based on gender, all other things being equal. This act, incorporated into the Civil Rights Act of 1964, allows different amounts of pay to be bestowed for seniority, merit, production differences, and situations in which pay is based on any factor other than sex, race, color, religion, and national origin. (Alexander & Alexander, 1985).

Insurance

Employee benefits may include insurance, maternity leave, paid time off, paternity leave, program management, retirement income, disability income, tuition credits, time off without pay, temporary health leaves, accumulated sick days, health insurance, maternity leaves, paternity leaves, and sabbatical leaves.

Disability insurance is usually an optional benefit for which teachers must pay in addition to their regular insurance. Disability insurance pays employees a significant percentage of their salary if they become disabled.

Generally, school districts provide some type of health insurance for their employees, with the employee usually paying for additional family coverage and dental insurance. Premiums for group insurance are much lower than for individuals, so it is in the employees' best interest to sign up for group coverage. Basic health insurance coverage may cover most medical expenses for hospitalization and related medical expenses.

Health Maintenance Organization (HMO) insurance is an alternative to standard health insurance. Employees in an HMO plan can only use the services of physicians preapproved by the HMO. The use of physicians attached to other HMOs or completely independent is sometimes permitted if their specialty is not available in the employee's HMO or at increased cost to the employee. There are many variations of standard HMOs.

Life insurance, usually an optional benefit, is especially important for employees with younger children. These employees need to know that their spouses and children will have financial security. Premiums are lower when employees are younger and group plans are even less expensive.

Annuities are similar to life insurance policies, but in reverse. After making payments into the policy during the working years, the policy pays retirement income to the employee after retirement. The longer the employee has worked, the greater the amount paid to the employee upon retirement. There is no time limit on the length of the payments made, since the payments are based on actuarial tables used to compute life expectancy. Older employees may wish to have an annuity to add to the pension benefit. Annuities often offer the employee tax-sheltered annuity payments; that is, taxes on those amounts are only paid when the employee is retired and collecting the annuity. The employee is usually in a lower tax bracket at that time resulting in a lower tax rate.

Workers Compensation

Workers' compensation is an insurance program required by states to cover injuries on the job. If an employee is injured on the job, there are funds available for medical expenses and employee income. Usually, the employer pays a percentage of the employee salary into this insurance fund. The insurance rates increase based on the history of the work organization or the type of job held by the employee. For example, the premiums for bus drivers may be higher than for teachers because of higher occupational exposure to risk.

Unemployment Insurance

Employers are required by their states to pay into a pool from which funds are drawn to pay unemployed persons for short periods of time between jobs. The amount an employer must pay is often based on its rate of firings and layoffs. The more often the district lays off or fires its employees, the higher their unemployment premiums. Teachers are not entitled to unemployment benefits during their usual period of summer unemployment.

Occupational Safety and Health Act (OSHA)

Occupational safety issues may be difficult in any workplace, but when a community's children are in the same buildings, an extra measure of caution is strongly advised. The public will not tolerate any inaction in dealing with any questionable margin of safety. If a safety issue affects the employees, assume that it also affects students and is a sensitive issue in the school district. OSHA specifies the levels of safety required in various situations. Its tough enforcement standards have been blamed for placing undue pressure on organizations to spend large amounts of money for questionable additions to margins of safety. However, those same tough standards have made very significant gains in employee safety. School decision making ought to err on the side of safety as it affects everyone.

Community Issues in Personnel Administration

Much of what is decided by school boards occurs at informal private meetings or in discussions over the telephone with other board members and the superintendent of schools. Even sunshine laws, which require decisions to be made in public, cannot prevent board members from discussing their business informally. Often there are extensive discussions among various public constituencies influencing the thinking and the votes of board members. Behind each school board member there is likely to be a group that is informally influential in the viewpoint of that board member. It could be a church, a synagogue, a social group or club, a volunteer fire department, or an active teachers union.

State laws governing education often severely limit the discretionary authority of school board members. Many board members are elected on their promise to effect change, but. subsequent to their election, they are likely to realize their limitations.

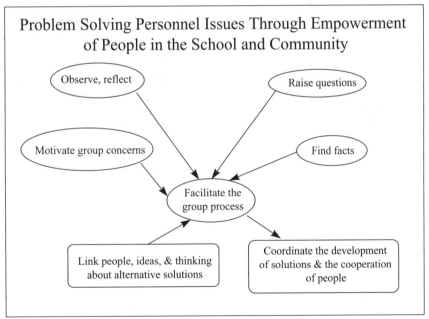

Figure 8-7

Summary

Community, student, faculty, and staff participation in schools will be enhanced by fostering greater involvement in the personnel function. Empowering people has long been the key to increasing commitment, raising performance levels, and decreasing negative conflict. This chapter provided information about many legal and regulatory requirements affecting the personnel function. While legal and regulatory compliance is mandatory, it will not cultivate trust among the many special interest groups in education. Trust can only come from a history of true respect for the values of people. Faculty and staff are expensive resources requiring maintenance and development to ensure flexibility and performance over time.

Case Problem: Cleaver School District

The Cleaver School District, a small city school district located in the Midwest, is in a relatively isolated city, mostly populated with descendants of Irish and Polish immigrants. Most of the African-American and Hispanic minorities of the community live together close to School Three, a small neighborhood school with 300 children in grades K-5.

Three years ago, the school district received a large five-year grant for a needed bilingual program for 75 Hispanic children. The bilingual program at that time was housed entirely in School Three. Other than a Chapter I resource program and a Title IV migrant education program, there were no efforts giving any kind of recognition to the needs of African-American students. The bilingual program required the hiring of teachers who could speak Spanish and English. They would engage the elementary students in the development of English language learning and a program of basic literacy skills in Spanish.

By the summer of last year the school had formulated a procedure for institutionalizing the program through local positions and hiring bilingual teachers who could teach in English and Spanish. There was a need, however, to hire a third grade bilingual teacher. In a year of teacher surplus in the Cleaver School District, approximately 160 applications were received for the opening. The principal screened the folders personally. A systematic procedure using a grid system was used to evaluate all the folders fairly and objectively.

The principal selected a committee of people including the nonbilingual teacher at the third grade level, the bilingual teacher for the second grade, a bilingual parent, the supervisor for the bilingual program, the Spanish-speaking home-school coordinator, and the president of the school's parent association. The principal chaired the sessions where the prospective teachers were interviewed.

Ten teacher candidates were interviewed. That included all candidates who appeared on paper as possibilities in being able to fulfill the language requirement. Approximately half the interview time was to be conducted in Spanish. Each member of the interview committee asked one question of each candidate. Most of the teacher candidates were unable to fulfill the Spanish language requirement since a high level of proficiency was required for modeling native language literacy to elementary students who are native speakers of Spanish.

Among the teacher candidates invited was a teacher who was in fact on strike in a much larger city but who said he was unemployed. He was an African-American teacher who normally was employed by the larger Great Lakes City School District. Upon being asked whether he was able to speak Spanish, he said that he spoke a little Spanish but was not really proficient in the language. The rest of the interview politely continued in English. Near the end of the interview, the teacher was asked about his plans for the future. He was rather ambiguous, so he was asked if he would be interested in a position at the school as a paraprofessional (there were two paraprofessionals at the school who were certified teachers).

Shortly after the interview, the school district received complaints from the State Department of Human Rights; the U. S. Department of Health, Education and Welfare, Division of Human Affairs; and the U.S. Department of Civil Rights complaining of discrimination in hiring practices. Investigations continued for the next 2 years from all three departments. Each department sent a person to the school district for an entire day to interview the people involved in the selection. One department sent out a Spanish-speaking legal investigator to interview the hired teacher in Spanish and to observe in the classroom.

When the investigations were completed, the findings indicated that there was nothing wrong with the hiring of the teacher, but that the African-American candidate should not have been asked if he was interested in being a paraprofessional, because this was viewed as demeaning. Findings on the history of the school district also included a history of not hiring minorities, and difficulties for minority employees who were hired in finding housing in the community. Recommendations were made for a more active affirmative action program.

References

Alexander, K. & Alexander, M. D. (1985). *American public school law* (2nd ed.) St. Paul: West Publishing Company.

Bittel, L.R. (1987). *The complete guide to supervisory training and development.* Reading, MA. Addison-Wesley.

Carlson, R.V. & Awkerman, G. (Eds.). (1991). *Educational planning: Concepts, Strategies, practices.* New York: Longman Publishing Company.

Castetter, W.B. (1986). *The personnel function in educational administration,* (4th ed.) New York: Macmillan Publishing Company.

Drucker, P. F. (1990*). Managing the non-profit organization: Principles and Practices.* New York: Harper Collins Publishers.

Glatthorn, A.A. (1990) *Supervisory leadership.* Glenview, IL: Scott Foresman/Little Brown Higher Education.

Heilman, M.E. & Hornstein, H.A. (1982). *Managing human forces in organizations.* Homewood, IL: Richard D. Irwin, Inc.

Henderson, R. I. (1982). *Influencing employee behavior at work.* Atlanta: Georgia State University, College of Business Administration.

Ivancevich, J.M. & Glueck, W.F. (1986*) Foundations of personnel/human resource management.* Plano, Texas: Business Publications.

Johnson, S. M. (1991). *Teachers at work: Achieving success in our schools.* New York: Basic Books, Inc.

Keith, S. and Girling, R. H. (1991). *Education management and participation.* Boston: Allyn & Bacon.

Lieberman, A. & Miller, L. (1984*). Teachers, their world & their work: Implications for school improvement.* Alexandria, VA: Association for Supervision and Curriculum Development.

Morrison, J.H. (1970*). Human factors in supervising minority group employees: Conference leaders guide.* Chicago: Public Personnel Association.

Nadler, L. (Ed.). (1984). *The handbook of human resource development.* New York: John Wiley & Sons.

Rebore, Ronald W. (1991). *Personnel administration in education: a management approach.* Englewood Cliffs, NJ: Prentice-Hall.

Sergiovanni, T.J. (1990). *Value-added leadership: how to get extraordinary performance in schools.* San Diego: Harcourt Brace Jovanovich.

Sergiovanni, T.J. (1984). *Handbook for effective department leadership* (2nd ed.). Bost).on: Allyn & Bacon

Stanton, E.S. (1982). *Reality-centered people management: key to improved productivity.* New York: American Management Association.

Chapter 9
Staff Development

Linda J. Schmidt*

This chapter will define staff development and its accompanying philosophies, recommend the timing of various program elements, furnish planning methods, and present mechanisms for administering staff development programs.

Introduction

At no time has staff development been more important than it is today. The profession of teaching is currently undergoing profound changes, and an effective school administrator will use staff development to help staff understand and adapt to these changes. The changes, at their most basic level, relate to what is to be taught and the methods by which to teach it. Beyond basic levels, they involve new state or federal teaching mandates that directly affect the operation of schools, such as those that relate to teaching children with special needs. The changes relate to new laws or new interpretations of laws that seriously affect the teacher's responsibilities and behavior (Petzko, 1998). The changes also relate to rapid shifts in the school's student population as new people come into a district, either from other parts of the country or as immigrants from foreign countries. Teachers must learn about cultures that are very different from those in which they grew up (Gibson and Follo, 1998).

More hostile work environments also create the need for change. The pressures put on today's young people to succeed are not only making students more volatile and hard to control, but they are also making parents and community members more hostile. Personal safety is increasingly a matter of concern for teachers in schools far beyond the inner city (Reglin & Reitzammer, 1998). Indeed, teacher burnout is becoming one of the critical issues affecting the functioning of our schools.

The changes also concern new ways of evaluating a school's effectiveness. In large urban school districts, staff development can make the difference between whether a school meets its set goals or whether it is put on probation. Finally, we are in an era of profound technological change. The advent of the Internet is having a huge effect on teaching and on students. No longer is the school the only portal of knowledge for students. Many students are coming to schools with a knowledge base that, in some aspects far surpasses that of students even 20 years ago. They and their parents are more sophisticated and less forgiving than in the past, and this will add immensely to the pressures placed on the teaching staff. An effective staff development program will help teachers acknowledge and come to terms with the implications of these profound technological changes, and to become effective participants in the information environment (Meltzer & Sherman, 1997).

---

*Linda J. Schmidt and Michael H. Jacobson authored the chapter Staff Development in Kaiser, J.,*Educational Administration, 2nd. ed.* (1993), Mequon, WI: Stylex Publishing Co., Inc.

What is Staff Development?

Staff development is "any planned program of learning opportunities afforded staff members of schools, colleges or other educational agencies for purposes of improving the performance of individuals in already assigned positions" (Harris, 1989, p. 18.). Orlich (1989) provides another definition: "Inservice education denotes programs or activities that are based on identified needs; that are collaboratively planned and designed for a specific group of individuals in the school district; that have a very specific set of learning objectives and activities; and that are designed to extend, add, or improve immediate job-oriented skills, competencies, or knowledge with the employer paying the cost" (p. 5). Staff development takes two major forms: those activities designed to help the individual function better as a professional and those that are designed to help all personnel work together in a harmonious and pleasant environment. The first form deals at a basic job-related level, helping teachers or staff members improve their professional skills and knowledge base. However, it also relates to helping individuals in other ways, for instance, giving them a chance to step back and reflect critically on what they do, allowing them to have their mental space (Darling-Hammond & Cobb, 1995).

To help individual staff members function as a team, staff development should be focused on learning to work together with other teachers, with teachers from other disciplines, with school and district administrators, with teacher's aides, and with all the ancillary personnel that make up a school. By learning to work together, educational professionals will better understand the constraints and burdens felt by others and will be able to contribute to making the work environment a safe and pleasant place.

Staff development helps individual teachers and other school staff members mature as professionals dedicated to helping young people learn. Staff development bonds and molds individuals into an effective team working together for a common end.

To summarize the above, staff development should be able to help teachers and educational professionals to:

- Increase and expand their job awareness, skill acquisition, and knowledge base in their area of expertise
- Be aware of the legal implications that affect their behavior and that of their students
- Come to terms with and embrace change as a constant, not only in their teaching content, but in the students whom they teach
- Recognize telltale signs of external factors that may affect a student's engagement in the classroom, such as drug or alcohol addiction, gang involvement, or emotional or physical abuse at home.
- Develop an awareness of and respect for cultures different from their own
- Recognize the stressors that affect their colleagues and learn what actions they can take to help relieve their stress

- Handle hostile or potentially hostile situations both in class and outside the classroom
- Promote a safe environment for students and staff
- Become competent in managing the technological advances that affect teaching, learning, and the search for information

Not only is the content of staff development important, but also the form. It must be very different than that which has been frequently offered in the past. Staff development programs are unsuccessful if they expect teachers to sit relatively passively while an expert exposes them to new ideas or practices, and where the success of this effort is judged by a measurement of participants' satisfaction with the experience and with the expert's assessment regarding its usefulness to the improvement of student performance. This chapter will provide a theoretical framework and practical ideas for the creation of effective staff development programs.

Who Does Staff Development?

The National Staff Development Council (2002) defines any person who performs the functions of staff development as a trainer. A trainer is a person who helps adults learn through specialized instruction. There exists no restriction in the definition as to whom that person may or should be. Very often, the trainer is someone from outside the organization, perhaps someone from a local college of education or someone from a school that is implementing a program that could be of benefit to the staff, such as operating a year-round program, or implementing a new dress code policy. Some outside experts can be very effective and can offer a perspective that will expand the horizons for the staff. However, sometimes, outside experts come in with little understanding or appreciation for the problems particular to the school to which they are providing staff development. They may bring a one-size-fits-all-prescription, which can sometimes be totally ineffective, and indeed counter-productive. Staff resent giving up valuable time to listen to someone who is ill prepared to offer advice on their specific problems or concerns.

Inservice training by outside experts should be supplemented with training by inside experts. People within the school or school district should also conduct staff development. Superintendents, assistant superintendents, curriculum supervisors, and principals must recognize that they have an obligation to provide and actively participate in staff development. In addition, wise administrators will recognize that there is a wealth of talent and expertise resident in their own teaching staff. The best way to accomplish this is to set up a small committee of either two or three staff members. The money that would have been spent on an outside expert could be allocated to them to attend a conference or visit schools that exemplify the practice they want to research. The benefits of using inside expertise are that 1) the trainers will be around after the inservice training has been completed, 2) the trainers know intimately the issues and context of the school, and 3) staff feel good in that it shows that internal abilities are recognized and respected. School administrations that prohibit teacher involvement in the planning of staff development programs are doomed to failure.

Who Needs Staff Development?

There is little debate here. Staff development activities benefit all members of any organization. The exclusion of any category of employee from staff development activities will be counter productive; it will promote negative feelings from other elements within the school toward that class of employee, and will engender feelings of resentment by the excluded employees who will feel that they are taken for granted and may tend to work accordingly. Staff development helps to prevent people from being stale and may make a difference in reducing turnover of staff, which can be very expensive and disruptive to the functioning of the school. Failure to train and failure to upgrade skills will lead to a diminution of skills and general functional malaise.

The Timing of Staff Development

Most staff development researchers will readily agree that staff development should be continuous. At all times there should be regular meetings where employees are being trained in new skills, new developments in the profession, and team-building activities. This is true despite the annual influx of new employees and the lack of long periods of time available for the presentations.

Orientation of New Staff

The field of education is unique in its scheduling of the arrival of new employees and the transition of seasoned employees. Administrators can count on receiving the bulk of new employees at the beginning of each school year or semester. This is both a problem and an opportunity.

There is an inherent problem in the short period between the arrival date of teachers and that of students. Students arrive expecting to find an educational program in place. The same period of time must also be used by administrators to implement staff development modules available for the entire staff.

This preschool period available for the setup of school and staff development runs from two weeks in some districts to one day in others. This time is often the most important spent with new arrivals to the school, and should not be wasted. Often, however, inservice training for new teachers is reduced to distribution of keys, lesson plans, grade books, the teachers' handbook, a map of the building, the name of the assigned department chairperson, and a request to attend the kickoff faculty meeting. This type of quick orientation does not provide the new teachers with an understanding or even awareness of the school's philosophy, expectations, and policies. The new staff member may feel alienated due to what may be perceived as administrative incompetence at worst or administrative carelessness at best.

The staff development program for new teachers should begin the first day they arrive at school. It should be a concentrated effort aimed not only at making sure that the new teacher has all the initial survival skills and information at hand, but that the new staff member feels welcome as a member of the faculty. No matter how crowded the first day's agenda, the most important item on that agenda is the initial staff development of the new teacher.

This initial day should be the first step in a well-thought-out, well-planned staff development program. What was summarized on the first day and the first week should be reviewed and explored in detail during the teacher's first year at the school. The more that support is given to the new teacher, the lower the probability that the teacher will need assistance.

Continuing Development of Experienced Staff

Professional staff developers maintain that an ongoing staff development program can prevent stagnation. Programs providing teachers with updated information on their areas of expertise ensure a knowledgeable faculty. The acquisition of specific teaching skills provides teachers with the ability to transfer their knowledge to students. Further, the updated information and skills increase teachers' competence and confidence. The behavioral changes are a manifestation of theory into practice. Teachers do change through growth to higher order abilities. The entire basis for all this growth is the belief in the ability that staff can achieve.

All educational staff bring with them a continuum of skills developed through time and training. However, due to the pressures of the job, these skills start to decay. Many of these skills are not regularly used. Skills erode through disuse, but the ability to learn does not. The emerging role of teachers in school management calls for enlightened, informed faculty. Education is one of many professions where there has been a vast knowledge explosion from a rapidly increasing body of research. The results of school reform research have had great effect on teacher behavior. Teachers must be informed of new knowledge and teaching skills to keep current. School administrators can ensure greater levels of staff achievement through continuous staff development designed to provide reinforcement of present skills, new information, and development of new skills.

In addition to improving the skills and competencies of the teacher in the classroom, experienced staff must be helped to learn about the challenges affecting them from outside the classroom. They need to learn about the constraints in the community that affect their students' ability to study at home or to come to school with a mind prepared to learn, especially when it affects other cultures or socioeconomic groups different from their own. They need to know about signs of gang involvement or drug and alcohol addiction, and they need to recognize that they can play an active part in promoting a safe environment in the school–safe for the students and safe for themselves. With more and more students who previously were confined to special education classrooms now being mainstreamed into the regular classroom, there is a greater urgency to form staff development programs to help the teacher create a classroom atmosphere where all students can be accommodated and feel connected.

Planning for Staff Development

The most important stage in providing the staff development program is the planning of the program. The planning process is critical to ensure a relevant program with current and timely topics.

While administrators may have the ultimate responsibility for development of continuous staff development programs, as many faculty members as possible should be involved in the planning of the program. This involvement will ensure sufficient input to provide relevance. Teachers need to feel that they have input and ownership of the program.

The Planning Team

Creation of any staff development plan cannot be a haphazard activity. There needs to be systematic input from the faculty, evaluation of suggestions, evaluation of the feedback received from previous inservice efforts, and utilization of internal resources. One manner in which this can be structured is through the development of a staff development planning team.

Administrators should develop a plan of action ensuring representation from all members of the planning team. In addition, the responsible administrator should make sure that the general staff has some participation in the selection of the personnel who serve on the planning team. Administrative steps for formation of a staff development planning team are listed in Figure 9-1.

Steps in Forming a Staff Development Team

1. Information regarding the nature of the inservice program should be given to the faculty
2. Opportunity for feedback should be given to the faculty
3. Input about the nature of the planning team should be solicited from the faculty
4. The planning team should be announced to the faculty
5. Sufficient time for the planning team members to obtain data from the faculty should be given
6. The planning team should meet periodically with the faculty to assure two-way communication about the inservice program

---

Figure 9-1

These steps are most important in the initiation of a comprehensive staff development program. All communication about the initiation of a staff development program should be clear, concise, and comprehensive. Staff members should receive information regarding the program before the initiation phase, and sufficient time should be provided for staff feedback. When the staff feels they are participating in the initiation of the program, they will not resist it.

If the staff is given opportunity for input about the nature of the planning team, they will feel invested in the program. By allowing the planning team sufficient time to give suggestions regarding the nature of the inservice program, the program will become the staff's program and not the administration's. The planning team thus becomes a realistic and viable means of having the staff identify with the goals and objectives of the program.

The two-way communications element serves not only to obtain additional suggestions about the nature of the inservice program but also serves to allow for open feedback from the staff about the success of the program. Without the opportunity for valid feedback, there will not be an honest evaluation of the program, and without the staff feeling that their feedback is important, the value of the program will be weakened in their eyes.

Methods of Planning for Staff Development

The planning team is the most important factor in planning in staff development. Once a representative planning team is selected, it must be allowed to operate as both an information-gathering team and a topic-selecting team. Both functions are equally important for the development of a successful program.

Assessing Staff Development Needs

The central purpose of staff development programs is to bring about the improvement of teaching, but other issues of interest to staff must not be ignored, as these have a direct effect on their teaching ability. Getting teachers involved in the process of staff development as early as possible is vital for willing participation in staff development activities.

An effective way to find out about the issues of interest to staff is to administer a survey. The survey might also collect other data, such as recommendations for who should run the workshop or staff development activity, and preferences for time and credits. A sample survey is shown in Figure 9-2.

Sample Survey to Assess Staff Development Needs

Name: _____

Staff development is vital to all of us if we are to continue to meet the needs of our students. Please help
us to plan our upcoming staff development activities by letting us know your preferences.

Check the areas that are of interest to you:
_____ Classroom management
_____ Curriculum development in my subject area
_____ Team teaching
_____ Classroom climate/academic climate
_____ Test anxiety/improving testing climate
_____ Safety in the classroom/school
_____ Technology in the classroom
_____ Inter-classroom visitation program
_____ Inter-school visitation program
_____ Multi-cultural awareness
_____ Other. Please specify:

_____

Which curriculum area is of most concern to you?

_____

Who would you like to present this workshop? (Check your preference.)

_____ Teacher in this school. Recommendation?
_____ Teacher in this district. Recommendation?
_____ District personnel. Recommendation?
_____ Consultant. Recommendation?
_____ Other. _____

What times are convenient for you?

_____ After-school hours
_____ Inservice days only
_____ Summer
_____ Other:

_____

Participation incentive
_____ Continuing service credits
_____ Stipend
_____ Release time for curriculum development
_____ Course credit
_____ Other:_____

Figure 9-2

When the results are collected and tabulated, they can be used to generate a rank order of topics for the annual plan for staff development.

Developing Goals and Objectives

The same care in planning that takes place for the education of students should take place for the education of staff members. The selection of topics from a staff needs assessment is only the first step in planning the staff development program (Figure 9-3).

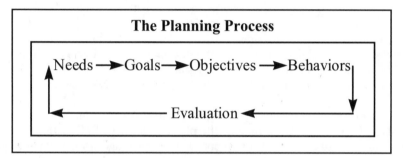

Figure 9-3

The second step in this process is to establish exactly what is to be accomplished through the staff development program. The staff development planning team should indicate what the specific goals of the training should be. Once the goals of the training have been defined, it will be easy to make other decisions about the duration and nature of the training.

Without the establishment of clear-cut goals, it will be impossible to develop a comprehensive program for staff development that will satisfy the needs and desires of the faculty. In addition, it will be impossible to evaluate the success/failure of the program. Finally, it will be impossible to develop a set of behavioral objectives that will state what the desired changes in staff behavior will be as the result of the development activities.

The primary goal of staff development is, as with the goals of education, a change in behavior. Without the specification of what direction that change is to take, it is difficult to develop a program that will result in the desired change.

Under each goal, there should be some clearly defined objectives, preferably specified in such a way that they refer to observable behavior, either on the part of the training participants or, preferably, as evidenced by the students themselves. These objectives should drive the nature of the staff development program and should indicate how they are to be evaluated. From the number of objectives so defined, and the approximate time needed to meet these objectives, it will be easy to determine what length of training should be budgeted to meet the objectives of the program. In addition, from the objectives, it will be possible to define baseline behavior and to evaluate any changes that will occur (see Figure 9-8 for evaluating staff development programs).

Scheduling for Staff Development

Often the most difficult part of planning for a comprehensive staff development program is finding the time in the school day for staff development activities. In many schools, there are few blocks of time available to most of the faculty to use for staff training. In addition, administrators find that it is difficult to schedule staff development activities that consider the different needs of the various grade levels or departments within the school building.

Many school districts are now operating close to the minimum number of days of school allowed by law, and thus cannot have the flexibility to cancel classes to provide for staff development. It has long been recognized that staff development activities, while important before beginning the school year, must continue throughout the school term.

The solution is to use the staff development planning team to develop a plan for continual staff development. Utilization of the planning team will allow the administrator to seek creative methods of ensuring that a comprehensive, ongoing staff development program is initiated. Without faculty involvement in the development of the time schedule, faculty members will simply not buy into creative solutions to the problem.

In many school districts, elementary teachers start their school day at least one-half hour before the arrival of the students. Some of this time is reserved as preparation time for teachers, and some of this time is available to the school administration. One solution to the staff development scheduling problem is for the administrator to yield some of this time for staff development. The utilization of this time also will serve another purpose. By scheduling the teachers into departmental (grade level) segments, this time can be used for targeted staff development—that is, staff development activities that are specifically designed for the staff who will be present. This will eliminate one complaint often received from faculty members:"The material was fine, but I cannot use it . . . why am I here?"

Unfortunately, a half-hour segment of time is usually insufficient time for a comprehensive staff development activity to take place. Here, the administrator must use some innovative practices to ensure the delivery of staff development. Some administrators have developed teacher scheduling so that all the members of a particular department have common preparation periods during the school day. If the teachers have accepted and are committed to the staff development model, they will be willing occasionally to give up a preparation period to participate in a staff development activity. Through creatively scheduling the common preparation period back-to-back with the one-half hour pre-school A.M. inservice time, an hour will be available for the conduct of a staff development program. An hour will suffice for many staff development sessions.

One problem exists in using the above models: the teachers are using a preparation period to receive inservice training. Both activities are important to a teacher, and one should not supplant the other. This model can be used when teachers are willing to arrive earlier or stay later than the normal school day, or if the funds are available to pay the teachers for extending the school day. This will, again, allow for a longer term of staff development without removing preparation time from the teachers' schedules. Unfortunately, this model calls for teachers to be involved in staff development activities before their school day, when they are anticipating the activities of the day, or after the school day, when they are likely to be worn out.

A fourth model calls for inservice activities to occur on a specially called staff development day, either a half-day program or a full day program. Students are either dismissed for this time, or the program is held on a nonschool day. Although this removes some barriers, the lack of available days makes it difficult for the program to be continuous. This will be the case of the one-shot staff development program in many districts.

Fortunately, there is an answer to this dilemma. The combination of a staff development day, followed by a series of brief staff development activities following any of the other models, has long been found to yield great benefit (Dodd, 1987). Usually, in any program, the initial presentation has to be of some length to allow for not only the presentation of the development activities, but to deal with the basis of the program and to establish follow-up activities.

The most important element here is the establishment of the follow-up activities. Without follow-up, staff development may not result in any new behavior. Follow-up is important to give the staff a chance to apply what they have learned and to modify it to their own purposes based on the feedback they receive.

Selecting the Staff Development Provider

After the decisions on topic, goals and objectives, and timeframe have been made, it is important to decide who will provide the staff development activities. Although staff development may have a greater effect when provided by an internal staff member, there are cases where outside personnel should be the inservice providers.

In those cases where no member of the staff has the expertise in the topic to deliver the staff development activities, an outside provider should be selected. When making this decision, these should be some important considerations:

- Outside providers should have credibility in the area in which they are delivering the staff development activities.

- Outside providers should agree to adopt the goals and objectives of the staff development design, while making only approved modifications to the plan.

- Outside providers should be available for continual follow-up activities or should be willing to train members of the staff to provide for follow-up.

- Outside providers should provide references and should have a proven track record in the provision of staff development.

- Outside providers should have some experience in education to lend credence to their presentation.

When making the decision about who should provide staff development, there should be a design to help with the decision making. There is a preferential order for making this decision. This order is:

1. Members of the school staff with demonstrated expertise in the area to be covered by the staff development activities and with experience in staff development

2. Members of the school staff with demonstrated expertise in the area to be covered by the staff development activities but no experience in staff development

3. District-level personnel who have expertise in the area to be covered by the staff development activities

4. Personnel from other districts who have expertise in the area to be covered by staff development activities

5. University personnel who have expertise or training experience in the area to be covered by the staff development activities

6. Professional staff development personnel who have a program in the area to be covered by the staff development activities

7. Professional staff development personnel who will develop and present a staff development program for your district

If expertise in conducting inservice programs does not exist at the school level, other resource people in the school district should be sought. Again, it is important for the activities to be conducted by personnel known and trusted by the teachers. If these resource people are unavailable, local personnel from other districts who might have the necessary expertise to conduct the inservice program should be contacted.

University personnel often prove to be good providers of staff development. They have experience working with teachers and teacher-candidates. They speak the same language as the staff. Often, there is an established relationship between the university and the school district, and this relationship can be the basis of trust. In those cases where no relationship exists, one can be cultivated. In addition, teaching faculty know that the university is not transient and will be available for future feedback.

There are many professional staff development providers who will take a school's goals and objectives and turn them into staff development programs. This may be expensive and will require time for the provider to develop media materials and handouts specifically for that school.

Professional staff developers tend to be well organized and excellent presenters. They represent the best value because:

- Their materials and presentations are usually based on much experience.

- Their presentations are field tested with hours of platform (presentation) experience.

- They are hired on a daily basis. Their fees usually translate into a very minor expenditure per teacher.

- Outside providers are usually very willing to work with the staff development Team. The possibility of contract renewal and long-term contracting is usually an incentive to provide excellent services.

For presentations on topics not specific to any particular school in any particular district, it is the experienced outside provider who offers the very best quality, experience, and value.

Training for Effective Staff Development

Staff development will never be successful if the trainers themselves are not effectively trained for their role. Teachers view themselves as professionals, and resent being the recipients of poorly planned and poorly delivered instruction. No matter how important the subject matter presented during the staff development session, the mode of presentation is equally important.

When the quality of the subject matter is held constant, faculty evaluations of inservice training programs improve with the quality of presentation. While the subject matter is important, it often takes a back seat to the manner in which it is presented. As such, it is often the perceived teaching ability that is evaluated, and not how much is learned. This is a problem whenever students evaluate teachers. It is also true when teachers evaluate presenters. The following cliché is common among management trainers and is becoming well known among educational inservice program providers:

> *The balance between the sizzle and the steak is achieved through judgment.*

There is a danger in placing too much emphasis on method and not enough on the content of the material being covered. This controversy also exists in teacher training institutions over the relative time devoted to methods courses compared with subject matter courses. A similar controversy exists in the restaurant industry over the importance of the taste of the food or the presentation of the food. "It's the sizzle, not the steak" voices the need to attend to presentation. Such sizzle in a staff development training session can result in a thoroughly entertained teaching staff who carry away very few new skills with them when they return to teaching. However, there is an equal danger resulting from poor methods of presentation: a bored group of participants who lose their attentiveness and carry few new skills with them when they return to teaching. The result is the same, and the answer is balance. The balance between the sizzle and the steak is achieved through judgment. Good judgment is achieved through wisdom gained from evaluating feedback from previous programs and watching the resultant behavior changes in participants.

A common complaint from teachers is that trainers are occasionally condescending to participants. Good human relations skills are important for the inservice educator. Trainers must be reminded that participants have pedagogical skills and talents that can contribute to the program.

The nature of the training of staff developers is dependent upon the model of delivery selected by the district. Each delivery model has its own characteristics to be addressed in the training of the personnel responsible for delivery.

Another benefit of using experienced outside providers is that little effort is necessary in training the trainer. However, post-program follow through from within the district often requires district personnel to be familiar with the outside provider's materials, goals, and objectives. This may require district personnel to meet with the outside provider and be fully trained for follow-up sessions. The outside provider should meet with district staff to tailor the program to district needs. Outside providers who are unaware of internal specifics might provide a program that would fit well into one district's needs but would be completely inappropriate to another. The result could be a poorly received program and a poor attitude of staff toward future programs.

The use of internal providers somewhat assures the provider's future services. It is the wise district that develops personnel who are trained in inservice education and in the district's training programs. The development of a trained inservice cadre should be a high priority; such a cadre is recognized by the staff of the school as competent inservice educators who know the faculty and its students.

Thus a train the trainer program can be developed. For the program to be successful, it must model for the participants all the elements that it holds as desired outcomes for the participants to master. The initial assumption of this program is that well-trained teachers will have the knowledge base and initial skills for effective teaching and will be able to impart the knowledge and skills to teachers. A secondary assumption is that the graduates of the train-the-trainers program will be skillful trainers of teachers, able to impart a strong knowledge base to participants.

It is also assumed that graduates will be able to take the goals and objectives provided to them by the staff development planning team and identify an organizing theme for the program. This theme will be the basis for their staff development efforts.

Subsequent evaluation must be based on the goals and objectives agreed upon from the start. The assumption is that the graduates of the training program will be able to use the goals and objectives of the program to develop high- and low-priority performance outcomes that will lend themselves to an objective evaluation of the success of the inservice programs.

From the realization of the nature of the training program, the district must identify the personnel who will serve as the trainers of trainers. Usually, the district will be best served by going out of district to identify a person who has been recognized as having specific skills in this area. While it may not be considered essential for the personnel who run the actual inservice programs to have impressive credentials, it is vital that those who do the training of the inservice leaders should be sufficiently qualified.

It is important to have follow-up sessions built into the training model to allow for periodical retraining of the trainers, and to allow for an opportunity for the trainers to ask questions that have arisen from their training experiences.

Providing Staff Development

All the staff development plans in the world will not have any effect on the educational program of a school unless there is a definite implementation plan for the staff development efforts. Three major elements must be present in this plan: an administrative component, an allotment of resources for the implementation of the plan, and a provision of an adequate budget for the program.

Administration of the Program

While administration may have made an initial commitment to a staff development program through formation of a staff development planning team, it does not relinquish its responsibilities for success of the program. There are many administrative responsibilities that must be completed if the program is to be a success. These responsibilities are listed in Figure 9-5.

Effective school research has shown that a strong leader will result in an effective school. One area in which this has the most impact is in the staff development program, where the role that the administrator takes can make or break the program. The administrator must be active in the program from its inception. The more active the administrator is, the more successful the program. In most of those cases where the administrator is taking a facilitator role, the administrator also must take a participant role. The attitude in which the administration expresses its involvement is most important.

By being a participant, the administrator shows a strong commitment to the program and is in a prime position to evaluate the nature of the program in terms of the philosophy of the school. In addition, this places the administrator in the role of critical evaluator of the program's success from inception through actualization.

Simultaneously, the administrator cannot relinquish essential administrative functions. There should be a consistent level of reporting to both internal and external publics about the nature of the inservice program. The district needs to know about the program; the staff needs to know about the plans, the scope and nature of the program and the level of involvement required; and the public should be informed about the efforts of the school to ensure a quality education.

The administrator has the responsibility of ensuring that all programs within the building are of quality. This responsibility can be discharged only through the maintenance of an ongoing program of evaluation. Evaluation should not take place only after the program is completed but at every phase of the program.

Programs cannot exist without administrative support. Not only does this mean that the administrator endorses the program in spirit, but that the administrator ensures that there are sufficient resources available to support the program. Without the active participation of the administrator to ensure that the program is properly supported, the program will suffer for lack of resources.

Administrative Responsibilities for Staff Development

1. Establishing the program and giving the program its initial direction
2. Functioning as an active member of the staff development planning team
3. Securing trainers
4. Assisting in the development of the staff development program
5. Assisting in the training of the staff development providers
6. Developing the program timetable
7. Allocating resources to the program
8. Budgeting for effective staff development
9. Providing for follow-up activities
10. Participating in evaluation activities
11. Showing a consistent level of support for the program

Figure 9-5

Resource Utilization

Allocation of resources, a prime administrative function, is necessary for program viability. Without resources, any program will wither and die. Without administrative participation, the program will not be a success. Inservice training takes place during school hours, before school, after school and on nonschool days. Without the proper allocation of resources, this would not be possible, because teachers have instructional commitments during school hours and often have work-related tasks to perform during other hours. They also may have personal restrictions on the availability of their nonwork hours.

There are many administrative models that ensure the success of inservice programs presented during school hours. Some of these are:

- Common preparation periods for specific subject area (grade level) teachers
- Restructured school day to provide for blocks of time available for inservice education
- Periodic release time to allow for blocks of staff development time
- Substitute cadre to allow teachers to be released to participate in staff development activities
- Release time for teachers to participate in professional development activities and professional organization meetings
- Providing physical resources for staff development

One major complaint of teachers regarding the delivery of inservice programs to large groups of teachers is that the programs are not focused on the specific needs of the various groups of teachers. Through the scheduling of preparation periods allowing teachers with common preparation periods to meet together, this problem could be alleviated. Teachers will have inservice and staff development activities focused on their needs at a time specifically engineered for this purpose.

A traditional schedule for inservice activities is the period between when the teachers arrive at school and when school begins. In those schools where all teachers start at the same time and all students arrive later, this allows for large groupings of teachers for inservice. However, there are two problems with this: the time allotted is too short, and the activities must be sufficiently general to fit the needs of large segments of the staff. In some schools, the day has been restructured to allow for greater blocks of time for staff development. This restructuring could be done in such a manner as to allow for different groupings of teachers to have a long day on different days of the week and to have a shortened day the balance of the days. The time developed by the long day would be used for staff development activities.

A traditional manner for providing for staff development time is to release students from schools for periods of time, within the constraints of state requirements, to allow release time for the teachers to participate in staff development activities. There are two major problems with this model: 1) students lose instructional time and 2) the time allocated, although in large blocks, is allocated infrequently.

Large blocks of time are helpful, but the infrequency of their occurrence makes a comprehensive program of staff development difficult to administer. Another model provides for students to be released for smaller blocks of time to allow for more frequent staff development activities.

It is often difficult to release staff members designated and trained as staff development providers. This difficulty results in trained personnel who are unable to use all their training. The development of a substitute cadre will solve many of these problems.

Teachers feel hesitant about leaving their classroom in the hands of a substitute. They need assurance that their students will be receiving quality instruction. The development of a substitute cadre is important. When the substitute cadre is considered an integral part of the staff, and have themselves participated in the school's inservice program, the teachers and the students will react to them as *regular* teachers. This will free the teachers for a more active role in staff development.

Physical resources for staff development must be provided. For many staff development programs, all that might be necessary are a classroom and a blackboard. However, for larger groups, or for special presentations, physical arrangements might have to be made to ensure the success of the staff development program. Many districts use private meeting rooms in hotels equipped to arrange for group meetings of various sizes. Some restaurants have private dining facilities that are often used for luncheon presentations.

Too often, the administration leaves all this planning and organizing to the person implementing a specific staff development program. If the school uses a staff member to present the program, that person may feel overwhelmed by organizing the presentation, preparing materials and methods for the presentation, setting up the physical site, giving the actual presentation, conducting the evaluation, and analyzing the feedback. The more that can be done for the presenter, the better. Custodial personnel are more appropriate than a presenter for setting up tables and fetching equipment. The presenter should be given access to the facilities at least 30 minutes before the start of the session for last-minute adjustments of facilities, placements of handouts, focusing of equipment, and setting of lighting.

Online Staff Development

Staff development will grow in new directions in the 21st century as new communications technology will allow for asynchronous staff development. That is, learners will be able to participate in learning events when they can fit them into their personal schedules. This has already begun as online courses allow teachers and administrators to learn from their homes, offices, libraries, and media centers via computer linkage. As communications utilize increasingly wider broadband channels, real time Television-quality home video conferencing looms on the horizon. It is already available albeit in a less-than-smooth milieu. Online computer-based courses proliferate. Las Vegas's Clark County School District already offers computer-based staff development courses on a variety of subjects. The image of classroom-based learning is merging with computer-based learning. Kaiser (2002) writes:

Governors State University in University Park, Illinois offers Web-based graduate courses in educational administration. Students attend on campus only when necessary for face-to-face demonstrations, simulations, management training films, and on-campus exams. Audio lectures are online, as are various course modules, including professionally-developed graphics, student chat rooms, bulletin boards, communication pages, and quizzes. This combination of online and on-campus learning allows students partially familiar with technology to catch up and serves as an interim step allowing technology to catch up with more technologically oriented students. Band broadening over the next decade should allow even greater asynchronous learning as well as the ability for real-time live audio-video communication among all class participants no matter what their locations.

Richardson (2001) writes:

In today's rapidly expanding world of e-learning, both images are possible. Online staff development offers enormous opportunities to customize learning around individual teacher needs and to make learning convenient for teachers. Learning can be just in time' when teachers need it most. E-learning provides a confidential setting in which teachers can learn basic skills or it can open doors to allow teachers to network with colleagues across their districts or across the county.

Budgeting for Staff Development

Planning, training, and providing for staff development has implications for budgetary provisions. As with any program, the amount and nature of the budget must come from long range planning. Too often, schools budget for staff development by using a haphazard approach. The result is that schools are often unable to provide the program or send representatives to one provided elsewhere.

Enlightened school districts place a staff development line in their budget, and have sufficient experience in using that line so that they can ensure sufficient funds for carrying out programs. Those districts that have not had experience in this area need to develop the kind of familiarity that will carry them through at least one year of operation. This way, they can draw from experience to develop a second year's budget. However, for continuity, the staff development budget should be part of a multiyear plan.

This plan should follow the same general outline of the planning done by the staff development planning team. The first step is for the school to develop a program model, including the scope of the program and the methods of delivery. Many schools make the assumption that the provider model will be a combination of provider types, depending on the material to be used in staff development.

One way of developing a multiyear program is to use outside providers and gradually phase in inside providers as more staff members become experienced trainers. Once the necessary number of trained trainers has been ascertained, the budget for them can be worked out. It should include funds for materials, training, release time to receive training, and fees for the trainers.

The staff development planning team also must consider the nature of the programs to be brought to the faculty. Programs that are vendor based have licensing requirements, and while the cost to train the smaller trainer group will be less expensive than having the presentation for the entire staff, it will pose a budgetary consideration. Funds should be budgeted for the presentation of the program to the trainers, for the licensing, and for the materials. Additional follow-through funds should be budgeted so that new staff members who are hired after the primary training also can receive training.

Facilities planning is also an important aspect of the inservice budget. Before school, after school, and non-school-day programs may incur additional facilities expenses. A weekend training session often meets at a site different from school. Funds will have to be budgeted for the utilization of this site. Sometimes, the facilities have additional fees for audio-visual equipment. Professional staff development firms make the assumption that school districts have the audio-visual equipment necessary for them to make their presentation. Thus, it is the responsibility of the school to have this equipment available. It might be necessary for the district to rent the equipment for the program. The district might consider budgeting for the rental or purchase of this equipment for the smooth operation of the staff development program.

The comfort and ease of the participants is also of a budgetary consideration. Coffee, tea, and cookies or doughnuts are commonplace. Too often, these are last-minute considerations, purchased out of some school source other than the inservice budget. These items, as trivial as they may seem, should be budgeted for out of the inservice budget.

Professional Organizations

Staff members should be encouraged to participate in professional organizations, conferences, and training sessions. Many organizations hold periodic conferences that consist of meetings where current trends, research, and skills are discussed. Conferences usually bring together many experts in the field. This is an excellent chance for members of the staff to become acquainted with new information and to have the opportunity to discuss the information with the experts. Even more important, most of these conferences are preceded and followed by training sessions. Local school trainers can avail themselves of this training and then bring this knowledge back to the school in the form of an inservice program.

Schools are often offered institutional memberships that afford them all the rights and privileges of membership, including publications, conferences, and training sessions. The education profession is fortunate to have professional organizations for teachers of specific subjects, teachers of students with special needs, staff developers, curriculum developers, teacher educators, and educational administrators. Most organizations have publications, such as newsletters and journals, that give the members information on current trends and the results of current research. This information is invaluable to the educational practitioner and can be used by the person responsible for staff development in the school to assist in the improvement of teaching skills.

Dues for memberships should be anticipated expenditures in regular budgets. Registration fees for sending personnel to meetings and training sessions should be provided by the school. Substitute teachers for covering classes of those teachers participating in professional organization offerings should be provided from an anticipated staff development substitute cadre fund.

Many professional organizations have joined the ranks of those who prepare staff development materials and programs. These are outstanding, because they are prepared by teachers for teachers, and are professional in their execution. Of utmost importance to budget-conscious administrators is that they are often considered as services by the organization to the membership, and are thus priced more economically than other packaged staff development materials.

Clinical Supervision

Clinical supervision, which focuses on the individual rather than the entire staff, is also a form of staff development. Clinical supervision involves the improvement of an individual teacher's teaching skills through a combination of conferences, observation of that teacher, training, and reobservation. Often, the cycle can be modified to be one of training, conferences, observation, retraining and reobservation (see Figure 9-6).

Two Cycles of Clinical Supervision

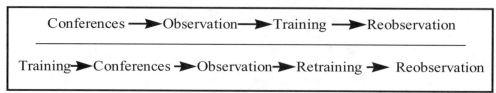

Figure 9-6

There are many skills important to teaching success that should be presented to the entire staff in individual and group conferences and in flexible venues. The presentation may be an initial introduction or a reinforcement activity. Individual instruction, large group instruction, and small group instruction are all applicable. Whatever the vehicle, sufficient practice time should be allocated before becoming engaged in the clinical supervision model.

Administrative and faculty presence are both important. To ensure a high level of staff confidence, administrators and the staff development team should work together to develop the inservice activities in clinical supervision.

Mentoring

One means of developing new teachers or remediating the problems of seasoned teachers is the assignment of a mentor teacher. This is being used more and more for the training of the beginning teacher (Ganser, 1996). The mentor teacher, usually more experienced in teaching, serves as a trainer to assist the newer teacher in developing an acceptable level of performance in a somewhat short period. Huling-Austin (1989) describes five basic goals for mentoring: (1) to improve teaching performance, (2) to increase teacher retention, (3) to make experienced teachers feel that their experience is valued, (4) to meet mandated requirements about certification, and (5) to pass on the operational philosophy of the school building and school system.

Peer Coaching

Peer coaching is similar to mentoring but is generally associated with more specific training goals. In a peer coaching model, an effective teacher desiring to improve in a specific area of teaching will be paired with a staff member who has shown skill and expertise in that area. This coaching model provides individualized instruction in the area, mentoring, and the ability to observe an expert in actual performance of the desired skills.

Just as there must be trust and respect by participants toward presenters in inservice presentations, there also must be trust and respect by teachers toward trainers, coaches, and mentors in clinical supervision. If the teacher does not have trust in the person performing the training, there may be dishonesty about feelings and about initial teaching skills. This lack of trust may result in the effects listed in Figure 9-7.

The Effect of Lack of Trust on Clinical Supervision

- There may not be a true analysis of the teacher's desired learning outcomes
- There may not be a true focus upon improvement of the teacher
- There may not be a true understanding of sufficient improvement
- There may be an overestimation of progress
- There may be disillusionment when the eventual summative evaluation occurs

---

Figure 9-7

Non-Peer Coaching

A third model of clinical supervision uses a department chair or an assistant principal as the coach. Since this type of coach may not have teaching responsibilities, this approach has two common drawbacks: 1) the teacher may not be able to observe the coach in action, and 2) the coach may be perceived as a possible adversary. However, this model may be useful when the teacher needs assistance regarding personality traits. This is important, because often, personality traits that affect the relationship between teachers and students also affect the relationships between teachers and other teachers or administrators. In these cases, it can be very beneficial to receive coaching from a nonteacher perspective.

Supervisor Formative Evaluation

There are two types of evaluation, formative and summative. Formative evaluation is ongoing evaluation, where the trainee's supervisor makes continuous assessments of learning progress and offers continuous suggestions and corrections. Summative evaluation is the evaluation done when the training has been completed. Summative evaluation assesses whether or not the person undergoing the training did indeed achieve the training objectives.

In formative evaluation, the supervisor may make multiple classroom visitations over many months before any summative evaluation is made. Each observation is specific to the areas discussed in the pre-observation conference and should be measured against some clear and reasonable standards discussed in that conference. After the classroom observation is completed, the supervisor and the teacher hold a post observation conference, where the results of the observation are discussed and areas for improvement agreed on.

The inservice training supervisor may choose to make suggestions involving the coach or mentor models of staff development. The supervisor may set a reasonable timeframe for the development or improvement of the skills in question, along with some standards for acceptance. After the time has expired, the administrator holds an additional preobservation conference with the teacher, observes the teacher in class, and holds a postobservation conference.

Evaluating Staff Development

Participants should evaluate the mode of presentation and the quality of the information received at each session. This provides the administration and staff development team with data from which to decide on renewing outside developer's contracts. It also provides the presenter with immediate feedback on the presentation's reception by participants.

The entire staff development plan also should be periodically reviewed and evaluated. The needs assessment at the start of the cycle provides baseline data which are the benchmarks from which to measure progress toward goals. Although feedback must be a continuous process, there must also be occasional freeze points in time where measurements of progress are taken, and where those measurements are compared with the original plans for the freeze point. If the extent of success matches the plans, it can be assumed that the program is functioning adequately. If not, then the program must be modified to remedy its insufficiencies so that its deficiencies are not repeated.

Although staff development is never complete, there is a need to bring closure to cycles. This is necessary to assure that the staff development program is accomplishing its goals and objectives. Feedback systems must be designed and implemented at the start of a cycle to provide information on whether the planned improvement in performance is achieved. Just as the purpose of evaluation of teacher performance is to improve teacher performance, the evaluation of a staff development program has the purpose of improving the program in the next cycle. Without the development of baseline data, the effectiveness of the staff development program cannot be evaluated. Evaluations also measure what long-term effects have been achieved because of the training. They also can pinpoint the type of support needed to ensure the success of the changes that have been instituted as the result of the training.

The following questions are merely illustrative. They are recommended for incorporation within a larger evaluation of a staff development presentation. Evaluation instruments are usually tailored to the needs of a specific school, relate to the specific objectives of that staff development presentation, and are completed after each presentation in a manner similar to formative evaluations of teaching. Summative evaluation forms can be developed from similar questions to gather data on staff perceptions of the accomplishments of long-term goals. Figure 9-8 lists questions appropriate at the formative stage in the evaluation of the attainment of short-term objectives, and at the summative stage in the evaluation of the goals of an entire staff development program.

Evaluating Staff Development Programs

1. Was the program content relevant to the identified objectives or goals?
2. Was the program relevant to the participants' perceived instructional needs?
3. Was the program relevant to the perceived problems experienced by the staff in the area presented?
4. Were the program information and materials transferable to the teaching strategies or curriculum planning skills of the participants?
5. What was the quality of the instruction?
6. What was the quality of the materials used?
7. Was there a mechanism for gathering open-ended evaluative statements from the participants?
8. Was there a mechanism for gathering suggestions for follow-up activities and programs from the participants?
9. Was there sufficient faculty involvement in the development of objectives, goals, curriculum, and methodology of training?

Figure 9-8

These questions, when combined with more school-specific evaluation techniques, will yield valuable information, not only regarding the participants' view of sessions and programs but information that will help in the planning of future staff development activities.

Case Problem: Staff Development According to Hoyle

Susan. Hoyle, the new principal at Liberty Elementary School has been asked to take charge of the entire school district's staff development program. Although she asked for guidance from the superintendent, she received nothing but encouragement. Her superintendent said, "You just finished your M.A. in Educational Administration, Susan. You certainly should know how to do this." How would you advise Susan in planning who should be involved, the structure of the process, the timelines, the assessment process, and the implementation of the plan?

Summary

Staff development activities should pervade the atmosphere of the school. Instructional improvement is directly related to the extent of planned changes incorporated into the staff development program. While outsider personnel may be employed, and in certain situations should be employed, to perform staff development, in-house, full-time staff will have a higher level of insight and sensitivity for the needs of the specific school. Involvement of full-time staff is essential in the planning, implementation, and evaluation of the entire staff development program.

References

Darling-Hammond, L. and Cobb, V., Eds. (1995). *Teacher preparation and professional development in APEC members: a comparative study.* Washington, DC: U.S. Department of Education.

Dodd, A.W. (1987). Getting Results from a one-day inservice program, *Principal.* 66, (5), 29-30.

Gibson, S.L. and Follo, E. J. (1998, Winter*)* The status of multicultural education in Michigan, *Multicultural Education.* 6, (2), 17-22.

Ganser, T. (1996, Fall) Preparing Mentors of Beginning Teachers: An Overview for Staff Developers, *Journal of Staff Development.* 17 (4), 8-11.

Harris, B. M. (1989) *In-service education for staff development.* Needham Heights, MA: Allyn and Bacon.

Huling-Austin, L. (1989). Beginning teacher assistance programs: an overview. In L. Huling-Austin, S. Odell, P. Ishler, R. Kay, R. Edelfelt (Ed.), *Assisting the Beginning Teacher.* Reston, VA: Association of Teacher Educators.

Kaiser, J. (2002, January) Interview. Mequon, Wisconsin

Meltzer, J. and . Sherman, T.M.. (1997, January) Ten commandments for successful technology implementation for staff development, *NASSP Bulletin.* 81, (585), 223-32.

National Staff Development Council (2002) Retrieved on October 7, 2002 from http://www.nsdc.org/.

Orlich, D.C. (1989*).* Staff development: Enhancing human potential.* Needham Heights, MA: Allyn and Bacon.

Petzko, V.N. (1998, December) Preventing legal headaches through staff development: Considerations and recommendations, *NASSP Bulletin.* 82, (602), 35-42.

Reglin, G..L. and Reitzammer. R.F., (1998, Summer) *Dealing with the Stress of Teaching,* Education, 118, (4), 590-596.

Richardson, Joan (September 2001) *E-learning potential: Online staff development has great possibilities and pitfalls.* National Staff Development Council. Retrieved September 2001 from http://www.nsdc.org/educatorindex.htm

Chapter 10
Microcomputers in Educational Administration

J. Fred Schouten and Jeffrey S. Kaiser

This chapter examines the impact of microcomputers on administration and, more specifically, how four general areas of computer use enhance the efficiency of educational administrators: productivity software tools, data management tools, specialized productivity tools, networking and the Internet, and other computerized devices.

Introduction

The advent of microcomputers has been the most significant advancement in school management history. With the rapid development of computerized tools and software, administrators can gain instant access to student, personnel, inventory, and financial information and can communicate instantly with others around the world. A few decades ago, these solutions would have required a mainframe computer. Now, desktop and laptop computers not only have the power to rival mainframe computers, but they do so in much less space and with many fewer location restraints. Wireless technologies are providing even more ubiquitous access to networked resources.

Secretaries and other essential office support staff can learn data entry and retrieval processes easily. The use of password-protected databases helps to insure the integrity of the data and limit access to those people who have a need for such information. Networks allow administrators, faculty, and support staff shared access to essential information and expensive shared resources.

Microcomputers have decreased in price so much that most administrators also have a computer system at home. Works in progress (e.g., word processing documents, statistical information in spreadsheets) may be transferred from home to work and back on a floppy disk, on high-capacity removable disks (e.g., Iomega Zip or Jaz disks), on rewritable CD discs, or via the Internet using e-mail or file transfer (FTP).

Perhaps the biggest decision in determining what technologies to use in the administration of schools is the identification of the tasks to be supported. Once these tasks are specified, it is relatively easy to find the software and hardware to accomplish them. It is important that school administrators become familiar with the wide range of electronic solutions available, so that informed decisions may be made.

Typical administrative tasks may be accomplished with four general categories of technologies. These include productivity software tools, data management software tools, specialized productivity tools, networking and the Internet, and other computerized devices. These technologies allow administrators to perform many types of tasks, including word processing, spreadsheet calculations, database management, electronic communication, researching topics of interest, and managing personal information. Not included in this discussion are microcomputer solutions related to classroom-level management (e.g., electronic gradebooks, curriculum tools, etc.).

Productivity Software Tools

Administrators may use a variety of general and specialized software tools to increase efficiency. General-use tools include word processing programs, spreadsheets, databases, and suites of integrated applications. The comments that follow are not specific to any computer platform, except as noted. In this chapter, the word "platform" refers to the two main computer operating systems available today. Those are Microsoft Windows (currently available as Windows 95, Windows 98, Windows 2000, Windows-ME, and Windows-XP) and Macintosh (currently Mac OS 8.6, Mac OS 9.0, and Mac OS X).

Most of the general productivity applications are now cross-platform, meaning that files created on Windows may be used on Macintosh and vice versa. To do so requires saving the file on a PC-formatted disk. It is best to use the older DOS file-naming convention of a maximum of eight characters for the file name and a three-letter extension representing the application used for creating the file. An example of a file name for a yearly report created in Microsoft Word would be "rpt99-00.doc". If different applications are to be used in different locations, generic file types are available in all modern applications. To move a document from one word processor to another while retaining formatting, save the file in rich text format (RTF). To move a spreadsheet among applications, save the file in symbolic link format (SYLK). To share a database file among applications, save in the database format (DBF). By allowing the administrator to take work home, these processes allow for enhanced flexibility and productivity.

Word Processing

Some of the tasks that may be accomplished with general productivity tools include creation of personal and professional correspondence, memoranda, proposals, reports, and more. These types of documents are typically handled with a word processor. Some of the more common word processors are Microsoft Word, Corel WordPerfect, and Sun StarOffice. The AppleWorks and Microsoft Works integrated suites also contain a word processing module. All of these products are available for either the Windows or Macintosh operating systems.

Editing, Revising and Formatting. Editing and revising, or the ability to make changes to the text before saving and printing it, is a major strength of a word processing program. When additional text is inserted, the entire document is reformatted automatically. Similarly, text may be deleted at any point, and the document is automatically reformatted. Text may also be moved from one location to another by using the "cut and paste" features of the software. Many newer word processors allow for "drag-and-drop" movement of text. In this process, the desired block of text is highlighted, then dragged to a new location, where it is inserted, and the document automatically reformats itself.

Formatting word-processed text is also very easy to do. Text may be bolded, underlined, and italicized. The font (typeface) and size of the text may be changed at any time. Paragraphs may be formatted with the text aligned to the right or left margin, centered on the page, or fully justified (with the text aligned to both the left and right margins). Margins and tabs may be set for the whole document or for selected paragraphs within the document. A variety of tabs may be selected, allowing for alignment to the left or right of the tab setting, centered on the tab setting, or aligned to a decimal point (useful for aligning columns of numbers). Tabs may also be set with a "leader." This instructs the software to fill in the space up to the tab with a line of periods, an underscore, a line of hyphens, or a line of customized characters. Documents may also be formatted to contain headers and footers. These are blocks of text that appear on each page of the document and are useful for placing the document title on every page, for automatic numbering of every page, etc.

Advanced Features of Word Processors. Most of the newer word processor applications contain several advanced features that enhance productivity. The first feature is called either a "wizard" or an "assistant." These are automated features that assist the administrator in creating a formatted calendar, fax cover, memorandum, business report, or other type of standard document. Typically a wizard or assistant will step the user through the creation process by providing questions, and the answers are incorporated into a preformatted document.

A second common feature is a set of templates (also sometimes called stationery). These are collections of preformatted documents that an administrator can open, complete by filling in the blanks or replacing placeholder text, save, and print. The templates are reusable because, when used, a copy is opened, thereby leaving the original template unchanged. Common templates include: certificate, course syllabus, invoice, meeting agenda, newsletter, press release, resume, and letters for a variety of purposes.

A third common feature is the ability to create recordings of keystrokes (also called macros). Typical uses of this feature include the "recording" of a signature block or of a block of text commonly used in a standard discipline letter. To create the macro, the administrator activates the recording feature in the word processing software, assigns an unused keystroke to the macro (e.g., shift-control-8), types the text exactly as it is to appear, and deactivates the recording. To use, the administrator begins a new document (perhaps using a wizard or template), types in the new content up to the place where the prerecorded text is desired, then types the keystroke. At this time the recorded text will be entered into the document at the location of the cursor. The judicious use of macros can greatly reduce the time it takes to create documents that call for repetitive entry of text.

Additional advanced features that enhance productivity include:

- Importing files (text, graphics) from other applications.
- Exporting files in generic formats for use in other word processing applications.
- Reformatting into columns
- Inserting tables (sometimes with mathematical computation capabilities).
- Automatic date and time stamping (with the capability of updating the date or time when the document is opened at a later date).
- Automatic outlining in a variety of formats.
- Word wrapping (allowing text to flow around graphics)

Most current word processors (listed above) share these features. Most all use both text-based menus and icon-based toolbars to select functions within the word processor. Most come with "translators" that allow them to read documents created in a variety of other word processing applications, and offer the reciprocal function of saving a file in formats compatible with a variety of other word processing applications.

In summary, administrators make use of word processing applications in many ways, creating the plethora of daily documents necessary to the management of human and physical resources. Advanced features such as wizards and templates boost productivity. The ability to share word-processed files among platforms and applications provides the flexibility needed to function efficiently in this electronic world.

Spreadsheets. Spreadsheets are another category of general productivity tools that greatly enhance the work of school administrators. Spreadsheet software may be used to create tables of information, to compute simple or complex mathematical formulas, and to develop visual representations of data. Information from spreadsheets may be incorporated into other types of documents, such as word processing reports.

The most common spreadsheet applications are Microsoft Excel (Windows and Macintosh) and Lotus 1-2-3 (Windows only). The AppleWorks and Microsoft Works integrated suites also contain a spreadsheet module. The major difference between the stand-alone applications and the modules that are a part of the suites is the number of advanced features that are available.

The most frequently used features of spreadsheets allow the user to present information in a tabular layout, to perform calculations, and to represent numerical information in a visual format. Additional features of more powerful spreadsheet applications allow for statistical analyses and limited database functions. Administrators will find spreadsheets useful for tracking budgets, forecasting total costs during salary negotiations, projecting enrollments, preparing data for reports, and performing related tasks that require multiple calculations or frequent recalculations.

A spreadsheet file is typically called a worksheet. Data in spreadsheets is organized into rows and columns. The intersection of a row and column is called a cell. Cells may contain labels (combinations of text and numbers), numbers, or formulas (mathematical instructions).

At times, administrators may decide not to use a spreadsheet for mathematical calculations. Because cells may also hold text or combinations of text and numbers, one frequent use is the tabular presentation of information. For example, a spreadsheet may be used to lay out a faculty directory, where names are placed into one column, telephone numbers are placed into another column, school assignment is placed in another column, and grade level or department name is placed into another column. The sorting function of a spreadsheet may be used to order the directory alphabetically by name, numerically by grade level, and so on.

The power of these software solutions lies in their ability to do mathematical calculations with spreadsheet formulas. Formulas may be as simple as an instruction to display the sum of two other cells, or they may be as complex as instructions to display an advanced statistical calculation. A formula may also consist of a conditional calculation, where the result will be one answer if a certain condition exists or a different answer if the condition does not exist.

Charting and Graphing. The ability to convert numerical data into visual representations is one of the most frequently used features of spreadsheet applications. A variety of representations are available in modern spreadsheet software. These include many types of bar charts, pie charts, area graphs, line charts, scatter plots, pictograms, high-low graphs, and more. Most allow for "stacked" charts representing multiple variables. Most provide advanced types of charting, such as X-Y line and scatter plots. Most allow for the creation of black-and-white charts and graphs (most suitable for typical printing and reproduction) or for colored versions (most suitable for electronic presentations and transparencies). Most of the spreadsheets also provide the ability to create most of these charts and graphs in a three-dimensional representation. For advanced graphing and charting capabilities, administrators may choose a more specialized application such as SPSS Incorporated's DeltaGraph (Windows or Macintosh).

The charts and graphs created in modern spreadsheets are linked to the original numerical data. Changing any of the numerical data forces an automatic redraw of the chart or graph. This allows the administrator to adjust budget numbers or enrollment projections and receive immediate visual feedback on the impact of the forecasted change.

Spreadsheets and/or their related charts and graphs may be printed for distribution. Many times, however, the charts and graphs are placed into word processing documents as integral parts of reports or proposals. This is accomplished in one of several ways. The most common method is to copy the chart in the spreadsheet and paste it into the word processing document. Spreadsheet software also allows the user to save (or export) the chart as a graphic that may be inserted (or imported) into the word processing document. Advanced users may also save the graphic in a special interactive format (also sometimes called "publishing") that may be inserted into the word processing document (sometimes called "subscribing"). When this process is used, any changes in the numerical data in the spreadsheet that results in a change in the chart will cause the chart to be updated in the word processing document. These types of advanced features go far to enhance the productivity of a school administrator.

In summary, administrators make use of spreadsheet applications in many ways, creating the variety of daily documents necessary to the management of data. Advanced features such as repetitive calculations, advanced statistical analyses, and sophisticated charting and graphing boost productivity. The ability to integrate numerical and visual data from spreadsheets into word-processed documents provides the flexibility needed to function even more efficiently in this electronic world.

Data Management Tools

Databases are yet another category of general productivity tools that greatly enhance the work of school administrators. Database software is a data management tool used to store, organize, manipulate, retrieve, and summarize data. Administrators use databases for managing general student records, health and immunization records, discipline records, transportation routes, inventories, personnel records, and many other tasks that require the maintenance of information from a centralized location. Information from databases may be incorporated into other types of documents, such as word processing reports, mailing lists, or spreadsheets.

The most common general database applications include Microsoft Access and Corel Paradox (Windows only), and FileMaker Pro (Windows and Macintosh). The AppleWorks and Microsoft Works integrated suites also contain a database module. The major difference between the stand-alone applications and the modules that are a part of the suites is the number of advanced features available. These database solutions also come with wizards (assistants) and/or templates (stationery) to facilitate the creation of a database.

Some data management needs are beyond the capabilities of simple software solutions, however. Very powerful database tools (which require an extremely advanced level of database and programming knowledge) include Microsoft's FoxPro and ACI's 4D (both available for either Windows or Macintosh). Most administrators would need to employ the services of a programming consultant to use these applications.

Database Structures and Functions

A database consists of fields, records, and files. A field is a single piece of information, a record is one complete set of fields, and a file is a collection of records. For example, a staff directory is analogous to a file. It contains a list of records, each of which consists of several common fields, usually including name, address, telephone number, building, grade or department assignment, office phone extension, etc.

Databases are usually constructed in one of two ways; they are either "flat file" or "relational." A flat file database is a collection of information stored in one table. A relational database comprises several individual databases (or tables of information) that are related by common fields. The staff directory used as the illustration above could be created and maintained as a flat file database. It could also be a part of a larger relational database, where staff names are in one file, telephone numbers and addresses are in another file, building and grade or department assignments are in another file, and all of the files have the field "staff identification number" in common. When an identification number is entered into the "assignment" database file, the file looks into the "staff name" file and enters the person's name into the appropriate field. It then looks into the "telephone numbers" file and enters the person's office number and extension into the appropriate field. Relational databases allow for the entry of a piece of information one time and the use of that information in multiple locations and for multiple purposes, thereby saving data entry time and enhancing productivity.

The power of databases comes from both the warehousing of information in a centralized location (e.g. a database file or files) and from the relative ease with which information may be retrieved from the database for multiple uses. Once the data is entered into the files, the administrator may sort it alphabetically, numerically, or chronologically using a desired field or multiple fields. Information that matches specific criteria may be isolated in the database by using the search or find feature.

Information may be viewed or printed using the report or layout feature. A report or layout is analogous to a window into the collection of information. If one were to look into a house through a window, information could be obtained about the household furnishings or the layout of the house. This information would be limited, however, and would be quite different if the observation were accomplished through a different window. Reports or layouts allow for the same type of data access. A report may contain a limited amount of information from the large collection, and the information may be physically arranged on the page to accommodate its desired use. For example, an administrator may need a listing of teachers and their room numbers. A report could be constructed to display only teacher name and room assignment. The report could also be constructed to display this information with each department on a separate page and with the listing alphabetized by teacher's last name. A second report could be generated that provides an entire faculty listing organized by room number.

Database Design

The most important part of database design is identifying the purposes for which the information is to be used. Once that is decided, the individual pieces of related information may be identified. Usually, smaller "pieces" of information allow for more flexible use of the database. For example, the city, state, and zip code of a person's address could be entered as one piece (field) of information. This limits the future use of the information. If the data were entered as three separate fields (one each for city, state, and zip code), then the data could be sorted by zip code, by city, or by state. This determination of information chunking should be given much consideration during the initial database design.

The next part of the design is to decide on the format of the data to be entered. For example, are birth dates to be entered as numerical (date) information or merely as text? If entered as text (e.g., "June 19, 1993"), the dates cannot be sorted chronologically. Sorting would result in a listing that is alphabetical by first letter of the month.

While databases may be redesigned after initial use, this usually results in the loss of previously entered data. If, for example, we were to decide to change the birth date information from text to numerical data, all of the dates would probably have to be entered again. For this reason, the initial design of the database is critical. Administrators who are interested in designing their own databases should consult the manuals that accompany the software for more specific information.

Once the uses for the data are identified, and the complexity of the data is determined, then the administrator may select the type of database (flat file or relational) and the specific software solution to be employed. Additional features such as automatic page numbering, automatically generated summaries and calculations of information, headers and footers, print preview features, multiple report or layout selections, complex methods of finding information ("querying") within the database, and the like should also be considered when selecting database management software.

Embedding Information into Standard Documents

Older database software only allowed for the entry, storage, sorting, and printing of information in tabular format. These applications provided a feature termed "mail merge" to allow fields of information to be embedded into a word processing document. In this process, a generic letter or report is created in a word processor. Whenever an individualized piece of information is desired, a link is made to the related field in a database file. When printed, multiple copies of the document are generated, each with information from a different record in the database file. This is useful for creating "personalized" letters to parents informing them of upcoming events that feature their child. It may also be used for generating purchase orders or classroom inventory lists on school letterhead. The uses of this feature are limited only by the creativity of the administrator. Newer database software allows for this word processing to be accomplished within the database file itself, eliminating the need to link to a word processing document. The letter is created as another report or layout, and fields are inserted where desired.

Administrators make use of database management software in many ways, creating the variety of daily documents necessary to the management of data. Advanced features such as the elimination of the repetitive entry of information and the automatic calculation of summary data boost productivity. The ability to use information for multiple purposes and in a variety of formats provides the flexibility needed to function even more efficiently in this electronic world.

Data Management Software Tools

In addition to general and specialized productivity tools, administrators use specialized software solutions to manage data related to human and physical resources. These include tools to manage student data, libraries and textbooks, financial information, and transportation. The Schools Interoperability Framework offers the standardization needed to allow these various applications to share data in a seamless manner.

Student Data Management

The management of student data is one of the largest and most critical tasks in the successful administration of schools. The functions built into these solutions vary, and many of the packages are modular, allowing the school to purchase the features it needs. The types of data managed by these tools include information related to student demographics, parent or guardian contact, emergency contact, health and immunization, attendance, scheduling, student grade reporting, transcripts, discipline, guidance and career choices, teacher demographics, resource allocation (teachers and rooms), etc.

The software packages used to manage student data are actually very large, specialized relational databases, and all feature built-in report formats or templates and the ability to create additional reports that meet local needs. Examples of such software include: NCS' SASIxp (modules for: Student & Enrollment, Attendance, Scheduling, Health, Discipline, Non-Student Info, File Management, Test History, Grade Reporting & Course History, Special Education, Period Attendance, and Scanning for data entry), Chancery's MacSchool and WinSchool (modules for Student & Contacts Demographics, Discipline, Health & Immunization, Report Cards & Transcripts, electronic Scanning for data entry, Attendance, Scheduling, Guidance, Health, Query, and Report Manager), and Tremont Software/DPconsultants' Student Management System (SMwin) (modules for Student and Family Database, Medical - Health and Immunization, Attendance Reporting, Discipline, Grade Reporting and Transcripts, Class Scheduling, Activities Eligibility, Fee Billing, Textbook Fees and Inventory, Query Tools, Reporting Tools, E-mail Merge and Mail Merge, and Security). All of these examples include several levels of password security to prevent unauthorized access to viewing and/or editing information contained in the database. All function as a centralized database that is available from multiple locations simultaneously.

In addition to general student data management software, specialized solutions exist for administering schools. Most states use software solutions for the reporting of data related to vocational education. Recent advances in software also address the unique data management needs of special education. Examples of this software include Horizon Systems Software's Excent for the management of individualized education plans (IEPs), Orion Systems Group's IEP Plus for IEP management, Total Recall Software's IEP Maker, and more.

Library and Textbook Management

A variety of software solutions exists for the management of libraries and textbooks. One of the central functions of school libraries is the warehousing and circulation of books and other media. Many of the data needs for this function are facilitated by software applications. These solutions provide for storage of MARC (MAchine-Readable Cataloging) records for all books, patron information, circulation functions and statistics, automatic generation of fines and reminders, inventory, online searching of the card catalog from multiple locations, and bar code entry of data for circulation and inventory. Examples of this software include Horizon by Epixtech, Mandarin by SIRS, Winnebago Spectrum by Sagebrush Corporation, Circulation Plus and Union Catalog Plus by Follett Software Company, and Library Pro by Chancery.

Suites

Included in the foregoing discussion of word processing, spreadsheets, and database management was the mention of software suites, such as Microsoft Works and AppleWorks (formerly ClarisWorks). These applications integrate several productivity tools into one piece of software. Microsoft Works contains an integrated word processor, calendar, spreadsheet, address book, and database, plus Web and e-mail connectivity. AppleWorks contains an integrated word processor, spreadsheet, database, and paint and drawing graphics, plus a communications module for connecting to remote servers. Both suites offer many wizards (assistants) and templates (stationery) to facilitate the creation of a wide variety of documents. Because these applications were designed as an integrated suite of tools, they provide a somewhat easier path for embedding one type of information (e.g. a spreadsheet) into another document (e.g. a word processing report). Their limitation is that they do not provide the number of advanced features that are available in stand-alone applications. For most common administrative tasks, however, these suites offer sufficient features to help make the user much more productive.

Specialized Productivity Tools

A variety of specialized tools exist that can assist the administrator. Three of these include graphic organizers, electronic presentation tools, and project management tools.

Graphic Organizer Software

Visual brainstorming, semantic maps, and flow charts or organizational charts are examples of the kind of information that may be useful to administrators. A software solution that allows for the easy creation of these products is Inspiration by Inspiration Software. This application comes with a large variety of templates. It has a "rapid fire" feature that assists the user in recording information in a brainstorming session. As ideas are generated, they are associated with broader ideas or grouped into clusters. Once the visual grouping is complete, one click on an icon transforms the diagram into an outline. The visual diagram may be exported for use in a report or on a Web page. The outline may be exported for use in a word processor or an electronic slide show presentation.

Presentation Software

Presenting ideas to groups of people in an effective manner requires the use of visual aids. Most presentations now are supported by electronic slide shows or by colorful transparencies. Both may be created with presentation software. Although some software applications allow for the creation of simple slide shows (e.g. Microsoft Excel, AppleWorks), by far the most popular application for this purpose is Microsoft PowerPoint. This allows the administrator to create slide shows that can be used electronically or printed onto transparencies in full color.

A picture is worth a thousand words. A picture may also greatly distract or mislead. This is perhaps the most important concept to keep in mind when designing a visual aid, such as an electronic slide show. Applications like PowerPoint come with a library of clip art. When used appropriately, the graphic can enhance the message, although it is difficult at times to select the best graphic to support a message. At such times, it may be the best decision to allow the text to speak for itself. A second consideration is that a visual aid, such as a slide or transparency, should contain only the outline of an idea. The presenter should provide the information; the slide is there to provide a focus for the audience.

Presentation software allows the user to add sophisticated effects between slides (called "transitions") as well as effects for animating information on the individual slides (called "builds"). These transitions and builds may be accompanied by sound effects. Once again, the administrator is cautioned to use these effects appropriately, consistently, and sparingly (in the case of the sound effects). The slide show should support the presentation, not detract from it. Other features provide for the integration of graphics files (e.g., pictures taken with a digital camera) and movies (perhaps recorded with a digital video camera) into slides. Slide shows may also be configured to advance automatically. This feature is useful when used as a "greeting" to parents entering the school for an open house or for providing the daily schedule for students via a video distribution system.

To use the slide show, the administrator must have a means of connecting the computer to a larger monitor or projector. Products marketed by AverMedia, Focus Enhancements, and others convert the computer's video signal so that it may be used with a television monitor. InFocus, Sony, Epson, Dukane, and other companies market video projectors that allow for a direct connection of the computer's video output. These machines then project the image onto a screen. When purchasing a video projector, the main consideration should be the brightness of the projection. A projector that offers 900 lumens or more can be used in typical school conditions (i.e., lights on, windows uncovered).

Presentation software gives the administrator access to the tools necessary to create a professional visual aid. The quality of the final product is directly related to the message being delivered and the judicious use of the features of the software.

Project Management Software

Project management software is another type of productivity tool that may be used by administrators. This software allows the user to track a project from inception to completion. Intermediate goals and timelines are entered, along with available resources (such as people and money). The software will graphically display the timeline and internal checkpoints for the project. Using this type of application allows the administrator to manage all aspects of a large project in a way that helps to keep everyone and everything on task. An example of this kind of application is Microsoft Project.

School Finance Software

Several software solutions exist to help the administrator manage financial data in the two main areas of accounts payable and payroll. Accounts payable software allows for the generation and tracking of purchase orders, for generating invoices, for printing checks to vendors, and for viewing and printing current budget balance reports. Payroll software provides the features necessary to generate periodic payroll checks (including salary, benefits, deductions, etc.), maintain cumulative records (taxes withheld, pension contributions, etc.), and track used vacation and sick leave days. Examples of this software include Infinite Visions by Windsor Management Group, CIMS G/T by NCS; Payroll, Financials, Purchasing by School Data Systems (SDS); and Financial Management System (FMwin) by Tremont Software/DPconsultants.

Transportation Software

Schools that own and operate their own fleet of transportation vehicles can also benefit from electronic data management. Specific solutions for this area allow for scheduling, routing, mapping, and other related functions. Examples of these applications include: School Bus Management System (SBMS) and Graphic Routing System (GRS) by Northwoods Computer Software, MasterPlan by Planware Systems, MapNet by Trapeze, and School Transportation Manager by Dynacomp Software.

Schools Interoperability Framework

Early in 1999, Microsoft launched the Schools Interoperability Framework (SIF) initiative. In November of that year, the initiative was given over to the Software and Information Industry Association, and many more companies decided to participate. This project has developed standards, or specifications, that will allow a variety of school software solutions to interact and share data seamlessly. Rather than each software package having its own method for storing and retrieving data, applications that are developed using this "technical blueprint" will share the common data that is prevalent in schools. This will result in standard data formats, rules for naming standard data, and rules for interaction among applications.

Schools will benefit from the elimination of the need for redundant entry of common data (such as student demographics), from the interaction of various software solutions with one another, from the enhanced ability to create reports that extract data from multiple applications, and from the increased ability to electronically move data and reports over the Internet to other organizations (such as annual reports to their state departments of education).

Networking and the Internet

People in organizations no longer have to operate in isolation from one another. The advent of affordable networking capabilities allows schools to connect teachers, students, classrooms, and schools to each other and to the world. This section will explore the basic concepts of networking and the uses of networks in the administrative environment.

Networks

Networks are usually labeled by the scope of their use. A network that exists in a classroom, in an administrative office complex, or within a single building is called a local area network, or LAN. A network that exists between or among schools and locations is called a wide area network, or WAN. Networks may be constructed by physically connecting all of the resources in a building (or among buildings) with wires or fiber optic cable. Networks may also be constructed to take advantage of the developments in the use of wireless, or radio frequency, devices.

A typical LAN would consist of a centralized wiring closet that serves as the "hub" for the network. From this closet, wires are installed to each classroom or office, where they terminate in ports into which a computer, printer, or other networkable device is plugged. All of the network devices must have a network card and proper software installed in order to take advantage of the resources. The wiring closet contains hubs (centralized units into which the individual wires are connected) and/or switches (units that direct network signals into the proper paths). A school's LAN may also be connected to a robust Internet connection (such as a leased T-1 telephone line) by means of a digital modem (CSU/DSU) and a router.

A district may connect all of its schools and offices together into a WAN by connecting the routers in the various locations together. This may be accomplished via a dedicated fiber optic cable between the buildings' routers, via leased T-1 lines that connect the routers, or via wireless antennas and receivers that are connected into the routers.

Wireless networking within buildings has become stable and affordable for schools. This type of networking involves the installation of transceivers in various locations in the school. Computers (and other networkable devices) must have special hardware and software installed to communicate with the transceivers. Once a wireless connection has been negotiated between the device and the transceiver, the user has the same access to network resources as with traditional wired connections. The user, however, has the increased ability to move about and remain connected. This allows the easy reorganization of office space as needed, as well as easy access for users of laptop computers. Wireless networking between buildings involves the installation of antennas that are connected to transceivers that are in turn connected into the main router in the building. Once the link between antennas is established, all of the users in the buildings may share the resources in the wider network. Current wireless technology allows line-of-sight wireless connection of buildings that are up to 25 miles apart.

Uses of Networks

There are four main uses for administrators with access to building and between-building networks. These include sharing expensive resources, enhanced communication among administrative offices and personnel, access to groupware applications, and access to the vast resources of the Internet.

Many network resources are too expensive to purchase for each individual user. An example is a high-quality laser printer. Instead, a few of these printers are installed in strategic locations around the school, and users share them. Typically, an administrative office will have one installed laser printer that is shared by the building administrators and support staff. Another network resource that may be shared is a file server (a computer with a large-capacity hard drive and other specialized software). This file server provides secure, password-protected space for storing an individual's files; secure, password-protected space where members of specific groups may share common files (such as a student management database); and access to shared applications.

A second use of administrative networks is communication among the administrative team and/or support staff. With instant messaging software, it is possible to carry on discussions in near "real time" from one computer to another. This capability enhances the quality and quantity of communication between and among administrators and their faculty and staff.

A third use of networks that can greatly enhance collaboration is the access to groupware applications. These software solutions allow multiple people to share in the task of creating or maintaining common documents. The documents may be Board reports, policy revisions, or group appointment calendars. Examples of these applications include Microsoft NetMeeting, Lotus Notes, Microsoft Outlook (when used with Microsoft Exchange Server), Novell Groupwise, and Netscape Calendar.

The Internet as a Massive Information Network

The fourth use of administrative networks is to access resources on the Internet. These resources may include access to state or federal agencies or professional organizations, professional discussions with other administrators, instant messaging around the world, and access to news and weather information.

Many governmental agencies and professional organizations maintain Internet sites that offer access to a wealth of information (conference schedules, statistics, legislative updates, etc.). You can locate many of the professional organization sites with the generic URL (Uniform Resource Locator or Internet address) of www.acronym.org, where the word "acronym" is replaced by the organization's acronym. Example: The acronym for the American Association of School Administrators is "AASA". Their Web site is located at http://www.aasa.org. Similarly, the generic address for the homepage of any state in the United States is http://www.state.__ __.us, where the two blanks are to be replaced with the two-letter postal abbreviation for that state. Example: The homepage for the state of Wisconsin is http://www.state.wi.us. State Web addresses may automatically transfer you to updated addresses as Web protocol changes and the Web grows over time. From the state homepage, you have access to all of that state's governmental agencies.

At times, administrators need to seek the experiences and opinions of their peers on a specific topic. Access to the Internet allows an administrator to seek this type of information from peers around the world. This is done via a listserv (an E-mail based discussion group). There is no fee for membership, and the information to be gained from participation is sometimes invaluable. Three listservs of particular interest to school administrators are the K12ADMIN listserv (established for discussion of topics and issues related to the administration of K-12 schools), the EDTECH listserv (established for the discussion of topics related to the use of technology in education), and the SUPER-LIST listserv (established for the discussion of topics and issues related to the central office in school districts). More information on how to join and how to access the archives of these and other listservs may be found on the Internet at http://www.ericir.syr.edu/Virtual/Listserv_Archives/.

Access to the Internet also provides administrators with instant messaging capabilities. The person on the receiving end of the message may be in the next room or somewhere on the other side of the world. Two of the most popular methods for accomplishing this type of communication are: ICQ (http://www.icq.com) and the AOL Instant Messenger (available from America OnLine at http://www.aol.com, or from Netscape Communications at http://www.netscape.com).

As speeds of data transfer grow, great use is being made of very inexpensive live video conferencing. Cameras and microphones attached to computers allow people to see and talk with each other in private conversations and in video chat rooms where multiple people meet. MS-NetMeeting software has been included with MS-Windows-XP since its inception and may be download for other operating systems. Microsoft runs software on its own servers that allow free video/audio connections with anyone else having a microphone and camera. White Pine CU-SeeMe has played a lesser role in this type of free videoconferencing since Microsoft and others have begun to offer free services. B4Udirect (http://www.b4udirect.com) is another free service offering private or multiple-user videoconferencing. With most of these free services, a $20 camera and a $5 microphone allows any user participation. With cable, DSL, or T1 connections to the Internet, video movement and synchronous audio have begun to approach TV quality. With slow 56K phone modem connections, video quality is clear, but movement jumps comparable to old-time movies. These inexpensive cameras also allow recording of video for storage as computer files in a variety of formats (WAV, MPG, MPEG, WMV, etc.).

This allows the user to attach a video to an e-mail message. While this is not live broadcasting, it provides a convenience for persons unable to attend live conferences. It also permits the storage of videos on Web sites for click access by the public. Ramifications for on line courses proliferate.

Finally, access to the Internet helps busy administrators stay informed of events in the world, nation, and state. Most major newspapers, television stations, radio stations, and related news organizations now maintain Web sites with current news. Local Doppler radar may also be accessed at any time from the Internet. For the administrator who likes to keep things simple, a company called Essential Links (www.el.com) has positioned itself as a portal to the Internet offering links to just about every type of news and information source you may want to access. Administrators who prefer to have news headlines, sports results, financial information, weather forecasts, and more automatically arrive in their e-mail boxes at specified intervals may wish to obtain a free subscription to these services at InfoBeat (www.infobeat.com). Upon first entering the Web site, users are prompted to establish a personal profile of the types of information and the delivery schedule desired. After that, everything happens per schedule until the profile is changed or deleted.

District and School Web Sites

Most school districts have their own Web sites on the Internet. These provide the public with a wide variety of information such as:

- Faculty and administrator profiles
- Board member listings
- Phone and e-mail directories
- Alumni accomplishments and gathering dates
- Athletics and recreation department procedures and events
- Guidance services including college search guides and links, scholarship searches, career descriptions, college testing schedules and procedures, career interest assessments
- School calendars
- PTA events
- School foundation activities
- School store products, prices, and hours
- Bus services, bus schedule, contact number, daily delay information
- Press releases
- Employment vacancy notices
- Listings of upcoming deadlines
- Upcoming events
- Cafeteria menus
- School, faculty, staff, and student accomplishments
- Curriculum
- Emergency announcements

School and district Web sites also provide the public with a quick way to communicate with the school by using on line forms and accesses to data bases. Students and parents can use passwords to retrieve student grades.

While a comprehensive Web site can provide the public with a wealth of information and services, it may necessitate many hours each day of an employee's time to program changes and manage services. Although a comprehensive Web site increases parent involvement in their children's education, it also increases the administrative, faculty, and staff time necessary to serve the community.

Creating a district or school Web site is serious business. In earlier years, these Web sites were left to the uncoordinated creativity of students, teachers, and administrators. This often resulted in unprofessional, unorganized, and artistically displeasing public representations of districts and schools to their communities. One staff member should be selected to manage the Web site. The usual title for such a person is "Webmaster."

There are many different types of software necessary for developing and maintaining a Web site. School Webmasters should be familiar with all of the following:

- Word Processor software necessary for creating lengthy documents for eventual uploading.
- HTML editor software necessary for quick changes to Web page code.
- Graphics design software such as MS-PowerPoint
- Image editing software such as Adobe PhotoShop and Adobe ImageReady (embedded in recent versions of PhotoShop). ImageReady provides the Webmaster with the ability to optimize images allowing for smaller file size with faster loading abilities.
- Image conversion software providing the Webmaster with the ability to change image types to the GIF or JPG formats necessary for Web visibility
- WYSIWYG Graphical Web Editor software, stands for What You See is What You'll Get. Products such as Dreamweaver and Front page provide the Webmaster with a graphical interface for the development of Web pages. Most professional Webmasters prefer to program in HTML language and not to use graphical interfaces for their development. They maintain that the graphical interface packages are too limiting on element placement and action commands. The benefits of WYSIWYG software is that the nonprogrammer can get a Web site up in a shorter time than might be necessary to learn HTML programming language. Additionally, programs such as Front Page provide a limited selection of server-side applications. These applications reside on the Webserver and allow Webmasters to connect their users with more robust functions.
- Audio production and audio editing software provides the Webmaster with the ability to incorporate music and voice within a Web site. The ability to record files in a ".wav" format and to convert them to RealAudio files (RA and RM) allows the end

user to hear at the click of a button.

- Video editors and cameras provide the school district with the ability to edit short video clips on line. That basket at the final second of the game looks great on line. So do science demonstrations.
- Course development software provides districts with the ability to place entire lessons and courses on line. Although entire courses can be produced using combinations of the software listed above, course development software such as Blackboard and WebCT include server-side programs enabling testing, chat rooms, bulletin boards, and other interactive course features normally unavailable with self-hosted Web sites. Districts having their Web sites hosted by large Internet Service Providers (ISPs) can take advantage of many server-side programs without the need for course development software.

Administrators make use of networks in many ways to help stretch budgets and foster increased communication. The Internet provides access to a wealth of timely information and the ability to share school and district information with others. The ability to use networks and Internet resources allows for great efficiency of service.

Other Computerized Devices

In addition to the technologies presented above, several other computer-related devices allow administrators to function in a more productive manner. These include handheld personal computers and integrated technologies.

Handheld Personal Computers

The advances in microminiaturization have introduced of a variety of small personal devices that are of use to the administrator. Handheld personal computers (HPC), which run the Microsoft Windows CE operating system, also come with a useful selection of software, including versions of Microsoft Word, Excel, Access, and Internet Explorer. The HPCs also have an address book, interactive calendar and task list, and other features. This gives administrators access to word processing, spreadsheets, databases, presentations, calendars, names and addresses, telephone numbers, the Internet, e-mail, and other features available through applications that may be downloaded from sites on the Internet. Many handheld devices also come with a built-in modem for connection to the Internet. Examples of these HPCs include Jornada by Hewlett-Packard and Velo by Philips.

Related to these devices are palmtop computers. Some palmtop devices use the Windows CE operating system, while others use the palmtop's proprietary system. Most offer a core set of applications that include Date Book, Address Book, To Do List, and Memo Pad. Additional software may be downloaded from sites on the Internet. Newer versions of palmtop computers feature a built-in wireless modem for connection to the Internet. Examples of these devices include PalmPilot by 3Com, Aero by Compaq, and Cassiopeia by Casio.

One feature common among handheld PCs and palmtop computers is the ability to connect to the administrator's desktop computer. Accompanying software may be configured to synchronize files between the personal device and the desktop. For example, the administrator may be working on a report in Microsoft Word on the desktop computer in the office. When the devices are connected, the newest draft of the document is loaded into the personal device. During a break at a conference, the administrator makes some changes to the report. Back at the office, when the devices are reconnected, the changes are uploaded to the desktop. This same process works with spreadsheets, task lists, and calendar changes. Because of the portability of HPCs and palmtops, and because they offer this synchronization feature, the use of these devices can greatly enhance the productivity of the administrator.

Integrated Technologies

The future of microminiature personal devices is filled with much promise. These *personal digital assistants* (PDAs) are now featuring a variety of technologies integrated into one device. Models now feature wireless/cellular telephones with e-mail, pager, Internet browsing, and intercom capabilities.

In summary, administrators make use of other computerized devices in many ways to help increase productivity. Handheld, palmtop, and integrated computer-based technologies provide the tools necessary for functioning in a global society. Access to these devices will enable the administrator to function even more efficiently in this electronic world.

File Storage and Backup

Administrators use file cabinets for storing important paper documents. Similarly, electronic documents are stored. Options for this process includes floppy disks (typically 3.5" disks) and the built-in hard drives on desktop and laptop computers. Hard drives hold much more data, but they are not portable. Floppy disks are portable, but they hold a limited amount of data, and they are also much more subject to data loss. Fortunately, advances in removable storage have brought solutions to the administrator. Specialized removable disks now hold 10 to 20 times the amount of data that the 3.5" floppy could store. Examples of these include Zip and Jaz disks by Iomega and SuperDisk by Imation. Technology is also available that allows the administrator to store information on compact discs (CDs). Some devices allow the user to write the information onto the CD once (CD-W), and some allow for writing multiple times (CD-RW).

When people use computers, one fact is certain. At some point, the computer will malfunction. Many times, this results in loss of data. The only way to protect from this catastrophe is to back up all critical files on a regular schedule. This back-up procedure may be as simple as keeping copies of important files on more than one disk. Optionally, the administrator may wish to store copies of the files on the network file server. Usually, these servers have very large hard drives to accommodate the storage needs of multiple users, and they are protected through the use of software that automatically copies these files to other media on a daily schedule. The servers in a network are usually further protected by an uninterruptable power supply (UPS) that provides battery power to keep the server running during a power outage.

Planning for Technology

Effective and efficient administration of schools requires planning. The use of microcomputers for administration is an area that should be an integral part of any school planning process. Most states require a specific planning process for technology, but these processes usually focus on the instructional use of computers. This chapter is not an appropriate location for details on planning for technology, but the process may be simplified if the following steps are followed:

1. First, decide what you want to accomplish. List the tasks that you wish to perform electronically.
2. Next, investigate how you might accomplish these tasks with computers
3. Only after the first two steps are completed should you begin looking for the software and hardware needed to realize these tasks

Too often, decisions are made to purchase equipment (computers, accessories, and networks) only to have the installation followed by discussions on how to use the new technology. The unfortunate result of this sequence is that many times the administrator realizes that the purchased equipment is insufficient to perform the critical tasks that are a part of school administration. The planning process, when completed logically and deliberately, can help to avoid these problems.

Summary

This chapter briefly examined the impact of microcomputers on administration and, more specifically, how four general areas of computer use enhance the efficiency of educational administrators: productivity tools, data management tools, networking and the Internet, and miniaturized, integrated devices. Computer-based technology is changing at an exponential rate. Every day, new innovations in computer processing speed, electronic data storage, networking connection speeds, and ways to interconnect are announced. Technology frees the administrator from mundane office tasks, and it provides increased access to larger amounts of information in less time. Managing this information wisely and efficiently is the challenge of the future.

Case Problem: Joining the 21st Century At Last

Everyone respects Michael Soft, the principal of Cook Middle School. He is the most computer-literate employee in the district and was indeed the most logical choice to head the technology advancement effort in the district. Michael's superintendent, the board of education, all the district's teachers, and all the students are looking forward to Michael's leadership in updating the districts paltry computer labs from its older 20th century hardware and in installing updated computers and software in all the classrooms. Using the planning advice presented in the section above this case problem, the information throughout this chapter, the leadership skills you know work best, and any other information available to you, advise Michael Soft on the design and implementation of a technology update plan for his district.

References

Leiserson, A.B., (Ed.) (2001). *Guide to Automated Library Systems, Library Software, Hardware and consulting companies*. AcqWeb, Nashville, TN: Vanderbilt Law Library. Retrieved September 25, 2002 from http://acqweb.library.vanderbilt.edu/acqweb/pubr/opac.html

No author. (2002). *Webopedia: Online computer dictionary for internet terms and technical support*. Darien, CT: Internet.com Corporation. Retrieved September 25, 2002 from http://webopedia.internet.com/ .

Power, D.J. (2000). *Brief history of spreadsheets*. Cedar Falls, IA: DSSResourcesRetrieved September 25, 2002 from http://dssresources.com/history/sshistory.html.

Software and Information Industry Association. (2002). *Schools Interoperability Framework.* Washington, DC: Software and Information Industry Association. Retrieved September 25, 2002 from http://www.siia.net/sif/.

Tang Sha, V. (2002). *Library automated systems*. Cranberry Twp., PA: InfoWorks Technology Company. Retrieved September 25, 2002 from http://itcompany.com/inforetriever/sys.htm..

Copyrights, Trademarks, and Acknowledgments

The following listings identify the owners of the copyrights or trademarks.

Copyrights

4D is copyrighted by ACI Corporation. Instant Messenger is copyrighted by America Online. AppleWorks is copyrighted by Apple Computer. MacSchool, WinSchool, and Library Pro are copyrighted by Chancery Software. WordPerfect and Paradox are copyrighted by Corel. School Transportation Manager is copyrighted by Dynacomp Software. Horizon is copyrighted by epixtech. FileMaker Pro is copyrighted by FileMaker. Circulation Plus and Union Catalog Plus are copyrighted by Follett Software Company. Exent is copyrighted by Horizon Systems Software. Inspiration is copyrighted by Inspiration Software. Lotus Notes is copyrighted by Lotus. Microsoft Word, Microsoft Excel, Microsoft PowerPoint, Microsoft Access, Microsoft FoxPro, Microsoft Project, Microsoft Works, Microsoft NetMeeting, Microsoft Outlook, and Microsoft Exchange Server are copyrighted by Microsoft Corporation. SASIxp is copyrighted by NCS. Netscape Calendar is copyrighted by Netscape. School Bus Management System (SBMS) and Graphic Routing System (GRS) are copyrighted by Northwoods Computer Software. IEP Plus is copyrighted by Orion Systems Group. MasterPlan is copyrighted by Planware Systems. Mandarin is copyrighted by SIRS. IEP Maker is copyrighted by Total Recall Software. MapNet is copyrighted by Trapeze. SMwin is copyrighted by Tremont Software.

Trademarks

PalmPilot is a registered trademark of 3Com Corporation. AOL is a registered trademark of America Online. Macintosh and Mac OS are registered trademarks of Apple Computer. Cassiopeia is a registered trademark of DBA Casio Computer. Jornada is a registered trademark of Hewlett-Packard Company. SuperDisk is a registered trademark of Imation Corporation. InfoBeat is a registered trademark of InfoBeat Inc. Zip and Jaz are registered trademarks of Iomega Corporation. 1-2-3 is a registered trademark of Lotus. Windows is a registered trademark of Microsoft Corporation. ICQ is a registered trademark of Mirabilis Ltd. Corporation. Winnebago Spectrum is a registered trademark of Sagebrush Software. DeltaGraph is a registered trademark of SPSS. StarOffice is a registered trademark of Sun Microsystems.

Acknowledgement

Thanks goes to David Blood, who worked on the 1990s versions of this chapter.

Chapter 11
Conflict

Jeffrey S. Kaiser

> The manner in which administrators react to job pressure can reduce the negative effects of stress. This chapter examines ways to prevent stress from negatively affecting productivity. Effective conflict management can greatly reduce the upward spiraling of pressure.

Conflict with People

Conflicts with people and time are the most serious contributors to stress. Recent work in conflict management and time management have provided administrators with the knowledge and skills necessary to lower stress levels and maintain higher levels of performance.

Conflict of interest, conflict of personalities, conflict of ethics, and conflict involving turf are only some of the aspects that make most administrative jobs less pleasant than desired. But conflict can be a challenge rather than a drudgery, a challenge that can come from an attempt to traverse conflict using the skills of conflict management. These skills can be applied through a process of objectification. The process begins with a clear understanding that conflict is inevitable in organizations.

Typical Administrator/Staff Misunderstandings

Some conflict can be avoided with all the people all the time and all conflict can be avoided with all the people some of the time, but all conflict cannot be avoided with all the people all the time. As overplayed as that type of statement may be, it is exactly what must be understood as a first step in handling interpersonal problems. Major problems with interpersonal conflict always come from passive or active emotional reactions that are usually absent in reactions to mechanical breakdowns.

A conflict is only a problem. When treated as routine, problem solving can be very pleasurable. It provides a sense of task completion, closure, success, growth, and even a sense of rebirth and freedom to look for new problems. That breath of fresh air can be very satisfying. It can come from completing a major report, finishing a well-developed schedule of classes, graduating from an administrative certification program, or finally being awarded a doctorate.

The process of resolving the conflict can be just as challenging and just as pleasurable as seeing the conflict in its final state of resolution. It is that process that is to be examined in this chapter.

Consider Figure 11-1. There will always be a certain amount of misunderstanding between administrators and faculty

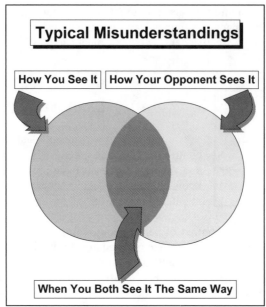

Figure 11-1

The causes for the differences fit nicely into two categories: perception and communication. Administrators, by the nature of their responsibilities alone, have a different perspective. They have the distinct advantage of seeing whole pictures from the vantage point of their position in the hierarchy. While administrators' perspectives are certainly wider than those of classroom teachers, it must understood that it is exactly those differences that may cause conflict. The shaded areas in Figure 11-1 will always exist; however, the relative size of the areas is somewhat within the control of the administrator.

An administrator's decision about how much administrative perspective, how much vantage point is shared with faculty will have a significant effect on the level of faculty resistance to decisions. It stands to reason that the more faculty know about "the big picture," the more they will understand the reasoning behind major policy decisions. The more understanding, the less resistance.

Administrators often explain that there are many facets of administration that cannot be shared with subordinates. Those facets usually have to do with forthcoming personnel decisions, budgetary constraints, and personal politics. This is certainly true. But the trade off for secrecy and lack of sharing will always be a widening of the gap between the way teachers see things and the way administrators see things. Administrators who accept that reality, and are not surprised when conflict increases, will be better decision makers.

There will be times when administrators may be willing to accept the increase in tension and conflict to protect confidences. The extent to which one can limit that type of secrecy will extend one's efficacy. Administrators can withhold information for only so long before faculty become confused, frustrated, and eventually hostile (see Figure 11-2).

Faculty confusion will increase as administrative deceit increases. Without any understanding of the reasons for this newly perceived deception, faculty will at first make overtures of collegiality with the administration in an attempt to lesson the dissonance between what is and what faculty want it to be. Receiving no feedback, or perhaps even more secrecy and deceit, faculty will experience much frustration, then worry, then fear, and then anger, as their puzzlement and confusion grow through emotional stages into hostility.

> When you stop hitting your head against the wall, it stops hurting.

Since stages of anger and hostility come from the original feeling of being left out of decision-making for what appears to be no reason, it is the wise administrator who prevents the start of such an emotional syndrome by sharing as much as possible with subordinates.

If a continually hostile faculty finds no change in administrative behavior, it will eventually become resigned to what is. To such a faculty, the only way to stop feeling bad will be to stop trying to change things. This type of resignation is not too dissimilar to the resignation of a person who leaves. In either case, productivity ceases.

Faculty resigned to an atmosphere of intimidation, while maintaining an outward appearance of having fallen into line, have been transformed into true bureaucrats. They can be characterized by their somewhat mediocre performance. The most that can be expected from such a faculty is a day's work for a day's pay. They will do what they are specifically told to do, no more, no less. And administrators will have caused this type of behavior, sometimes with smiles on their faces. Such smiles signal the loss of self-trust and self-honesty in relations with others. They may also signal a loss in commitment towards creativity. Creativity is no longer worth the risk for faculty who have experienced this.

With no rewards available for creativity, there are no longer any reasons for it, hence, the consummate bureaucrat. Bureaucrats can be a source of conflict, because they contribute nothing to the organization. They merely exist on the payroll. They are what Marilyn Kennedy (1980) calls barnacles. The organization cannot get rid of them and they live off the ship forever.

Principals and superintendents come and go, but faculty positions rarely turn over. Administrators only maintain hierarchical positions through secrecy and deceit if held there by their own superordinates. When the superordinates fall, the secret and deceitful administrator falls with them.

Emotional vs. Substantive Conflict

All the problems depicted in Figure 11-2 may well be misunderstandings by a faculty that feels isolated from the administration. Whether these misunderstandings come from perceived or real problems, it is the administration that must take responsibility for the cause. Part of an administrator's job is to prevent such things from happening. A confused faculty becomes frustrated as lack of trust in the administration grows. Frustration leads to hostility and the eventual *resignation* that this is the way life is going to be around here. A deceitful administration will dash any hope for light at the end of the tunnel, and eventually a *cover-thyself*, noncreative faculty bureaucracy will result.

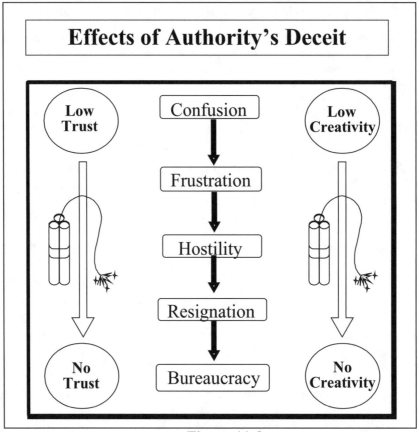

Figure 11-2

The results are the same emotional responses regardless of the original intent. Emotional conflict is draining. It begins with those valid psychological constructs referred to as personality conflict, resentment, fear, dislike, distrust, and anger (see Figure 11-3).

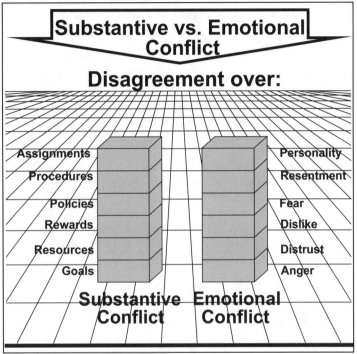

Figure 11-3

Fear is bad for the organization. Fearful employees behave in bureaucratic ways. They perform at the minimally permissible standards, just enough to keep their jobs. They lack creativity and exhibit no motivation. Since the danger of what might happen to them if they fail at an attempt at creativity outweighs any benefits if they succeed, they do not try. They are motivated, but all their motivation will be directed toward outside activities where there is the possibility of success. The motivation of great teachers can be easily lost to volunteer work elsewhere.

Anger is also bad for the organization. Angry employees engage in antiorganizational behavior. Their motivation is to hurt the organization that they feel has hurt them, so they will subvert administrative efforts and do whatever they can to get even. This is nothing new. We learned this from the original studies at the Hawthorn Plant of Western Electric decades ago. Because employees have been known to sabotage their companies by "throwing a monkey wrench into the works", administrators are ill-advised to create situations that result in angry employees.

Another even bad for the organization is anxiety, defined as "fear in the absence of specific danger." Anxious employees behave the same as fearful or angry ones. They make efforts to lower their own anxiety levels by either avoiding all conflict and becoming docile bureaucrats, or by releasing their anxiety via hostile behavior that, paradoxically, gives them temporary peace. Administrators are also ill-advised to create situations that create or enhance levels of anxiety in their faculty.

Substantive conflict may be good or bad for an organization. It results from disagreement over assignments, procedures, policies, rewards, resources, and goals in the organization. When such disagreement is channeled toward creative problem solving, an organization can grow. It is only when disagreement takes on a life of its own that it becomes detrimental to organizational functioning.

Disagreements may be normal and healthy, and serve the organization well. Even disagreement over district-wide policies can be healthy. Hegel, a well known philosopher, wrote of the classic clash of opposites as the seeds of growth. The clash of thesis with antithesis can result in synthesis (growth), which is often called *creative conflict*. Conflict over limited resources can result in prudent spending and purchasing policies. Conflict over assignments can result in clarification of responsibility. Conflict over procedures can result in better ones. Substantive conflict can be a sign of a very healthy organization. It is only when the disagreements over substance become emotional that efforts need to be made to reduce conflict levels.

Interdepartmental Quarrels

Three conditions are necessary for interdepartmental conflict. The departments must have:

1) interdependent goals
2) incompatible goals
3) the ability to interfere with each other.

First, the interdependency of goals is necessary for conflict to exist, because without such interdependency, there would be little need to interact. And without interaction, there can be no conflict. The goals must be so interdependent as to require interaction between members of one department with members of another department.

Second, the goals of two departments must be incompatible. If one department's goal accomplishment means trouble for another department's goal accomplishment, conflict is inevitable. Although the goals are interdependent, incompatibility can cause conflict.

Third, at least one department must have the ability to interfere with the other department. Without interference, there can be no conflict.

An administrator's ability to control the interdepartmental conflict in a school may rest on the ability to prevent interference. Since departmental goals ought to automatically reflect school-wide and district-wide goals, their interdependency may be a given, and their incompatibility may be one of those troublesome things that comes with the territory.

The concentration should be on the prevention of interference. That can be done with clear-cut procedures for each department to follow while working on its goal. Procedures should be structured and include specification of tasks and schedules. Although administrators are not normally this involved with the *administrivia* of a department, it is advisable to become this involved under such circumstances. Once such details are specified, the administrator's need for involvement will decrease.

When to Resolve and When to Stimulate Conflict

There are times when it is very appropriate for an administrator to stir up a little trouble. Other times, the administrative role requires more the role to be that of moderator, mediator, referee, or arbitrator. Figure 11-4 is a checklist for stimulating or resolving conflict.

Stepping in to resolve conflict when it has become too disruptive is a role of administration. Once the level of conflict begins to interfere with teaching or learning, it has gone too far. Monitoring organizational climate can be aided by spending time in the faculty lounge, asking direct questions of individuals, discussing climate and problems at faculty meetings, and distributing climate surveys. Once parents or students begin to discuss the problem, though, it has gone too far.

It is time to intervene when conflict has become personal. Personal conflict is usually emotional rather than substantive, and is rarely creative. It is important to balance the need to allow people the usual, day-to-day

Benign neglect can become carcinogenic.

arguments that characterize the human existence and the need to intervene when the problem becomes severe and affects teaching and learning.

Intervention is necessary whenever the conflict, whether substantive or emotional, becomes so severe as to outweigh the need to attend to the tasks assigned. Whenever a conflict becomes that highly elevated, it must be resolved. Trivial arguments over trivial matters are not trivial if they interfere with teaching or learning. Administrators must be sure that the interference is real and of sufficient severity to warrant involvement. Otherwise, they must stay out of it.

There are times when administrators must become involved with conflicts that are not concerned with district-wide goals. The reasoning here is that as long as the conflicts are goal-oriented and as long as the goals are those of the entire school district, the conflict may indeed be necessary and even creative. But, if the conflict is within one department or between two departments and has little to do with the over-all district mission or goals, it may be better off resolved.

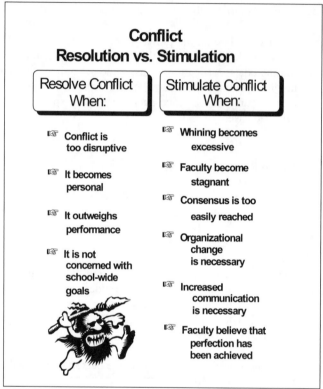

Figure 11-4

It does become necessary to stimulate some conflict on occasion. Administrators have long known that bored faculty with too little to do can often become thorns in the sides of administrators. Evidence of excessive whining, or constant complaining about seemingly minute problems, may signal the need for stimulation.

When faculty become so relaxed as to not care about issues that need to be fully examined or when faculty rush toward consensus on most issues to adjourn meetings early, they are usually in need of some very active leadership. This may necessitate administrative involvement in one or two departmental meetings to assure that agenda items are completed and to present a clear role model of concern about the topics.

When organizational change is necessary, the change itself may be self-stimulating, and controversial issues serve well the need to stimulate general creativity. To suggest to faculty that departments may need to be reorganized is usually sufficient to begin the process of self-reflection. Ask faculty for their opinions on some models for reorganization. Form a committee to examine various models and recommend new models to the administration.

Stirring up the organization is often necessary to increase communication among departments and within the same department. Although nobody needs a boss on his or her back all the time, a faculty that rests on its accomplishments for too long will soon be passed by. Faculty who believe that perfection has been achieved need to understand that there is always much to do. Schools are only one part of a much larger environment that never stops changing. And while continuous organizational change may seem oppressive, it is only a reflection of environmental reality. (See Chapter 6 on Strategic Planning)

Organizations have a life cycle. They are born, grow, level off into middle age, and then begin the downward slide toward death. The only organizations that have been able to survive are those that continually meet the need for change caused by the changes in their environments. The March of Dimes set the end of polio as its goal. When this was generally achieved, they switched to birth defects. The organization is intact, the jobs are intact, and it is still serving the needs of its environment. It learned to adapt.

Distinguishing between Healthy and Unhealthy Conflict

Healthy conflict usually involves compatible goals between conflicting parties. Achieving such goals may require some competition, but the goals themselves do not compete with each other. Therefore, one might expect the competition on the way to the goals to be somewhat healthy and to fall largely in the substantive realm.

Any emotional conflict will be the result of emotional problems within the individual or in the administration's misjudgments regarding the compatibility of the goals. For example, if administrators mistakenly judge the goals to be compatible, but in reality the goals will result in severe losses to either of the competing parties, then administrators have an unclear perception of the goals. Figure 11-5 lists differences and similarities between healthy and unhealthy conflict.

Conflict remains healthy when competing faculty members or competing departments have a clear understanding of what is being contested and what is not being contested, what allowable limits exist on the extent of competition, and what is considered appropriate and inappropriate behavior in the school among competing parties. Just as time on task is important for students, it is important as well for adults engaged in goal-oriented competition. The time spent on the competitive endeavor should be oriented to accomplishing the task, not on destroying the competitor.

Healthy & Unhealthy Conflict

Healthy	Unhealthy
Goals are compatible	Goals are incompatible
Agreed-upon limits to competition	A fight to the death
Focus is on goals	Focus is away from goals
Willing participation	Either competitor may feel forced to play
Some opposing behaviors, some cooperative behaviors	Behaviors are in opposition
Appropriateness of behavior is well understood	No holds barred, few ethics
Risk of "we-they" attitudes	Risk of "we-they" attitudes
One party wins more, but all parties win something	One wins, one loses
Post game strength	Post game scars
Time well spent, goal oriented	Some time wasted fighting opposition

Figure 11-5

Conflicting faculty or departments must be willing to engage in competition. If either competitor feels forced to "play", competition will be unhealthy. There needs to be something for everyone, no matter who wins the conflict. By assuring such, "cut-throat" competition will be prevented and no injury will occur to the fragile egos involved. This is crucial to behavior during the competition and to behavior of everyone involved after the competition. Upon the completion of the competition, all parties should have learned much and grown in strength from their newly acquired skills. Scars to the ego, political status, or pocketbook will only result in emotional conflict. If the rules and goals of the competition are kept substantive, the aftermath will be substantive as well.

These suggestions for maintaining a healthy competitive atmosphere are rarely placed in writing for competing faculty or departments to read and sign. This is probably best for two reasons. First, most conflict is not planned. It occurs out of a natural series of nonpredictable events and is short-lived. Therefore, it is impossible and inappropriate to develop rules for the many different aspects of normal human interaction. Second, rule-making regarding human relations borders on legislating morality. It just doesn't work. Instead, it must come naturally out of the organizational culture itself.

Although all the factors in Figure 11-5 should be considered, the clearest role in all of this should be in the way administrators model behavior for subordinates to copy. If faculty see administrators as highly motivated, high-energy persons engaged in continuous goal acquisition for the good of the school district (not for self-serving good), they will understand what is valued. On occasion, frank discussions may be necessary with people involved in conflict. Rarely, if ever, ought these things be reduced to writing except in situations that require legal documentation in preparation for future legal or quasi-legal actions, such as dismissal for cause.

Personal Approaches to Conflict

Because personal approaches to conflict differ, they are the most important factor in dealing with the difficult people and personal opponents in schools, districts, and communities. Administrators aware of their own conflict approaches and the conflict styles of others can predict the outcomes of conflict. Even more important, that knowledge empowers administrators with the possibility to change their own approaches and, hence, the conflict outcome.

The terminology *opponents* and *difficult people* is not to suggest that these people must be beaten as in a contest, nor that there is something bad about the basic fabric of their being. That is very unlikely. The terminology simply refers to the people with whom one is in conflict. Opponents and the difficult people can be turned around with skillful management. In the end, everyone comes out a winner. And since leaders set the tone for entire organizations, the net effect should appear in the classroom.

Figure 11-6 lists the character, philosophy, strategy, and behavior of five administrator approaches to school conflict.

5 Approaches to School Conflict

	Approach						
	Warrior		**Placator**		**Leader**	**Avoider**	**Appeaser**
Philo-sophy	**Barbarism**		**Civilized**		**Teaming**	**Isolation**	**Serve others**
Strategy	Suppres-sion	Full war	Limited war	Bargain-ing	Cooperation	Hide	Giving
Behavior	•Intimidate •Isolate •Order •Coerce •Duress	•Over-throw •Destroy •Fire	•Convince •Mediate •Slow but steady	•Nego-tiate •Arbitrate	•Pluralistic •Collegial •Use classic problem-solving process: —Define problem —Search for alternatives —Evaluate —Pilot —Implemement —Reevaluate	•Low profile •Low assertiv-ness •Low care for others	•Low Assertiv-ness •Give anything to keep job •Wimpy •No opinions •Want to be liked •Keep people happy

Figure 11-6

The Warrior: The warrior uses the philosophy of barbarism. Characterized by an almost insatiable desire to get one's own way, the warrior will ignore facts, hard data, and the feelings of subordinates. They are extremely closed-minded, dogmatic, and bullheaded. Some warriors may not only desire to win on all fronts in the conflict, but, additionally, to defeat their opponent absolutely,

> The gunman appeared early in the morning. He had a job to do and no one was going to get in his way. He pulled out his six-guns and began to fire. He fired all day and all night for five years. When the smoke from his guns and the dust from the turmoil cleared, all the buildings remained and the train tracks ran in the same direction as before he came. Just the people were dead.

completely. Warriors often take joy and pride in the failure of all others around them. While they may extol the virtues of school spirit, they care more about themselves than about the goals and objectives of the school district.

Warriors use their offices for the suppression of others. They allow no one to achieve except themselves. To keep teachers and subordinate administrators in line, they withhold information through isolation, give direct orders that demand absolute compliance, and use coercion, intimidation, and duress. If necessary, they will destroy their opponents by taking away all decision-making power, and even fire them. Beware, especially when the warrior smiles.

The Placator: Placators appear to be quite civilized. They are not as assertive as warriors and have a desire to make sure there is "something for everyone" in every decision. When conflict becomes too tough, they are willing to take the time to convince their opponents

> I'm just trying to keep everyone happy. After all, isn't that my role?

(politely). They will negotiate and compromise if necessary and are willing to bring in third-party mediators to help with the process. Should mediation fail, the placator will defer to third-party arbitration for the final decision.

Placators are not bad at handling conflict and not bad at keeping their school districts moving toward goals and objectives in a slow and steady pace with little chaos and low levels of controversy.

The Leader: Leaders are very assertive. They are determined to achieve their goals and objectives. They are equally determined to cooperate with all people involved in any conflict to be sure that everyone comes out of the conflict a winner, not just the leader. For this reason, leaders often form their own goals and objectives only after gathering information from all people involved with the topic under consideration.

Administrators using the leader approach to conflict adopt cooperation as their major strategy. Their decision-making is pluralistic and collegial. They rely on their team, of which they are a member, to help them define problems. Then the team helps select a few appropriate alternatives for consideration. The team evaluates all proposed alternatives and selects one alternative for implementation. If possible, a smaller, less obtrusive pilot project is attempted and evaluated before a "full blown" implementation begins. The team also designs procedures to assure continual reevaluation of the process and product. Such reevaluation plans include the dates, sequence, and measurement tools for reevaluation.

The leader is not at all afraid of making the final decision. However, final decisions are made as a result of input from all appropriate sources. Communication is open, and all-channels are encouraged and expected. Administrators using the leader style are rarely satisfied with the status quo. They have a high energy level and operate in an atmosphere of openness, consultiveness, honesty, and trust. Warning: Leaders can be corrupted by the warriors above them. Either the leader falls in line according to the warrior's demands, or the leader must leave.

The Avoider: Administrators who maintain a low profile fall into this category. This approach is characterized by low administrator assertiveness on all issues, especially those that may be controversial. Neither does the avoider care about anyone else's concerns. The avoider will do whatever is necessary to get the paperwork in on time and to abstain from dissension. The avoider wants no trouble. Avoiders' goals are to remain invisible, keep their jobs, work as little as possible, and eventually retire. The problem with avoiders is that they are already retired from everything except the payroll.

Avoiders are difficult to work for because they provide no leadership at all. They do not solve problems. They would rather look the other way. Creative people are stifled because of their administrator's attempt to keep everything calm and stagnant.

We have a fine school here. We don't get involved in all this nonsense regarding school reform, left-brain-right-brain, cooperative learning, quality circles, at-risk students, or that Hunter model. And we certainly aren't involved with critical thinking.

The Appeaser: There are those administrators who seem concerned with appeasing everyone around them. They have no assertiveness to speak of. Although like the avoiders, they dodge all conflict, appeasers are different. They maintain their positions by doing whatever their faculty and staff want. They have no opinions of their own and are only strong on giving lip service to other people's ideas. They want to be liked. They want to be accepted. They have no ideas, goals, or objectives. They appear to be wimpy, and are. Their philosophy, if any, is that they exist to serve the needs of everyone else. They will give away the whole store (if given access to it).

Appeasers only last as long as they can serve the needs of the creative people around them. But after a while, creative people need the strength of leadership to help get to their goals. Then, appeasers can no longer appease.

Figure 11-7 depicts all five approaches in relationship to assertiveness and cooperativeness . *Assertiveness* refers to the extent of the administrator's desire to win. *Cooperativeness* refers to the administrator's desire to help the opponent win. Careful attention to the directions for Figure 11-7 can help identify the conflict style of an administrator and opponent.

It appears from all the data gathered and from everyone's opinion that we ought to do it. Let's get started on developing the process. I'll need some help figuring out how we're going to measure whether we're successful with this. I'll take all the recommendations and work up a budget to fund this thing. John, can you get your department to develop the curricula before the end of this semester?

Directions for Determining Your Conflict Style

1. On a scale from 0-9, ask yourself how much you really desire to win in this conflict (O means low desire to win, 9 means high desire to win). That will be a measure of your assertiveness. Write your score here: _____

2. On a scale from 0-9, rate your desire to help your opponent (0 means low desire to help your opponent, 9 means high desire to help your opponent). That will be a measure of your cooperativeness. Write your score here: _____

3. Take your score from #1 above and find it on the vertical axis (at the left side of Figure 11-6).

4. Draw a horizontal line from that vertical axis score all the way through the graph from left to right.

5. Take your score from #2 above and find it on the horizontal axis (at the bottom of Figure 11-6).

6. Draw a vertical line from that horizontal axis score all the way through the graph from the bottom to the top.

7. Note where your two lines intersect each other.

8. The box closest to the intersection is your conflict style with this particular opponent for this particular circumstance.

9. On a scale from 0-9, do your best to estimate how much your opponent really desires to win in this conflict (O means low desire to win, 9 means high desire to win). That will be a measure of your opponent's assertiveness. Write your opponent's score here: _____

10. On a scale from 0-9, do your best to estimate how much your opponent really desires to help you (0 means your opponent has a low desire to help you, 9 means your opponent has a high desire to help you). That will be a measure of your opponent's cooperativeness. Write your opponent's score here: _____

11. The box closest to the intersection of the score from #9 with the score from #10 is your opponent's conflict style with you for this particular circumstance.

12. Refer to Figure 11-8 to determine the likelihood of winning this conflict.

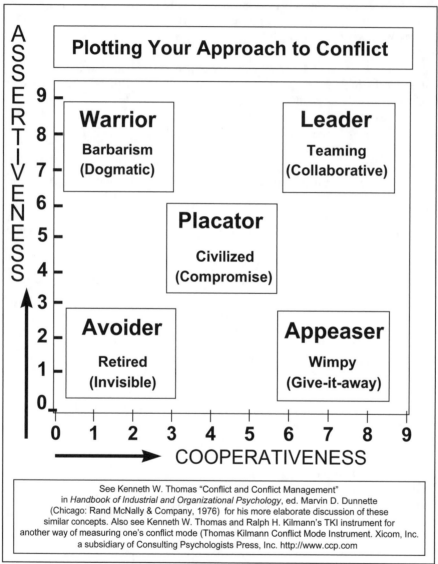

Plotting Your Approach to Conflict

ASSERTIVENESS

Warrior
Barbarism
(Dogmatic)

Leader
Teaming
(Collaborative)

Placator
Civilized
(Compromise)

Avoider
Retired
(Invisible)

Appeaser
Wimpy
(Give-it-away)

COOPERATIVENESS

See Kenneth W. Thomas "Conflict and Conflict Management"
in *Handbook of Industrial and Organizational Psychology*, ed. Marvin D. Dunnette
(Chicago: Rand McNally & Company, 1976) for his more elaborate discussion of these
similar concepts. Also see Kenneth W. Thomas and Ralph H. Kilmann's TKI instrument for
another way of measuring one's conflict mode (Thomas Kilmann Conflict Mode Instrument. Xicom, Inc.
a subsidiary of Consulting Psychologists Press, Inc. http://www.ccp.com

Figure 11-7

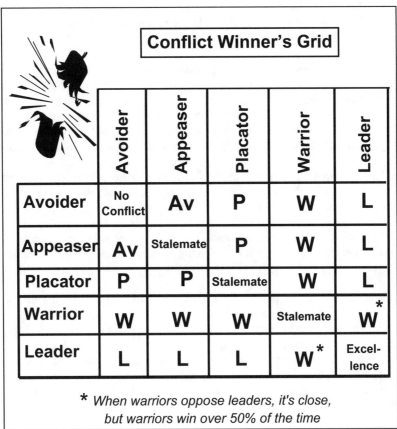

Figure 11-8

Predicting the Winner

It is possible to reliably predict the winner in any particular conflict once the conflict approach of both opponents is known. The validity and reliability of the prediction depends on how accurate are analyses of the opponents' approaches to conflict.

Now look at Figure 11-8 to determine the outcome based on both opponents' approaches to a particular conflict situation. If both are in the warrior mode, they will never settle the conflict. That is probably because things have escalated to an emotional level of conflict where the original substance of the conflict in no longer the issue. Until one of the opponents deescalates, no one can win. The opponents are better off discussing this problem. If both back off from warrior mode, the problem is solvable. Figure 11-8 shows that if one opponent backs off first, the other is placed in the advantageous position. There is a solution to this dilemma.

The solution lies in a completely different approach to this entire problem. It will require a big change on the part of either opponent. The approach is to back off a little and send verbal and nonverbal signs of "liking" to the opponent. If the opponent becomes convinced that the other opponent may indeed find him or her to be an "okay" person, perhaps even likeable, or better yet "lovable," the result will encourage delectation on both parts. The positive signs will eventually be returned to the sending opponent. Patience will be the order of the day.

This new approach is going to take tremendous effort on the sender's part, because the sender may not be used to sending such information to opponents and opponents may not be used to or trust what they are receiving. By forcing oneself to be a sender, one will soon begin to feel better about all opponents. The strong negative emotions will have dissipated, the positive Pygmalion effect will have begun, and the sender will feel better about the job of leading someone who used to be such a difficult person. This is exactly where human relations skills are put to use.

Senders need to be prepared for no visible signs of change during the first day of implementation with an archenemy. The change may take a week or two. It has nothing to do with magic. It all has to do with verbal and nonverbal behavior and people wanting to feel good about themselves and their environment. If they feel bad whenever they are in someone's presence, perhaps even threatened, they will act very negatively. This is a protection and a defense mechanism. Remove the threat and negative vibrations, and opponent will no longer feel as threatened or negative. These are the basic tenets of the self-fulfilling prophecy, the Pygmalion effect.

While the winners listed in the intersections in Figure 11-8 for various pairs of opponents seem quite appropriate, one is quite disconcerting. The warrior tends to win over the leader.

When warriors oppose leaders, it is a close battle. But warriors tend to win over 50% of the time. The reasons are simple: Warriors' guns are bigger and their ethics are of questionable morality. However, leaders eventually win. Perhaps not this battle, perhaps not the next, but in the long term, the warrior becomes obvious to all, even the school board. The challenge here is to wait long enough to win the war while all the battles are being lost. It may take a change in management philosophy, and that can be a long wait.

There will always be victims so long as bullies are protected by the power structure.

Warriors cannot be defeated by placating, appeasing, avoiding, or leading. People cannot be beaten when they play by tougher rules. Disappointment awaits those who escalate to a warrior's level of behavior and find themselves to be as adept at war as the warrior, because a fight between two warriors results in stalemate. The only winners in such battles are those who can persist through support from higher levels. The avenues above the opponent must be examined with extreme care. It may be necessary to back off until the warrior leaves. Backing off is also a sign of leadership. It suggests an ability to forgo the immediate for the future.

Considering the Subject of the Disagreement

It is also useful to examine the subject of the disagreement. Resolving differences over facts, methods, goals, or values can be easier if the correct method of resolution is used.

Differences over facts: To resolve differences over facts, both opponents should share all information. It is important to agree first on the criteria for judging the validity of facts before the facts themselves are presented. Agreement on mutually acceptable sources for facts is also important.

Differences over methods: To resolve differences over methods requires a change in attitude by both parties to the disagreement. Methods, unless dangerous or immoral, are less consequential than goals to disagree over. It is the goals that are important, not the methods of achieving them. Opponents need to address goals and objectives instead of methods. Methods are means, not ends. Disagreement over methods should always signal the need to move the discussion to the level of goals and objectives toward which the methods aim.

Differences over goals: To resolve differences over goals, the focus of the conversation should be raised to that of the mission of the school district. Since all goals should reflect the mission, it may be that the mission is the culprit and needs to be addressed. If the goal in question does not directly relate to the mission, then work needs to be done to assure closer ties between the two levels.

Differences over values Resolving differences over values may be the most difficult challenge. The best approach is to avoid discussion of the differences and build on the similarities. Look for any overlap between opponents' values. Trying to reach agreement on even the most basic similarities is often helpful. The success with gang problems, albeit minor success, has come from the mutual desire of both sides to stay alive. The value of one's own life may be enough to initiate a cease fire. Building on that value may take time, but it is a start. Point systems used in behavior modification systems for behaviorally disturbed and Emotionally Disturbed children utilize the same approach to ending conflict among students. Accumulated points may be traded for school privileges. To the extent that those privileges are valued, conflicting students disengage.

The Difficult People Cube

The Difficult People Cube (Figure 11-9) is an extremely useful tool for understanding the motivations of difficult people and for planning your own behavior to deal with their difficulties. The first part of this section will describe the front face of the Difficult People Cube.

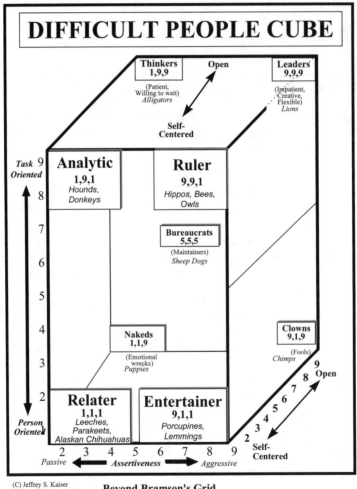

(C) Jeffrey S. Kaiser
Stylex Publishing Co., Inc.   **Beyond Bramson's Grid**

Figure 11-9

The front face of the cube forms a chart. Thanks goes to Bramson (1981), who explored these first two dimensions forming just the front-most face many years ago. His original explorations are what provided the impetus for what grew into the work presented here.

Front Face Dimensions

The front-most face of the cube has two dimensions. The horizontal dimension (the X-axis) of Assertiveness runs from Passive on the left to Aggressive on the right. The vertical dimension (the Y-axis) runs from Task-Oriented behavior at the top to Person-Oriented behavior at the bottom. To understand the coordinates, the X-axis is always presented first, followed by the Y-axis, followed by the Z-Axis.

The Quadrants

These two dimensions provide us with four quadrants on the front face, the quadrant in the upper right (Ruler), lower right (Entertainer), lower left (Relater), and upper left (Analytic). The general characteristics of the four quadrants will be examined first and then some of the personality characters that fit into those quadrants will be discussed.

Rulers (9, 9, 1) is a great label for difficult people whose behavior places them in the upper right quadrant. The label is apt, because difficult people in this quadrant are task oriented and aggressive. They tend to be autocratic. Their speed of operation is usually fast, and they are motivated by their fear of loss of control. They love efficiency. Their need for speed and aggressiveness often take a precedence over a more advisable and reasoned thought process. Instead, they often use a *ready-fire-aim* mode of behavior. *Hippos*, *Bees*, and *Owls* are the names chosen for variations of personalities that may easily be seen as part of the *Ruler* category of difficult people.

Hippos (9, 9, 1) can be characterized by the following stereotypical case.

> *Ms. Johnson, principal of the Happy Apple school, was sitting at her desk at 7:30 AM when the door flew open and in stormed Mr. Sandstorm. Mr. Sandstorm moved quickly to the front of Ms. Johnson's desk and began to yell, "Your 5th grade teacher Mrs. Thompson has been harassing my daughter and I want it stopped immediately. I am sick and tired of this going on. I hold you completely responsible for allowing a teacher to do this to a student, and I intend to sue this school district, this school, and you personally for everything you own.*

Dealing with a stampeding hippo like Mr. Sandstorm requires that you do nothing to enrage him further.

Dealing with a Stampeding Hippo

1. Wait until your own emotions are under control. You are being attacked and may need to compose yourself before acting. Let him run down. Do not try to stand in the way of a stampeding hippo. You are liable to get run over. It is better to let the hippo go through a catharsis, getting all of this off his chest. The likelihood is that he will eventually get it all out and calm down. Then, perhaps, you can have a reasonable conversation with him and begin to gather the facts about the alleged situation.

2. Pace the hippo. This means that you need to bring your attention level up to his. For you to sit and merely stare off into space with a disgusted look on your face would serve to anger the hippo further. Sit up straight in your chair and pay attention to the hippo. Show concern for what he is saying. You might even want to tell him that you are very interested in hearing what he has to say about what is going on in Ms. Thompson's classroom, because you, as principal, need to know these things.

3. Use assertive behavior, but be careful not to become aggressive. This is not the time to tell the hippo that he has no right to talk to you this way. That would be aggression on your part, whether it is true or not. It is better if you invite the hippo to sit down so that you can get to the bottom of this.

4. Interrupt the hippo. Sometimes, a stampeding hippo can get worked up into an emotional state that becomes a mental cloud around his consciousness. This cloud disconnects him from the reality around him. If his yelling becomes out of control, you may need to break through that cloud by saying his name a few times. Mr. Sandstorm. Mr. Sandstorm. Mr. Sandstorm! Hearing his name may be all that is necessary to bring him back to the recognition of his environment.

5. If you can get a postponement to give you time to gather facts, do so. Either way, plan your present or future encounter very carefully. Without a postponement, you will be forced to do a great deal of planning on your feet. That is difficult if you are emotional yourself. If the hippo does not calm down, consider postponing the conversation. The acceptance of a postponement will be more likely if you take some sort of blame for not being able to proceed at the moment. Consider telling the hippo that you want to get to the bottom of this situation and intend to discuss this with Ms. Thompson during her planning period this morning, but that you feel caught quite unprepared at the moment. You might even admit that you are feeling a bit nervous from what he has told you and don't want to say anything while feeling this way. Ask the hippo if he would be willing to meet with you later this afternoon or tomorrow to continue this discussion.

6. Schedule the next meeting at a time and place where you won't be interrupted or rushed. Hold all calls and turn off your pager, two-way radio, cell phone, and computer. Use the intervening time to do some serious planning. Meet with Ms. Thompson and find out whether there are any bases to the hippos's allegations. Get her perspective on the situation. Gather the student's files. Speak with any guidance counselors who may have had dealings with the student. Decide on where to hold the afternoon meeting with the hippo. Sometimes it is better to hold such a discussion in a conference room where you can sit diagonally from each other instead of you sitting in an authoritarian position behind your desk. Sometimes exactly he opposite is true. Bring the student's files with you. Greet the hippo with a big smile and thank him very much for coming back. Briefly, go through pleasantries, such as a comment about the weather. Offer him some coffee or a soft drink. Direct him to the seat by motioning toward it and saying, "Please sit down." All of your behaviors will serve to set a noncompetitive, nonconfrontational milieu for discussion, a far cry from the environment when he stormed in earlier today.

7. Preset a time limit. Ask the hippo to meet with you at 2:PM because you have a half-hour free at that time. In that way, the hippo will know that you will both need to conclude that meeting in 30 minutes. If your meeting is unexpected, tell the hippo that you have another meeting scheduled at a specific time and will have to leave then, but that you would like to hear all he has to say right now.

8. Focus on one issue at a time. If the hippo appears to divert the conversation into multiple directions simultaneously, bring it back to one issue at a time.

9. Use exploratory language, such as, "Help me understand. . ." "I am concerned about . . ."

10. Avoid an accusatory style, such as, "I have documentation. . ." "I heard that you said. . "

11. Give feedback to the hippo such as, "It sounds to me as if you feel. . ." Then, thank the hippo for telling you.

12. Finally, move back to your initial concern and continue the discussion until you resolve the problem and have a clear understanding of how things are going to change.

Figure 11-10

Understand that Hippos come in all sorts of flavors. Another stereotypical Hippo might be the boss on a Monday morning after she has spent the weekend coming up with ideas. Bosses with hippo behavior can come in on a Monday shouting directives to everyone in sight without taking the time to discuss these ideas with those involved in implementing them. Again, don't stand in the path of a stampeding hippo. Use modifications of the approaches discussed above to let the hippo run down before attempting a more rational approach to problem solving. Remember, your boss is more likely to have more stampeding power than you.

Kosmoski and Pollack (2000) provide insight into why Hippos often calm down when treated the way Figure 11-10 suggests. The Hippo's issue becomes co-opted. The issue is no longer just his or her issue. It now belongs to both the Hippo and the person being confronted. The burden to find a solution is now in both persons' hands, and the transfer of much of the burden lessens to weight on the Hippo.

Bees (9, 9, 1) are also in the _Ruler_ quadrant. They are also aggressive and task oriented, but operate a bit differently from _Hippos_.

The stereotypical bee is one who might sit in the back of the room at a meeting, making snide remarks about the person leading the meeting. Bees often do their stinging just loud enough to be heard by those around them. The bee's purpose is indeed to control the situation. After all, bees are in the Ruler quadrant. By making these snide remarks, they take attention away from the leader and bring the attention to themselves, giving them a sense of control. They also may sting loudly enough to disrupt the train of thought of the meeting leader and all of those in the meeting.

Consider Ms. Betty B. Stinger, the bee who interrupts the meeting by saying, "You would say that. You always agree with central office." What the bee wants is to immediately put you on the defensive and destroy what you are trying to implement. The bee hopes you will ignore the sting. In fact, leaders often make the mistake of hoping bee stings will cease if ignored. The opposite is usually the case. Bees will have succeeded in getting their point across and disrupting the meeting and your train of thought. Instead of ignoring Betty's sting, consider stopping the meeting and confronting the situation by asking, "Is what Betty says true? Do I usually just accept what central office says?" In all likelihood, others at the meeting will support you instead of Betty and she will have lost the issue and even some "face." She won't stop being a bee. That is her nature, but she may think twice about stinging you again.

Another example of a bee sting can come when you are standing with a group of people and one of them says, "That is a nice tie you are wearing. I heard that those are coming back into style soon." Of course the bee wishes to catch you off guard, embarrass you, and control the moment. Do not ignore the bee sting. Stop what you are doing and turn to the others around you and say, "Is Betty right? Is my tie too out of style?" In all likelihood, others will come to your rescue and the bee will lose with you again. Your goal is not to change the bee's personality, but merely to make the bee sting elsewhere.

Consider the list below to help you with the stinging bees in your life:

Dealing with Bees

1. There are times when you might be able to provide an alternative to open confrontation with the bee. Try to bring the bee's grievance to the surface in a private meeting between the bee and yourself. It just may be that the bee is targeting you because of a specific problem he or she has with some decision you have made. If you can find out what that was, perhaps you can remedy the situation. However, don't get your hopes up. Bees usually sting because it is part of their general behavior pattern, not because their opponents deserve the sting.

2. Consider the possibility of always confronting the bee when he or she stings. The bee will then be in a defensive position instead of you.

3. Find out if others agree with the bee. In all likelihood, they do not. If they do, consider modifications to your behavior that trips off the stings.

4. Ask the bee to be specific. Don't allow bees to sting you with generalities, such as when a bee says, "You would say that!" Stop what you are doing and ask the bee to be specific. Exactly what is it that the bee is stinging about? In this way, you can deal with specific issues and not generalities.

Figure 11-11

Owls (9, 9, 1) also belong in the _Ruler_ quadrant. They are aggressive and task oriented. They also may be more knowledgeable than you about the subject matter being discussed. While this might be considered an asset for you rather than a liability, it is not always so. For example, their ability to out talk you about a particular subject might result in their being able to lead all of your subordinates away from what you need to accomplish.

Be well prepared for discussions with an owl about the subject matter, but don't try to appear more knowledgeable than the owl unless you actually are. Instead, acknowledge the owl's knowledge. Let the owl be the expert.

Use *backtracking*. Backtracking is different from paraphrasing. Backtracking requires you to use the exact same wording as your opponent when clarifying a situation. For example, if your opponent says, "The famous Iowa Schools Study found that the Jones reading series is much better for students with advanced reading ability than the Smith reading series," don't paraphrase by saying, "So what you are saying is that you think we ought to adopt the Jones series." That is not what the owl said. You are likely to elicit an angry response from the owl. Instead, use backtracking. Say, "So you are saying that in the Iowa study, they found that the Jones reading series is much better for students with advanced reading ability than the Smith reading series." Such backtracking placers your difficult person in the position of now agreeing with you. You might explain to the owl that if the other series (the Smith series) is adopted, you will need his expertise in these matters to provide for recommendations for reading materials for advanced. In fact, you might ask the owl if he would be willing to chair a committee to study and discuss the materials that need to be ordered to address the needs of advanced readers. Such a move on your part takes into account the need for the owl to be in control of something while simultaneously diminishing his need to defeat you. In this way, you will have created a situation where he will be considerate of your alternatives while you are considerate of his.

Entertainers (9, 1, 1) is a great label for difficult people whose behavior places them in the bottom right quadrant. The label is apt, because difficult people in this quadrant are people oriented and aggressive. They tend to be enthusiastic. Their speed of operation is usually fast, and they are motivated by their need for approval and prestige. Their need for speed often takes precedence over a more advisable and reasoned thought process. The stereotypic used car salesman would fit easily into the *Entertainer* quadrant. Like *Rulers*, *Entertainers* often use a *ready-fire-aim* mode of behavior. *Porcupines and Lemmings* are the names chosen for variations of personalities that may easily be seen as part of the *Entertainer* category of difficult people.

Porcupines (9, 1, 1), while normally happy, person-oriented, aggressive people. can be very difficult when they explode. The easiest way to deal with exploding porcupines is to treat them in a similar way that you treat Hippos.

The following is a list that you may want to consider in dealing with an exploding porcupine.

Dealing with Porcupines

1. Help them regain their self-control by getting their attention.
2. Show your concern.
3. Take time out away from each other
4. Discover what trips them off and avoid those topics if possible and if appropriate.

Figure 11-12

Lemmings (9, 1, 1) also fit within the *Entertainer* quadrant. Lemmings are a type of animal that is known for scurrying to the edge of a cliff and jumping off to their death. Other lemmings follow the first lemming in a long line and proceed to jump to their deaths, too. The lemming is person oriented and aggressive. Lemmings have a great way of convincing others to follow them. Although they are not as knowledgeable as Owls, they are convincing talkers. Lemmings can lead your subordinates away from your direction into the wrong direction, resulting in disaster.

Here are some ways to deal with lemmings:

Dealing with Lemmings

1. Don't try to be more convincing than the lemming. The lemming will win. Remember that they are usually better than you at convincing others that their ideas are the best.

2. Don't let lemmings win just because they are intimidating to you. If their statements are false, accepting their intimidating personalities can hurt your organization.

3. Don't directly challenge lemmings. They will become defensive and out talk you, especially in front of others.

4. State your facts using the "I" statements you were taught not to use as a child. "I just don't feel that is the right path to take." "I don't want to." "I don't like that." "I don't know why, but I just don't want o do that."

5. Always give the lemming a way out.

Figure 11-13

You are standing outside your office with four others who are all ready to go out to lunch for Chinese food with you. Along comes the Laura the lemming and says in an excited voice, "There is a great new Mexican restaurant that just opened this week down the block. Let's go there." While normally others would give in to the lemming simply because they don't care enough to get into an argument, try the following: "Laura, we have all already decided to go out for Chinese food. That Mexican restaurant sounds great, though. Are you going to be around tomorrow for lunch? Maybe we can go there. I know I want to."

**Relaters** (1, 1, 1) is a great label for difficult people whose behavior places them in the bottom left quadrant. The label is apt, because difficult people in this quadrant are people oriented and passive. They are more sensitive than most people and have a greater need to be liked. Their speed of operation is usually slow and they avoid conflict. _Parakeets, Leaches,_ and _Alaskan Chihuahuas_ are the names chosen for variations of personalities that may easily be seen as part of the _Relater_ category of difficult people.

Leaches (1, 1, 1) are those within the Relater quadrant who love to hang around the boss's office to be sure the boss likes them. You can spot them with coffee mug in hand, dropping in at all times of the day to chat. They are looking for affirmation and reaffirmation. If you are the boss, they can eat up your entire day. Here are some things to consider when dealing with leaches:

Dealing with Leaches

1. Stop encouraging them with those big smiles and that big "Hi! How are you?"
2. Keep silent while they leach. If they are in your office again wasting your time, keep silent and keep working.
3. Simply tell them you are too busy to chat right now.
4. Assertively discourage their continual interruptions by saying the following when they leach: "Larry, while you are here, can you tell me how you are doing reaching the goals and objectives set forth in your last evaluation"?

Figure 11-14

Parakeets and _Alaskan Chihuahuas_ (1, 1, 1) also fit into the Relater quadrant. Parakeets are those characters that always parrot what the boss says. They haven'tenough of their own fortitude to merit the name parrot, just parakeet. Of course, they act the way they do because they also have high security needs and want to be liked and loved. Alaskan Chihuahuas are a new breed of the stereotypical Mexican chihuahua. The difference is that a Chihuahua in Alaska can be pictured as siting by a nice warm fire and often getting up to scratch on the door to go outside. The problem is that whenever the door is opened for an Alaskan Chihuahuas to go outside, it will merely turn around at the first feeling of cold air and scurry back to the fireplace. They can drive you crazy with their inability to make decisions for fear of offending someone.

Consider the following in dealing with Parakeets and Alaskan Chihuahuas. Understand that because they are Relaters, you will fail in getting much work out of them by appealing to any task orientation. They have none. What they do have is a great need to be liked and loved. So if they are way behind in a project that must be combined with your own before submittal to your own boss, consider approaching the Parakeet or Alaskan Chihuahua as follows:

Dealing with Parakeets and Alaskan Chihuahuas

1. Tell them that your relationship with them will improve by them honestly telling you why they haven't given you their assignment. Ask them if they are angry with you and watch them go to lengths to tell you that is not the case. Maybe they'll finish their project to assure a continuing good relationship with you. Tell them you need to count on them.

2. Ask them to consider the awkward situation in which you find yourself because of their lack of project completion.

3. Use them for cooperative problem-solving discussions and give them all the credit for anything you solve together. They need that confirmation of their worth.

4. Never assume that they will complete the action phase of a co-solved problem. Although you need to give them credit for co-problem solving, assume the action phase of a project for yourself. They probably wouldn't complete it anyway. They are not task oriented, and they are very passive individuals.

Figure 11-15

**Analytics** (1, 9, 1) is a great label for difficult people whose behavior places them in the top left quadrant. They are the former gatherers of humanity, except now they often consume their day with gathering and processing data. The label is apt, because difficult people in this quadrant are task oriented but passive. These are the bean counters. Their speed of operation is usually slow, and they can enjoy spending an entire day balancing a spreadsheet on their computer. _Hounds_ and _Donkeys_ are the names chosen for variations of personalities that may easily be seen as part of the _Analytics_ category of difficult people.

Hounds (1, 9, 1) are always whining and complaining. They usually have very little to whine or complain about, but they do it anyway because that is their nature. Often, their complaints are nonspecific, such as, "You know how it is around this joint." "Forget about being able to get anything done around here." "You know how this place is."

Consider the following when dealing with *Hounds*.

Dealing with Hounds

1. Ask them to be specific when they whine. Ask them exactly what they mean when thy whine about the way "this place" is.
2. Get them to solve their own problems. Never be the sole solver of a hound's problems. For example, if they ask you to use your influence to get their window shade repaired, ask them to fill out the standard custodial request form that everyone else fills out. Let them solve their own problems. Otherwise, they will whine to you all the time, and you will waste your own time doing their work.
3. Often excessive whining by a hound comes from the fact that the hound doesn't have enough work to do or has been slacking off. Decrease the hound's slack and increase the hound's structure.
4. Be sure the hound is indeed a hound. Someone who has a legitimate complaint does not necessarily fall into this quadrant.

Figure 11-16

Donkeys (1, 9, 1) are those in the Analytics quadrant who are notorious for being stubborn. Their favorite answer to a request is a perfunctory "No!" The stereotypic budget manager who refuses to approve a requested expense fits well into this category.

Consider the following ways to deal with Donkeys.

Dealing with Donkeys

1. Be prepared for their "no's."
2. Be prepared to go it alone. Don't assume they will say "yes". You can't count on that. You may have to figure out your own way to solve this problem.
3. Be very specific in your requests of a donkey. For example, if you need a $50 allocation so that you can provide coffee and donuts at your next meeting, do not ask the Donkey if there are funds available for "social events for staff meetings." The donkey will likely laugh and say, "Are you kidding? With the budget this year we are lucky to have any money at all. Money for social events? Ha!" It would be wiser to ask specifically if there is a way for him to get you $50 for coffee and donuts.

Figure 11-17

The Third Dimension

An important third dimension has been added to the front face. It is the Z-axis which runs from the front of the *Difficult People Cube* to the back. The front most end of the Z-axis is called *Self Centered*. This dimension of difficult people is characterized by those who are concerned more with themselves than they ought to be. The entire front face of the *Difficult People Cube* discussed so far is made up of self-centered people.

The other end of the Z-axis is characterized by people more in tune with the reactions of others. This can be positive or negative.

Clowns (9, 1, 9) are those difficult people who are typical entertainers, but are so open to the reactions and interactions of others that they forget the need to care for their own self image. The act like a chimp at a zoo, trying to draw attention to themselves at the expense of their own self-esteem.

Chimps (9, 1, 9) fit well into the Clown category. Consider the following when dealing with *Chimps*.

Dealing with Chimps

1. Understand that they have a great need for attention. Although they are not as sensitive as Relaters, they seek attention for the purpose of controlling the moment.

2. Let them finish their joke or their clowning around before you attempt to work with them.
3. Note by their placement in the *Difficult People Cube* that they are sufficiently assertive, but lack a task orientation. You can do well when you solve problems with them, but their lack of task orientation and lack of self-centeredness will likely interfere with their ability to complete projects on time, if at all.
4. If you have clowns as subordinates, structure their work for them. Set up schedules, timelines, and deadlines. Monitor their progress.

Figure 11-18

Nakeds (1, 1, 9) are those difficult people who are typical relaters, but are so opened to the way others perceive them that they often bare their souls to others. They become extremely vulnerable and may often find themselves crying because of something they perceived as a criticism. They can easily become whimpering puppies.

Puppies (1, 1, 9) fit well into the *Nakeds* category.

Dealing with Puppies

1. Understand that their sensitivity to the way they perceive others' approval is far from healthy.
2. Be very careful with a Naked's' feelings. Nakeds need continuous reinforcement, much more so than self-centered Relaters.
3. Ask them for their opinions. Let them know you are seeking their help in solving problems because you so value their opinions.
4. Understand that because they are not task oriented, you'll need to carefully plan the flow of projects. Ask them to have a look at your schedule of their work to see if it makes sense to them. Ask them if it will be okay if you check back with them from time to time to see if you can help them with any obstacles that might get into their way. In this way, you can monitor their progress without them feeling that you are accusing them of being too slow.
5. You may have to assign the action part of a project to yourself instead of to them. They are people oriented, passive, and emotionally open to the point where their personalities interfere with their ability to get their work done.

Figure 11-19

Thinkers (1, 9, 9) are task oriented, passive, and open. Their openness makes them different from the self-centered Analytics already discussed. Unlike *Hounds* or *Donkeys*, *Thinkers* can be very creative. They seek out the thoughts of others, research and study the facts, and engage in excellent decision making and planning. They just don't seem to be sufficiently assertive to enter the action phase of their plans and develop their thoughts into immediately useful products. Thinkers can be excellent advisors. They are patient and willing to wait for the right solutions. They can also hamper project flow by becoming overly zealous in gathering volumes of data for the consumption of their statistical programs. In a way, they can be like alligators in a swamp, becoming so patient with their own projects that their very presence can be deleterious to organizational health.

Alligators (1, 9, 9) fit well into the *Thinkers* category.

Dealing with Alligators

1. Spend time with them discussing as many aspects of a problem as possible.
2. Give them lists of subtopics for which you need information and recommendations.
3. Specify how much time they are to spend on each aspect of all problems
4. Specify aspects of problems that you do not want them to work on.
5. Supply them with computers and databases for their research and problem-solving.
6. Delegate to them the authority to ask questions of others.
7. Have them trained in project management techniques, project management software, and time management.
8. Remember, thinkers are indispensable people to have on your staff so long as their reports and recommendations come in on schedule.

Figure 11-20

Bureaucrats (5, 5, 9) are necessary for the smooth maintenance of an organization, but can stifle the organizational creativity and progress. They are indispensable when they function to keep people on track. Bureaucrats function as the enforcers of rules, policies, and procedures. There is just as much need for people to follow acceptable procedures in dealing with problems as there is for people to fill out travel expense forms properly. Those aspects of bureaucracy are far from negative. They provide structure to goal-oriented organizations and prevent people and departments from going on tangents that unnecessarily divert organizational resources.

However, *Bureaucrats* can too easily subvert the leadership role in an organization by stifling creativity and hampering project completion. When bureaucrats live off of the enforcement of organizational rules, they function as sheep dogs, biting at the feet of those who are trying to march forward, not just keeping meanderers goal oriented.

Sheep Dogs (5, 5, 9) fall well into the category of *Bureaucrats*.

Dealing with Sheep Dogs

1. Use them for the creation of forms and the standardization of procedures, but only for those that need to be standardized.
2. Their design of forms and standardized procedures must be overseen by members of the organization more interested in progress than in the control of others.
3. The overseers of bureaucrats must have the ability to undo the strangle hold of bureaucrats.
4. While bureaucrats must have the ability to enforce rules, the rules must only function to keep everyone goal oriented. Never allow bureaucratic functions to impede the speed of movement toward organizational goals.

Figure 11-21

Leaders (9, 9, 9) are those persons in an organization who are task oriented and highly assertive, but not as self-centered as Rulers. Leaders listen to the thoughts of others, have the task orientation to focus on project goals, and are sufficiently assertive to move toward their goals quickly for project completion. They function like *Lions*, impatient, focused, and sufficiently flexible to work with varying targets and with varying people.

Lions (9, 9, 9) fall well into the category of *Leaders*.

Dealing with Lions

1. Relish their existence. Lions move your organization forward.
2. Encourage their project leadership. Allow them to lead. Encourage them to lead. Empower them to lead.
3. Protect them from Machiavellians who care more for themselves than they do for the organization.
4. Understand that Lions often ignore rules and standardized procedures when such rules and procedures interfere with project completion. While that can be a positive aspect of Lion behavior, it can also interfere with a sense of fairness when some people must follow procedures and some can ignore them. Better to modify the official rules to accommodate lion behavior than to engage in what some organizational members might perceive as arbitrary and capricious enforcement for some people and not for others. Of course, be sure that all rules encourage creativity and goal attainment. Be careful not to strangle a true lion, or you will encourage an over-manifestation of bureaucratic behavior throughout the organization.

Figure 11-22

Of course the characterizations on *The Difficult People Cube* cannot fit every difficult personality you meet through life. The purpose of viewing difficult people along these three axes (Assertiveness, Task vs. Person Orientation, and Openness) allows for a less emotional more objective approach to dealing with difficult people. Such an approach allows you to reflect upon the situation within which you find yourself and to plan not only a response to categories of difficult people, but to take a more proactive role in leading difficult people toward organizational goals.

Summary

The objectification of what are normally emotional responses to conflict situations becomes habitual over time. Such objectification provides us with a control over our own emotional responses. The resultant lessening of emotional responses and the heightening of objective considerations for problem solving serve to strengthen the overall health of organizations. Objectification also provides us with insight into our own behavior. After all, we are often the difficult people in the lives of others.

Case Problem: Valium High School

Valium High School (VHS) has department chairpersons for each academic area. The superintendent of the district has made it clear to the principal of VHS that department chairpersons are now responsible for implementing the new School Improvement Plan, requiring redesign of all course curricula to meet new state standards. As the department chairperson for social studies, you are finding it exceedingly difficult to gain the cooperation of Betsy, one of your faculty members. Betsy never gets her work into you on time and breaks into tears whenever you mention it to her. It is not that she doesn't want to do the work, it is just that she always has some sort of excuse for not getting it done. She is honestly sorry for holding up the project, but being sorry doesn't seem to motivate her, nor does it help you fulfill your own responsibilities. Since she is the only faculty member in your department with expertise over her particular aspect of social studies, you cannot merely assign her work to someone else. You have three more weeks until the entire social studies portion of the School Improvement Plan must be submitted to the principal. The principal relies on you to get your department's work in on time and holds you responsible for doing so.

References

Bramson, R. M. (1981) *Coping with difficult people* NY: Ballantine Books (and Bantam Doubleday Dell Publishing Group, Inc.)

Kennedy, M. M. (1980) *Office politics: seizing power and wielding clout* New York: Warner.

Kosmoski, G. J. , Pollack, D. R. (2000) *Managing difficult, frustrating, and hostile conversations: Strategies for savvy administrators.* Thousand Oaks, CA: Corwin Press, Inc.

Thomas, K.W. (1976) *Conflict and Conflict Management* in Handbook of Industrial and Organizational Psychology, Ed. Marvin D. Dunnette. Chicago: Rand McNally & Company, 1976.

Thomas, K.W. , Kilman, R. H. (2002) TKI Instrument Xicom, Inc., a subsidiary of Consulting Psychologists Press, Inc. Available http://www.ccp.com

Chapter 12
Violence and Safe Schools

Sandra L. Harris, Garth Petrie, and Jamey E. Harris-Pinkerton

---

This chapter presents the factors contributing to school violence, early warning signs, and techniques of prevention, intervention, and crisis management

---

Introduction

In recent years, the U.S. public has ranked violence and crime in schools as the most important problems that face our educational system (Phi Delta Kappa/Gallup Poll, 1998). In fact, in a recent survey, 77 % of Americans say they worry about school safety today and fear that their children are no longer safe at their schools (*Public Agenda Online*, 2000). Yet according to the *1999 Annual Report on School Safety* (U.S. Department of Education (USDOE) and U.S. Department of Justice [USDOJ], 1999), the vast majority of schools are safe. Homicides at school are very rare events. From July 1, 1997, to December 31, 1997, less than one percent of the more than 2,500 murders or suicides involving children nationwide took place at school. For that school year, there were only 46 school-associated violent deaths. In fact, most injuries that occur at school are not the result of violence but of falls and sports-related incidents. Additionally, students in school today are less likely to be victimized than in previous years. The overall crime rate at school for students ages 12 to 18 has declined from about 155 crimes for every 1,000 students in 1993 to about 102 crimes in 1997. This number has also declined for students outside of school.

While positive statistics are very encouraging, terrorism in America and abroad brings attention to violence. Undoubtedly, disturbing events do happen on school grounds, such as:

- A reported 135,000 students carry guns to school each day (Brock, Nelson, Grady, & Losh, 1998).
- One in four students nationally will be threatened with violence in school (1998).
- Approximately three million crimes occur on or near school property each year (1998).
- There were two events in the 1992-93 school year of multiple victim homicides, and there has been at least one multiple victim homicide event every year (except for 1993-94), leading to five events in 1997-98 (DOE and DOJ, 1999).
- Suspensions in the state of Maryland for false alarms and bomb threats increased by 44% from the 1997-98 school year to the 1998-99 year (McQueen, April 12, 2000).
- From 1989 to 1995, the percentage of students who reported that they feared being harmed at school increased by 3 percent, the percentage of students who reported being fearful of being attacked while traveling to and from school rose 3 percent, and the percentage of students who reported that they avoided certain

areas in the school, such as stairwells, from fear rose 4 percent (DOE and DOJ, 1998).

- Terrorist attacks on America present an adult, albeit disgusting model of behavior as an attempt toward problem solving. The glorification of martyrdom feeds well into a perverted sense of adventure.

Considering these statistics and the horrors of Butte, Montana; Jonesboro, Arkansas; Paducah, Kentucky; Springfield, Oregon; Columbine, Colorado; and the shooting and subsequent death of 6-year old Kayla Rolland, security in America's schools must continue to be a major concern for all who are associated with education. In fact, Ordovensky (1993) posits that school principals are suspected of actually underreporting violence on their campuses, fearing that they would be perceived as poor administrators. Clearly, teachers cannot teach effectively in an atmosphere of violence, and students cannot learn when the school climate is one of fear for personal safety.

Media, video games, and music all tell kids that the way to solve interpersonal problems is through violence. In the '70s, kids used to fight with their fists; now, when kids have arguments, one of them goes home and gets his Uzi

-Kevin Dwyer-
President of the National Association
for School Psychologists
(Violence and Safety, 2000, p. 1).

Factors that Contribute to Juvenile Crime

While it is generally believed that school violence is a result of emotional and physical abuse, there are many factors that contribute to juveniles committing crimes. Racism, drug abuse, access to weapons, child abuse and neglect, inadequate parenting, poverty, unemployment, and exposure to violence in the media have an effect on children that contributes to violence. In addition, biological factors, cognitive development, developmental traits beginning in early childhood, and cultural and psychological factors all play a significant role that leads to violence (National Association for the Education of Young Children, 1993; *Violence & Youth*, 1993). We live in a culture of violence that surrounds our children with violent scenes from the media, whether they are watching the evening news or watching other media events on television for recreation. A Northwestern University study reported that three-fifths of Chicago local news was devoted to coverage of violence, and a study by Sen. Byron Dorgan (D-N.D.) recorded 1,000 violent acts on television weekly (Sautter, 1995).

In July 1994, the U.S. Department of Justice reported that the number of violent crimes *against* juveniles aged 12 to 17 had risen nearly 24 percent between 1988 and 1992. While these juveniles only account for one-tenth of the population over 12 years old, almost one in four crimes of violence involved a juvenile victim. Almost one in 13 young people becomes a victim of violence, compared to a ratio of one in 35 for adults over the age of 35 (Sautter, 1995). At the same time, statistics indicate that, by the early 1990s, violence *caused* by young people reached unparalleled levels in American society (American Psychological Association [APA], 2000).

Even prior to birth, violence can effect a young person's life. A study by Prothrow-Stith and Quaday (1995) indicates that pregnant women who experience physical abuse often deliver low-birth-weight babies who are at risk for developmental problems. Shaking an infant can result in irreversible physical and neural injuries such as blindness, seizures, or even death (Poussaint & Linn, 1997; Shore, 1997). Too often, children who come from homes where parents model violent behavior display an array of behavioral disturbances, including poor self-esteem and aggression against others (Peled, Jaffe, & Edleson, 1995). According to the American Psychological Association (APA), the strongest predictor that a child will become violent is being a victim of abuse. Nearly 70 percent of men who become part of the criminal justice system have been abused as children (*Violence & Youth*, 1993). Children's odds of committing murder are nearly doubled when they come from violent families, have a history of abuse, belong to gangs, and are involved in substance abuse. The chance that children will kill are tripled when, along with these factors, they have access to weapons, or have prior arrests or neurological disorders, or *"when they skip school and have other school-related problems"* (Williams, 1998).

According to the APA, there is no doubt that the breakdown of the family contributes to young people developing the antisocial behaviors that often result in violence. Lack of parental supervision is another strong predictor of the development of conduct problems leading to delinquency (*Violence & Youth*, 1993; Sampson & Laub, 1993). The lack of bonding with adults has far-reaching implications for children emotionally and cognitively, including an inability to cope effectively with stress (Lerner, 1992). Researchers have found that the involvement *of "just one caring adult can make all the difference in the life of an 'at-risk' youth"* (Sautter, 1995, p. K8).

When violence is part of a child's life, it negatively affects a child's learning ability (Prothrow-Stith & Quaday, 1995; Shore, 1997; Massey, 2000) While the APA does not blame schools, it does indicate that there are several components of a school organization that create a climate that leads to aggression. Schools that are over crowded, impose overly restrictive behavioral routines, or even have poor building designs may all create a climate conducive to violence. Other problems are brought to school by the students, such as gang activity, the belief that one is entitled to be violent, and emotional problems (Sautter, 1995; Dill, 1998). However, after 50 years of studying juvenile aggression, the APA feels strongly that much of the violence within our society today is learned behavior and therefore can be unlearned. Thus, it is imperative that addressing school violence become a collaborative effort within the entire community. This involves the juvenile system; federal, state, and local agencies; businesses; parents; and the schools themselves (Sautter, 1995).

Descriptors of a Safe School

Research has demonstrated consistently that school communities can do much to prevent violence by providing a safe and responsive climate. Therefore, in an effort to provide a guide for educators while president, President Bill Clinton requested that the U.S. Departments of Education and Justice collaborate with many agencies of law enforcement juvenile justice, mental health, and education associations to compile a guide to help educators stop school violence. Included in this guide, *Early Warning, Timely Response: A Guide to Safe Schools* (Dwyer, Osher, & Warger, 1998), is a list of characteristics of safe schools. Safe schools support learning and socially appropriate behaviors. These schools focus strongly on creating a support base for academics, high standards, positive relationships between students and staff, and meaningful involvement within the community. Safe schools understand that safety and order are necessary for children to develop appropriate social, emotional, and academic skills. This guide identifies a set of descriptors for school communities where safe schools are being responsive to the needs of children. These descriptors include:

- Focusing on academic achievement for all students, while allowing for individual differences.
- Involving families in meaningful ways. This makes parents feel welcome and works to keep families positively engaged in their children's education.
- Developing links to the community to enhance the use of all resources.
- Helping children develop positive relationships with faculty and with one another.
- Discussing safety issues by teaching about the dangers of firearms, and teaching strategies for dealing with anger and conflicts.
- Treating students with equal respect. Safe schools establish understandings that all children are valued and respected, and that caring attitudes for all must be displayed.
- Creating ways for students to safely report their concerns about potentially dangerous situations.
- Having a system for referring children who are suspected victims of neglect or abuse.
- Offering programs for children before and after school.
- Promoting good citizenship and character.
- Identifying potential safety problems and evaluating progress toward solutions.
- Helping students make the transition to adulthood and the workplace responsibly.

Verdugo and Schneider (1999) studied the characteristics of quality schools and the characteristics of safe schools. Research suggests that quality schools hold five very broad traits in common: 1) a shared commitment to high student achievement; 2) open communication and collaboration; 3) continuous assessment for learning and teaching; 4) personal and professional learning; and 5) availability of resources to support teaching and learning. They found important relationships between school quality, safe school components, and the seriousness of school violence. Quality schools are less likely to be characterized by serious crime or violence and are more likely to have safe school components in place.

How to Identify Early Warning Signs of Violence

Predicting behavior that will lead to violence is not always possible. However, training educators, parents, and students to be alert to situations where violence is highly probable, or recognizing students whose behavior is at risk of leading to violence, is important. Staff members who are aware of warning signs that lead to violence and then take conscious, visible steps to eliminate or control these factors ensure a safe environment for children at all grade levels and in all areas of the school environment (Dill, 1998).

Gangs

According to the U.S. Department of Justice, students were almost twice as likely to report the presence of gangs at their school in 1995 as they were in 1989, and this increase occurred in all schools, regardless of income level, place of residence, or race (Glazer, 1992; Stephens, 1994). Miami, Florida, reported a 1,000 percent increase in gang membership and activity during a 5-year period (Today's gangs cross cultural and geographic boundaries, 1992). Chapter 4 in the book you are reading offers advice on gang problems in schools and communities. Dill (1998) indicates that the signs of possible presence of gangs in a school include:

- Gang presence in the community.
- Groups of students congregating by race and calling their group a name that solidifies their identity, such as, "The Red Rozes" or "The Perfect Perils" (p. 22).
- An increasing number of racially based violent incidents.
- An absenteeism rate that is increasing and community crimes committed by truants.
- The visibility of graffiti on or near the school.
- Students wearing colors symbolic of a group; students using hand signals.
- Students wearing unique symbols on T-shirts or jewelry
- Students carrying beepers, cell telephones, or pagers.

Bullying Behaviors

When aggressive behaviors such as taunting, stealing, constant hitting, or intimidating other children are left unattended, they can escalate into much more serious behaviors. Additionally, the emotional abuse these acts inflict on others can lead to a circle of violence. According to a conference sponsored by the FBI in 1999, one theory of school "shooters" is that the shooters themselves are victims who have been repeatedly bullied. The rage at injustice then erupts in a major act of violence. Although it is the bully who commits an initial act of aggression, in many cases it is the victim who carries out the final deadly act. "Once the roles of bully and victim become 'fixed' and the victim cannot move from that role, the stage is set for violence carried out by the victim," (Underwood, Lewis, Pickett, & Worona, 2000, p. 2). To combat bullying, a change in school culture is necessary. An environment must be created where the relationship between students and adults is one of mutual respect, and students must feel comfortable telling authority figures when they feel their safety is in jeopardy (USDOE & USDOJ, 1998).

Other Warning Signs

None of the signs identified by *Early Warning—Timely Response: A Guide to Safe Schools* (Dwyer, Osher, & Warger, 1998) is sufficient alone to predict violence, but these are indications to aid in the identification of children who may need help:

- Appearing socially withdrawn and exhibiting excessive feelings of isolation.
- Exhibiting excessive feelings of rejection.
- Being a victim of violence in the community, at school, or at home.
- Feeling picked on and persecuted.
- Losing interest in school and not achieving academically.
- Expressing violence in writings and drawings.
- Expressing uncontrollable anger.
- Having a history of chronic discipline problems at home and in school.
- Having a history of violent and aggressive behavior,.
- Being intolerant of differences and exhibiting prejudicial attitudes toward others based on racial, ethnic, religious, language, gender, sexual orientation, ability, and physical appearance.
- Having inappropriate access to firearms.
- Making serious threats of violence.

Research suggests that age of onset of these behaviors may be a critical factor in interpreting these warning signs. For example, children who are aggressive and already involved in drug abuse before age 12 are more likely to become violent than are children who do not exhibit such behavior until they are older (Dwyer, Osher, & Warger, 1998). It is important, when considering all of these warning signs, to review a child's history with counselors and other behavioral experts, and to communicate with parents to seek additional insights.

The Role of Administrators and Teachers in Creating Safe Schools

Administrators and teachers must be responsive and current on educational research in order to lead curricular change for a safe school. In-school factors that place studer• at risk for engaging in violent behavior must be addressed by the administration and faculty. Two of these risk factors are academic failure and alienation from other schoolmates. One approach for schools to promote higher achievement and increased competency in higher-level reasoning by students is to emphasize cooperative learning more than competitive learning. Helping students to analyze situations and think through decisions encourages them to accept responsibility for their own actions and engage in creative problem solving. In creating an environment that provides personal and academic support, schools must encourage long-term caring and committed relationships. One way to do this is to form cooperative groups that last for a number of years, with teachers following cohorts of students through several grades (Johnson & Johnson, 1995).

Schools can create conditions that contribute to violent behavior when educators' actions, school policies, and the general school climate are filled with tension, rather than a climate of respect for all. A certain amount of rebellion and self-doubt is normal in adolescent development; however, among children of poverty, those not achieving academically, and children who are fragile emotionally, these feelings can escalate to forms of violence. Therefore, it is vital that administrators and teachers understand the nature of problems contributing to violent behavior that may be caused by school climate or even by individual faculty. Possible problems include: failure to respond to circumstances of violence; lack of a vision for school safety or policies involving tracking students; high rates of failure; the use of too many suspensions and expulsions to control behavior; mandated transfers of difficult students; the use of humiliating forms of discipline and corporal punishment; crowded conditions in classrooms and in the school; and authoritarian rules that are quick to punish (Dill, 1998).

Administrators must have a vision that leads to a well-developed plan for preventing violence. Too often in the past, teachers have been left to deal with potentially violent situations in whatever way they chose. Boards of education, reacting impulsively and without careful thought, can impose plans that are simplistic and heavily authoritarian. This has been observed in some zero-tolerance policies that have mandated predetermined consequences for specific offenses, regardless of the circumstances or disciplinary history of the student involved. Occasionally, this blanket enforcement of discipline policies has backfired. For example, a 6-year old with a plastic knife placed in his lunch box by his grandmother was disciplined. A middle school girl who shared her asthma inhaler on the school bus with a friend having a wheezing attack was suspended for drug trafficking (Tebo, 2000).

While zero tolerance policies have been effective in some areas of the country, these policies must be implemented with discernment (Underwood, Lewis, Pickett, & Worona, 2000). A well-thought-out plan, collaboratively developed with input from teachers as well as students and parents, can help prevent violence. Texas has devised an innovative approach to zero tolerance that sets out three levels of violations. At the most serious level are offenses such as bringing a gun or long-bladed knife to school, that merit expulsion and the requirement to attend a county alternative school. The next level includes misdemeanor drug possession and simple assault, which temporarily removes students from school and places them in an alternative education setting within their own school district. The lowest level of offense includes inappropriate actions, such as acting out within the classroom, where school officials have discretion to determine the consequences (Tebo, 2000).

School faculty, led by the principal, must be committed to maintaining high academic standards for all children. Principals and teachers must support and be responsive to curriculum reform where conflict resolution skills are taught and lived on the school campus. Conflict tends to be resolved most constructively in a cooperative context rather than in a competitive environment. Other schools are implementing violence prevention programs into the curriculum, such as The Second Step, which has measurably reduced aggressive behavior among second and third graders who have gone through the program ("This is the hand . . ., 1999). Urban (1999) maintains that students benefit more from caring, compassionate faculty who respect them as individuals. *"Most of the students we work with daily . . . are anonymous nobodies. It is through the way that they are treated, challenged and coached that they become somebodies"* (Wesley, 1999, p.43).

Administrators and teachers must model ways for children to control anger in order to change the destructive path of violence. Curwin (1995) suggests several steps in this process to reduce violence:

- Teach students alternatives to violence.
- Teach students how to make more effective choices.
- Model alternative expressions of anger, frustration, and impatience.
- Reduce cynicism.
- Welcome all students.
- Replace discipline based on rewards and punishments with values.
- Ask students to contribute (pp. 73-75).

Systemic Changes to the School Environment

Many issues that are inherent in the nature of the school system itself are being explored as signals that schools are beginning to reject the depersonalization of schooling in a variety of ways (Lewis, 1999). These issues are generally addressed by looking at the structure, size, and climate of the school.

Structure of the School Organization

How schools are structured appears to affect student achievement and attendance. This structure appears to have a greater impact on disadvantaged young people than on those who are not (Bryk & Thum, 1989; Lee, Smith, & Croninger, 1995). Charter schools, career academies, and "schools-within-schools" are efforts to develop a sense of community among students (Lewis, 1999; Verdugo & Schneider, 1999). A study by Drug Strategies, Inc. (1998), identified organizational aspects such as physical and administrative changes to promote a positive school climate, adopt culturally sensitive material, and provide teacher training.

Frequently, the structure of a school is built around tracking, where students are grouped homogeneously by academic performance. Often, this tracking divides the school into classes of poor performers and college-bound students. Typically, students in the lower-level tracks do not experience high expectations from teachers, have limited curriculum opportunities, have a diminished opportunity to work with students from diverse backgrounds, are not assigned the best teachers, and are restricted in later career opportunities (Marsh & Raywid, 1994). On the other hand, heterogeneous, mixed-ability classes tend to encourage young people to build relationships with individuals who are quite different in interests and abilities. This opportunity to learn together, cooperate, and complete tasks builds skills that are necessary in our society. It also encourages positive values and attitudes toward learning for all students (Chase & Doan, 1994).

School Size

Incidents of violence on school campuses have brought the issue of school size to the attention of educators and others. The U.S. Secretary of Education and several state governors have spoken in favor of small schools and praised the resistance to consolidating schools in rural communities (Bickel & Howley, 2000). There is a preponderance of evidence in the research on school size that suggests that smaller school size improves education, especially in lower socioeconomic communities. Raywid (1998) reports findings that reveal a consistency of academic success factors in student achievement when school size is considered. National studies confirm that young people learn more in math, reading, history, and science in small schools than in large ones, especially if they are disadvantaged students. Other studies document that small schools are far more apt to be free of violence than large ones. Small schools appear to encourage greater connectedness to others, thus enabling school faculty to affect children's positive personal decisions.

Recent evidence suggests that the influence of school district size on aggregate performance is related to socioeconomic status. This effect has implicated small size as better for the performance of districts that serve more impoverished communities. The equity effects of district size appear to be more consistent and more impressive even than achievement effects (Bickel & Howley, 2000). Thus, increasingly, research is suggesting the need to create smaller districts as well as smaller schools in order to achieve both excellence and equity of school outcomes.

Climate

Leaders for nonviolent schools must model a culture that resonates with communication and relationship development. Studies report that successful principals in schools where students are poor, at-risk, and exposed to violence outside the school have core beliefs that are communicated to students, teachers, parents, and the community. These beliefs, when translated into action, demonstrate leadership, create a visible commitment to learning, turn theory into practice, help faculty understand the role of the school for at-risk students, lead change, evaluate school and personal success, make clear decisions, build a positive school climate, admit when they are wrong, build strong relationships with parents and the community, and take responsibility for student safety (Haberman, 1996). According to Dill (1998), to build a culture of nonviolence in schools today, educators must model "a different way of thinking and believing that builds respect and caring among those for whom respect is a rare commodity. . . . [The behavior of violent children] covers fragile egos in a frightening world" (p. 93).

In studying the lives of shooters in school violence tragedies, a common thread is that they felt rejected and disconnected from their peers (Friedland, 1999). Therefore, it is important to look closely at a school's "places, policies, people, programs and processes" in order to create an "invitational education" (p. 15). Berreth and Berman (1997) list principles for a moral school as including collaboration, adult role models with positive values, involvement of students in decision making, and the use of problem-solving approaches to discipline. They recommend that, to experience being part of the solution, students be involved in discussing topics such as school violence..

Fostering a safe learning environment requires that the school climate be one of tolerance for student diversity. Too often, conflict occurs in many schools just because of bias toward children who are different. These incidents are termed "hate crimes" and are defined as those ". . .crimes against individuals where the victim was selected because of the race, skin color, ethnicity/national origin, sexual orientation, gender, religion or disability of any person" (USDOE & USDOJ, 1999, p. 8). The Health Behavior of School Children Survey indicates that approximately 15% of youths who had been bullied or harassed had been treated in this manner because of their religion or race. Another 30% had been bullied by sexual jokes, comments, or inappropriate gestures. Therefore, a number of schools are creating anti-hate policies and programs to foster an equitable, supportive, safe environment for all (1999).

Dealing with Crisis Situations

> *The best defense against random violence is a comprehensive school security plan that is as concerned with routine fist fights among students as it is with the attack by an armed intruder. . .*
>
> (Baldwin, 1999, p. 11).

Preparation of school personnel to deal with a crisis can build confidence and cohesiveness between the school and community. All schools should have a crisis plan that establishes clear district policy in at least eight areas:

- Major school bus accident
- Fire or explosion at school
- Event requiring immediate evacuation
- Weather disaster
- Bomb threat to the school
- Kidnapping or terrorist situation
- Personal crisis situations
- Weapons and other police emergencies

The following steps should be used in creating a crisis management plan:

1) Establish a district policy and a safety and crisis management mission statement
2) Appoint a district-wide task force.
3) Survey surrounding school districts and your own to evaluate how vulnerable the campuses are.
4) Assess the physical security of the building and grounds for crime prevention.
5) Identify current and proposed safety features to evaluate what is reasonable to prevent criminal or dangerous situations.
6) Identify, designate, and document who is a part of the team.
7) Set goals and guidelines for developing building-level plans.
8) Develop a table of contents for the plan to prevent omission of any major part.
9) Develop the plan.
10) Distribute the plan to all stakeholders (Decker, 1997). Of course, this program should be part of a larger, districtwide emergency crisis plan.

When a crisis occurs, generally the building administrator is responsible for informing the faculty and student body. It is important to consider the age of the students and their involvement with the individual or situation. Emotional reactions should be anticipated and appropriate responses planned. Decker (1997) recommends that the curriculum be altered to include conflict resolution training to avoid exacerbating difficult situations. Occasionally, faculty themselves find it difficult to control their own emotions during crisis times, but faculty need to keep in mind that true emotion may be the catalyst for students to release built-up emotion. Crises are human situations, not times to fear the demonstration of emotion.

Informing the Media

In the last few years, nearly every school district in the U.S. has developed a specific plan for dealing with the media. Along with adoption of this plan, staff development should be provided so that appropriate implementation can be assured should a crisis occur. When informing the media, school personnel must remember that it is imperative to keep a positive attitude; no matter what the crisis, every attempt must be made for calmness to prevail. The following are some suggested guidelines for handling the media:

- Do not panic.
- Appoint a spokesperson.
- Develop a written statement concerning the crisis (when possible).
- Contact the press before they contact you.
- Develop media-on-campus guidelines and restrictions.
- Never refuse to speak to the media.
- Do not overreact or exaggerate any situation.
- Give only factual and verified informational statements
- Do not lie.
- Do not try to avoid blame by using a scapegoat.
- Stress positive action taken by the school district.
- Do not talk off the record.
- Do not argue with media personnel (Decker, 1997, p. 56).

Sample Plan to Follow

A sample plan to follow when a bomb threat has been made over the telephone would be as follows. The plan should be disseminated to all faculty, administrators, and staff.

- Never hang up on telephone threats; try to keep the caller talking.
- Notify the principal immediately.
- Attempt a trace through the police or the telephone company.
- Document the telephone threat immediately.
- Document in writing, as soon as possible, a bomb threat, or any other type of threat. Include the specific time the message was received, the date and day of week, and the exact wording of the message. Attempt to discern the sex, race, age, or any other information about the person making the threat. Also include any unusual circumstances, such as background noises, etc.
- Follow the district crisis management plan to determine which authorities should be notified, such as the police department, superintendent, or others.

- Have the principal evaluate the seriousness of the bomb threat using input from as many sources as are available. Then she should act quickly in a manner that reflects the greatest safety for all of those in her charge.
- If the decision is to evacuate the building, use the public address system to inform teachers and students to use standard fire drill procedure.
- Notify the predetermined individuals who will search the building.
- Have students remain with their teachers and off-duty teachers should help as needed.
- If an explosion should occur, move students to designated areas. (Decker, 1997; Baldwin, 1999).

Collaborative Support Efforts

The APA recommends that schools proceed with caution in adopting new programs and develop programs that share two basic characteristics: 1) an understanding of developmental and sociocultural factors of risk that contribute to antisocial behavior and 2) intervention strategies that have been researched and demonstrate effectiveness in changing behavior. Programs should begin early, and their components should reinforce the child's daily social contexts: family, school, peer groups, and the community (Sautter, 1995). According to Dill (1998), support services should be of two primary types: those that are preventive and those that intervene after an incident. Preventive programs create after-school activities, offer training in peer mediation and/or conflict resolution, and offer young people help in resisting gangs and drugs. Intervention programs that have the most positive, long-term effect require restitution from the offender and compensation of victims. These programs distinguish between punishment and restitution. For example, the consequence or punishment of misbehaving in class might be to pick up trash in the lunchroom, but restitution requires that the offender accept responsibility for the act, in some way, such as by apologizing (Dill, 1998).

How the juvenile justice system can collaborate with schools

The first juvenile court, separate from the adult system, was created in Cook County, Illinois, in 1899, with the stated purpose to act as a parent for children whose parents had failed to supervise and train their children properly (*In Re Gault*, 387, U.S. 1, 14, 1967). This rehabilitation system was based on two premises: that good parenting molds a child's behavior, which will either increase or decrease the tendency toward criminal behavior; and that the developmental differences between children and adults make young people more amenable to rehabilitation. By the early 1960s, all states in the U.S. had adopted a juvenile system following the Illinois model (Harris & Harris, 2001).

In July and early September 1999, the Federal Bureau of Investigation (FBI) met with over 100 educators, law enforcement officials, victim assistance advocates, and mental health professionals for a discussion of school violence that would help everyone learn from the school-related tragedies that have occurred since 1993. They were disappointed at the lack of communication between many schools and local law enforcement agencies. Their goal was to encourage better information sharing so that the school and the community could see problems and patterns that were emerging and thus prevent future violence (Underwood, Lewis, Pickett & Worona, 2000).

Courts and legislatures have begun to focus on ways to positively affect choices of juveniles. For example, Texas, in 1995, required the public schools and the juvenile justice system to develop a code of conduct jointly within each school district. Additionally, Senate Bill I mandated the creation of Juvenile Justice Alternative Educational Programs (JJAEP) in counties with a population over 125,000. These charter schools were developed to serve students between the ages of 10 and 17 who had been expelled and who had engaged in delinquent behavior. This educational program operates 7 hours per day, 180 days per year, and focuses on the core curriculum and self-discipline (Kemerer & Walsh, 1996).

Other communities have adopted the balanced and restorative justice concept, which has three goals: protect the community, insist that criminals be accountable to victims for restitution, and help offenders develop competencies to prevent a return to crime. These justice programs usually require mediation sessions between the victims and offenders to help offenders understand the implications of their behavior (Coordinating Council on Juvenile Justice and Delinquency Prevention [CCJJDP], 1996).

Other suggestions for the juvenile justice system to collaborate with the schools include establishing a positive working relationship with the schools, patrolling the school grounds, responding quickly to reports of criminal activities in the school, consulting with school authorities and parents regarding school security, and working directly with youth to maintain a constructive relationship (USDOE & USDOJ, 1998).

How Parents Can Collaborate with Schools

Researchers, theorists, and legislators are questioning whether or not the parents of juvenile delinquents should shoulder some of the blame for their actions. In President Bill Clinton's State of the Union Address in 1994, he said, "As you demand tougher penalties for those who choose violence, let us also remember how we came to this sad point. . . . We have seen a stunning and simultaneous breakdown of community, family and work. This has created a vast vacuum which has been filled by violence. . . ." (Harris & Harris, 2001, p.22). Parents are now working more than in previous years; in fact, statistics indicate that children spend 11 fewer hours with parents each week compared with children in the 1960s (Cloud, 1999). Today's parents spend an average of 2 minutes a day communicating with their child, yet children watch an average of 3 1/2 hours a day of television. Reports of child abuse have increased dramatically within the past 30 years. According to the U.S. Department of Health and Human Services, in 1997, 42 out of every 1,000 children in the U.S. were reported as victims of child abuse, a 320% leap from 10 per 1,000 in 1976 (Portner, 2000). To change this trend, schools are developing parent support teams (which allow parents to help each other), while encouraging parents to become involved making decisions in their children's educational progress to improve student success (Friedland, 1999).

Studies have consistently reported a reduction in the involvement between schools and low-income and minority parents. School districts have begun to address this by creating parenting programs that address good parenting methods and child development, encouraging parents to be come involved with their child's education in ways other than just attending an occasional PTA meeting or helping with fundraisers. Training sessions for parents should include specific violence prevention skills, such as anger management, impulse control, stress management, and positive communication methods (Dwyer, Osher, & Warger, 1998). Lists of parenting resources and hotline numbers should be made available to parents (Massey, 2000). Many schools are conducting home visits to improve relationships between parents and the schools. The *Annual Report on School Safety* (USDOE & USDOJ, 1998) recommends that parents should collaborate with their schools in the following ways:

- Make sure children attend class daily and complete homework.
- Get to know teachers and administrators.
- Encourage children to participate in extracurricular activities.
- Read to children and listen and offer help when they are practicing reading.
- Inform the school if their child expresses a concern or problem about school
- Attend school conferences and school board meetings, and volunteer when possible.
- Know the school's discipline policy and discuss it with the child.
- Cooperate with the school when a child has been victimized at school.
- Work with other parents to ensure that children are safe going to and from school

How Federal, State, and Local Agencies can Collaborate with Schools

The federal government has sponsored many local and state safety initiatives:

- The 1993 Safe Schools Act offers grants, research, and technical assistance that undergirds state and local programs (Dill, 1998).
- In 1994, Congress enacted the Gun-Free Schools Act, 20 USC. § 8921, which requires that schools, in order to receive Elementary and Secondary Education Act (ESEA) funds, must have a policy mandating a one-year expulsion for students who bring a firearm to school (Dill, 1998)
- In spring 1999, then-President Clinton announced the Safe Schools/Healthy Students Initiative, a grant program jointly administered by the U.S. Departments of Education, Health and Human Services, and Justice. This Initiative promotes comprehensive, integrated communitywide strategies to promote school safety and healthy child development across the country (USDOE & USDOJ, 1997).

In fall 1998, President Clinton convened the first-ever White House Conference on School Safety, declaring the importance of investing in prevention. The federal government was challenged to play a greater role in making schools safer. From this dialogue came many of the strategies of the Safe Schools/Healthy Students Initiative, which uniquely provides students, schools, and communities enhanced educational, mental health, social service, law enforcement, and, when needed, juvenile justice system services that strengthen healthy childhood development and prevent violence and alcohol and drug abuse. In 1999, the agencies awarded 54 initiative grants to local educational agencies in partnership with local law enforcement and public mental health authorities (USDOE & USDOJ, 1999).

The U.S. Department of Justice Office of Juvenile Justice and Delinquency Prevention works closely with the U.S. Department of Education in the Safe and Drug-Free Schools Program to find ways to improve communication between juvenile justice and public school initiatives. These groups produce materials on school safety, violence prevention efforts, and intervention programs, and they disseminate successful programs nationwide through books and pamphlets, and electronically. State departments of education and state departments of health work closely to publish curricula to prevent school violence, develop pilot programs, and collect research on effective programs. Project Head Start is an example of a successful violence prevention program that targets the very young, low-income children and their parents. Research reports that this program has been one of the most effective inner-city crime and drug prevention strategies yet developed (Dill, 1998).

Additionally, the *Annual Report of School Safety* (USDOE & USDOJ, 1998) recommends that these agencies continue to:

- Provide leadership for school crime prevention by introducing and supporting legislation that promotes school safety, holding conferences to raise awareness, attending school events for violence prevention, educating the public through speeches about crime prevention, and endorsing official initiatives on school crime.
- Support school crime prevention research; quality evaluations need to be financed through funding for research projects.
- Encourage all schools to monitor and report crime. These efforts require their advocacy for funding.
- Begin a discussion of key legislative issues in school violence prevention. Some of the questions to be answered include what type of data should be needed, what types of information should be shared between government agencies and schools, and who should receive comprehensive risk screening.
- Build collaborations between and among local, state, and federal agencies to share resources and maximize effective approaches to school safety.

How Business and Community-based Organizations Can Collaborate with Schools

Businesses support nonviolent cultures by providing activities during after school hours because this time period, according to the CCJJDP (1996), has the greatest incidence of juvenile crimes, which peak at 3:00 p.m. during the week. Community programs and nonprofit organizations provide counseling, recreational opportunities, library facilities, and Internet access to both parents and students after hours in the schools. Funding for these programs is critical, and even with business support, many of these programs rely on volunteers. Local places of worship are also an important support component to the schools. Regardless of the faith, these organizations provide moral growth for young people. Many of them provide their facilities after school that encourage young people to fill their time with positive activities (Dill, 1998). An example of an educational program in San Antonio, Texas, a free program called Great Start, is a collaborative effort among four nonprofit groups (Baptist Children's Home Ministries, Avance, the Family Service Association, and Healthy Families) to provide parental education to at-risk families where abuse or neglect has been present (Hoholik, 1999)..

Other suggestions for businesses and communities to collaborate with schools to reduce violence include:

- Adopt a local school.
- Provide training in basic job skills.
- Provide internships and employment opportunities through after-school jobs and summer employment.
- Provide scholarships to deserving students distributed on the basis of need and performance.
- Offer resources to local schools.
- Provide release time to parents and volunteers to attend children's school activities and serve as mentors, coaches, and tutors.
- Establish school-community partnerships.
- Identify and measure the problem within the community.
- Set measurable goals and objectives for the community (USDOE & USDOJ, 1998).

Conclusion

Schools and communities must continue to work on preventing school violence and creating safer schools. However, because violence permeates all levels of society in America, it cannot be addressed in isolation. It is imperative that all must work together as a community to keep children safe in local schools. While prevention strategies are necessary, intervention strategies will provide the greatest security for the future. Marian Wright Edelman, president of the Children's Defense Fund, challenges school leaders to "never give in to the urge to give up, no matter how hard it gets. . . . Every youngster is entitled to an equal share of the American Dream. . . . We need every one of them to be productive and educated and healthy" (1993, p. 26). Every child in America needs to be safe from violence in school.

See this chapter's appendix for resources and Internet Web sites on school safety.

Case Problem: Tranquility High School

Tranquility high school has been a relatively safe school. However, a few years ago, things began to change. The number of student fights increased, there have been three separate assaults on teachers, there have been numerous bomb threats, and 9 students have been expelled for bringing weapons into school. The administrative team recognizes that there are many factors involved in the escalating level of violence at Tranquility, but they have only been partially successful at curbing it. They recognize a need to do more. How would you advise them regarding 1) systemic changes to the school environment, 2) collaboration with the community, 3) federal, state, and local help available, and 4) specific crisis management procedures?

References

American Psychological Association (2000). *Warning signs*. [Brochure]. Washington, D.C.: Author.

Baldwin, H. (1999). *Planning for disaster: A guide for school administrators*. Bloomington, IN: Phi Delta Kappa Educational Foundation.

Berreth, D. & Berman, S. (1997). The moral dimension of schools. *Educational Leadership*, *54* (8), 24-27.

Bickel, R. & Howley, C. (2000). The influence of scale on school performance: A multi-level extension of the Matthew Principle. *Education Policy Analysis Archives, 8* (22). [On-line]. Retrieved September 10, 2002 from http://epaa.asu.edu/epaa/v8n22/.

Brock, B., Nelson, L., Grady, M., & Losh, M. (1998). Public schools and law enforcement agencies joining forces for school safety. *Connections*, 1 (1), 21-27.

Bryk, A. & Thum, Y. (1989). The effects of high school organization on dropping out: An exploratory investigation. *American Educational Research Journal*, 26, 353-383.

Chase, P. & Doan, J. (1994). *Full Circle: A new look at Multiage Education.* Portsmouth, NH.: Heinemann, 1994.

Cloud, J. (1999, May 3). What can the schools do? *Time*, 153 (17), 38-40.

Coordinating Council on Juvenile Justice and Delinquency Prevention (CCJJDP). (1996). *Combating Violence and Delinquency: The National Juvenile Justice Action Plan.* Washington, D.C.

Curwin, R. (1995). A humane approach to reducing violence in schools. *Educational Leadership, 52* (5), 70-75.

Decker, R. (1997). *When a crisis hits will your school be ready?* Thousand Oaks, CA.: Corwin Press, Inc.

Dill, V. (1998). *A peaceable school.* Bloomington, IN.: Phi Delta Kappa .Educational Foundation.

Drug Strategies, Inc. (1998). Safe schools, safe students: A guide to violence prevention strategies. Washington, D.C.: Author.

Dwyer, K., Osher, D., & Warger, C. (1998*). Early warning, timely response: A guide to safe schools*. Washington, D.C.: U.S. Department of Education.

Edelman, M. (1993, March). Investing in our children: A struggle for America's conscience and future. *USA Today Magazine*.

Friedland, S. (1999). Violence reduction: Start with school culture. *The School Administrator, 56* (5), 14-16.

Glazer, S. (1992). Violence in schools. *CQ Researcher, 2*, 787-807.

Haberman, (1996). *The star administrator selection interview.* [Brochure]. Houston: Haberman Educational Foundation.

Harris, S. & Harris, J. (2001). Youth violence and suggestions for schools to reduce the violence. *The Journal of At Risk Issues, 7* (2), 21-28.

Hoholik, S. (1999, September 4). Programs provide parent coaching. *The San Antonio Express-News,* pp. B1, B4.

In Re Gault, 387, U.S. 1 (1967), 14.

Johnson, D. & Johnson, R. (1995*).* Why violence prevention programs don't work—and what does. *Educational Leadership 52*, (5), 63-67.

Kemerer, F. & Walsh, J. (1996).   The educator's guide to Texas school law, 4th Edition. Austin, TX.: University of Texas Press.

Lee, V., Smith, J., & Croninger, R. (1995). *Understanding high school restructuring effects on the equitable distribution of learning in mathematics and science.* Madison, WI.: National Center on the Organization and Restructuring of Schools.

Lerner, R. (1992). Bonding is the key. *Adolescent Counselor, 13,* 15.

Lewis, A. (1999). Listen to the children. *Phi Delta Kappan, 80* (10), 723-724.

Marsh, R. & Raywid, M. (1994). How to make detracking work. Phi Delta Kappan, *75* (4), 314-317.

Massey, M. (2000*).* The effects of violence on young children. *The ERIC Review: School Safety: A Collaborative Effort,* 7 (1). ED 424032 Retrieved June 2, 2002 from http://www.accesseric.org/resources/ericreview/vol7no1/effects.html.
McQueen, A. (2000, April 12). Despite decline in youth violence, schools establish a stricter tone. *San Antonio Express-News*, p. 11A.

National Association for the Education of Young Children. (1993). NAEYC position statement on violence in the lives of children. *Young Children, 48* (6), 80-84.

Ordovensky, P. (1993). Facing up to the violence. *The Executive Educator, 15* (1), 22-24.

Peled, E., Jaffe, P., & Edleson, J. (Eds.). (1995). *Ending the cycle of violence: Community responses to children of battered women.* Thousand Oaks, CA: Sage Publications.

Phi   Delta   Kappan/Gallup   Poll.   (1998).   Retrieved   April   11,   2002   from http://www.pdkintl.org/kappan/kp9809-3.htm.

Portner, J. (2000). Complex set of ills spurs rising teen suicide rate. *Education Week*. [On-line]. Available: http://www.edweek.org/ew/ewstory.cfm?slug=31problems.h19.

Poussaint, A. & Linn, S. (1997). Fragile: Handle with care. *Newsweek* 33 (Special Edition).

Prothrow-Stith, D. & Quaday, S. (1995, April 25th). *Hidden casualties: The relationship between violence and learning.* Washington, D.C.: National Health and Education Consortium and National Consortium for African-American Children. ERIC Document Reproduction Service No. ED 390 552.

Raywid, M. (1998). Small schools: A reform that works. *Educational Leadership*, *55* (4), 34-39.

Public agenda online. (2,000). Retrieved April 25, 2002 from http://www.publicagenda.org/issues/pcc_detail.cfm?issue_type=crime& list=7.

Sampson, R. & Laub, J. (1993). *Crime in the making: Pathways and turning points through life.* Cambridge, MA.: Harvard University Pres.

Sautter, R. (1995). Standing up to violence. *Phi Delta Kappan*, 76 (5), K1-K12.

Shore, R. (1997). *Rethinking the brain: New insights into early development: Executive summary.* New York: Families and Work Institute.

Stephens, R. (1994, January). *Gangs, guns, and school violence.* USA Today Magazine, 122, 29-33.

Tebo, M. (2000). Zero tolerance, zero sense. *ABA Journal*, *86*, 40-47.

This is the hand of a high school kid. These are the bullets taken out of his body. He was shot by another kid at school. Almost every day in America, one kid kills another. What can we do? (1999, June l). *Life*, *22* (7), 112 - 113.

Today's gangs cross cultural and geographic boundaries. (1992, May). *Educational Digest*, 57, 8-11.

Underwood, J., Lewis, J., Pickett, D., & Worona, J. (2000). *School safety: Working together to keep schools safe.* Retrieved April 11, 2000 http://www.keepschoolssafe.org/school.html

Urban, V. (1999). Eugene's story: A case for caring. *Educational Leadership*, *56* (6), 69-70.

U.S. Department of Education (DOE) and U.S Department of Justice (DOJ). 1998. *Annual Report on School Safety, 1998.* Washington, D.C.: Authors. Retrieved on April 11, 2000 from http://www.ed.gov/pubs/AnnSchoolRept98.

U.S Department of Education (DOE) and U.S Department of Justice (DOJ). (1999). 1999 *Annual report on school safety.* Washington, D.C.: Authors.

Verdugo, R. & Schneider, J. (1999). Quality schools, safe schools: A theoretical and empirical discussion. *Education & Urban Society*, *31* (3), 286 -308.

Violence and safety. (2000, April). *Education Week*. Retrieved April 11, 2000 from: http://www.edweek.org/context/topics/violence.htm.

Violence & youth: Psychology's response, Vol. 1. (1993). Washington, D.C.: American Psychological Association.

Wesley, D. (1999). Believing in our students. *Educational Leadership*, *56* (4), 42-44.

Williams, W. (1998). Preventing violence in school: What can principals do? *NASSP Bulletin*, *82* (603), 10-17.

Chapter Appendix: Resources and Web sites on School Safety

Annual Report on School Safety, 1998 http://www.ed.gov/pubs/AnnSchoolRept98

Blueprints for Violence Prevention http://www.Colorado.EDU/cspv/blueprints

Center for the Study and Prevention of Violence http://www.colorado.edu/cspv/

Combating Fear and Restoring Safety in School http://www.ncjrs.org/jjvict.htm

Hamilton Fish National Institute on School and Community Violence http://www.hamfish.org

Indicators of School Crime and Safety, 1999 http://www.nces.ed.gov

Institute on Violence and Destructive Behavior http://www.uoregon.edu/~ivdb/

Law-Related Education http://www.okbar.org/lre

Mentoring: A Proven Delinquency Prevention Study http://www.ncjrs.org/jjdp.htm.

National Association of Secondary School Principals http://www.nassp.org

National Center for Juvenile Justice http://www.ncjj.org

National Center for the Prevention of School Violence http://www.ncsu.edu/cpsv

National Council on Child Abuse and Family Violence http://nccafv.org/

National Institute of Justice http://www.ojp.usdoj.gov/nij

National Resource Center for Safe Schools http://www.safetyzone.org

National School Safety Center http://www.nsscl.org

National Youth Gang Center http://www.iir.com/nygc

Partnerships Against Violence Network http://www.pavnet.org

Preventing Crime: What Works, What Doesn't, What's Promising http://www.ncjrs.org

Safe and Smart: Making the After-School Hours Safe for Kids
http://www.ed.gov/pubs/safeandsmart

Safe Schools Now Network http://www.nea.org/issues/safescho/echostar/safeschools/index.html

School Violence Resource Center http://www.svrc.net/Coalitions.asp

The Office of Juvenile Justice and Delinquency Prevention http://www.ojjdp.ncjrs.org

U.S. Department of Justice http://www.usdoj.gov

Violence Prevention Coordinating Center
http://www.informdurham.com/informdurham/details.asp?RSN=2935

Chapter 13
Educational Choice
Bernard Brogan

In a 5-4 decision, the U.S. Supreme Court approved the use of vouchers for private and parochial schools (Zernike, 2002). This chapter provides a brief history of educational choice, including legal and philosophical arguments for and against it, and a description of *choice, charter, voucher, open enrollment,* and *magnet,* concepts.

Introduction

The debate over whether families should have a greater voice in where they send their children to school has persisted since the establishment of public education. In recent years, however, educational choice has emerged as a dominant theme in the school reform movement. Nearly every state has some form of tax-supported choice option, including a growing number of states that are considering private school voucher legislation (Bowman, 2000). It is estimated that 15 percent of public school students attend schools of choice (Hardy, 1999). The number of charter schools have grown from two in the 1992-93 school year to more than 1,250 now, serving over 350,000 students (Watkins, 1999).

The extent to which educational choice will enhance or hamper overall school renewal efforts depends in large measure on the type of educational choice plan and on the conditions that guide the implementation of that specific choice plan. As the choice movement expands, school administrators will be called upon to take an active role in representing the interests of their school communities. In some cases, this will mean developing policies that address how best to expand school choice options for families. In other cases, where school choice proposals are seen as harmful to the quality of schooling in their community, school administrators will need to effectively lobby against such plans.

This chapter provides educators with a framework from which to better understand the issues surrounding the choice movement. First, a brief history of educational choice is presented. This is followed by a careful look into the arguments fueling the choice debate. Next, the features, benefits, and potential consequences of specific school choice plans are defined. The chapter concludes with a discussion of the implications of school choice for local school communities and recommendations for how school administrators can best prepare themselves and their school communities for the promise and challenge that educational choice presents.

A Brief History of Educational Choice

The roots of educational choice go back to the beginning of the nation itself. In 1776, Scottish economist Adam Smith in *The Wealth of Nations* recommended that money be given by the government to parents for the purpose of buying educational services. Smith's argument was that giving parents the right to choose schools in an open market would make schools more competitive and responsive to the needs of students. This, in turn, would lead to better education. Thomas Paine introduced Smith's ideas to America in 1792. Paine elaborated on Smith's concept of schooling by suggesting that the lower-class families be given the opportunity for schooling through what might today be called a negative income tax, scaled progressively in favor of the poor and coupled with a parental duty to purchase adequate education (Coons & Sugarman, 1978). In his 1859 essay, "On Liberty", John Stuart Mill proposed that education was a right of all children, that parents should provide an adequate education in the school of their choice, and that the government should assist those who could not otherwise afford to do so.

Peterson (1988) argues that the recent interest in giving families more choice in education is only the latest in a continual challenge to break the monopoly of public schools: *"The quasi-monopoly in public education is today so pervasive a fact of American life that it is taken for granted. But a century ago the place of public schools in the American educational system was not something that could simply be assumed. Nearly one-third of all high school students were being privately educated as late as 1890. Religious groups were establishing their own schools and business groups were proposing the establishment of a vocational education system apart from the public school"* (p. 5).

Public school advocates were able to achieve the dominance of the common school over the private school in part because of the need to provide the great streams of immigrants flooding into the United States from all over the world a degree of conformity and the common values essential to a stable society (Friedman, 1962). The enthusiasm for this mission of public education was such that it required a Supreme Court decision to establish the right of families to choose other than public schools. In Pierce v. Society of Sisters (1925), the Court held that the *due process* clause of the Fourteenth Amendment protected private education and added that the family had a right to choose such education where it met reasonable state standards for quality.

In 1962, Milton Friedman gave renewal to the question of educational choice in his work, *Capitalism and Freedom*. Arguing that a stronger case could have been made at the turn of the century for an all-inclusive public school system, Friedman wrote, "Our problem today is not to enforce conformity; it is rather that we are threatened with an excess of conformity. Our problem is to foster diversity, and the alternative [a private school system] would do this far more effectively than a nationalized school system" (p. 97).

Friedman, a conservative economist, influenced the thinking of Christopher Jencks, a democratic socialist, who, in 1972, proposed vouchers as a means to equalize educational opportunity for all citizens. In the early 1970s, an Office of Economic Opportunity-sponsored experiment with educational vouchers was conducted in a suburb of San Jose, California, called Alum Rock. The educational demonstration project began in the Alum Rock Union Elementary School district during the 1972-73 school year. Under the voucher concept, parents freely selected a school for their children and received a credit or voucher equal to the cost of the child's education that was paid to the school upon enrollment. It was presumed that this form of school finance would foster competition among schools by making schools more responsive to students' needs. A number of school districts did not participate, and no private schools were involved. There were no rewards or sanctions for those schools that gained or lost students, and teachers had considerable job security. Because of these and other limitations, the Alum Rock experiment has historical significance but limited value in determining the effect of parental choice, and the data collected is of marginal use (Goldhaber, 1999; Wortman, 1978).

Beginning in the 1970s, educational choice surfaced most notably in the form of magnet schools, where specialty programs were created to achieve voluntary integration and interest-driven student performance. Magnet schools offered an alternative to mandatory assignment, and they provided incentives aimed at decreasing the number of white families leaving urban school districts (Blank & Archbald, 1992). By 1983, one-third of the largest urban school systems had magnet schools. Today, most urban school districts have at least one magnet school.

Political support for educational choice mounted during the Reagan administration. Support for educational choice was driven in part by the widespread disappointment in the progress of educational reform that was fueled by reports such as *A Nation at Risk* (1983). Near the end of his tenure in office, Reagan remarked that "Choice works, and it works with a vengeance. Choice is the most exciting thing that's going on in America today" (Paulu, 1989, p. 29).

The George Bush (Sr.) administration considered school choice a high priority and expanding parent's right to choose their schools a national imperative (Education Week, January 18, 1989). Increased parental choice was included as a component of the America 2000 initiative. Although clearly not in favor of spending public tax money on private vouchers, the Clinton administration enthusiastically supported public choice plans such as charter schools.

This brief history of educational choice was presented to establish the point that giving parents choice in school selection is not a new concept. As we embark on our journey into the 21st century, however, school administrators need to be aware of the profound impact that certain school choice plans may have on their school communities. This is especially so in light of the dramatic increase in charter schools (including on-line virtual charter schools) and the significant number of states that are proposing voucher legislation. The next section of this chapter presents the political, social, and economic arguments that frame the educational choice debate.

The Choice Debate

Choice in American education remains one of the more important and controversial issues facing the nation (Witte & Thorn, 1996). The subject of educational choice will likely continue to dominate the school reform conversation and remain a persistent topic at education meetings and on various special interest group agendas. In this section, some of the general arguments in favor of expanding educational choice are presented, followed by some of the general arguments against such expansion.

The Arguments in Support of Educational Choice

Levin (1989) identifies three major arguments supporting educational choice: (1) families should have the right to choose the type of education they want for their children, (2) even among schools of the same type, families should be able to choose the schools that best fits the specific education needs of their children, and (3) choice will lead to greater competition for students and improvements in student achievement.

A number of supporters of expanding educational choice believe that academic performance (or lack of academic performance) can be traced to the monopoly of public education systems (Spicer & Hill, 1990). Walberg (1996) asserted that, although education may be the largest American enterprise in terms of numbers of people involved, the value of human time required, and the capital invested, it is the institution with the least amount of accountability for results. Choice advocates believe that public schools would be more productive, more efficient, and more effective if they were not a monopoly. That is, requiring schools to compete for students encourages those providing substandard education to be more accountable for their educational programs. As better schools attract students from inferior schools, the inferior schools will be more easily identified and helped to improve. This, in turn, will force educators to either make the needed changes or risk closing their doors. These free market forces work because they are in harmony with fundamental economic laws that motivate human behavior (Borden & Rauchut, 1998; Doyle, 1988). When parents and students have a choice of which school they attend, accountability will follow (Brandl, 1988).

There is also the argument that lack of choice may harm disadvantaged families because (1) poorer families are less able to furnish home remedies for educational difficiencies, (2) poorer families have more difficulty escaping inferior schools by changing their residence, and (3) poorer families are less able to induce the public school system to provide the alternative classroom or program they prefer (Coons & Sugarman, 1978). Through educational choice, the less advantaged may gain the same access to quality education for their children that affluent parents achieve by living in expensive residential communities or by paying private school tuition (Nathan, 1996). Glenn (1989) maintains that educational choice can do much to promote equity by creating conditions that encourage schools to become more effective and by allowing schools to be more responsive to the special needs of their students.

Hansen (1986) provides a final summation of support, stating that educational choice is fundamentally related to the following: (1) the right of the families, whether rich or poor, to bring up their children in their own value system, (2) successful learning, and (3) political empowerment to improve education when it is unsatisfactory.

Arguments Against Educational Choice

Choice is an appealing value in a free and democratic society. It is difficult, therefore, to argue against expanding choice unless such expansion is at the expense of other values considered important to public education in a democracy. One such value is equity. Equity is defined as an educational system that provides all students with equal opportunity to an education that will enable them to succeed in society after school. (Bowles, 1989).

Although equity and choice may be fundamental goals of a democratic education, they are often in conflict (Spicer & Hill, 1990). One of the strongest criticisms of some choice plans is that they will make the good schools better and the bad schools worse. Giving disadvantaged families more choice in where they send their children to school would seem to provide immediate expansion of their equal educational opportunity, yet opponents see choice as a serious threat to the health and even survival of a strong public school system and, therefore, as ultimately detrimental to disadvantaged families. Schools with limited budgets have a difficult time providing the necessary resources for a quality education, and any exodus of students would likely make the situation worse (Apple, 1989).

Another concern with expanding educational choice is grounded in the belief that public education should be a common experience for all children. Here, opponents argue that parental choice can work against the necessary conditions of a common educational experience. Ackerman (1984) contends that a liberal education in a pluralistic society should expose children to beliefs and group values different from those of their parents, and that the danger of parent choice is that it allows parents to practice "horticulture," trying to reproduce their children in their own image.

Glenn (1989) emphasized than any plan to promote choice will have to deal with the fact that some schools will attract more students than they can accommodate and other schools too few students to operate adequate programs, and this could result in significant inadequacies and racial segregation. When choice is strongly influenced by a desire to affiliate with certain groups, competition promotes segregation by class and race and limits the ability of schools to transmit common social values (Spicer & Hill, 1990).

Arguments against educational choice are also rooted in the interest of the community. Advocates of strong neighborhoods believe that schools should be the center of the community. When families leave the local schools, they do so at the expense of others in the community because they no longer have a vested interest in making the community schools better. Hansen (1985) argues that increased choice would only be exercised by the more informed, active, and educationally ambitious parents, thereby leading to some schools becoming hotbeds of parent support and involvement, with others becoming pockets of apathy.

A final argument against educational choice is that the educational system might be dominated by the profit motive. The burgeoning number of individuals and businesses that have entered the K-12 education-for-profit business magnifies this worry. These for-profit charter and contract schools may be concerned primarily with cost-efficiency, as opposed to diversity of content and methods (Zollers & Ramanathan, 1998). The student might be treated like a product through packaging, advertising, and promotion. The goal of cost efficiency might emphasize performance on standardized tests as opposed to empowering students with the knowledge and abilities with which to succeed (Molnar, 1996; Spicer & Hill, 1990). Hawley comments that the more choice is maximized, the more likely it is that we will also:

- Sort students by race, income, and religion, and increase social conflict and economic disparity.
- Reduce financial support for public education, and for programs serving children with special needs.
- Increase the cost of good private schools.
- Lower standards of academic performance overall and simultaneously decrease the demand for school reform at the grassroots and among elites (1998, p. 190).

Understanding what effect educational choice will have on student performance and parental involvement clearly requires continued and ongoing research. Before school administrators can evaluate the impact of school choice on their school community, choice must be defined in specific terms. Otherwise, as Rosenberg argues, there is created the misunderstanding that educational choice is a singular policy rather than an assortment of policies and programs (1989). The next section of this chapter defines the features, benefits, and consequences of specific choice plans.

What Do We Mean by Educational Choice?

By some standards, the current organization of public education allows students ample opportunity to get out of school what they want. Although not ordinarily considered in the context of "choice," students—often influenced by their parents—choose how much time and energy they spend on school. This simplest form of choice has a major impact on how well students do in school (Elmore, 1988). At the secondary level, there is often considerable choice in what courses students take. Students who choose a rigorous college preparatory program will get out of school something different than those who choose a "general education" program. One could argue that these programmatic choices are narrowed considerably by student ability and course availability. Nevertheless, the amount of time and energy, the types of courses students take, and the program they pursue are all choices generally available to students and their families in the existing public school system.

The existing system, however, does not provide equal access to choice opportunities. Families with the financial ability can move to a neighborhood that has the type of school they want. Although they do not generally participate in decisions about the school, they can select a school that comports with their values, expectations, and standards. This same opportunity exists for parents who choose schools outside the public domain. Private schools, however, can be a costly choice. The cost of private school tuition limits access to those who are willing and able to pay the price.

Open Enrollment

There are two general types of open enrollment: interdistrict open enrollment and intradistrict open enrollment. Interdistrict open enrollment permits parents to enroll their children in the public school of their choice, regardless of the family's residence. This type of choice is important to the discussion because it is feasible in rural and suburban areas as well as urban areas. Minnesota began offering parents interdistrict open enrollment in 1987. There, school districts have a right not to participate in the plan, but no district is permitted to prohibit a student from leaving.

One potential advantage of an interdistrict choice plan is that it can encourage local school districts to be more responsive to parents and students, especially if they fear losing students (and the associated dollars) to another school district. Another advantage is that it does provide families a choice. Even though fewer than 2% of the students in Minnesota attend a school outside their district (Goldhaber, 1999), 100 percent of the families have a choice. It should be noted that there is no direct evidence that this form of educational choice has an impact on student outcomes (Armor & Peiser, 1998; Goldhaber, 1999).

Intradistrict open enrollment allows parents to choose any public school within the district. School choice within districts has existed in varying degrees since the inception of public schools in the United States. Common reasons for permitting enrollment outside the attendance area include special needs and programs, students changing residence close to their graduation date, and brothers or sisters attending different schools (Witte, 1991).

Magnet Schools

The most popular version of intradistrict open enrollment is magnet schools. Magnet schools tend to specialize in one of a variety of academic areas and generally enroll students from within the public school district boundaries (Goldhaber, 1999). The first magnet schools were based on models from speciality schools such as the Bronx School of Science or Boston Latin School, which have offered advanced programs to highly selected students for many years. The idea of a magnet school, however, was to attract and enroll students on their interests, not ability level (Blank & Archbald, 1992).

> *"By attracting students with common education interests but diverse abilities and socioeconomic backgrounds, a magnet school can enroll a racially heterogeneous student body and provide a unique educational experience through a curriculum organized around a specific theme or instructional approach"*
> (Blank and Archbald , p. 82).

Magnet schools are particularly popular in urban school systems and have been used as a strategy for desegregation. Magnet schools were implemented in Buffalo, New York in response to a 1976 court determination that segregation existed in the district's schools. In St.

Louis, 26 magnet schools are currently offered under a magnet school program that has been operating for 20 years. All eighth grade students in Rochester, New York, choose among 18 magnet schools. Placements in all schools are contingent upon available space and racial balance (Council of Great City Schools, 1996).

It is also believed that magnet schools can work toward improving student attendance, dropout rate, suspensions, and other discipline problems (Black, 1996). Magnet schools have also been shown to generate renewed motivation for education among students, parents, and teachers and, in some magnet schools, to improve academic performance (Gamoran, 1996; Blank & Archbald, 1992).

Blank (1988)cdescribes 10 steps in the effective planning and development of magnet schools that are useful for school administrators to consider (see Figure 13-1).

Blank's 10 Steps for Effective Planning and Development of Magnet Schools

Step 1. Identify Needs for Magnet Schools - Interests in magnets, types of themes - Status of desegregation - Quality concerns - Building capacity and utilization	**Step 6.** Design and Staff Individual Magnet Schools - Design appropriate to theme - Principal and teacher selection - Staff development and commitment
Step 2. Establish District Desegregation and Educational Objectives - District plans versus area of school focus - Increase options, improve academic curriculum, career preparation - Leadership concerns	**Step 7.** Development Curriculum Around Magnet Theme - Integration of theme - Relation to district-wide curriculum - Innovation methods - Experiential education
Step 3. Develop District Program Strategy - Broad versus limited - Location, type, theme - Participation by staff and community - Themes that are definite, distinctive, appealing	**Step 8.** Publicize the Program and Recruit Students - District and school-level efforts - Equal access - Broad public support - Selection method
Step 4. Select Leaders for the Program and Schools - District central leadership - School leaders - Direction, coordination, and flexibility	**Step 9.** Organize Students and Staff - Part-time, whole-school - Building magnet identity - Expectations and attitudes
Step 5. Identify and Allocate Resources - Start-up funds - Planning staff - Community involvement - Facilities and equipment	**Step 10.** Maintain Support - Funding and resource support - Community roles - Publicity with outcomes and innovations - Spin-offs and expansion
Source: Rolf K. Blank, Local Planning and Development of Magnet Schools: 10 Steps to Success. ERS Spectrum 6 (1), Winter, 1988, 12.	

Figure 13-1

Charter Schools

Most states define charter schools as public schools that operate under a special contract or charter. Depending on the state, the charter sponsor might be a school district, a university, a state board of education, or some other public entity. Charter schools are intended to be nonselective, tuition-free, nonsectarian, and based on choice (Molnar, 1996). During the 1990s, the number of charter schools in the United States dramatically increased, and the growth is likely to continue (Watkins, 1999).

Proponents of charter schools argue that these schools are held more accountable for student outcomes, enjoy greater freedom from cumbersome mandates, operate more efficiently, provide educational choice to families, infuse healthy competition into an otherwise unresponsive bureaucracy, and model innovative practice for other schools to follow (Wells, 1998). Advocating for charter schools, the Hudson Institute (1996), offered five key features of these schools:

1. Charter schools are small, even intimate places where everyone knows each other. They have clearly articulated missions that can be pursued without unacceptable constraints or distractions.
2. Charter schools offer havens to people who badly need and want alternatives to schools that have not served them well.
3. Charter schools are genuinely innovative, with imaginative curricula and truly inventive ways of doing things.
4. Charter schools establish a much-needed measure of accountability. They will be abandoned if they do not serve their customers or closed by public authorities if they do not serve their communities.
5. Charter schools serve the public in a different way and are anchored to their communities in ways more reminiscent of Horace Mann's day than today's bureaucracies.

Watkins (1999) categorizes charter school advocates into three main groups:

1. *Zealots and Ideologues*: These individuals view charter schools passionately as an immediate answer to public education problems. Their enthusiasm and devotion blinds them to the complexities of operating effective schools.

2. *Entrepreneurial Scoundrels*: These vultures are circling charter schools with no real regard for the educational outcomes of the children in them. Their slick proposals look good on the surface, but their long-term prospects for bringing beneficial change for students are very limited.

3. *Child-, Parent-, and Teacher-Centered Reformers*: These are individuals who believe strongly in the value of public education, yet realize that public schools are flawed, and in some cases, near the breaking point. These people see charters not as anti-public education but rather as prochild and propublic school choice.

Although Watkins believes that many charter advocates are motivated by the best interest of children, Molnar (1996) maintains that "Despite the rosy image provided by the child-centered reformers, most of the money and political influence driving the charter movement have been provided by the zealots and the profiteers" (p. 10).

Lack of money has proven to be a problem for those interested in starting charter schools. Although charter schools usually receive the same per-pupil funding as do other schools in the district, they do not typically get start-up funds or assistance with legal matters, payroll, or other support services. Another major problem facing some charter school founders is finding a place to house their school. There have been a number of charters granted to well-intended individuals that have scrambled at the last minute for a place to call school.

Accountability is the cornerstone of the charter school movement. Nathan (1996) is among a number of charter school supporters who argue that charter schools will improve academic performance because they are required to do so if they want to have their contract renewed. It should be noted, however, that there is scant evidence thus far that charter schools are, in fact, more accountable. A UCLA study of charter schools in California, for example, found little evidence that charter schools live up to the accountability claims made by their advocates (Wells, 1998).

School administrators need to take the rapidly expanding charter school movement seriously. Unlike magnet schools, where the funding remains within a district's oversight, charter schools siphon valuable resources from a district's budget. Even if some students gain from the charter school experience, the rest of the students may suffer. "Charter schools, like private school vouchers, are built on the illusion that our society can be held together solely by the self-interested pursuit of our individual purposes" (Molnar, 1996, p. 15).

Public/Private Choice Plan

Educational choice includes public/private plans that use some form of public funds to subsidize private school education. A modest example of this support is found in those states where transportation and support services, such as school nursing, are provided by the local school district to parochial schools. There are also a growing number of school districts that offer home-schoolers access to their schools on a part-time basis, and some that even offer special programs for families who choose to teach their children at home (Dahm, 1996; Lines, 1996). Private school vouchers are the form of private/public school choice that receive the most attention, but some postsecondary options plans also serve as an example of private/public school funding.

Postsecondary Options

Postsecondary options is defined as a policy that allows junior and senior public high school students to take courses for high school or college credit at institutions such as community colleges, vocational/technical institutions, and four-year colleges and universities. Tuition for these courses is generally paid by the student's resident school district, and admission is determined by the postsecondary institution. Minnesota passed the first postsecondary option legislation in 1985 (Greenburg, 1989).

One distinguishing feature of some postsecondary choice options is that they can include private, sectarian colleges. In some cases, this means that public tax money generated for use in the local school districts may now be given to religious colleges. This raises the question of whether it is constitutional under the Establishment Clause of the First Amendment to support private institutions with public taxes. In *Minnesota Federation of Teachers v. Thomas A. Nelson*, a U.S. District Court ruled that, because the money being paid is attributed to individual action of the student and not a state decision to make a grant, there should be no concern with what eligible institutions do with the postsecondary option funds (Mantano, 1989). This court decision could impact other educational choice proposals such as vouchers.

Vouchers

The type of educational choice that offers families the greatest freedom of school choice, that provides the strongest test of the competitive market effects on education, and that stirs up the most opposition is vouchers (Goldhaber, 1999). Wisconsin, Ohio, and Florida are among the states that have legislated some form of voucher plan. Lawmakers in more than a dozen other states are considering bills to start voucher plans. The basic question that school administrators must ask themselves in forming their opinion on vouchers is this: Who is best suited to spend the large sum of money involved in providing public education—those who provide the education or those families that consume it?

Under a voucher plan, parents are given a specific sum of money each year that they can apply to any public or private school. Tuition vouchers are funded with public tax dollars. Depending on the type of voucher system, these funds could be used for public schools outside a child's local community or applied to a private or parochial school. Florida's contested voucher plan, for example, offered parents of students in the state's "failed" public schools the opportunity to send their children to a higher-performing public school or private school of their choice.

Many of the general arguments for and against educational choice discussed earlier in this chapter have specific application to school vouchers. The tension between voucher supporters and opponents is high. In his attempt to get at the heart of the voucher debate, Levin (1989) explains that since the birth of the common school, it has generally been agreed that our society must rely on its public schools to provide students with common values and knowledge in order that they can serve as informed, thoughtful citizens in a democratic society. Levin goes on to say that in recent years, the primary importance of this concern for the common good has been challenged by those who argue that parents are best suited to choose the experiences, influences, and values to which they expose their children, and that providing such choice through public tax money will result in a more responsive pubic school experience for all other students.

One of the most pressing arguments raised by proponents of vouchers is that they afford the less advantaged the same opportunity as the more advantaged (Miller, 1999). Friedman (1997) contends that enabling parents to choose freely the schools their children attend is the most feasible way to improve education. The argument here is that public schools fail to serve their full purpose because they are controlled almost exclusively through regulation, and alternatives are precluded by this monopoly status. Private schools, through a market economy, can determine how well they are doing by the number of students enrolled.

McClaren (1994) writes *"Letting the market equalize education through vouchers will only exacerbate the disparity of chances between rich and poor students - inner-city schools will collapse. 'Choice' means that the poor are 'free' to become poorer while the rich are given the 'choice' of becoming richer. Choice means Jim Crow education for the 1990s. Choice schemes need to improve the conditions of low performing schools or else state funding will shrink due to declining enrollment, and students and teachers will transfer to other schools"* (p. 172).

The constitutionality of publicly funded educational vouchers is a central concern, because 85 percent of private schools are religiously affiliated (Kemerer & King, 1995). Critics argue that government-funded vouchers for religious schooling violate the separation of church and state. In June of 2002, in a 5-4 decision, the U.S. Supreme Court approved the use of vouchers for parochial and private schools (Zernike, 2002).

While some educators support expanded public school choice, few are in favor of vouchers. Raywid (1987) cites the positive benefits to be gained from diversifying the public school system and allowing a wider choice in school selection, but cautions that problems would ensue from establishing an educational voucher system. Raywid raises three concerns about vouchers:

1. Many educators are seriously questioning whether the public schools can survive. Under these circumstances, we ought to be doing everything possible to shore up the public schools, not stimulate the flow of students and resources out of those schools.

2. To assign parents full and unfettered responsibility for choosing their children's education in an open market is to telegraph the message that the matter is solely their affair and not the community's concern.

3. Vouchers would quickly solidify a two-tiered educational system consisting of nonpublic schools and pauper schools. That development would impoverish us all, because it would represent an abandonment of efforts to improve education for disadvantaged youngsters, who are already a majority in most U.S. cities. (p. 763).

In his book *The Case Against School Vouchers,* Doerr (1995) sums up some of the major arguments against vouchers by stating that they undermine religious liberty, clash with the Establishment Clause of the Constitution, run counter to public opinion, provide funding to fundamentalist Christian schools that teach bigotry, and conflict with the major tenets of American democracy—respect for diversity, intellectual freedom, and religious tolerance.

Figure 13-2 presents an overview of other concerns about a voucher system that uses public tax money to fund nonpublic schools.

Concerns About a Voucher System.

- Anyone could open a school and accept vouchers.

- Nonpublic voucher schools could deny admission to children based on race, religion, gender, economic status, physical ability, mental capacity, or other arbitrary criteria.

- Nonpublic schools provide no guarantee for public review or oversight.

- Vouchers for nonpublic schools do not link funding to increased achievement, accountability, or basic public school regulations.

- It is difficult to estimate the costs for transportation, administration, etc. Busing one child at a time to a voucher school is an expensive proposition.

- Real choice and equal opportunities mean that every child must be able to select any school and have all of the funding needed to attend that school.

Source: Pennsylvania Coalition for Public Education, 1994.

Figure 13-2

Schlecty (1997) cautions, *"If the forces of privatization and vouchers carry the day, public schools will not disappear. Rather, they will become increasingly pathetic reminders of the fact that the present times are the good old days for the generation that follows this one"* (p. 18).

Conclusion

Boyd and Kerchner (1989) noted that educational practitioners have generally been silent or reluctant about the idea of expanding educational choice. Glenn (1989) agrees in observing that ". . . there is a puzzling resistance among educators to the extension of parent choice" (p. 87). Perhaps this resistance is because educational choice might threaten the security that educational administrators find in the existing system, as Chubb and Moe argue (1990). Possibly it is because ". . . *they cling to the administrative tradition and convenience of the 'one best system' approach to the provision of school"* (Boyd & Kerchner, 1988, p.5). It is equally important to recognize that public school administrator resistance to certain forms of educational choice may be attributed to the close connection that administrators have to their school community. Unlike politicians, business leaders, and educational theorists, public school administrators have first-hand knowledge of the conditions that influence the quality of education in their school districts. Because they are in an appropriate position to assess the likely impact of educational choice on their schools and their school districts, school administrators have important insight into judging the likely effect of educational choice on their school community. It is therefore important that public school administrators recognize their role in ensuring that families in their school communities are not adversely affected by the implementation of public school choice. The following recommendations may guide public schhol administrators in their effort to achieve this purpose.

Recommendations for Public School Administrators

The school choice movement has many avenues. Ideas such as open enrollment, charter schools, magnet schools, and voucher plans have many approaches. Avoid closed mindedness to these idea. Instead, work within the culture of your district to help everyone understand the costs and benefits of their options.

1. **Know where you stand on educational choice**. As a school leader, you need to make a decision on where you stand in the educational choice debate. Are you really against expanding family choice? Or do you support choice arrangements that may benefit the individual needs of students in your school community, so long as the price is not a general deterioration of the education for all students? Are you in favor of allowing seniors to take advantage of postsecondary options? Do you believe charter schools would strengthen or weaken public education in your community? Would a magnet school serve the needs and interests of some students in your community? Understanding where you stand on the issue of educational choice will enable you to participate more fully in the choice debate.

2. **Challenge the assumption that public schools don't work**. The most strident argument that educational choice proponents make is that public schools are failing. An elaboration of this argument is provided in an earlier section of this chapter. As a school leader, you should not accept this premise without question. Berliner and Biddle (1995) provides a convincing counterargument that this assault against public education is a "manufactured crisis." Bracey (1997) writes that those who want to introduce privatized education look only for bad news about our schools and fail to fairly interpret the available data. Using extensive educational statistics, Bracey reports on the significant progress American education is making in comparison to other industrialized nations. The good news about public education can also be found in studies published by the National Center for Educational Statistics, which reports that fewer students are dropping out of school, SAT scores are up, and student mathematics and science achievement is improving (1998). The point here, however, is not for school leaders to become complacent in their efforts. There will always be the need for continuous improvement. Yet, unless you as a school leader recognize the accomplishments of the students in your school community, it will be difficult for you to spread the good news.

3. **Market the achievements of your school community**. Proponents of vouchers and charters are quick to point out the failings in the system. This is an effective strategy to promote their argument for expanding choice. School administrators need to broadcast the accomplishments of the students, teachers, and support staff and help cultivate a sense of pride in the greater school community

4. **Know what impact educational choice will have on your school community**. This chapter highlighted a number of different choice arrangements. Some choice plans, such as interdistrict open enrollment, may have little impact on your school community. On the other hand, one or more charter schools could dramatically impact your school district budget and ability to provide support services to your students. Once you know what impact specific choice plans will have on the ability of your school district to deliver quality education, you will be in a position to take a stand on what forms of educational choice you support.

5. **Become an information source for your school community.** Eighty-one percent of the adults surveyed said they knew very little about charter schools, and 63 percent were likewise uninformed about vouchers (Hardy, 1999). There is no question that the choice debate is driven by special interests. Information sources such as the Internet are often partial to one perspective and generally lack balance. It is important that school leaders provide information and resources that educate families in their school district on current choice options as well as the advantages and disadvantages of expanding educational choice.

Case Problem: A Chance to Explain

As the most knowledgeable administrator in her school district on the topic of school choice, Elizabeth Chance has agreed to her board of education's request for her to run a public presentation on the topic. If you were advising Elizabeth, what would you tell her to to include in the development of a plan for the presentation? Include 1) the topics to be covered, 2) the subtopics to be covered, 3) a preliminary list of pros and cons on each topic, 4) the people to be invited to attend, and 5) the people to be invited to speak, and your rationale for each of these recommendations.

References

Ackerman, S. (1984). Pluralism, equal liberty, and public education. In C. Marshner (Ed.), *A blueprint for educational reform*. Chicago: Regney-Gateway Publishers.

A Nation at Risk (National Commission on Excellence on Education, 1983).

Armor, D., & Peiser, B. (1998). Interdistrict choice in Massachusetts. In P. Peterson & B. Hassel (Eds.), Learning from school choice . Washington, D.C.: The Brookings Institute.

Apple, M. (1989). The politics of common-sense: Schooling, popularism and the new right. Unpublished manuscript.

Berliner, D. & Biddle, B. (1995). The manufactured crisis: Myths, fraud, and the attack on America's public schools. Reading, MA: Addison Wesley.

Black, S. (1996). The pull of magnets. The American School Board Journal 183 (9), 34-36.

Blank, R. (1988). Local planning and development of magnet schools: Ten steps to success. ERS Spectrum 6 (1), 11-20.

Blank, R. & Archbald, D. (1992). Magnet schools and issues of educational quality. The Clearing House 66 (2), 81-86.

Borden, K,. & Rauchut, E. (1998). School choice II. Thoughtful teachers, thoughtful schools. in Editorial Projects in Education. Needham Hills, MA: Allyn and Bacon.

Boyd, W.L., & Kerchner, C.T. (1988). The politics of excellence and choice. New York: Falmer Press.

Brandl, J. (1988). An educational policy agenda for legislators. In J. Nathan (Ed.), Public schools by choice. St. Paul, MN: The Institute for Learning and Teaching.

Bowles, B.D. (1989). Gaining support for change: the politics of strategic planning. In J.T. Mauriel (Ed.), Strategic leadership for schools.. San Francisco: Jossey-Bass.

Bowman, D. (2000). Charter school movement growing rapidly, study shows. Education Week 19 (23), 5.

Bracey, G. (1997). What happened to America's public school? American Heritage 48 (7), 38-52.

Brandl, J. (1988). An education policy agenda for legislators. In J. Nathan (Ed.) Public schools by choice. St Paul, MN: The Institute for Learning and Teaching.

Chubb, J., & Moe, T. (1990). Politics, markets and American schools. Washington, DC: The Brookings Institute.

Coons, J., & Sugarman, S. (1978). Private wealth and public education. Cambridge: Harvard University Press.

Council of Great City Schools (1996, May). Open enrollment and school choice programs in the Great City Schools. Retrieved May, 2000 from http://www.cgcs.org/services/fastresp/open.htm.

Dahm, L. (1996). Education at home, with help from school. Educational Leadership, 54 (2), 68-71.

Doerr, E. (1995). The case against vouchers. Amherst, NY: Prometheus Books

Doyle, D. (1988). The excellence movement, academic standards, a core curriculum, and choice: How do they connect?" In W. L. Boyd & C.T. Kerchner (Eds.), The politics of excellence and choice in education. New York: The Falmer Press.

Education Week (1989, January).

Elmore, R. F. (1988). Choice in public education. Washington, D.C.: The Center for Policy Research in Education.

Fowler, F. (1988). The politics of school reform in Tennessee: A view from the classroom. In W. L. Boyd & C.T. Kerchner (Eds.), The politics of excellence and choice in education, New York: Falmer Press.

Friedman. M. (1997). Public schools: Make them private. Education Economics, 5 (3), 341-344.

Friedman, M. (1962). Capitalism and freedom. Chicago: The University of Chicago Press.

Gamoran, A. (1996). Do magnet schools boost achievement? Educational Leadership, 54 (2), 9-15.

Glenn, C. (1989). Putting choice in place. In J. Nathan (Ed.), Public schools by choice. St Paul, MN: The Institute for Learning and Teaching.

Goldhaber, D. (1999). School Choice: An examination of the empirical evidence on achievement, parental decision making, and equity. Educational Research, 28 (9), 16-35.

Greenburg, A. (1989). Concurrent enrollment programs: College credit for high school students. Bloomington, IN: Phi Delta Kappa Education Foundation.

Hansen, K. (1985). Choice within the system: An analysis. Portland, OR: Northwest Regional Educational Laboratory

Hardy, L. (1999). Public school choice. American School Board Journal 187 (2), 22-26.

Hawley, W. (1998). School choice I. Thoughtful teachers, thoughtful schools. in Editorial Projects in Education. Needham Heights, MA: Allyn Bacon.

Hudson Institute (1996). Charter schools in action. Retrieved March 15, 2000 from http://www.Hudson.org/Hudson/Charters/TOC.html.

Kemerer, F., & King, L. (1995). Are school vouchers constitutional? Phi Delta Kappan, 77 (4), 307-11.

Levin, H. (1989). The theory of choice applied to education. In W. Clune and J. Witte (Eds.), Choice and control in American education Vol. 1: The theory of choice and control in education. New York: The Falmer Press.

Lines, P. (1996). Home schooling comes of age. Educational Leadership, 54 (2), 63-67.

McClaren, P. (1994). Life in schools. New York: Longman.

Miller, M. (1999). A bold experience to fix city schools. The Atlantic Monthly 284 (1), 15-31.

Molnar, A. (1996). Charter schools: The smiling face of disinvestment. Educational Leadership 54 (2), 9-15.

Montano, J. (1989). Choice comes to Minnesota. In J. Nathan (Ed.), Public schools by choice. St. Paul, MN: The Institute for Learning and Teaching.

Nathan, J. (1996). Charter schools: Hope and opportunity in American schools. San Francisco: Jossey-Bass.

National Center for Educational Statistics (1998). Digest of Educational Statistics, 1998. Washington, D.C.: U.S. Department of Education, Office of Educational Research and Improvement.

National Commission on Excellence in Education (1983). A nation at risk: The imperative for educational reform. Washington, D.C.: Author.

Paulu, N. (1989). Improving schools and empowering parents: Choice in American education. A report based on the White House workshop on choice in education. Washington, DC: U.S. Department of Education.

Pennsylvania Coalition for Public Education (1994, June). School vouchers. Available through Pennsylvania Coalition of Public Education. P.O. Box 6993, Harrisburg, PA 17112.

Peterson, P.E. (1988). The public schools: monopoly or choice? In W. Clune and J. Witte (Eds.), Choice and control in American education Vol. 1: The theory of choice and control in education. New York: The Falmer Press.

Raywid, M.A. (1987). Public school, yes; vouchers, no! Phi Delta Kappan, 68 (10), 762-769.

Rosenberg, B. (1989). Public school choice: Can we find the right balance? American Educator, 13 (2), 8-14.

Schlecty, P. (1987). Inventing better schools. San Francisco: Jossey-Bass.

Smith, A. (1976). The Wealth of Nations Books I-III. London: Penguin Books.

Spicer, M., & Hill, E. (1990). Evaluating educational choice in public education: Policy beyond the monopoly model. American Journal of Education, 98 (2), 97-113.

Walberg, H. (1996). Educational productivity and choice. In J. Nathan (Ed.), Public schools by choice. St Paul, MN: The Institute for Learning and Teaching.

Watkins, T. (1999). The charter challenge. American School Board Journal, 186 (12), 34-36.

Wells, A. (1998). Charter school reform in California. Phi Delta Kappan 81 (4), 305-312.

Witte, J. & Thorn, C. (1996). Vouchers and the inner-district choice programs in Milwaukee. American Journal of Education 104 (3), 186-217.

Witte, J. (1992). Choice in American education. Educational Considerations 19 (1), 12-19.

Wortman, P. (1978). The first year of the educational voucher demonstration: A secondary analysis of student achievement test scores. Evaluation Quarterly 2 (2), 193-214.

Zernike, K. (2002, June 30,) Vouchers: A shift, but just how big? The New York Times, p.3

Zollers, N., & Ramanathan, A. (1998). For-profit charter schools and students with disabilities: The sordid side of the business of schooling. Phi Delta Kappan, 80 (4), 297-304.

Chapter 14
Stress and Time Management

Jeffrey S. Kaiser

Knowledge of the causes and effects of stress on educators continues to grow. Attention to the topic grew with what appeared to be the identification of the culprit in the 1970s. The culprit was the demands of the school system and society. In the 1980s, the culprit was redefined as coming from within those educators who simply had not the ability to cope with hard work or with change. The cure in the '70s was to fix the environment within which educators worked. The cure in the '80s was to cure the educator. The cure in the '90s and the first decade of the new century is to cure both.

Stress reduction includes the acceptance of, but not surrender to, the environment. This attitude, coupled with increased knowledge of coping skills, has provided educators with a more utilitarian and pragmatic approach to reality. It suggests that educators must learn to make peace with what cannot be changed and choose their battles more carefully. Such an approach is indicative of maturation in our understanding of stress. It is not a capitulation.

Make peace with what cannot be changed and choose battles carefully.

Figure 14-1 lists two types of errors made when an administrator chooses to fight: 1) choosing to fight battles that cannot be won and 2) choosing too many winnable battles, thereby decreasing the odds of winning. Both types of error increase stress not caused by the environment but by the administrator's free choice. And, to the extent that winning is improbable, the resultant stress is for naught.

Engagement Choice Errors

1) Choosing battles that cannot be won
2) Choosing too many winnable battles

Figure 14-1

Students do not create stress. Neither do old buildings, poor facilities, bureaucratic administrators, incompetent colleagues, school board members, nor declining enrollment. Stress is a syndrome of biochemical events that may result from a change in a person's physical or psychological environment. Such a reaction to environmental change is person-specific. Some people withdraw from the change, some fight the change, and some are barely affected by it (Kaiser, 1991).

The Physiological Meaning of the Stress Response

Cannon (1935) describes stress as a body's natural resistance to change. The resistance is in the form of flight or fight. This is true of all living organisms, including humans. Submission to the change has traditionally been seen as a path to death—death of the original self by modification or death through complete disintegration.

Selye (1974) refers to the stimulating conditions that produce stress reactions in humans as the stressors. The state of the human—the reaction itself—is termed stress. According to Selye, stress is a state that is manifested by a specific syndrome of biological events.

Selye defines the mobilization of the body's defenses as the General Adaptation Syndrome. This syndrome, depicted in Figure 14-2, consists of three stages: alarm, resistance, and exhaustion.

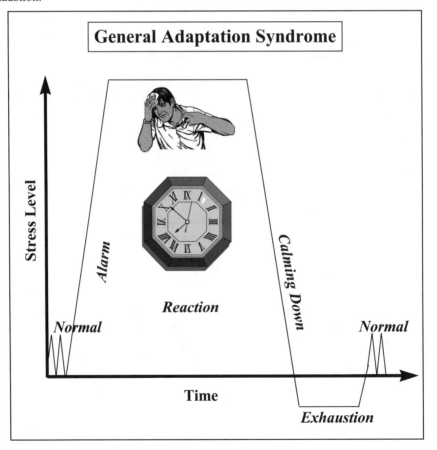

Figure 14-2

The alarm stage occurs when the stressor is first experienced. Anything tripping off the alarm stage can be considered a stressor. Examples of stressors are loud noises, the unexpected visit of an irate parent, or the wrath of one's boss. The alarm stage is characterized by the brain alerting the pituitary gland, resulting in a general biochemical alert to the entire body. The pituitary gland signals the adrenal system to secrete adrenaline, which in turn, converts muscle-stored glycogen into glucose (a form of sugar). The glucose enters the bloodstream, resulting in increased blood pressure, an increased pulse rate, and a general increase in energy to all parts of the body.

The resistance stage may last for a few hours, during which the body's blood pressure, respiration, and pulse are high. These conditions result in increased alertness and even increased physical strength. It is this stage, for example, that enabled cavemen to fight wild animals and run for a long distance when necessary. It is an expected reaction to stress.

The exhaustion stage results from the body's attempt to lower these abnormally high levels. It does so by secreting insulin to pull excess sugar out of the bloodstream and reverse the process. However, this may result in reducing blood sugar to such a low level as to result in temporary hypoglycemia (low blood sugar). It is not unusual for people to feel exhausted a few hours after the alarm stage.

> *Women have a dual problem: They hold a disproportionate number of high strain jobs and the stress tends not to let up at home.*
> -John Tierney-

Prolonged stress may damage the adrenal system, the lymph glands, and the thymus. Malfunctioning adrenals can result in low blood sugar. Damaged thymus and lymph glands can result in insufficient production of antibodies, thereby heightening the body's susceptibility to disease. This exhaustion stage may result in wear and tear and even death. Stress does not cause the body's reaction—it *is* the body's reaction.

Educational Stressors

Factors intrinsic to the job have received much attention from researchers studying working conditions and work overload. The findings of Marcson (1970) and Sheppard (1971) show that physical and mental health are adversely affected by repetitive and dehumanizing environments. Kornhauser (1965) indicates that mental health is positively related to working conditions. French and Caplan's (1973) research on the effects of qualitative and quantitative work overload reveals that job dissatisfaction, job tension, lowered self-esteem, threat, embarrassment, high cholesterol levels, and increased heart rate can result from work overload. Class size, number of preparations, and availability of teacher aides are a few of the factors that may affect perceived work overload and, therefore, stress levels in teachers and administrators.

Ambiguity increases when individuals have inadequate information concerning their work roles. Kahn (1973) found that individuals suffering from role ambiguity experience job dissatisfaction, job-related tension, feelings of futility, and lowered self-confidence. French and Caplan concludes that individuals who have conflicts in role responsibilities that concern other people experience more cardiovascular heart disease than those who have conflicts in role responsibilities that concern things. Cooper and Marshall (1977) determined that these factors are role stressors: too little responsibility, inadequate support from top administrators, and increasing standards of performance and technological change. Katz and Kahn (1966) define role conflict as the simultaneous occurrence of two or more role sendings that counteract each other in terms of compliance. Four types of role conflict are directly applicable to educational organizations: intrasender, intersender, interrole, and person-role (see Figure 14-3).

Four Types of Role Conflict

Intrasender conflict exists when an individual is asked by another to accomplish two objectives that are in apparent conflict. A principal's request that teachers complete test grading earlier than usual and with fewer mistakes is an example of intrasender conflict.

Intersender conflict exists when an individual receives incompatible directions from two or more people. For example, teachers often complain that their principal encourages them to confront classroom discipline problems but that district policy prohibits any real support from the administration.

Interrole conflict exists when an individual is forced to assume two or more incompatible roles. For example, an administrator must frequently conduct business after school and in the evening. This aspect of the job role may conflict with the administrator's roles as a spouse and parent.

Person-role conflict exists when people are asked to do things that contradict their personal values. The pressure to pass unqualified students is an example of person-role conflict.

Figure 14-3

Causes of stress can also vary with the personality of the individual. Relationships within the school also may be related to stress among educators. French and Caplan (1973) conclude that job dissatisfaction, job tension, lowered self-esteem, threat, embarrassment, high cholesterol levels, and increased heart rate result from work overload. Decreasing school budgets, increasing student-teacher ratios, and multiplying numbers of preparations are other factors that contribute to work overload.

The following highlights additional stressors particular to the environment of educators:

The changing roles of teachers and administrators are not easily identified. Although everyone agrees on the need to increase the level of educator performance, little agreement exists on what constitutes excellence. To some, political survival has become a role model. Excellence in community relations may not be related to heightened student achievement levels, but it is increasingly perceived as a very tangible, desirable, and measurable goal in education. The ambiguity of one's role as an educator is certainly as important a stress factor as poor interpersonal relations with colleagues, subordinates, and students.

Most teachers attain their highest job title upon entering the teaching profession. Relatively few chances for career development exist within the profession, and American schools frequently grant the same job title to new and to experienced teachers. Moreover, a move from teaching into administration is usually perceived as a job change, not as a promotion to a higher teaching rank (see Chapter 1). For the vast majority who remain in teaching, the organizational structure may be perceived as a threat to autonomy, freedom, and identity. Lack of participation in the decision-making process, poor communication, and mistrust of fellow workers may lead to poor communication, low job satisfaction, and feelings of job-related threats, all of which result in added tensions and frustrations.

Lipsky (1980) describes teachers as "street-level bureaucrats [who] work in situations which tend to maximize the likelihood of debilitating job stress." Much teacher behavior is obviously devoted to bureaucratic processes. Taking attendance, handing out detentions, and monitoring the cafeteria and halls are within the realm of maintaining order, not that of motivating students to higher levels of world comprehension." High student-teacher ratios also mean that teachers must attend to maintaining order and have less attention for learning activities.

Bureaucratic behavior affects different teachers in different ways. It will cause stress in goal-oriented individuals, and it will be welcomed and assimilated by those who thrive in an ordered environment. Cannon (1935) and Selye (1974) fail to sufficiently address this variable of "individual orientation" (Kaiser, 1991, p. 290-291).

Regardless of orientation, stressors in education have increased considerably in the few years since the end of the 20th century. Most exacerbated stressors fall within the realm of eroding educator decision-making authority stemming from economic crises in public schools and from a legal environment which encourages law suites.

Stress-Prone Educators

In a famous study conducted by Friedman and Rosenman (1974), 3500 male subjects, ages 39-59, with no known history of heart disease, were classified as Type A or Type B personalities. Seventy percent of the subjects who subsequently developed coronary heart disease were from the Type A group. Type A personalities are often characterized as impatient, quick anger, abrupt, worried, overcommitted, highly ambitious, and, frequently, highly successful. In contrast, Type B personalities are more relaxed and easygoing, generally lacking Type A characteristics.

As expected, an attempt to divide people into two discreet categories may have been overly simplistic. There is a newer expectation that Type A people who are go-getters, rather than hostiles, have a greater survival rate. And, as with all endeavors to understand human psychology, there eventually arises the question of appropriate intervention techniques to change behaviors rather than dwelling on underlying causes.

Holmes and Rahe (1967) developed the Social Readjustment Rating Scale, an instrument that measures the amount of stress arising from positive or negative changes in a person's life over a period of 1 year, without regard to their Type A or Type B behavior patterns. Persons with high scores on the scale have perhaps three times the probability of serious illness within 2 years from measurement as those with low scores. Preliminary findings also indicate the possibility of a direct relationship between suspected hypoglycemic individuals and Holmes-Rahe life change scores ($R = .4$, $p < .02$). Such results, if confirmed by blood-sugar analysis, would be of no surprise to those describing stress as the wear and tear of life.

The origins of Type A behavior vary. It may stem from an insatiable need to know all the facts, to maintain self-esteem, or to allay a fear of appearing ignorant. It may be the result of experiences early in life that have created Type A characteristics. It may even derive from poor work habits.

Hodge and Marker (1978) relate that secondary teachers rank class interruptions, special events, announcements, tardy pupils, and other time management problems among the most bothersome job factors. Seventy-three percent of the teachers studied by Sparks (1979) reported feeling "pulled in different directions" by the expectations of students, administrators, and the general public. Bortner (1969) uses an 8-point scale to measure the intensity or frequency of seven behaviors: appointment time consciousness, competitiveness, feelings of being rushed or under pressure, attempting multiple tasks at one time, speed of eating and walking and such, tendency to express feelings, and lack of interests outside of work. Bortner suggests that high scores on the scale are representative of Type A behavior.

Stress Carriers

Administrators can be a source of stress for teachers and subordinate administrators. Administrator stress carriers are often unaware of the stress they carry and spread to others. Figure 14-4 lists some ways administrators create climates of anxiety for others.

> . . . *sometimes the stressful conditions of the school and the personality of the principal warp the formal structures and relational features that develop between administrators* (Rothstein, 1991).

All people bring to their jobs a predisposition created by their individual emotional and intellectual life histories. Occasionally, bad attitudes result from such backgrounds. Figure 14-5 lists four techniques for the administrator to use when dealing with gripers, complainers, and people with bad attitudes.

How Administrators Create Climates of Anxiety

- Keeping people in the dark
- Putting people on the defensive
- Undermining confidences
- Not letting people know where they stand
- No priorities—just piling on the work
- Approving a subordinate's work before the subordinate's immediate supervisor has had a chance to approve it
- Not overlooking a few negatives
- Allowing politics to reign supreme

Figure 14-4

Stress Reduction Techniques

The most effective means of reducing one's stress is to eliminate the pressure, the source of that stress. Although a double martini, a tranquilizer pill, or jogging can relieve the symptoms of that pressure, it does not eliminate the pressure. If the source is one's boss, that source will still be there the next morning. The danger of treating the stress instead of the source of the stress is that a cycle of treatment dependency can emerge.

Although it would be wrong to suggest that stress comes only from bosses with bad attitudes, Figure 14-5 gives suggestions for administrators who might need to control their own attitudes to avoid being contagious to faculty.

Dealing With Bad Attitudes

- Understand that employees' defensiveness may seem reasonable to them because of their backgrounds. It may, in fact, be the long history of poor administration that has contributed to this attitude.
- Be open. Create an environment where employees feel free to discuss the impact of their attitudes on their job performance.
- Be prepared for emotional outbursts and emotional emergencies. They are a part of many people's lives. Be a good listener. Help employees see the situation objectively.
- Give it time with attention, but be sure that employees understand that excellent performance is expected regardless of personal feelings.

Figure 14-5

The conflict management techniques presented in this book can serve to eliminate some of the sources. Figure 14-6 is a list of methods of stress reduction. The list is presented with the understanding that people are individuals, and as such, must choose what is most useful for them and for their situations.

Manera and Wright (1981) report that educators rank poor time management as highest among stress-producing factors.

Stress Reduction Techniques		
• Biofeedback • Exercise • Meditation • Medication • Hotlines • Inservice and Staff Development Programs • Support Groups • Detached Concern • Compartmentalization (leaving your work troubles at work and your home troubles at home) • Maintaining professional but emotionally detached concern • Changing one's job to one with more motivating factors • Taking advantage of Employee Assistance Programs (health benefits, psychological counseling, workshops)	• Giving yourself an annual mental health checkup (How are you doing this year compared to last year?) • Heed other people's warnings (they might spot your stress before you do) • Concentrate on causes, not just symptoms • Give of yourself e.g. volunteer work • Keep in touch with your friends • Carve out personal time • Take all your vacation • Control your daily amount of bad news intake • Avoid unhealthy confrontation • Live one day at a time • Give in sometimes • Avoid constant covering up • Slow down in talk, walk • Concentrate on enjoying events and experiences as they take place	• Establish reasonable life goals • Accept the incompleteness of life • Attempt to achieve completeness through nonmaterial things • Reengineer hostility • Change bad habits to good • Get enough rest • Don't overwork to improve your self-image • Advance a plan for leisure • Try loafing now and then • Join a regular group (sport, entertainment, hobby) • Get away from home • Don't overschedule • Listen to your body • Accept your imperfections • Laugh or cry for relief • Build a support group • Don't attend or initiate self-pity parties

Figure 14-6

Time Management

Time management works. It allows for more important things to get done in less time. It lowers the emotional tone of human interaction and increases effectiveness by maximizing results with minimum costs. The byproduct is reduced stress accompanying increased performance.

No one has any more time than anyone else. Whether rich or poor, everyone has approximately 70 years. Everyone has all the time that there is. It is equally distributed. Time cannot be hoarded, overspent, or saved. Once it is gone, it is gone.

Time Allocation

How our time is allocated appears to be largely in our hands, a matter of free choice. That is not to say that our allocations are not encumbered by the environment within which we work. To be sure, no one can do everything. In fact, much of what can be accomplished depends on whether one is positioned at the top or the bottom of the administrative hierarchy. The available time is the same, no matter where positioned. However, how it is utilized depends partially on the relative position.

Figure 14-7 represents the allocation of time between management functions (planning, organizing, staffing, directing, controlling) and operative functions (the day-to-day tasks associated with specific jobs).

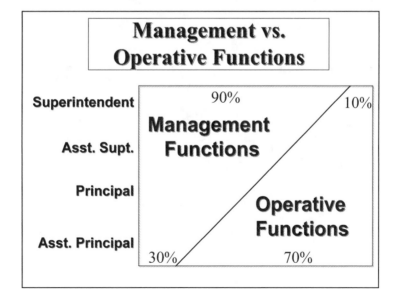

Figure 14-7

It is apparent that the lower one's administrative position, the less time is available for management functions. This is largely because higher-level administrators delegate as many operative functions as possible to lower-level administrators. In this way, higher level administrators are free to spend their own time on management functions. See Chapter 1 for specifics on management functions.

Notice that superintendents are likely to have 90% of their time available for planning, organizing, staffing, directing, and controlling. They do not escape operative functions completely. In contrast, assistant principals have only 30% of their time available for management functions, because 70% is encumbered with day-to-day operations.

The time available for specific management functions also varies with organizational level. Although superintendents and assistant principals spend time on management functions, their management functions time differs. Of all the management time superintendents have available (90%), approximately 33% of it is spent on planning. Of all the management time assistant principals have available (30%), approximately 10% of it is spent on planning. Figure 14-8 displays the differences in the way management function time is used by organizational level.

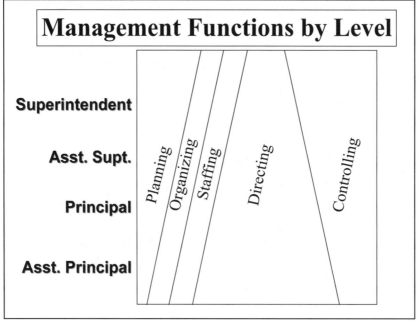

Figure 14-8

Timewasters

Mackenzie (1972) identifies 40 timewasters that fit within the 7 management functions depicted in Figure 14-9. The timewasters most often identified in the U.S. are the telephone, drop-in visitors, and meetings. Controlling these interruptions takes practice, and often, a heightened respect for oneself.

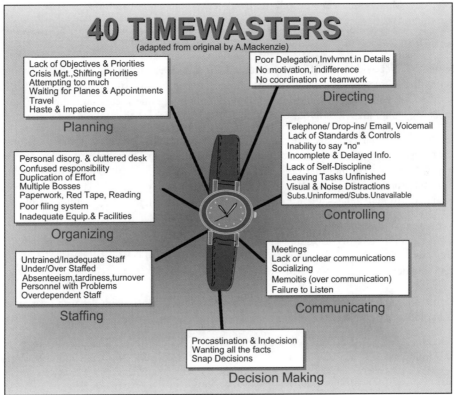

Figure 14-9

<u>Telephone and E-mail</u>

Controlling your telephone and e-mail requires increasing your awareness that the telephone is just a machine and your e-mail is run by one. Although this seems apparent to the intellect, the recognition is often clouded by emotion and bad habit. The following is a list of problems and bad habits connected to telephone and e-mail usage. along with some remedies.

The Habit: When the phone rings, I must answer it. When I have e-mail, I must respond.

Remedy: Answer the phone and e-mail when you want to, not always when it rings or arrives.. You cannot be available 24 hours a day whenever someone wants to call.

The Habit: I must be available to be a good administrator.

Remedy 1:. Set aside specific times during the day when you will be available to anyone who calls. Decide on the appropriate amount of time and schedule for that same time every day. Make your decisions public. Don't leave your e-mail alert on.

Remedy 2: Set aside a specific time period during which you will return all messages and take all calls.

Remedy 3: Set aside a quiet hour scheduled for the same time each day, during which you will not receive any calls accept those from your superordinates or significant members of your family. Send your secretary to a telephone reception course to learn screening techniques. Read your e-mail during set periods, not throughout the entire day.

Remedy 4: If your calls are automatically forwarded after a specified number of rings, ignore the ringing so that you can get your work done. Or, disconnect your phone by simply removing the modular plug. A phone on-off switch is available for a few dollars from electronic stores. The caller will not be aware that you are in your office. Your secretary will take a message. Return e-mail when you want, not always immediately.

Remedy 5: With prior approval from your superordinate, install an answering machine or get voice-mail ability. Be sure to arrange for remote retrieval to get your messages when away from the office. Think twice about having e-mail forwarded to your handheld device.

The Habit: I often contact someone and then have them get back to them because I forget all the things I want to say (or write).

Remedy: Always list all the points prior to making the call or drafting the message. As an administrator, you cannot afford to appear disorganized. Nor can you afford the wasted time.

The Habit: I have a tendency to talk for too long and spend way too long on e-mail.

Remedy: Obtain a small hourglass (egg timer) from the hardware or grocery store and place it next to your phone. Flip it over before taking or making a call or drafting an e-mail message. Watch the sand flow down while you talk or write. Get off before the sand runs out. After a few times, you will do fine without the hourglass.

The Habit: I can't get some people off the phone with me. They just keep talking.

Remedy: Set time limits as the conversation begins. For example, "Sure Frank, I can talk for about 30 seconds before my next meeting." Get talkers' attentions by calling their name: "Frank . . . Frank . . . Frank!" Another remedy is to foreshadow endings. For example, "Frank, before I get off, let me ask you this one last question." Be blunt,

"Frank, I can't talk any longer. I have to go now." If the person still continues to talk and you have no remedies left, try the ultimate remedy. Begin talking and hang up the phone in the middle of your own sentence. They will never guess that you hung up on yourself. But expect to receive a call back immediately. You may have to leave your office for a few minutes to attend to other business, so have your secretary take a message. Use this technique for extreme problems only.

The Habit: I have to answer the phone and check my e-mail because I must keep informed.

Remedy: Control your desire to know everything. Develop your own version of the *management by exception* principle. That is, let all of your subordinates know that you have faith enough in them that they do not have to report in when things are going as planned or when there is business as usual. They need to call or e-mail only when there are no school district or building-level policies in place to handle the problem and when they believe that they do not have the authority to make the decision.

The Problem: I have no secretary.

Remedy: Determine the financial cost to the school district from your salary (calculated per hour) for answering the time-wasted phone calls. Keep track. Present the financial facts to your boss. Consider a hideaway away from your office for a time each day so that you can get some work done. Understand that you are occasionally away from your phone and computer for meetings, lunch, and other reasons. The world does not fall apart.

The Habit: I like talking on the phone especially when I receive the call. Although I don't like to admit it, it makes me feel important. So does e-mail.

Remedy: Take heed of your own ego. Recognize that no one is indispensable. Consider the following adapted from an anonymous poem titled *The Indispensable Man*.

The Disposable Me

Sometime when you're feeling important, Sometime when your ego is in bloom,
Sometime when you're beginning to feel you're the most important one in the room,
Sometime when you feel that your going will leave an unfillable hole,
Just follow this little example and see how it humbles your soul.

Take a bucket and fill it with water. Put your hand in it up to your wrist.
Take it out and the hole that's remaining is a measure of how you'll be missed.

You can splash all you want as you enter. You can stir up the water galore.
But, stop, and you'll see in a moment, it looks just the same as before.

So the moral of this little example is to be just the best you can be,
Be proud of yourself but remember,. "They can always replace you and me. "

Drop-in Visitors

People who walk into your office without an appointment are a fact of life. This is true for administrators, teachers, subordinates, and community members. Occasionally, the number or frequency of drop-ins gets out of hand. The following is a list of remedies associated with the problem.

The Problem: People seem encouraged to walk in. When in, they seem to stay forever.

Remedy 1: Face your desk 90 degrees from the door. The inability to catch your eye will dissuade some of these interrupters, especially those dropping in to say "hi" or socialize.

Remedy 2: Stand up when someone comes into your office. That is often enough to dissuade them from sitting down.

Remedy 3: Walk quickly to situate yourself between the drop-in visitor and your guest chair. The odds are that the drop-in will not walk around you to sit down.

Remedy 4: If the visitor does get to the chair first, try not to look up from your work too quickly or too often. Use polite, nonverbal behavior to communicate that you are busy

Remedy 5:. Leave books, files, and paperwork on your guest chair to dissuade anyone from being seated. You can always remove them when you want someone to be seated.

Remedy 6: If necessary, be politely firm: "Frank, I'm going to have to excuse myself. I have a report due within the hour." Frank will usually leave.

Remedy 7: Schedule a quiet hour (for the same time each day) during which you accept no drop-ins.

Remedy 8: Find a hideaway somewhere else in the building to which you can escape to get some work done. Do not tell anyone where you are going.

Remedy 9: Have all scheduled meetings in the other person's office, not yours. In this way, you can easily get up and leave when the business is over.

Remedy 10: Refuse to solve your subordinates' problems for them. Do not encourage them to check with you. Use the *management-by-exception* principle.

Remedy 11: Recognize that an *open door policy* does not mean that you must always work with an open door. Close it whenever you do not want to be disturbed.

Meetings

     Meetings are thought to be among the biggest timewasters in America. Plus, they are very expensive to run. Imagine the cost in salary per minute of 20 professionals in one room. Figure 14-10 provides a good guideline:

Meeting Costs/Hour/Person			
Salary/Year	**Worth/Hour**	**Salary/Year**	**Worth/Hour**
$30,000	$15.37	$120,000	$61.48
$40,000	$20.49	$130,000	$66.60
$50,000	$25.61	$140,000	$71.72
$60,000	$30.74	$150,000	$76.84
$70,000	$35.86	$160,000	$81.97
$80,000	$40.98	$170,000	$87.09
$90,000	$46.10	$180,000	$92.21
$100,000	$51.23	$190,000	$97.34
$110,000	$56.35	$200,000	$102.46
(Based on 244, eight-hour working days per year)			

Figure 14-10

     A morning meeting of ten middle-management professionals will cost the school system over $1,000 in salary and more in lost productivity. The following is a list of meeting timewaster problems and remedies (Mackenzie, 1972).

The Problem: Meetings are costly and time consuming.

     Remedy 1: If the meeting is a regularly scheduled one, try canceling one of them one time and see what happens. Skip one week if the meeting is usually held once per week. Skip one month if the meeting is usually held once per month. In all likelihood, nothing will happen, life will go on, your school district will have saved all that salary, and all the time usually devoted to that meeting will become available to those people usually in attendance for getting some work done.

     Remedy 2: If nothing much happens when you cancel that meeting, try canceling alternate meeting times by scheduling only half as many meetings from then on.

     Remedy 3: If still nothing happens, try calling meetings only when absolutely necessary. Do not hold those regularly scheduled meetings.

     Remedy 4: Hold a telephone conference call among only those persons involved. This will eliminate the need for everyone to have to travel to the meeting location. If your phone system has no conference call mechanism, call the operator. Conference calls are very inexpensive.

Remedy 5: Make the decision yourself instead of calling an unnecessary meeting. Democratic decision making is not always preferable to monocratic decision making. Consider whether everyone really needs or even wants to be involved.

> *Dost thou love life?*
> *Then do not squander time*
> *For that is the stuff*
> *Life is made of.*
> -Benjamin Franklin-

The Problem: You must call a meeting and do not want to risk it being an unnecessary expense to salary and productivity.

Remedy 1: Limit attendance to only those who absolutely must be there

Remedy 2: Stagger attendance so that people attend only for the time necessary to make a contribution

Remedy 3: Pick the right time for the meeting to make it convenient for as many people as possible.

Remedy 4: Pick the right place to avoid interruptions. Consider a meeting place away from the school or away from central office, perhaps a conference room in a hotel or restaurant.

Remedy 5: Send a written agenda in advance to all those who will attend. This gives people time to prepare proposals and reports, and time for political lobbying to take place before the meeting begins.

Remedy 6: Limit the amount of time for each agenda item to prevent filibusters and to make priorities clear to all attending.

Remedy 7: Establish firm starting and ending times.

Remedy 8: Start the meeting exactly on time. Do not reward those who come late by waiting for them and punish those who come on time by having them wait for latecomers.

Remedy 9: Assign the minutes responsibility before the meeting begins. Consider that a secretary may not be the best person to take minutes if discussions involve sensitive areas or if political caution is necessary in the wording of published minutes. The leader of the meeting should never have to take minutes. The most common method of allocating responsibility for minute taking is alphabetical order of all those attending.

Remedy 10: Stick firmly to the agenda: old, unfinished business from the last meeting first, unexpected items at the end if time permits.

Remedy 11: Choose a leadership style appropriate for the purpose of the meeting: to inform, to generate creative solution proposals, to decide.

Remedy 12: Prevent all interruptions to meetings you lead by not allowing phone calls or secretarial interruptions for those attending.

The Problem: No follow through on what has been discussed or decided at previous meetings.

Remedy 1: Before the end of the meeting, restate all conclusions made during the meeting.

Remedy 2: Before the end of the meeting, restate all the "understandings" of who is going to do what. Clarify all assignments.

Remedy 3: Before the end of the meeting, restate the specific dates by which people have agreed to accomplish tasks and assignments emanating from meeting discussions.

The Problem: Minutes of meetings are distributed so long after the meeting that no one remembers what they mean and most people have forgotten their responsibilities.

Remedy 1: Minutes must be written, edited, typed, copied, and distributed no longer than 48 hours after the meeting.

Remedy 2: Minutes should always include all decisions, who is responsible for completing tasks, and deadlines.

Remedy 3: Wait a few days after the minutes have been distributed and call all of those who had any responsibilities emanating from the meeting. Ask them how they are progressing and if they need any help. This jogs their memory and implants the understanding of each responsibility.

The Problem: Meetings often drag on far longer than expected.

Remedy: Never violate the stated ending time of a meeting. Respect people's plans. They may have other appointments.

The Problem: There is no real evidence about whether these meetings are useful or even run appropriately.

Remedy: 1. Run occasional anonymous evaluations on meetings
    A. Was advance information adequate?
    B. Did the meeting start on time?
    C. Was the agenda followed?
    D. Were the right people attending?
    E. Was time wasted?
    F. Were the purposes of the meeting achieved?

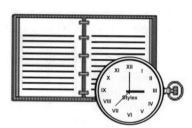

Remedy 2. Take an inventory of committees. Combine them if possible. Eliminate as many as possible.

The Problem: You are expected to be at a meeting but you do not believe you will get anything from it or offer anything to it. You would rather not attend and waste your time.

Remedy 1. If possible, discuss your feelings with the person requiring you to attend. Ask to be excused or even removed from further responsibility to attend.

Remedy 2. Ask the person requiring you to attend if you can be excused from this one meeting because of tremendous pressure to meet a deadline on another project.

Remedy 3. Delegate the responsibility for attendance to a subordinate who will attend on your behalf.

Remedy 4. Arrange with your secretary (or a colleague) to interrupt you with an emergency shortly after the meeting begins. Be sure to take all your materials with you when you leave the meeting room.

General Interruption Control

Mackenzie (1972) identifies six ways in which managers are responsible for their own interruptions. See Figure 14-11 for these and more.

```
┌─────────────────────────────────────────┐
│     Typical Causes Of Interruptions     │
│                                         │
│   •  Illusion of courtesy               │
│   •  Image of availability              │
│   •  Presumption of the legitimacy      │
│      of the interruption                │
│   •  Need to socialize                  │
│   •  Desire to be informed              │
│   •  Low value of one's own time        │
│   •  Mistaken notion that completing     │
│      many small tasks means progress    │
│   •  Mistaken notion that an empty      │
│      inbasket allows for concentration  │
│      on important projects              │
└─────────────────────────────────────────┘
```

Figure 14-11

The *illusion of courtesy* refers to the mistaken notion that by refusing an interruption, one is being discourteous. Of course, no discourtesy may have been intended by the interrupter, but certainly none is intended by refusing to be interrupted. This illusion often manifests itself in administrators personally answering all phone calls and allowing anyone to come into their office at any time. The techniques specified earlier in this chapter in no way suggest discourtesy to the interrupter, who, in the case of a potential telephone interruption, may actually be unaware that the administrator is even hearing the telephone ring.

The *image of availability* refers to the mistaken notion that one must be available to all persons at all times. Wise administrators schedule their availability or risk the possibility of lowering their own performance.

The *presumption of the legitimacy of the interruption* refers to the mistaken notion that if someone calls or drops in unexpectedly, their interruption merits immediate attention. It may indeed be important for the interrupter's purposes to get your immediate attention. However, the interruption may not be of such high priority to the office interrupted or even to the school system as a whole. The danger in presuming that every interruption is legitimate is that it encourages such interruptions in the future

The *need to socialize* encourages interruptions and wastes time. While socializing is necessary in human organizations, it can get out of hand. Socialization is best reserved for lunchtime and work breaks.

The *desire to be informed* is dangerous. It encourages subordinates to waste their time reporting in, and it confuses the informed person with more facts and figures than any one person needs or can handle. Implement a management-by-exception system and require people to report only exceptions to standard events and variations in standard operating procedure.

The *low value of one's own time* encourages others to take advantage. Such low self-value provides others with the instant ability to fulfill their own performance objectives at someone else's expense.

The *notion that completing many small tasks means progress* is a mistaken one. It is very easy to believe that crossing many items off a list of things to do is accomplishing something or is freeing up future time to work on the important tasks of the day. The opposite is usually true. Working on small, insignificant tasks results in accomplishing small, insignificant tasks, albeit many of them. It is much more advisable to work on very important projects of high priority and leave the many small tasks for a less encumbered time.

Attempting to empty one's inbasket may be futile. While an empty inbasket may appear satisfying, it may simply be evidence of spending too much time on the multitude of low-priority tasks. After all, the low-priority tasks are what usually fill the inbasket.

General Solutions to Time Management Problems

It is highly advisable for administrators periodically to monitor their own activities. Logging one's own activities as they occur can be very helpful in identifying key timewasters and poor habits, because remedies cannot be applied until problems are identified. The blank time log template (Figure 14-12) can be utilized to log all activities as they occur. It should not be surprising to learn from your time log that something interrupts administrators an average of every eight minutes throughout the day.

Decide what objectives need to be accomplished each day and place them in the space provided, along with today's deadlines for them. Start to log each activity as soon as you arrive at work. Log them as they occur. Place the number (1-4) corresponding to the priority on each line. Save the comment section for a spare moment when you can reflect on how well that time was used. At the end of each day, notice how much time you have spent on high-priority (Priority 1) objectives. Most people notice improvement in their time management as soon as they begin their time log. A new time consciousness sets in quickly.

> *He who rushes ahead doesn't go far.*
> -Lao-tsu-

Daily Time Log				
Name: _____		**Date:** _____		
Today's Tasks/Deadline		**Today's Tasks/Deadline**		
1) _____ _____		4) _____ _____		
2) _____ _____		5) _____ _____		
3) _____ _____		6) _____ _____		
Priority: 1 = Most Important 2 = Medium Importance 3= Least Important				
Time	**Activity**	**Time Used**	**Priority**	**Comment**

Figure 14-12

Lakein (1973), Mackenzie (1972), Shipman et al. (1983), and others suggest many techniques for managers and administrators. Figure 14-13 consists of rules of thumb available to help with time management problems. None of these rules is presented as a cure-all or applicable to all situations. Any decisions on implementation of any of these suggestions require judgment and selective application to the specifics of administrative situations.

General Solutions to Time Management Problems

- Become a goal-oriented person.
- List your goals, set your priorities.
- Make a daily *to-do* list.
- Start with the most important project, not the least important tasks.
- Ask yourself: What is the best use of my time right now?
- After sorting, handle each piece of paper just once.
- Don't procrastinate, do it now.
- Discover what is blocking you.
- Value good attendance and punctuality.
- Avoid perfectionism.
- Strive for quantity and quality.
- Don't forget rest and stress reduction.
- Develop a strong work ethic.
- Work at a steady pace.
- Schedule similar tasks together.
- Organize your workspace.
- Time-limit your tasks.
- Clean up and throw out every six months.
- Control interruptions.
- Be decisive.
- Monitor and evaluate your progress

Figure 14-13

Summary

This chapter has presented concrete ideas for how to understand and manage stress and how to control the limited time available to perform an exceedingly difficult job. Each portion of this chapter might have been expanded to the size of an entire textbook to do honor to the topics involved. To the extent that the reader's appetite has been whetted, the job is done.

Better Done Than Perfect

Case Problem: Happy Apple School District

The Happy Apple School District has an Employee Assistance Program (EAP) contract for anonymous psychological services for district employees. The EAP is run by a local health care provider.

The Happy Apple superintendent has just handed the principal of Cortland High School (CHS), Barbara, a report received from the EAP Coordinator listing the percentages of faculty members in the district (by school) who have taken advantage of psychological counseling and stress management programs within the past 6-month period. The data suggest extremely high stress levels in the CHS building as follows:

- 25% of the CHS faculty have sought psychological or stress counseling in the past six months.

- CHS teacher absenteeism is up 50% over last year's rates and 40% higher than the district-wide average.

- 70% of eligible faculty have taken early retirement despite the fact that the board of education turned down the union proposal for special early retirement benefits.

- A local health care provider summary analysis of medical records for all CHS faculty lists incidences of ulcers, neurosis, and coronary artery disease far above the average for the entire district.

The superintendent is livid. "How is this going to look if the board gets hold of this data?, he asks in a stern voice. "We don't need any more trouble from the union rep in your school, Barbara. I brought you in as principal to run a clean show. What's going on in your shop, anyway?"

References

Bortner, R. W. (1969). A short rating scale as a potential measure of pattern A behavior. *The Journal of Chronic Diseases* 22.

Cannon, W. (1935). Stresses and strains of homeostasis. *American Journal of Medical Science.*

Cooper, C. and Marshall, J. (1977). *Understanding executive stress* New York: Petrocelli.

Franklin, B, (1757*). Poor Richard's almanac.*

French, J. R. P., and Caplan, R. (1973). Organizational stress and individual strain. In A. J. Marrow (Ed.) *The failure of success.* New York: Amacon.

French, J. R. P. (1972, January). In W. McQuade, *What stress can do to you.* Fortune.

Friedman, M., Rosenman, R. (1974). *Type A behavior and your heart* Greenwich, CT: Fawcett Press.

Hodge, J. , Marker, P. (1978, December). Assessing teacher stress: a beneficial task for the administrator, *American Secondary Education* 84, 49-57.

Holmes, T. H., and Rahe, R. H. (1967*).* The social readjustment rating scale, *Journal of Psychosomatic Research* 11.

Kahn, R. (1973) Conflict, ambiguity, and overload: Three elements in job stress. *Occupational mental health* 3.

Kaiser, J. (1985) *The Principalship* New York: Macmillan and (1991) Mequon, WI: Kaiser and Associates.

Katz, D., Kahn, R. (1966). *The social psychology of organizations.* New York: Wiley.

Kornhauser, A. (1965). *Mental health of the industrial worker.* New York: Wiley.

Lakein, A. (1973). *How to get control of your time and your life.* New York: Signet.

Lipsky, M. (1980). *Street level bureaucracy: Dilemmas of the individual in public services.* New York: Russel Sage Foundation.

Mackenzie, R. A. (1972*). The time trap* New York: McGraw-Hill.

Manera, E., Wright, R. (1981, October) Can you identify your source of stress*? Clearing House 55* (2), 53-58.

Marcson, S. (1970*). Automation, alienation, and anomie.* New York: Harper and Row.

Rothstein, S. W. (1991-1992) Personalized power in the principalship: some problems of dominance and submission in an administrative team. *National Forum of Educational Administration and Supervision Journal,* 8 (2).

Selye, H. (1974). *Stress without distress* New York: J.B. Lippincott.

Sheppard, J. (1971). *Automation and alienation.* Cambridge, MA. MIT Press.

Shipman, N. J., Martin, J. B., McKay, A. B., Anastas, R. E. (1983). *Effective time management techniques for school administrators.* Englewood Cliffs, NJ: Prentice-Hall.

Sparks, D. (1979, May) A biased look at teacher job satisfaction, *Clearing House 52,* 447-449.

Index

By Simon Scarrow

The *Roman* Series

Under the Eagle
The Eagle's Conquest
When the Eagle Hunts
The Eagle and the Wolves
The Eagle's Prey
The Eagle's Prophecy
The Eagle in the Sand
Centurion
The Gladiator
The Legion
Praetorian

The *Wellington and Napoleon* Quartet

Young Bloods
The Generals
Fire and Sword
The Fields of Death

Sword and Scimitar
Arena

ARENA

SIMON SCARROW

AND T. J. ANDREWS

ARENA

headline

First published in Great Britain in 2013
by HEADLINE PUBLISHING GROUP

2

Cataloguing in Publication Data is available from the British Library

ISBN 978 0 7553 9822 5 (Hardback)
ISBN 978 1 4722 0739 5 (Trade paperback)

Typeset in Bembo by Palimpsest Book Production Ltd, Falkirk, Stirlingshire

Printed and bound in Great Britain by Clays Ltd, St Ives plc

Headline's policy is to use papers that are natural, renewable and
recyclable products and made from wood grown in sustainable
forests. The logging and manufacturing processes are expected to conform
to the environmental regulations of the country of origin.

HEADLINE PUBLISHING GROUP
An Hachette UK Company
338 Euston Road
London NW1 3BH

www.headline.co.uk
www.hachette.co.uk